GW00371066

One Woman's Journey

Mary Potter

founder

Little Company of Mary

First published 2000
by Spectrum Publications
PO Box 75
Richmond Vic 3121
email: spectpub@ozemail.com.au

Copyright © Elizabeth West LCM

All rights reserved
No part of this publication may be reproduced in any manner
without prior written permission of the publisher.

ISBN 0 86786 302 1

Contents

Glossary

Approbation The process of gaining papal approval for the establishment of a religious congregation of pontifical right.

Beguines Women in the cities of northern Europe who, beginning in the Middle Ages, led lives of religious devotion without joining an approved religious order.

Charism of Religious life The particular gift or spiritual capacity contained within the founding vision of a religious order, which gives it a unique spiritual identity and mission in the church.

Charism (Lit. Gk. *charisma* from the verb *charidzomai* – "to bestow a gift or favour"). In its religious meaning, a free gift, a charism is a spiritual capacity resulting from God's favour, given for the building up of the church (cf. Paul, 1 Cor. 12:7).

Enclosure (clausura) The segregation of religious women under solemn vows within the environment of a convent or monastery.

Magisterium The authoritative teaching body of the Roman Catholic church, constituted by the college of bishops with the pope at its head.

Modernism Roman Catholic Modernism at the end of the nineteenth century took various forms. At its simplest level of definition, it was the attempt of many within the church to respond to the explosion of knowledge, critical theory and scientific discovery of the century.

Monastic Pertaining to the life of monks or nuns living in seclusion from the world under religious vows or resembling the life of same.

Mysticism The belief that direct knowledge of God, spiritual truth, or ultimate reality can be attained through subjective experience (as intuition or insight).

Nuns Strictly defined, nuns refer to those women who have taken solemn vows. Common usage has resulted in all women religious being identified by the term.

Prophet (Biblical) One who is called to assume the role of intermediary between God and the community, and who is given the task of proclaiming something of fundamental importance to the wider community.

Religious Congregation   A religious community in which members take simple vows. These may be of either diocesan or pontifical right. The former is under the direct control of a Bishop in a local diocese, the latter under the direct authority of the Holy See.

Religious Institute   Interchangeable with religious congregation.

Religious Order   By classical definition, a Religious Order is one in which members take solemn vows and are subject to enclosure.

Spirituality (1)   An individual's experience of "life in the Spirit". The existential understanding of God that influences, and is influenced by, the individual's experience of time and place and culture.

Spirituality (2)   Particular patterns of the spiritual life (ways of living the life of the Spirit), which become traditions or schools of spirituality.

Ultramontanism (Lit: beyond the mountains – Italian)   In Roman Catholicism the belief in the supreme power of the papacy as spiritual leader of the church. In the nineteenth century, a renewed interest in the "Roman" elements of Catholicism and a denial of, or reduction in national church interests.

Vows   Solemn and Simple. The public profession of perpetual observance of the three evangelical virtues of poverty, chastity and obedience. In the eyes of the church, solemn vows had a binding, quasi-sacramental character, and only the Holy See could grant dispensation from them. Associated with the life of enclosure and medieval monasticism, the vows signified a flight from the world in search of a spiritual perfection. Simple vows are distinguished from solemn vows only in so far as they were without the binding effect of solemn profession, may be temporary or perpetual, and exempted religious from the obligations of enclosure and monastic stability. Congregations of simple vows were considered less "perfect" than solemnly vowed religious orders.

Introduction

On January 14, 1877 a young woman made her way to the residence of the bishop of Nottingham, Edward Bagshawe.[1] She had come with a proposition to place before him – namely that he permit her to establish a new religious institution within his diocese. Her name was Mary Potter, and her hope was that, in spite of having been barred from such an action by Bishop Danell[2] of Southwark, told to "go home and care for her mother" by Cardinal Manning,[3] Bagshawe would hear her and give his consent. Ten days after this first visit, Bagshawe did give his consent to the establishment of a new order in his diocese, and with that decision, Mary Potter joined a small group of English women who founded religious communities in nineteenth-century Britain.

Following the Catholic Emancipation Act of 1829 and the restoration of the Catholic hierarchy in 1850, congregations of religious women within the Catholic church in England grew and expanded at an extraordinary rate. The reason for their rapid development lay in the need of the hierarchy to respond to the demand for education, nursing, and the provision of welfare services for an ever-increasing Catholic population.[4] Wiseman, Francesca Steele states, wanted to "build a wall of convents around London" to minister to the urban masses,[5] and to that end, encouraged the development of religious life for both men and women. By 1873 there were some 3,000 Roman Catholic nuns living in 253 convents in England and Wales.[6] By 1876, the number of women within Catholic religious communities had increased to approximately 4,200.[7] By the end of the century, those numbers had more than doubled, with between 8000 and 10,000 women in over ninety different congregations, working within the dioceses of England. These women religious taught in schools, ran orphanages, cared for the elderly, managed "lunatic" asylums, staffed houses of refuge and penitentiaries for "fallen" women, provided home nursing care, and did pastoral visitation in the slums of cities.[8] This small group of women – by mid-century, a tiny 0.036% of a total female population of 11,663,705 – was the heart of nineteenth-century Catholic social welfare endeavours.[9] They were the unpaid work force of a Catholic revivalism, which sought to restore English Catholicism to a position of power and authority, and to link it firmly to its point of origin, Rome.

As a phenomenon, it was to be expected that religious life would grow and develop within a revived Catholic tradition. The Oxford movement had already introduced the idea of religious communities for women into Anglican circles,[10] and while Catholic observance had never ceased to attract men and women to conventual or monastic life, such aspirants had been forced to enter European-based communities.[11] After the restoration of the hierarchy however, and due to encouragement from such men as Wiseman[12] and Manning as well as local bishops, religious life for women within English Catholicism once again became a reality, but a reality with a difference. In its new emergence, it was an active life, centred on the need for service to the poor, education for the community and the provision of welfare services within the structures of local churches.[13] The new groupings of women were not bound to strict cloister; they could take simple, not solemn vows,[14] and were conspicuous for their dedication, competence and service amid the degrading poverty of the new industrial poor.[15] In a church which had singularly few priests for the works of pastoral care and education[16] the work of women was both valuable and necessary. Thus women's communities were actively encouraged to participate in the life of the English Catholic church. At the invitation of Bishops, European congregations took root and established themselves in England.[17] They were, according to one contemporary reporter, "apostles of England", impelled by:

> an invincible desire for [its] conversion. Their looks bespeak their mission no less than their garb. They are calm, collected, gentle…The names of their several orders tell plainly on what their hearts are fixed. They belong to the "Good Shepherd;" they are the "Faithful Companions of Jesus;" they are handmaids of the "Holy Child Jesus," of "Notre Dame de Sion," of "Jesus in the Temple," of "Marie Répatrice." They are "Sisters of Mercy," of "Providence," of "the Poor," of "Nazareth," of "Penance," "of the "Holy Family," of "St. Joseph," of "St. Paul," of "the Cross." They address themselves to the heart rather than to the understanding, but they are not on that account less powerful instruments in the work of social improvement.[18]

If the Catholic view celebrated the achievements of these women, their presence within English society created debate and stirred conflict to the degree that historians Sheridan Gilley and Roger Swift could assert that nuns were the most unpopular single group in Victorian England.[19] Whilst the accuracy of that historical judgement may be open to debate, it is true that sisterhoods (both Anglican and Catholic), created tensions and ambiguity within the wider community.

The deep suspicion in the English imagination regarding convents was fuelled by their rapid increase throughout the century and accompanied by a fear of the encroachment of "Romanism."[20] Numerous lurid accounts of escaped nuns,[21] and a burgeoning business in artistic representation of religious sisters stirred the public imagination and added a piquant twist to the threat religious life appeared to pose to male control of female sexuality.[22] The political agitation of parliamentary member Charles Newdegate was a further stimulus for discussion. His conviction of the virulence of convents and their detrimental effect on British womanhood, ensured that debate, dissension and discourse continued in Parliament over years. His continued agitation on such issues as: the inspection of convents (1853); whether the inmates of such institutions and their property needed extra legislative protection (1853–1854); the rights of convents and monasteries to receive bequests (1863–4); alleged cruelty to nuns (1865); and the Great Convent Case of Susanna Mary Saurin (1869)[23] was representative of the peculiar threat that convents posed to the English imagination.

If convents and sisterhoods were lauded by some as places where female ingenuity could be expressed for the good of society; other members of the British public saw sisterhoods as hotbeds of repressed sexuality, representing wastage of womanhood.[24] Still others saw them as undermining the rights of fathers, brothers, and potential husbands to control their womenfolk and a wily plot of a papacy determined to undermine the rights of the empire.[25] At base, however, the antagonism to convents and conventual life rested in the disruption of middle-class and Protestant identity that was domestic for women and entre-preneurial for men. Convents were equivocal symbols in England,[26] and the alternative psychological and structural reality that they proposed to the public mind was sufficiently challenging to ensure an on-going turbulence into the early years of the twentieth century.[27]

Yet, for all the discussion that circled around religious sisters, and in spite of their obvi-ous presence and activity in England during the nineteenth century, Catholic sisterhoods remain absent from the major historical surveys of the Catholic revival. The history of the ill-named "second spring" of English Catholicism as presented by George Beck, John Bossy, Hugh McLeod, and David Mathew and Derek Holmes, gives but passing recogni-tion to the women who created, staffed and focused the Catholic systems of education, health and welfare services.[28] Where Anglican sisterhoods have been relatively well-served in women's studies and social history,[29] there are no parallel studies of Catholic women religious of the same period. The silence is vast, as Susan O'Brien notes, when she states that "the literature on Victorian religious culture and experience in England has barely acknowledged their presence."[30]

Even more invisible in that body of literature, is the small group of English founders – and the foundations that grew up around them – in the years following the restoration of the hierarchy.[31] These in general, remain "hidden and unknown" apart from hagiographic studies, congregational journals, or other privately published material. There are, however, exceptions. Various works exist on the founder of the Sisters of the Holy Child, Cornelia Connelly,[32] and a new and informative work has been published on Elizabeth Prout (1820–1864), founder of the Sisters of the Cross and Passion.[33] Apart from studies done for private circulation within communities, the lives of other nineteenth-century English founders remain trapped inside dusty covers of works published at the turn of the cen-tury,[34] or in the even dustier interiors of convent archives.

The silence that surrounds the inspirations that led these women to initiate religious communities is even more profound. Their invisibility in mainstream history, as Gail Malmgreen has pointed out, leaves a lacuna in knowledge regarding women, religion, and their relationship with their church and the wider world.[35]

That silence is slowly being broken in other countries by the voices of historians who have discovered the distinctive historical richness of the lives of women religious. Seminal works have appeared which appear to agree with Malmgreen's thesis that to ignore religion, or to confine research to the wilder fringes of female spirituality is to forfeit understanding of the mental universe of a substantial body of women historically important in their own right. Rapley's study of *The Dévotes* of seventeenth-century France explores the emergence of the new active religious congregations of women,[36] while American historians, Margaret Susan Thompson, Mary Ewens, Mary Oates and Mary Ann Donovan among others, have begun to chart the role and impact of women religious on American Catholic society and the wider culture.[37] More recently, Leslie Liedel has explored the relationship between bishops and women religious within the Catholic tradition[38] while Lyn Jarrell has turned attention to the impact of canon law upon their community lives.[39]

In Ireland, where Margaret McCurtain has named the history of Irish nuns as "late in the field",[40] the works of Anthony Fahey, Catriona Clear, Mary Luddy, and Mary Peckam Magray among others have provided insight into the purpose, history, and impact of nuns within Irish society.[41] In England, however, research is slow, with the historian Susan O'Brien (supported by the works of such women as Edna Hamer, and the late Caritas McCarthy,[42]) remaining the most significant contributor to the field of the history of women religious.

If the lives of the women who founded native English congregations during the nineteenth century are hidden from history, so too are the reasons for their foundations. Potter's life as a woman, mystic and founder of a religious institute indicates the close, even causal, relationship that linked Victorian religious life and religious experience to social action. The activism of many women in the last half of the decade found its roots in the religious motif, and as this study demonstrates, Potter's religious experience gave rise to a depth of creativity in the processes she used in order to effect both ecclesial and social reform. In this sense, Potter's life is part of a wider history of women and religion in Victorian England – a history that also remains relatively hidden from mainstream historiography. Religious experience empowered women. Under the influence of four intense religious or mystical experiences Florence Nightingale claimed her right to serve the sick,[43] and it was Josephine Butler's experience of what she perceived as a divine revelation that gave her the authority to commit herself to attacking the sexual double standard and the profligate actions of men.[44] Religious experience was an important factor in women's lives, and without recognition of that fact, or of the crisis such experiences brought with them, the tension such women generated within the community cannot be understood. Potter's life, just as much as the lives of Nightingale or Butler, was a life forged around the belief in a personal revelation of and intimacy with God. As this study will demonstrate, it was no easy path. The claim to a direct and unmediated relationship with a God who made his will known to women would be a source of conflict and suffering for Potter, for she was part of a church suspicious of things mystical, particularly as they related to women.

But the fact remains that women's religious experience is of crucial importance in understanding women's lives for, as Kerri Allen has pointed out, their religious conversions and convictions were often part of a quest for a coherent and authoritative sense of self.[45]

This study of the life of Mary Potter, as woman, mystic and founder of the religious institute known as the Sisters of the Little Company of Mary, seeks in part to redress the balance regarding Catholic women religious in nineteenth-century Britain. Her story, recorded in journals, letters, family reminiscences and memoirs, reveals an extraordinary religious virtuosity. Shaped by a culture and a religious framework which saw her as subordinate, Potter used that same framework to tap into a rich vein of spirituality which ultimately enabled her to break the restrictions that bound her to petty convention and the narrow confines of class and respectability. Unusual, in that she emerges from the silent ranks of lower middle-class respectability, her life reveals something of the nature of women's devotions, the status of the small and struggling Catholic community, and the difficulties faced by women, destined by God or circumstance, to a life of "redundancy."

Culture, class, and denomination all impacted upon Mary Potter. All focused her life and behaviour on the acquisition of virtue and domesticity described in Patmore's well-worn image of "the angel of the house." Shaped by her religious heritage to an affective piety, Potter's life was transformed by what she named as experiences of God. These were significant enough to shift her focus, impel her beyond her own limitations, and draw her to a new understanding of her life and purpose. Giving their own veridicality, the experiences became the means of empowerment by which she moved beyond the confines of domesticity and created a vision of possibility for women, for the church and for the wider world.

Forming the basis of her theological outlook, and giving her a reformer's zeal, Potter's spiritual life and mystical experiences framed her subsequent steps as founder of a religious institute. Convinced that religious orders were brought into existence to act as prophetic witnesses for renewal of the Christian life, her theological views and her belief in the meaning of religious life would bring her to face violent opposition. Her vision of, and belief in, the power of women to transform the church and the wider world was likewise called into question, as her views subverted the culturally bound "angelic ideal," even as they incorporated elements of it. More messianic and self-determining than Patmore's "angel," Potter laid claim to the right of women to participate in the evangelising mission of the church. Appropriating images from her culture, she used them to exploit the dominant cultural determinants for women. Maternal domesticity became subverted by a claim of maternal power in the reconstruction of a new world order. Claiming the right to emulate the "mother-love of the Good Shepherd" in his salvific role, she saw an unlimited and transforming power in women's maternal love. Sharing some of the insights of apocalyptic feminism, she believed that women were called to participate in the development of a new consciousness which could save the world and the church from the perils that assailed both. Her mysticism resulted in a radical re-defining not only of the notion of "separate spheres," but also of the theological awareness of the role of the church as "mother" of its members. This too shaped her actions and reactions to the church and her place within it.

As a founder of a religious institute, Potter stood in an uneasy alliance with the Roman Catholic church. As a woman, she was subordinate to its clerical authority. As a mystic, she stood outside its authoritative powers. Believing that she was called to found a new religious order[46] in the Catholic church, her quest for the legitimisation of her vision was to be compromised by centuries of tradition which had defined and limited the role of women and their particular expressions of religious life. Her theological arguments regarding the nature and meaning of religious life in the life of the Roman Catholic church were also negated, as was the fundamental spirit of the institute she eventually founded. As will be seen, her belief in the essentially charismatic and prophetic "spirit" of religious life stood in sharp contrast to that held by the church, as did her belief in the necessity of the integration of the contemplative with the active life. Quite simply, her vision did not meet the requirements of a church labouring to provide an infrastructure for a rapidly growing, predominantly urban population.

Conflict and compromise marked Potter's life as woman, mystic, and founder, but it is in the convergence of these three elements that the essential relationship between religion, spiritual experience, and social action intersect. Labelled as "unstable" and as a "self-proclaimed visionary" by clergy, Potter would withstand the criticism and condemnation heaped upon her, but she could not avoid the conflict generated between the authoritative and authoritarian voice of church and clerics and the inner vision and direction she followed.

Following the foundation of her institute in 1877, the struggles continued. Less readily accepted by English clergy than the European orders,[47] Potter's small institute would struggle for its survival. Deposed from office by her local bishop, exposed to ridicule both within and without the congregation and subjected to physical abuse by members of her own community, Potter's commitment to her vision remained true.[48] She believed she had been called to initiate a community that was marked by a specific inner "charism." It was a view foreign to many within the church, and stood in stark contrast to what one historian has termed the "instrumentalism" or functionalism of the majority of nineteenth-century foundations of religious women.[49]

Founders and Charisms

The particularity of Potter's view of religious life and spirituality are important considerations if understanding and insight are to be gained into the nature of the religious community she founded. Theologically, there is an intrinsic link between the founder of an institute and the particular "spirit" or "charism" that belongs to it. Born out of the lived experience of the founder, the "spirit" of a religious community is shaped by the particular vision of humanity grasped by the founder herself, in a process of spiritual growth and development that is at once personal and for a wider world. In biblical and theological terms, charisms are gifts of the Holy Spirit given to individuals, for the building up of the community of the church.[50] Those who are "called," or given the gift of establishing religious communities, may be seen as being given a specific charism, or gift. It is a concept simply expressed by the Jesuit Jerome Nadal in 1542. According to Nadal:

> When God wants to help his church, he first raises up a person and gives him or her a special grace and impulse, under which he or she may serve God in a particular manner. This is what he did in the case of St. Francis: God gave him a particular grace for his personal growth as well as for his companions. In the same way, he raised up Ignatius and granted him a grace, and through him to us…[51]

Highlighting the discussion on religious life that took place at the Second Vatican Council can expand Nadal's view of the nature of a founder and of the gift of the founding insight. On November 11, 1964 Cardinal Bea made a comment that was significant enough to change and orient the evolution of ideas on religious life within the Roman Catholic church. Religious life, he said, was the result of charismatic gifts that the Spirit has bestowed on founders. The use of these gifts has an ecclesial meaning: it aims to reflect the image of Christ more perfectly in the church. Bea went further still and stated that he believed that the charisms of the founders were conjoined to those of the followers. Each institute was charged with the faithful living out of the gifts and with reactivating them into life by putting them into practice, according to the possibilities and needs of the times.[52] These thoughts became the centre for much discussion and whilst the term "charism" did not emerge in any document from the Vatican until 1971, the seed had been sown for future consideration.

More detail of what was meant by the "charisms" of religious life emerged in 1978 in *Mutuae Relationes*,[53] a document that dealt with relationships between religious orders and bishops in the church. Chapter three of that document pointed out that, as a distinct and particular gift of the Spirit to the church, religious life enjoyed a unique share in the sacramental nature of the church. The consecration and testimony of religious tends to make visible certain aspects of the mystery of Christ.[54] The document argued for fidelity to the distinctive character of the various religious institutes and went on to say:

> This distinctive character also involves a particular style of sanctification and apostolate which creates a definite tradition so that its objective elements can easily be recognised…[55]

and that

> …every authentic charism brings an element of real originality in the spiritual life of the Church along with fresh initiatives for action. These may appear unseasonable to many and even cause difficulties, because it is not always easy to recognise at once that they originate from the Spirit.[56]

By 1984 John Paul II, writing in *Redemptionis donum*, clarified another connection between the various ways of serving the church in accordance with the particular apostolic mission of each institute, and the "particular gift of the founder." He pointed to the fact that there was an explicit relationship between the charism of an institute and that of its founder. The "particular gift" of a founder "[was] received from God and approved by the Church [and] becomes a charism for the whole community."[57] But elucidation of the particular "gift" of the founder requires a study of her life – a study that is at once historical and ecclesial. The theological understanding of charisms as "gifts of the Spirit" given in time and place and history "for the life of the church" indicates that charismatic gifts occur within history, and are thus able to be identified in the lives of those to whom they are given. They do not, however, transmute historical circumstance, but rest within it. This understanding of the charism of religious life, and of the nature of a founder is of importance in this study of Mary Potter, for her insights into the nature and purpose of religious communities bears remarkable resemblance to the post-Vatican II understanding of the charismatic quality of religious life. Her life reveals a particularly adept theological mind, and if she did not claim a role for herself as a theologian, she nonetheless claimed the right to use her theological acumen in her role as founder and primary articulator of the community charism. Her peculiar recognition of religious life as prophetic and charismatic, and her emphasis on the primacy of the "spirit" over the "works" give a particularly modern caste to her religious insight.

Mary Potter's liberation from the historical silence that surrounds her serves a multiplicity of purpose. It not only increases the growing body of knowledge about women's roles within the Catholic church in the years following the restoration of the hierarchy in Britain, but also serves to demonstrate the manner in which women created sacred spaces in which their undoubted religious virtuosity could take root and flourish.

In an age suspicious of mysticism and increasingly dependent upon rationalism, Potter's life stands as both challenge and discovery. Her charism was an unusual expression of a call to the church to renew itself in its fidelity to the Gospel. The distinctive elements of the spiritual path she promulgated for others are likewise worthy of record. Potter's devotional life demonstrates the manner in which currents of spirituality flowed down the ages and created new expressions of older realities. In the conjunction of two important elements – profound spiritual insights of divine realities, and equally profound recognition of historical realities – Potter's life as woman, mystic, and founder, becomes clear.

In the absence of any fully documented work on Potter's life and spirituality, or on the charism of the institute she founded,[58] this study seeks to explore three particular elements. Firstly, it provides a biographical study in the context of the world in which she lived. Secondly, it analyses her spirituality and those experiences which gave the insights that led to the founding the congregation of the Little Company of Mary. Thirdly, by exploring the manner in which her spiritual experiences shaped the vision she held regarding the church and the world, it reveals the charismatic underpinning of the religious project she initiated. Furthermore, these explorations expose the conflict and depth of ecclesial interference in and rejection of women's theological insight.

Examining the life of Mary Potter, woman, mystic, and prophetic founder, also reveals the complexity and experience of one human life. In that life can be found the ways in which women of insight and creativity were burdened, healed, oppressed or liberated through their spirituality, the structures of the church and of the society which surrounded them. Whilst Potter may not be representative of all English founders, her life reflects the tensions and the struggles women faced as they sought to integrate their religiosity and spirituality in a world which refused them credibility of theological insight. It reflects and refracts many of the themes and currents that swept around women throughout the nineteenth century.

In her history, and in the history of those who joined her community, common problems emerge. Problems of powerlessness, redundancy, poverty, illness, addiction and suffering emerge in the microcosm of community life, and give witness to the tensions faced by many. But, even in the struggles faced by Potter and her community, there emerges a belief in the essential power of women to make a difference in their world. Utilising a maternal rhetoric to destabilise the traditional role of women, Potter's vision provided a wider theological and spiritual meaning for women's lives and brought with it a claim to a specific "women's mission" in a world that refuted their public ministrations and beneficence. Pre-dating a culture of a self defined in psychological terms, Potter's life and vision also demonstrates the manner in which women's self-hood could be defined within a spiritual anthropology, in which barrier of gendered identity were crossed by an intimate and active sense of unity with God. In this, she was not unusual, for it was one way – albeit ill served by current historiography – in which women within the nineteenth century, found the motivation and the passion to become the reformers many of them were.

Biography must, of necessity, follow a paper trail, and Mary Potter left just such a trail. Over one thousand letters are held within the convent archives of the Little Company of Mary, along with notebooks, jottings, spiritual journals, published and unpublished conferences, and photographs. She was an established author of devotional literature and Marian spirituality in particular, so her published works also provide a fruitful source of information. All these records have been used in this reconstruction of her life and charism. Yet, in spite of such a vast body of material available for research, there remain gaps, silences, and shadows. She was a woman of her time and fortune, subject to all the limitations of humanity, and the documents that survive her life reveal only what she chose to reveal. Despite the rich sources available, the fact remains that the superficial interactions and daily routine of a life do not define an individual, who is always more and less than the parts made visible.

Schematically, this study of Mary Potter as woman, mystic and founder follows a straightforward chronological approach. Thus, section one examines her early years, tracing the patterns of her cultural and religious formation. Section two focuses on those elements of religious experience which led to the recognition of her mystical life, and the conflict these generated within the church, her home, and the wider society. Section three follows Potter's initial formation of the institute, the problems of ecclesial interference, and highlights the search and the difficulties of other women who sought to find ways to meaningful life by entering convents, and Potter's community in particular. Section four follows the pattern of expansion of the institute, the fight for recognition by the church, and the compromises made in the cause of legitimisation – compromises which ultimately led to the negation of the charismatic quality of the community, and its absorption into mainstream concepts of women religious.

SECTION I

The Early Years (1847–1870)

The Early Years (1847–1870)

The world into which Mary Potter was born on November 22, 1847 was that complex yet strangely cohesive period known as the Victorian era. Her England was in the throes of a revolution that would shatter old ideas, build great cities, and give rise to questions – unprecedented in its history – regarding the nature of God, the meaning of life and the nature of humanity. Having wrested the secret of steam from nature, Britain had embarked upon a voyage of inventiveness.[1] It was a country in which idyllic country land-scapes and dirty smoke-clad cities companioned each other in a mutual drive towards wealth, and the increasing riches of the few exacerbated the poverty of the many.[2] In the metropolis that was London, gentry sauntered through Belgravia's tree lined-streets and paraded wealth on Rotten Row while in the narrow streets of Stepney, Southwark, Bermondsey and Bethnal Green, east-end urchins played in lanes that ran with sewage.[3] Sharp contrasts marked Victorian London, and between the two extremes lay Mary Potter's world, the earnest, sombre life of middle-class merchants, small traders and the vast bulk of the British working classes.[4]

Governed by an intricate interplay of bridges and barriers, life within the mass of the middle-classes was delineated according to rank and status. Income mattered, as did pro-fession, and family life reflected the disparate elements of the sprawling mass of the mid-dle-classes. Within the hierarchy of values that determined position, the Potter family rested on the lower end of the scale. Members of the "lesser bourgeoisie," Mary Potter's family was marked by a well-regulated life, a capacity for apeish imitation of the class immediately above themselves, and a relentless drive to prove themselves worthy.[5] Rigorous standards dominated life within the lower middle-classes. Ambition was virtue, and if such ambition created a corset of behaviours and attitudes that tightly controlled family and social morality, it was a small penalty to pay for the chance of upward mobil-ity. As this section of the work will illustrate, however, within the mainly silent ranks of the lower middle-classes, such standards and the relentless drive for success brought their own dramas. Mary Potter's early years were marked by her family's shame of bankruptcy, a broken home, and a life of religious and social isolation.

Fifth child and only daughter of an absconded bankrupt, she lived circumscribed by the demands of a rigid code of morality which echoed the values of that "dull and temperate" virtue of the surrounding world.[6] Rigidly disciplined, yet coddled by her mother, she was shaped according to the patterns of Victorian ideology which Malmgreen states "paid effusive homage to women's higher spiritual nature and special nurturing mission."[7] Her socialisation and education conformed to that of women of her period. Limited by a vision of women's domestic role and virtue, her growing years illustrate the limited world of women. She, like other women, learned of her dependency upon men and of the necessity to conform to social expectation. Yet, for all that, class does not determine personality, and Potter's world view shifted and changed under the impact of her life circumstance and her own growing involvement in religion.

As her life shifted and changed Potter's spiritual sensitivities became of vital importance under the pressures of her church affiliation. Refused permission to marry by her bishop, she entered the convent of the Sisters of Mercy in Brighton. There, conflict erupted around her as her inner life began to take a shape and form that ill-fitted the highly apostolic life of a Sister of Mercy. Yet, within the process of her formation as a religious sister, a spiritual odyssey was begun which was to lead to her eventual removal from the Mercy community, and to a time of personal suffering both physical and spiritual.

In a society in which religion itself was "domesticated" to the world of women, Potter's early life reflects the polyvalent nature and power of religious experience. For her, as for many women, it provided an escape, a shelter, a source of comfort and a place of rebellion. If at times it was an opiate to dull the senses, it also held the potential to be a powerful source of transformation. As Potter grew to womanhood, she began to experience the capacity of religion and religious practice to transform an ordinary life.

Early Life

Potter's father, William Norwood Potter married Mary Ann Martin in 1837. He, the son of a chair-maker, and she, daughter of Thomas Martin, pawnbroker of Tooley Street, Southwark, no doubt believed that their lives would be successful and harmonious. It was, however, a relationship doomed to failure as William's poor business acumen and his dour, bleak personality, created tension between himself and his more able and business-like wife.

Like others of the period, William Potter sought to make his mark upon society. Eschewing the dying world of the artisan family to which he belonged, he became a pawnbroker, a trade which was not entirely "respectable," but which yet offered the potential for lucrative income.[8] For William's father-in-law, Thomas Martin, it had provided an income substantial enough to maintain two premises, and provide support for his wife and remaining unmarried daughter and for two apprentices and three servants – a not inconsiderable household.[9] It was, however, a risky business, subject to the same swings as the economy it served.[10]

Situated within the industrial classes, pawnbrokers and their shops enjoyed a mixed reception in the wider community. Extolled as "the poor man's friend," pawnshops and their brokers were attacked by those who believed that the system of pledging contributed to working-class vice.[11] Yet, as Tebbutt points out, brokers did provide a means of working class credit and, as a trade, had experienced a remarkable growth between the years 1820 and 1840[12]. It was a growth due in part to a change in the patterns of work within the cities. A growing irregularity of employment left the poor little option than to seek out pawnbrokers willing to give loans of short duration while among the "respectable" (the small trader or manufacturer), the pawnshop acted as a bank, where goods were pledged in order to gain capital to pay salaries.[13] The volatility of the profession was notorious, and as Britain started its slide into the economic depression that would mark the period as the 'hungry forties', it was a business which suffered badly. The volume of unredeemed pledges grew, and goods failed to sell, or were sold for less than the pledges given.[14] William Potter, with his poor business sense, and an evident inability to control finances, suffered the lean years with growing difficulty. As the depression bit deeper into the economy, it crippled the industry to which he belonged, and a combination of bad debts, poor trade and lack of financial acumen left the Potter household in desperate straits. By 1847, with four young children and another expected,[15] William Norwood Potter had fallen into serious debt.[16]

Both prudery and prudence marked much of Victorian morality.[17] The national morality, reinforced by the evangelical belief in the rewards of virtue, promised a new life for those who succeeded, and while the moral climate of Victorian industrialism could forgive the private peccadilloes of the individual, it could not forgive the public fall from grace that injured the financial advance of others. Bankruptcy, of all the "sins" of the nineteenth century, was a shameful and despicable reality.[18] In whatever class it occurred, it betrayed the prudence that was required of all, and brought not only the debtor but also his entire family into disrepute.[19] Failed businessmen were shunned socially, and suicide was considered one way of salvation from the shame of failure.[20] Private debtors, who were not covered by the laws of bankruptcy, faced debtors' prison and for some, migration to the colonies provided a solution. Emigration held a two-fold attraction for William Potter, for in reality, he was not simply facing accumulated debt and the prospect of debtor's prison, he was also facing a crisis in his marriage.

Family tension had been mounting for some years prior to William's slide into debt, as his wife had asserted her right to rule over the household. She had become a convert to Catholicism,[21] and in open and outrageous defiance of her husband's wishes, had her youngest son George baptised into the Catholic faith soon after his birth in 1845.[22] William, fairly understandably, was angered at this disobedience, yet Mary Ann, unrepentant, compounded the problem by having the three elder boys taken by a maid to the Catholic church in Hammersmith and baptised in secret.[23] On her daughter's birth in 1847, Mary Ann again contravened the wishes of her husband and had the child baptised a Catholic.[24]

The reason for Mary Ann Potter's conversion is unaccounted for within the family documents. What is recorded is that in 1847, Mary Ann was suffering from what Bunyan had called the "captain of all these men of death," tuberculosis.[25] The disease respected no one. Its victims were usually those with diminished resistance and those who worked or lived in poorly ventilated premises.[26] Living in the borough of Bermondsey, where, according to Charles Kingsley "there was no water to drink…but the water of the common sewer which stagnates full of …dead fish, cats and dogs, under their windows,"[27] the Potter family was subject to the common threats of the area. Cholera and typhoid were frequent visitors, and consumption merely another of the perils that faced the population.[28] In the May of 1847, fearful of losing her own life and that of the child she carried, Mary Ann sought spiritual comfort from Dr. Thomas Doyle, the energetic and zealous priest of St. George's church Southwark.[29] He advised her to make her Confirmation, and to place herself and her unborn child under the protection of the Virgin.[30] In a flush of fervour, she made a commitment to consecrate the child to the Virgin Mary and at midnight on November 22, 1847, following a long and difficult labour, she was safely delivered of her fifth child – a frail and sickly infant born with a congenital heart defect and a chronic tendency to lung infections.[31] True to her promise, Mary Ann Potter placed a medal of the Virgin on the newborn baby, whom she named "Mary."[32] She believed her safe delivery was a miracle and this belief was destined to have an enormous impact on the child, who heard the story of her birth told over and over again:

> Sitting in the twilight, which my mother loved, I used to hear from her over and over again, tales which told of God's providence in my regard…. An old Irish governess told my mother that her unborn infant would be so much better if she went to communion frequently, so she did so. Another, at my birth, putting on me before anything else, the silver medal of our Lady that mother had prepared to consecrate me to her and she, (as she used to tell me), keeping close to our Lord all the time with her crucifix in hand, would be reminded (by the nurse), "Now Mam, your little prayer," and she was saying the Memorare as I was born.[33]

As the baby grew, her small and circumscribed space was made secure by this refrain, its repetition resulting in a deep sense of the providence of God and a devotion to the Virgin Mary that remained with her all her life.

Shortly after Mary's birth, William Potter, outraged by his wife's intractability and powerless to change his economic circumstances, left home, setting his sights on Australian shores.[34] For some little time, he remained in contact with the family, but then, faced with what he considered the ultimate betrayal, he vanished forever from their lives. As recorded by one of Mary Ann's sons, the final separation occurred when a legacy, left by his brother Thomas, was refused him, and placed in trust for his wife and children. Then, and only then, did William make the separation permanent. As his son Thomas recalled:

> What estranged him from us was a question of property, for which his brother was trustee on behalf of my mother…He wrote saying that from that day forward, the date of the letter, we were, all of us, wife, children and brother, strangers to him, and he never broke the silence.[35]

For all the difficulties of the marriage, his absence was devastating. Supported by her family and by William's brothers, this "short, slight woman, full of energy and possessing an indomitable will,"[36] became, in the words of her grandchild Hilda, "a Queen Victoria in her own home."[37] It was not surprising. Mary Ann was faced with creating an environment within her home which would prepare her children for their adult years and at the same time, preserve them from the shame they bore. William's defection from home and his public shame as an absconded debtor left Mary Ann and her children vulnerable. The deserted wife was not above suspicion when the "the sacred place, the vestal temple" of home and family was broken apart.[38] Respectability meant that life mattered in a moral sense, and demanded marital fidelity.[39] If William had failed in the business of business, his wife had failed in the business of maintaining her home, and had lost the condition of respectability that marriage had given her. It was not a situation that could be easily explained, and when forced to do so, Mary Ann spoke of her circumstances with a strained dignity: "[My husband] left home when the youngest was but one year old. [He] was forced by adverse circumstances to leave me with five young children…there was no legal separation of any kind."[40] It was a statement of her own failure, as much as anything, for, the responsibility of a wife in the Victorian era was the preservation of the family, not its dissolution.[41]

It must be said, however, that William's departure gave his wife a freedom to establish herself and her children in a manner which living with her husband had not provided. Proud and determined, she refused to allow her young daughter to be raised by her childless sister[42] and though she accepted financial assistance from her own family, she set about establishing herself and her brood in what degree of comfort she could provide. Such was the hardiness and hard won dignity of the woman that she came to be held "in great respect and awe by all who knew her."[43]

From her children Mary Ann Potter demanded absolute obedience.[44] Obedience demanded conformity to the standards set for them, and the Potter children were expected to be dutiful, respectful, virtuous, and modest. Belonging to a class that Arlene Young has termed "more imitative than creative," their life, like the lives of the normal lower middle-class family, was governed by sternly evangelical notions of duty, and a "temperate, dull but comfortable domesticity."[45]

For all the rigidity that marked the childhood of the Potter children, they were a united brood. The young Mary Potter was well nurtured by her mother, and idolised by her brothers who provided a much-needed masculine presence. William and Thomas, the two older boys, held a special place in Mary's affections with Thomas assuming an almost parental role over his young sister. Henry and George, closer to her in age, were the playfellows of her early childhood, and if at times Mary irritated them, in later life each would provide a support for his sister as she sought to find her own path. Thomas, the second eldest, would "rescue" his sister from the Mercy community when her superior wrote of her illness. George and Henry would support her financially in publishing her books and, eventually, in providing her with some means to set up her infant community. They were, in the eyes of their young sister, models of manhood – heroes whose lives even provided her with images of what the person of Jesus might be like.[46]

Cocooned by the self-contained nature of the family, protected by her brothers, coddled by her mother, Potter came to understand herself as a well-loved child and recalled her youth as "a tale of love that reared a child to love everyone."[47] Financial difficulties not withstanding, all the children were given opportunities for parties and games, holidays by the sea, and visits to London relatives,[48] and if the young Mary Potter received more than the others did, it was with the blessing of her brothers. George, the youngest of the boys, recalled:

> At Christmas tide, we children used to go to many Christmas parties. I have vividly before my mind a tiny little girl dressed in white with a blue sash, and looking like a fairy. She is placed on a table for her brothers to admire. I think we were going to the house of Mr. Stevens, a wealthy iron-founder, whose Works and house were in Borough Road, near London Bridge.[49]

Yet, as much as she loved and was loved by her parent and elder brothers, the relationship between mother and daughter was often difficult. Towards her fragile and sickly daughter, Mary Ann was both overly protective and demanding. The child suffered frequent bouts of illness due to her heart defect and her weak lungs continue to be a cause of concern. They were, however, insufficient reasons to forgo the socialisation necessary to her successful integration within society. The young Miss Potter had to learn to take her place within her social boundaries, and Mrs. Potter was determined that her daughter should learn the ladylike behaviour demanded by a middle-class ideology.

As Potter grew, an even more rigid obedience was imposed upon the child. Unlike her brothers, who were allowed and encouraged in healthy pursuits, Mary was constrained into behaviours considered appropriate for girls. The separation between Mary and her brothers was so stringent that her youngest brother, George, when asked for memories of Mary's early life recalled that there was not much to record: "as our Mother kept us boys so much apart from Mary."[50]

Such insulation served to ensure that young girls learned the rituals necessary for their successful integration within their middle-class world, even as it taught them the necessary supportive role they were to assume in securing the domestic comfort of the male members of the family.[51] Hoydenish or boisterous behaviour was forbidden from early childhood,[52] and Potter, like other female children of the era, learnt to defer to her brothers, discovering that her role was to wait on them. She darned their socks, deferred to their presence and, even at the age of thirty, was forced to give up her bed so that her brother George could sleep comfortably.[53] For all that Mary loved her role as sister, and willingly served the needs of the boys whilst young, there was a slow-growing resentment at the distinction made between herself and the males in her family. It rankled that she was not allowed to do what her brothers could do:

> When little I must not play with them; when I grew up I must not go out with them. Nothing would ever move my mother on this point…My mother had some fixed idea that she could not be too careful of me, that it was a solemn charge given by God.[54]

However much the restrictions may have irritated, the fact was that the young girl adhered to what was demanded of her without obvious rebellion, and the restrictions of her home life were somewhat tempered by the affection of her aunts and uncles who proffered treats and summer holidays. The sheer enjoyment of such times drew the adolescent girl to small acts of rebellion, such as failing to return with her brothers from a visit to her Aunt and Uncle. "My Dear Mamma," wrote the thirteen year old Potter in 1860:

> I daresay you were very surprised at my not coming home on Monday evening with my brothers. I am going to stop with Aunt Saul till Saturday, and then Aunt will bring me home. I sleep in the front room by myself. It is next to Aunt's and opens into it by a door, which Aunt leaves open. Aunt took me to the Zoological Gardens yesterday, and I enjoyed myself very much. Aunt Saul is so kind. She has given me a pretty little box of Dominoes made of brass, I think, which Aunt said she had when she was only a year older than me.
>
> Aunt has gone out today, to dinner, and Uncle is going to take me on the water this afternoon. I am so happy Mamma, only George, I think, will be dull without me. You must ask my brothers to take him out.
>
> Dear Mamma, I would write you a longer letter and I intended to do so, only I am now going out for a walk with a friend of Aunt's, Mr. Church.
>
> With love to all my brothers, I am, dear Mamma, your very affectionate daughter,
>
> Mary Potter
> P.S. You will not be dull without me, as you have George with you.[55]

If holidays provided a means of escaping the rigid authority of her mother, the process of her socialisation continued at school. There too she was expected to exercise the virtues which would ensure she would become the ideal woman, one who would be "always charming, always sympathetic, conciliatory, sacrificing herself daily to others."[56]

Education

In early 1854, Mrs. Potter and her brood moved from Bermondsey to a new home in Falmouth Road, South East London. The following year, with the boys enrolled in public schools, the young Mary Potter began her education at Cupola House, 11 New Kent Road. She was eight years old and her education with the Misses Brennan, proprietors of this small boarding school for Catholic girls, would last for ten years.

Drawing its clientele from the less affluent members of the middle-classes, Cupola House, like other small academies of the period, was built around the keynote of domesticity. It promised a homely environment, one that allowed a "more personal influence" and would "tend more to the production and confirmation of gentle and feminine characteristics."[57] One of the few Catholic academies operating within the diocese of Southwark, it proudly publicised its presence in the Catholic Directory as:

> An establishment for Young Ladies, where only eight boarders are received, and where the domestic arrangements are in every respect the same as those in a respectable private

family. The house is admirably adapted for a school, being large and airy, and having a
spacious garden and playground attached to it. Terms moderate.[58]

In spite of its smallness, and its moderate fees, Cupola House professed to give instruction by the most "eminent masters" in French, Music and "other accomplishments."[59] If
it resembled the other small schools noted in the same directory of 1856, Potter also studied History, Geography, "[R]eading, simple and emphatical; Arithmetic and Writing; useful and ornamental Needlework."[60] Following the traditions of the period, her reading
matter was carefully selected.[61] Both at school and at home, bowdlerised versions of
Shakespeare, selections from her brother's encyclopaedia, and expurgated versions of the
Bible were staples,[62] and conformed to the belief of Sarah Stickney Ellis that a "prudent
and judicious mother [did not allow] … unrestrained … private reading … among her
children."[63] There was no emphasis on academic learning, which could foster what
Dyhouse calls "inappropriate vocational aspirations."[64] It was an education focused upon
the acquisition of those accomplishments that would make a young woman an asset for a
gentleman. It reinforced the virtues of piety, purity, submissiveness, and domesticity.
These blended to form the ideal of the Victorian "angel": mother, daughter, sister, wife, or
woman.[65]

Manners were of primary importance, and were for the Victorian era behaviours that
"vex or soothe, corrupt or purify, exalt or debase, barbarise or refine us, by a constant,
steady, uniform and insensible operation like that of the air we breath in."[66] If Potter, as
daughter of the house was to acquit herself well, manners – not intelligence, or education
– were of vital importance. They conveyed one's respectability, and responsibility and
manners began in the home. Potter's letters to her mother are studies of the stilted "man-
nerly" attitudes promoted by Cupola House. In 1862, Potter wrote to her mother of the
impending Christmas vacation:

> My dear Mamma,
>
> It is with great pleasure that I again avail myself of the opportunity afforded by the
> forthcoming season to thank you for the means you have so kindly taken for my
> improvement during the past year, and at the same time to inform you that the vaca-
> tion commences Decbr. 17th, 1862 and terminates Janry. 19th 1863.
>   Trusting that the progress I have made in my studies will merit a renewal of your
> kindness, and wishing you all the compliments of the season, I remain dear Mamma,
> your affectionate daughter, Mary Potter.
>
> P.S. The Misses Brennan desire their compliments to you and family.[67]

If Cupola House provided little in the way of an advanced education in a general sense,
it offered equally little in context of religious education. Obviously, in a Catholic academy,
prayers were said and taught, and religious observances upheld. Public devotion was signified by attendance at church-based services and private devotion along with a suitably

pious demeanour, was promulgated by the prayer books of the period, the most popular being Challoner's *Garden of the Soul*, which also aided and encouraged the good works so beloved of all Victorians.[68] Priests of the local parish prepared Mary for her first Communion and Confirmation, and in 1857, at ten years of age, she received both sacraments.[69] What religious consciousness she did have was formed by attendance at church for catechism classes. The classes were dull and incomprehensible to Potter's childish mind and in later years she wrote of the need to teach children simply and clearly:

> Very simple, plain language should be used in teaching children. Flowery expressions are quite out of place with them. I recollect, when a little child, hearing a priest preach about the creation. It was, I dare say, a very eloquent discourse, but it left a strange impression on my mind, especially when he said, 'God said, 'Let there be light, and a flood of light burst upon an astonished world.'
>
> The language of Scripture: 'Let there be light, and there was light' is beautifully simple, but the 'flood of light bursting upon an astonished world' set my mind to work wondering how the world looked when it was astonished, birds, flowers, trees etc., all astonished, not being aware of the fact that the light came before the animals, flowers etc. [70]

This capacity for imagination, a gift of childhood, was also stirred by the missions Potter attended as a young child. As Sharp points out, these were part of a Catholic revival, and some of them, specifically ordered towards children, were notable for their dreadful portrayals of the sufferings of the damned soul.[71] Mary, imaginative and receptive to the dire threats of hell and damnation, became terrified of "losing" God. This developed into a pattern of scrupulosity that plagued her childhood and early adult years. The potential for sin loomed everywhere, and her brother George recalled the difficulty Mary (and the family) suffered because of it:

> Her earlier life was not very bright, for she was troubled dreadfully with scrupulosity, and this extended to unthoughtup things. Poor Tom! He was very patient with her. At one time, she maintained that no good Catholic could use a frying pan for fish that had been used for meat.
>
> Father Woollett, the naval chaplain, happened to come and Mary put the matter to him. The dear old priest with a look of ineffable disgust uttered only one word, 'Bosh'![72]

Mary would recover from her scruples, but a growing awareness of the limits of her religious education led to a belief that children should not be raised under a regime of fear, proposing instead that religious instruction should focus on God's love for the individual.[73] There was a necessity, she believed, of teaching about Jesus "as he really is":

> not as we so often picture Him to ourselves, or as others wrongly picture him to us – severe. No, but as the Lord who so loved little children in his arms, and would not allow them to be sent away from him. … Teach them about the Man-God who so loves them, teach them about Jesus, the King of Kings; teach them how they are loved, that is the grand point. [74]

The "grand point" of teaching about the love of God would slowly but surely come to be part of Potter's own theological stance. As she matured and found the need for theological insight, the awareness of the limitations of her religious education became apparent: "I must say… I did not know my religion," she wrote to her confessor. "At twenty years old, I was ignoratnt of the most necessary things"[75] This awareness of her own ignorance would lead her to propose and promote the right of women and children to:

> extend their knowledge of religion…[and] encourage [their children] to the study of theology and the Fathers, impressing upon them that this is the noblest of all studies, and an inexhaustible source of delight.[76]

It was a view that would prove unacceptable for most. Women were to be formed in piety and the practice of prayer for others, but they were not to presume that the "Spirit of the Comforter" could lead them into understanding.[77] John Ruskin's eloquence spoke the words the general public tended to believe, namely that "There is one dangerous science for women – one which let them indeed beware how they profanely touch – that of theology."[78] This view of the exclusive, masculine nature of the "sacred sciences" would bring Potter into disrepute, as she sought to express her own theological insight to her confessors and, more publicly, through her devotional and spiritual writings. Ultimately, in 1912 she would be quietly advised to cease publication of religious or theological books, after the Vatican had received complaints that she was bordering on "modernism."[79]

In 1865, at the age of eighteen, Potter emerged from Cupola House, her education completed. She had been formed within the limits of the education provided her and her accomplishments were few. She was proficient in pianoforte, could speak some French, was an unremarkable artist, was versed in general knowledge and held the art of genial conversation. Having a sense of fashion, she loved nice clothes, and her sense of taste and flair for design were utilised by other members of her family in the creation of dresses for weddings and other special occasions.[80] According to those who knew her she was gay and bright, though somewhat shy, possessed of a keen sense of humour, certain stubbornness, impulsive generosity and little fear.[81] Catholic by upbringing, she was dutiful, if unremarkable, in her practice of her faith, and when she left Cupola House in 1865, her education halted because of a period of frail health, she was no more or less than a reasonably refined, semi-educated and somewhat reticent young woman. Her position in life was now that ambiguous and unsettling state of spinster-daughter.

Godfrey King and the marriage question

Potter's departure from school also marked her departure from London. Thomas Potter, the second eldest of the Potter boys, had become an employee of the rapidly expanding railways. Transferred to Portsmouth, he had invited his mother and sister to share his residence, and on Potter's departure from Cupola House, she joined her mother and brother in the bustling garrison town of Portsmouth. It was a noisy rumbustious place, filled with a population of mixed ethnicity, all of whom served, in one way or another, the needs of the naval fleet.[82]

Assuming the role of mistress of the house, Mrs. Potter now shared the domestic responsibility of keeping house with her daughter. It was a life of small pleasures and stultifying domestic routines. Potter's days were bordered by reading the books her mother still carefully selected for her, walking out with her mother or brother, sewing, and domestic duties within the house.[83] She played the organ at the small Catholic chapel in Prince George Street, and sang in the choir, but there was a growing sense of isolation. Mrs. Potter's dominance and her reluctance to allow her daughter to mix socially with the Catholic community of the area meant that Potter found no female friends of her own age. It was to become a source of irritation, and underscored the tension between mother and daughter. "I have mixed so little with the Church people," Mary wrote in 1876:

> My mother has been the obstacle. There is not a single house I visit. As regards young girls, there are few of the congregation my mother would consider in our position and she is very particular.[84]

Yet in spite of Mrs. Potter's control of the associations made by her daughter, the Potter household was one to which people were welcomed. Thomas, as master in his own house, brought his male friends to soirées that were attended by his mother and sister. He was undoubtedly careful in his choice of guests, those invited brought with them laughter and stimulation for his young sister. She contributed to their entertainment by accompanying them on the piano, and entering with alacrity into other home entertainments so beloved of the Victorians.[85] One frequent visitor to the Potter household was Godfrey King, a mathematics coach for the Indian Army examinations.

Godfrey King was, to all intents and purposes, a most suitable visitor to the home. He was quiet and serious, a "solid" Catholic possessed of impeccable manners. Well liked by his friend Thomas Potter, he was seen by Mrs. Potter as a model of rectitude and a very holy young man.[86] Sober, intelligent and obsessively committed to his Catholic faith, Godfrey began to take a deep, if surreptitious, interest in Thomas' young sister. As his visits to the Potter home continued, he became more attracted to the young woman who participated in the entertainment provided. Used to male companionship, Potter first accepted Godfrey as a friend of her beloved brother but, as he became more attentive, a romantic and innocent intimacy developed between the two.

King shared his religious aspirations with Potter and sought to interest her in a more intense practice of her own faith. A devotee of the writings of the Oratorian, Father William Fredrick Faber (1814–1863)[87] and European Catholicism in general, his piety was baroque, emotive, and shot through with a romantic idealism.[88] He lent Potter books, introduced her to the confraternity of Our Lady of the Immaculate Conception (more commonly known as the *Confraternity of Notre Dame des Victoires*), and urged her to commit herself to its aims – to combat religious indifference and convert sinners.[89] His interest and enthusiasm captivated Potter, and when he proposed that they should marry and live a life of marital virginity[90] like "Our Lady and St. Joseph," she accepted.[91] Godfrey was delighted. As a sign of his pleasure and affection, he presented his new fiancée with a book entitled *Instructions for Christians of a Timid Conscience who live in the World* with the inscription: "Mary Potter from Godfrey King, June 1867."[92] No ring was given to mark the engagement, the young couple opting instead to celebrate their betrothal by ordering a picture Our Lady of Victories from Paris, so that the "first present should be Our Lady."[93]

Mary's willingness to engage in marriage with Godfrey stunned her family. If they had noted the growing relationship, none had considered that "Trotty" – as Potter was called within the family – would leave the family home. The perennial child, she was simply "there" and her thoughts, wishes, and fantasies were totally unknown to those who believed they knew her best. But she was driven by her own longings. Reflecting on the whole experience, she later wrote: "From a child I wanted to be loved by others and to devote myself to them…When I grew to be a girl, the love of four elder brothers, and others was not sufficient for me. I wanted to have someone entirely devoted to me."[94] Godfrey provided that devotion and if an obsessive concern with moral purity and a high religious enthusiasm was exhibited in his proposal to Potter it reflects a Tennysonian adulation of chivalric love which had led others to embark upon the same course. The Ladies Lothian and Pembroke had entered such marriages, as Giroaurd illustrates,[95] and even if it was acceptable within the ranks of the upper classes, it was to find small encouragement from Potter's confessor.

For Potter, however, Godfrey King's offer of marriage with its utopian vision provided a means of escaping the family environment, and one may well speculate that the alleged equality of such a relationship was appealing precisely because it was untrammelled by notions of sexuality or gendered roles. As Giroaurd points out, such marriages had the distinct advantage of allowing women at least to move away from commonly accepted patterns of behaviour whilst at the same time allowing for friendship between men and women. They also had the effect of focusing emotions and sexual energies towards more "legitimate" ends, which for women were religious and philanthropic. [96]

Naïve and immature, Potter believed that her natural reserve regarding things sexual meant that she would never marry.[97] Religious life also held no attraction for her and to the time of Godfrey King's proposal, Potter's doom was to live as an unmarried daughter and sister in borrowed space by the whim of others. [98] Godfrey – and the fantasy of celibate marriage – offered a chance to move beyond the ancillary status accorded to her. It was the stuff of daydream. "I used to think how nice it would be to have a little house to ourselves and spend our lives in good works. We could be like Our Lady and St. Joseph," Potter wrote in her *Autobiographical Notes*,[99] and it came as a severe shock to both herself and Godfrey when Bishop Thomas Grant (1816–1870) of the Southwark diocese – Potter's confessor – ordered that the engagement be terminated.

Neither Godfrey King nor Mary Potter appeared to have considered that the church might not sanction such a marriage. Catholic doctrine was clear. The contract and the sacrament of marriage was "a lawful union of a man and woman by which they give themselves up one to the other for mutual society and the begetting of children."[100] For the marriage to be valid there had to be "the intention of living as man and wife."[101] When Mary went to share her good news with her confessor and family friend, Grant's reaction was swift and to the point. Mary could not marry under those circumstances, it was not the purpose of marriage within the church, and furthermore, it was his belief that marriage was not her vocation.[102] Grant followed up this interview with a letter to Potter's mother. She was to take her daughter to some convent and let her see what religious life was like.[103]

The instruction given by Grant to terminate her relationship with Godfrey came as a shock to Mary Potter, but, obedient to her confessor's command, she immediately wrote to her fiancé, telling him of what had happened, and calling the engagement off. Intensely hurt, Godfrey could not believe that the life he had planned together with Mary had been so summarily dismissed. In an outstanding breach of propriety that indicates the level of distress and agitation generated by Mary's letter, the normally conservative and restrained young man arrived at the Potter house at 8 o'clock one morning in an attempt to change Mary's mind and re-establish the relationship.[104] Mary would not see him. Grant again intervened and Godfrey was invited to call upon the bishop. He informed him that the engagement was invalid, and that Mary was no longer to be considered his fiancée.[105] The young man did not recover easily from the blow and friends and family alike remarked on his distress, Mary's brother Thomas going so far saying, "he never recovered from the disappointment. Half-insane for the rest of his days, he ended his life in a madhouse."[106]

Potter was as wounded by the event as Godfrey, but with Grant's encouragement, came to see that Godfrey had been simply "another brother" to her.[107] It was a recognition that did little to salve the hurt of the moment. Whatever her naivete, she had loved Godfrey in her own way, and her confessor's statement that she was "incapable of earthly love… [and] … called to be a Spouse of Jesus either in the convent or in the world,"[108] was hardly a consolation for the loss of the attentions of a personable, if somewhat peculiar, young man. After what she termed a "hard struggle," she followed the direction of the bishop and "gave up all [idea] of earthly love."[109]

Grant's exercise of power over Potter's life was not atypical of the role clergy played in regard to their women penitents, and it was a power resented by those who saw priests in both Anglican and Catholic persuasions usurping rights more properly belonging to male members of families.[110] But perhaps Mrs. Potter was glad of Bishop Grant's intervention, for she raised no objection to his interference in her daughter's life, nor did her brothers. In the absence of a husband, his control over the life of Potter appears absolute, and his decision once more thrust Potter into the dark reality of the life of a single woman dependent upon others for support. Outside employment was unthinkable, and the prospect of a convent held no appeal. But, by the bishop's command, Potter's choice was the acceptance of a virginal and self-sacrificing role either in the home or in the cloister. If she was not "made for man," she had few other options.

Spinster or nun: a dilemma of the times

From the middle of the century, the upsurge of religious orders in both Anglican and Catholic communities offered an alternative life to many single women.[111] Led by the Anglo-catholic revival of the Tractarians, religious communities of women began to appear in England in the 1840's. Promoted by such leaders as Newman and Pusey as a means whereby women could escape untenable marriages or the sterility of the single life, convents offered community, employment, stability and security.[112] They were, at least in the eyes of Dr. Newman, "the only shelter which a defenceless portion of the community has against the rude world …[saving them from] … the temptation of throwing themselves rustily away upon unworthy subjects."[113] Dedication to religious purpose was acceptable for women, and if convents did not suit all, single women like Potter could take advantage of what Charlotte M. Yonge saw as a solution to the apparent sterility of the single life – a devoted life of service:

> Wifehood was dignified by becoming a faint type or shadow of the union of the Church with her Lord. Motherhood was ennobled by the Birth that saves the world; and Maidenhood acquired a glory it had never had before, and which taught the unmarried to regard themselves, not as beings who had failed in the purpose of their existence, but as pure creatures, free to devote themselves to the service of their Lord; for as his Birth had consecrated Maternity; it had also consecrated Virginity. [114]

Such "consecrated virginity" did little to alleviate the stigma attached to the single woman. Philanthropy, as Frank Prochaska[115] and Anne Summers[116] have each pointed out, did provide an outlet for the energies of women. It was socially acceptable, and deemed particularly suitable for the female sex, who were perceived to be "possessed with an insatiable desire to have a finger in every benevolent pie, whether it's rubbing goose-oil on Mrs. Neighbour's croupy baby or working out some great plan for the world's reformation."[117] However, it was an unpaid work offering little in terms of security for middle-class single women. They remained locked in a state of dependency upon their families or forced as a means of survival into the world of employment, for which they were often ill equipped. Convent life, whether Anglican or Catholic, could focus and consolidate women's work. It had the appeal of providing a community of like-minded others, a means of becoming "helpers in all social good, not leaving …undirected energies to wear away … lives and sometimes trouble [the lives of men]."[118] Less altruistically, it also offered opportunity for revolt. Following the Catholic restoration of 1850, there was no better way for a daughter to defy and outrage the male dominion of the Victorian home than to remove herself from the control of father or brother and become a Catholic and a nun.[119]

Though society generally approved and blessed women's philanthropic endeavours as a true and right expression of both the virtues of religion and of women, not all agreed with the value or the validity of convent life. The Gothic revival in literature and publications of medieval romances depicting monks as ogres and nuns as examples of repressed female sexuality stimulated public imagination.[120] Protestant fears of sisterhoods grew and a general belief in the evil of female incarceration resulted in a backlash against convents, both Anglican and Catholic, finding them a seditious attack on that bastion of British society, the home.[121] After the restoration of the Catholic hierarchy in 1850, when anxiety about papal aggression became conflated with the rise of conventual life, convents came under further criticism. Deep suspicion of a celibate clergy and the convoluted Victorian obsession with sex combined to create patterns of sexual fantasy and social threat. Dominating all, however, was the perceived attack on the patriarchal power of husbands and fathers, and the function of women. These, as Ingham and Stone each suggest, were the cornerstones upon which anti-Catholicism was built.[122]

Whether perceived as places of terror and incarceration where hapless women were lured by the predatory desire of Rome and its celibate clergy, or as refuges for the lovelorn, the lonely or rebellious, convents drew much criticism and prurient interest from Victorian society.[123] Reporting attacks on nuns in Liverpool in 1853, *The Tablet* described religious women as "the most cherished objects of vituperation,"[124] and their exploits came under intense scrutiny. Tales of the imprisonment of orphans or sisters themselves were common, and at time brought before the courts.[125] The strands of criticism and concern that convents drew from the wider society were powerful agents for disturbance.[126]

Considering that the number of women entering religious communities was small,[127] the effect of their presence was immense, and spawned a new genre in art and literature throughout the nineteenth century.[128]

Both Potter and her mother appear to have shared in the general distaste for convent life. Having "vaguely thought about becoming a nun" as a child, Potter had put the thought aside with some repugnance.[129] Her convert mother, not finding any noticeable inclination to "religion" in her daughter, was even less enamoured of her leaving the family home to enter a convent, in spite of an earlier prophetic statement of Grant to that effect.[130] Grant, however, was firm on the issue of Potter's life direction. He believed that Potter had a vocation to live for God alone – either in the world or in the convent.[131] If the young woman was not to fritter her life away on useless daydreaming, she had to make a decision about her future. There seems little doubt that he believed entering a religious community would focus Potter's life on God, provide companionship and enable good works to be undertaken with impunity, but she was the only one able to make that decision.

In response to the bishop's statement, and having no real inclination to try her fortune as a religious, Mary sought to put aside her pain at the loss of Godfrey and set about to live as a "spouse of Jesus" in her world. In the belief that living a religious life in the world meant becoming more overtly pious, she increased her devotional practices and was noticed by the Catholic community for attending Mass and receiving communion "nearly every morning."[132] She began to attend the few organised church services at the Portsea parish[133] and adopted an air of intense piety. From the spring of 1868, she "came sometimes for Benediction [on] Wednesday and Fridays and of course, Sundays."[134] The Rosary was part of her life and she often made the Stations of the Cross in the local church.[135] Her high visibility and the overt nature of her devotional life, combined with a growing and zealous external charity, began to gain her a reputation. Local children such as Eleanor Smith remembered the impact the devout Miss Potter made upon her:

> To my childish mind she looked angelic, like one wrapped in God. Others noticed this and often I heard them say, "Ah, Miss Potter is very holy, she is a saint. For this reason and in order to be very good, I used to sit very near her.[136]

If the locals were impressed, her family was not. Mary was again disturbing the security of their world by this new "enthusiasm" for the spiritual life (an enthusiasm, it must be said, that Godfrey had played his part in developing). Her mother and brother complained to the bishop about her apparent excessive fervour in prayer, but he did nothing to curtail her activities. Local criticism became louder when her charitable actions became too "unseemly." Escorting an unknown drunken sailor through the gates of the Portsmouth Barracks, brought the wrath of "the Aunt Jane's" of society down upon her head,[137] while the complete unconcern with which she disposed of her own shoes and clothes drew her mother to despair.[138] Family correction brought no change as Potter, undismayed at the reaction she was causing, continued on her rounds of prayer and benevolent activity. The family's embarrassment at such "enthusiasm" was increased when Father Horan,[139] the parish priest of Portsmouth, arrived on the family doorstep to inform Thomas of his sister's profligate alms-giving and her excessive ardour for things religious.[140] In response to this complaint, Thomas attempted to curtail his sister's more extravagant benevolence. Her allowance from a legacy left to her was withheld, and in future, she was to request money for her needs from her mother.[141] He could do nothing about her life of prayer, but again Potter's freedom to determine her own life was curtailed, this time by her brother and her mother.

In the face of opposition to her full-blooded determination to live a spiritual life in the world, Mary continued on her rounds of prayer and good works, but she began to consider the opportunity offered by religious life. As a religious, she would not be subject to the control of brothers or mother, and her desire to engage in works of mercy would be normalised. Returning to speak with Bishop Grant, she told him of her growing interest in living as a nun. Grant, having been made aware of the difficulties surrounding Potter's practices of piety and charity, introduced her to a Redemptorist priest, Father Peter Burke,[142] to see if she truly felt drawn to the life of a religious. He wrote to Mrs. Mary Ann Potter, reminding her of the birth of this child, and of her promise to consecrate her to the Virgin Mary. "Do not be afraid of being alone, if she is called," he wrote, "as you always said when she was little that you hoped to be ready for this sacrifice."[143]

A young Mary Potter, circa 1860.

Bishop Grant, circa 1889.

The old stocking factory, Nottingham. It was to become the first home of Mary's order.

Mary, circa 1867.   *Mary, circa 1886.*

Potter began to correspond with Father Burke, and requested information regarding the different kinds of religious orders. He responded by providing her with literature on the different active and contemplative orders. The choice of a particular kind of religious life, he informed her, was based on a particular attraction to a given way of life or activity. Did she feel drawn by the silence, prayer, and solitude of the contemplative convent, or was she more at home with the idea of an active life, teaching, nursing, or caring for the poor?[144] He also made it quite clear that, in his opinion, Potter should look to particular congregations that would be prepared to accept her relative poverty and lower socio-economic status:

> I fancy you lean to some active Order. Then the question is: whether your attrait is merely for teaching children. In that case 'Notre Dame' would suit you and is easily entered. The order looks more to the subject than to her dowry. If you relish teaching and visiting the sick and poor, then, for my part, I should prefer the Sisters of Charity, otherwise known as 'of St. Vincent de Paul'. Money, I imagine, is no great difficulty there either…I have given you a standard or gauge by which you can measure yourself. Let me know the result, that is, your attrait. I shall probably consult the Bishop before I hear from you again.
>   No question of you being a lay sister. You need not wonder at any amount of temptation against a religious vocation.[145]

Potter was to read, reflect, and pray, to see if she could get some light on the subject of where she felt attracted to serve God. She set about the task with alacrity, and her reading and reflection bore fruit. The active life of a Sister of Mercy definitely did not appeal, but the contemplative life of the Carmelite community did.[146] "Such a strong light came to me that that was the one I must go to," she wrote "that, contrary to my usual custom of not troubling priests out of time, I went down to Portsea the same day to speak about it."[147] In spite of the strong "light" given that she was drawn to a contemplative community, neither Father Burke nor Bishop Grant considered it reasonable.

However, the reality was that Potter's desire to enter a community of contemplative nuns was beyond her reach. Traditionally the province of the aristocracy, the established Religious Orders[148] drew their choir membership from those who could afford the substantial dowry demanded.[149] In practical terms, as O'Brien[150] has pointed out, this ensured a class-based membership, ranked in terms of economic advantage rather that of spiritual virtuosity. Worker bees for the community hive, lay sisters within the contemplative communities were drawn from the ranks of the working classes, and theirs was a life of toil and drudgery. Separated from their more aristocratic sisters by different rules, habits, and prayer styles, they lived "humble and hidden lives" – often of severe hardship. In this segregation, as O'Brien states, there was a mirroring of "the status differences and the sexual divisions of the larger society in which the 'feminine' works of domestic labour and devotional ardour were simultaneously lauded and accorded lower status."[151]

Mary Potter, child of the lower middle-class, burdened with a family shame and tinged with the shade of "trade" was an uncomfortable fit for either choir or lay membership of a traditional contemplative community.[152] Her attraction was towards the contemplative life but it was an attraction that was to be denied. Following an interview with Bishop Grant in November 1868, she discovered that he had already decided on a plan of action for her. She and her mother were to follow his initial instruction to visit a convent and find out about the life of a religious. Writing to Mrs. Potter he explained his intent: "I think it would be well to take her to Brighton" he stated, "where she would see what convent life is like, as in all substantial matters, it resembles other orders."[153] In order to facilitate the investigation, he wrote to the Sisters of Mercy at the Brighton convent, telling of his interest in the Potter family and of his belief that God had some special designs in regard to the young woman. He asked that the community receive Mary and her mother so that she had some opportunity to learn about religious life.[154]

Obedient to the instruction of the bishop, Potter and her mother travelled to Brighton on December 7, 1868. They were to stay at the convent and Potter was to be provided with opportunity to see the life of the community. But on December 8, 1868 Mary Potter was received into the Sisters of Mercy as a postulant.[155]

The swiftness on the part of the community to receive the young woman as a postulant, and Mary's own decision to remain at the convent in that role, is curious. Neither the community nor Potter herself really knew if she had a vocation, and Grant's instructions to Mrs. Potter appeared clear. The visit was to help Mary gain some insight into the daily workings of a community in order to help her decide if religious life was really what she wanted. Certainly, Mrs. Potter's understanding of the journey was that it was a visit. Potter likewise did not intend to enter the community, and she was quick to point out to the superior, Mother Angela, that the Sisters of Mercy was the one community to which she felt positively unattracted.[156] So, what caused her to accept admission as a postulant and why had the community accepted her with such haste, particularly as she made clear her dislike of the Mercy order? Later, she would write that she thought Grant meant her to enter, but the fact remains that the two women expected to be received as guests within the house and Potter had brought no trousseau or dowry with her.[157] Far from being a considered choice, Potter's precipitous entry into the Mercy community appears to have been a moment of impulse and one might speculate if it was not – in part – motivated by the pressures she was experiencing at home.

In "giving up" marriage Mary Potter had also given up the chance to move away from home and family and assume an independent life. Tensions had been created within the family by her attempt to live "as spouse of Jesus" in the world. If there was to be freedom from the controls of family life in order to live for God alone, then entering the Mercy community provided an opportunity to make a necessary break. Perhaps her own fears and lack of attraction to the Mercy community were allayed by the discovery that Mother Mary Louis, the current Novice Mistress, was an old school friend, and by what appears as an overwhelming eagerness on the part of the community to receive her.[158] Speculation aside, it is a particularly clouded moment in Potter's life, but one destined to have an impact upon her. Furthermore, if her later writings are to be believed, the decision to enter was facilitated by the decision of the superior of the community that the simplest way for Mary to find out about religious life was to enter it.[159] If this was the case, it was against Catherine McAuley's own rule, in which it was stated that:

> Such as desire to embrace this Religious Institute shall be previously examined with respect to their vocation by the Bishop or priest delegated by him and by the Mother Superior.[160]

If the community had considered Grant's letter as one of recommendation of Potter as a postulant, it was not one he had conveyed to Potter and her mother. Whatever the reasons, it was a hasty and ill-prepared entrance, and, according to witnesses of the separation between mother and daughter, it was a painful break for both.[161]

Postulant and Novice in the Sisters of Mercy

On December 8, 1868 Mary Potter walked into a world unlike anything she had ever known. Founded upon the vision of Catherine McAuley (1787–1841),[162] the Brighton community in Bristol Road had been established from Bermondsey in June 1852 with Mother Angela Graham as its founder.[163] By 1868, the community had grown considerably. There were some forty members – twenty-nine professed sisters, eight novices and three postulants.[164]

The Brighton convent had been quick to establish its own particular works of mercy, which followed McAuley's desire to "make some lasting efforts for the relief of the suffering and instruction of the ignorant."[165] By 1865, it supported an Orphanage (capable of accommodating fifty girls), a Home of Preservation, which provided shelter for poor working women of the area, and a laundry in which "women and girls of good character [were] employed."[166] As with other Mercy communities, financial support was garnered from "[t]he pious sex [who were] specially invited to patronise this charity by laundry and needlework."[167] In addition, to these works, the community also staffed schools for girls and infants in the Brighton parish of St. John the Baptist, held instruction classes for adults and visited the poor.

As a postulant, Mary was introduced to the daily round of prayer practised by the Sisters of Mercy, and to the works of the order. For the first time in her life, she entered a process of prayer and work that imposed both discipline and structure. It was not an easy adjustment for one who, on her own admission, had "never even made [her] own bed,"[168] yet she threw herself into the task of living this new life as rigidly and perfectly as she was able.

Her day began at five-thirty each morning. At six o'clock there was communal morning prayer and meditation followed by Mass. Breakfast followed and after that, a half-hour spiritual reading in common, with the Superior, Mother Angela, or Novice Mistress, Mother Louis, presiding. Those engaged in the visitation of the sick were exempt from any 'choir duty' (i.e. chapel attendance) from ten until four 'clock, but all had to be together for the midday Office, and all had to attend lectures. Following dinner at twelve-thirty, there was a brief period of recreation followed by the communal recitation of Vespers, Compline and the Litany of Our Lady. Five-thirty saw a second half-hour of spiritual reading by the Superior, followed by the recitation of community prayers, and the offices of Matins and Lauds. A light meal was taken at six forty-five, followed by recreation. Night prayer ended the day and included the Litany of the Saints, a further general examen of conscience, and the preparation for the next morning's meditation. General silence was part of the convent daily discipline.[169]

Surrounded by all this prayer, were the works of the congregation. Teaching, care and supervision of the orphans, home visitation of the sick were all knit within the daily activities. As a postulant, Mary accompanied a professed sister on visitation of the sick, the poor, and the housebound.[170] She learned basic skills of attendance at the bedside of those suffering or dying, and followed the principles laid down in the constitutions of the Sisters of Mercy to care "with great tenderness" those who were ill, and "when death is not immediately expected … to relieve the distress first and to endeavour by every practicable means to promote the cleanliness, ease and comfort of the Patient."[171] She also taught in the parish school, St. Michael's, but it was noted that she "could not keep the attention of a class of children for any length of time, but could teach just a few beautifully."[172] In addition to prayer and professional duties, the works of everyday life had to be performed. Cooking, cleaning, polishing, washing, were all daily tasks to be squeezed into the times allocated. It was not a schedule for the faint hearted, or frail of constitution. For a delicate twenty-one year old postulant with no real skill, it was a race against time from the moment of rising to that of falling into bed at night.

In spite of the pressure, Mary survived her postulancy. Eight months after her entry, she received the habit of a novice in the Congregation of the Sisters of Mercy. The ceremony was held in the local parish church next to the convent, presided over by Canon Henry Rymer.[173] Admission was "by ticket," and an account of the reception appeared in the local paper. There it was recorded that Miss Potter from London: "attired in a rich white bridal dress, a long white lace veil flowing over her from a wreath of white flowers, which rested upon her head; her hair clustering in ringlets around her neck,"[174] was received as a novice. The building was three-parts filled when "the Lady Superioress and assistant … led the 'postulant' to the altar, where she knelt and remained upon her knees"[175] as the ceremony unfolded around her. She received the habit of the order, a new name (Sister Mary Aloysius), and the rules of the institute of the Sisters of Mercy. For all that it was a gala performance worthy of reporting, Potter's lasting memory was of the embarrassment the occasion afforded her. The "rich white bridal dress" was the cause of the problem, for Potter, schooled to severe modesty of manner and dress, found it far too revealing. She found it was:

> such a pain having to wear a dress, which left me very uncovered. I was afraid of being disobedient in spirit, and all I could do was to unite with our Lord stripped of his garments, as I had to go before a crowded congregation, band playing etc….I said after I would not like to go into my mother's presence like that, and my Novice Mistress consoled me saying she would not like it either.[176]

It is hard to imagine that the sisters would have dressed Mary in a gown of revealing cut. If anything, the anguish experienced over the dress reveals the limitations of Potter herself, and suggests that the young woman being clothed in the habit of religion was rather prudish, conforming to and expressive of a stereotype of Victorian lower middle-class respectability and repression.[177] The scrupulosity that had plagued her childhood years was not yet overcome, and her mother's rigid code of behaviour, fuelled by the scars of desertion and debt, resulted in a heightened moral sensitivity. Perhaps too, Potter's response to the "richness" and the low-cut nature of the dress was exacerbated by the absence of any family members at this very public reception. Mrs. Potter had not accepted her daughter's entry into religious life, and demonstrated her disapproval by non-attendance.

Following the ceremony, the new Sister Mary Aloysius had the task of entering a more intense study and experience of the Mercy way of life. In addition, she was expected to consolidate and deepen her relationship with God according to the spirit and spirituality of the institute. Withdrawn from the works of the order, her life was now surrounded by a domestic routine. The daily round of prayer remained the same, but there was increased emphasis on the spiritual life and a greater testing of the novice's capacity to conform herself to the spirit of the institute. Her spiritual formation rested in the hands of her novice mistress, her superior, and any priest appointed to act as the community's confessor or spiritual director. The next twelve months of Mary Potter's life were to prove of vital significance for her future development. As she entered the life of a Mercy novice, she was exposed to a sustained formation in the spiritual life. It was, however, a time of tension and conflict, for as Potter responded to the spiritual formation provided for her, it became increasingly obvious to those charged with her development, that her vocation did not lie with the Sisters of Mercy.

Mercy Spirituality

Mercy spirituality was an amalgam of McAuley's own historical traditions. Based upon a belief in the centrality of the Gospel values, the spiritual life of the Mercy institute required that the individual look to Jesus as the model and exemplar of all things. As McAuley had written, "our divine model, Jesus Christ, should be in regard of a Religious like a book, continually open before her, from which she must learn what she is to think, say and do."[178] Living according to the evangelical spirit of Jesus meant imitating the virtues and values of Jesus.[179] Thus each sister was admonished by the rule to "[b]e always striving to make yourselves like him – you should try to resemble him in some one thing at least, so that any person who sees you, or speaks with you, may be reminded of his blessed life of earth."[180]

This conformity to the spirit of Jesus was central to the Mercy vocation. Novices and postulants of the institute were to imitate by practice Christ's evangelical love of the poor and suffering. Their perfection as religious "depend[ed] not so much on doing extraordinary actions as one doing extraordinarily well the ordinary actions of every day."[181] Purity of intention was paramount, and McAuley's rule demanded all that the sisters did, be done "with the intention of pleasing God [for] God and God alone must be the principle motive of all action."[182] In order for this attitude to develop, the members of the community were to keep themselves mindful of the presence of God, "do the duty of every day, as if that day were to be their last of their mortal life,"[183] avoid idleness,[184] preserve a dignified and religious silence – which was "the faithful guardian of interior recollection,"[185] – and through the practice of charity maintain an inner unity within the congregation.[186]

McAuley's strong call to serve the needs of the poor and the ignorant, had been shaped by Quaker influences,[187] which, as Sheila Carney suggests, emphasised and valued as spiritual realities, belief in the indwelling Spirit and the power of redemptive love.[188] The Friends' conviction of the potential for good in each person and the consequent sensitivity to human degradation, ignorance, suffering, and injustice translated well into Catherine's vision for her congregation, becoming part of the practical training for those who would follow the Mercy way of life. "The spirit of the Institute," McAuley wrote, "is Mercy towards those who are afflicted with ignorance, suffering and like miseries. This requires such a combination of the spirit of Mary and Martha, that one does not hinder but helps the other."[189] In such a life, prayer was important, but it was blended within the daily works. Highly apostolic, McAuley's "walking nuns"[190] were to be living expressions of the charity of Jesus.

Formation for novices within the Sisters of Mercy was placed in the hands of the Novice Mistress who was to form her charges and "make them truly sensible of the end they should have in view in quitting the world."[191] "Judicious in discerning the dispositions of such as are under her care," she was to assist the novices to:

> unite their hearts perfectly to God by dying to themselves and to the world so as to apply all the powers and faculties of their souls to the service of their Heavenly Spouse, by a spirit of evangelical poverty, divested of all inordinate attachments, by the purest chastity and by an unlimited obedience, grounded on self-denial and an entire surrender of their own will; …in short, that this Institute is in a special manner founded on Calvery [sic], there to serve a crucified Redeemer. By whose example the Sisters ought to crucify their senses, imaginations[sic], passions, inclinations and caprices for the love of their Divine Master.[192]

Potter's response to this element of Mercy spirituality was enthusiastic. It met with her desire to live for God alone and provided a rationale for the self-denial and asceticism she began to practice. Mercy devotion to the Virgin Mary also drew Potter, for it asked of each sister the "warmest and most affectionate devotion," towards the Virgin, who was:

> the great Model they are obliged to imitate, that by Her intercession and Powerful protection, they may be enabled to fulfil the obligations of this Holy Institute, and implant Jesus Christ in the hearts of the poor, whom they are called to instruct.[193]

These two elements of Mercy spirituality – the redemptive power of the Cross and love for and emulation of the Virgin – profoundly impressed themselves upon Mary Potter, and these, along with a strong devotion to the Eucharist, were to be of fundamental importance to her own future development. But the months of her novitiate passed, tensions began to emerge, and questions were asked about Potter's suitability to the life of an active Sister of Mercy.

Along with her fellow novices, Potter was tested in her practice of the virtues – particularly obedience and humility. Religious obedience, the Mercy constitution named "the principal virtue of religious life," and it was seen as the "sacrifice of the soul to God."[194] Potter had little difficulty with this demand of the rule. Indeed, she succeeded so well in living a selfless life that her novice mistress wondered if she had any will of her own.[195] Submission to the will of another did not trouble her,[196] nor did the practice of self-denial.[197] In her eyes, she had done the most difficult thing she would have to do. "When I went to the convent they wondered that I took everything so easily," Potter wrote, and found it difficult that others did not understand what she knew about herself, namely "that nothing was difficult to me; … I had done everything before I went in, in giving up my engagement etc."[198] Indeed, Potter appeared to her those around her as an exemplary novice. She was perceived by those that knew her as "very good and holy," and remarkable "for [her] charity, humility, [and] strict observance of the rule." [199]

With certain simplicity she had entered religious life with an idea of loving God, and finding a niche for herself which would free her from the sterility of home and give her life meaning. To all appearances her naturally docile manner appeared to fit well into the conventual life, and if her goodness was unchallenged, those charged with her training were not convinced that her vocation was to the Mercy way of life. The question of health was always problematic for Mary's continuance as a Sister of Mercy, but the real difficulty for those responsible for her development came from an unexpected quarter, namely, her evolving piety.

Because it was an active institute of women, dedicated to the service of the poor, ignorant and sick, issues of prayer were important within the Mercy lifestyle, but were to be carefully balanced against the imperative of service. In 1841, a crisis had occurred in the Bermondsey (London) foundation of the Sisters of Mercy,[200] when the ministerial vocation of the community was threatened by the desire of the superior, Mother Clare Agnew for greater emphasis on the contemplative life.[201] Determined that the strong apostolic life of the community was to be preserved, Catherine McAuley removed Agnew from her office as superior, replaced her with Mother Clare Moore,[202] and prepared a document, which laid down the precise nature of the relationship between the spiritual and apostolic works of the order.[203] According to this statement, the Sisters of Mercy were called:

> To devote our lives to the accomplishment of our own salvation and to promote the salvation of others, [that] is the end and object of our Order of Mercy. These two works are so linked together by our rule and observances that they reciprocally help each other. We should often reflect that our progress in the spiritual life consists in the faithful discharge of the duties belonging to our state, as regards both our selves and our neighbour; and we must consider the time and exertion which we employ for the relief and instruction of the poor and ignorant as most conducive to our own advancement in perfection, and the time given to prayer and all other pious exercises we must consider as employed to obtain the grace, strength and animation which alone could enable us to persevere in the meritorious obligations of our state: and if we were to neglect these means of obtaining Divine Support, we would deserve that God should stop the course of His graces to make us sensible that all our efforts would be fruitless except we were continually renewed and replenished with his Divine Spirit.[204]

The fine tension of Catherine McAuley's institute depended upon a proper blend between the apostolic and contemplative dimensions. Differing from monastic spirituality in its originating focus, the contemplative dimension of Mercy life found its origin in the poor, sick and suffering, as the document on the spirit of the institute points out. There, among the poor was found the "stuff" of prayer, as Joanne Regan[205] and Mary Celeste Rouleau[206] have noted. Immersion in this world led to a contemplation of God in the mystery of his suffering people. Therefore, union with God would be achieved by *doing* the works of Mercy. In McAuley's spirituality, as Ann Scofield intimates, the sister "becomes" Mercy – unified with Jesus in his actions and desires.[207] For Catherine McAuley, the union between the creature and Creator was achieved through a loving attention and service to Jesus made visible in the persons of her beloved, suffering poor.[208]

For Mary Potter however, this path of Mercy spirituality was proving a particularly difficult passage. By nature she was reserved, less inclined to draw her spiritual resources from the world around her. More imaginative than practical, she began to experience difficulties in her prayer life which gradually drew her novice mistress to believe that the young woman she directed was more suited to a traditional contemplative community – as Potter's own prior discernment had indicated. It was a view that was also held by the Jesuit confessor to the community, Father George Lambert. [209]

No records exist of the precise details of Potter's spiritual development in the time of her novitiate in 1869 and 1870. The glimpses that do exist suggest that she was being drawn to a prayer life far different from that suggested by the Mercy rule. She could not pray as recommended, had developed a strong devotion to Eucharistic adoration, and had some intense religious experiences which both frightened and puzzled her.[210] Lambert, a skilled spiritual director formed by his Jesuit tradition of discernment,[211] believed that her religious experiences were genuine, and backed by his own training in Ignatian spirituality,[212] encouraged the young woman to pursue her life of prayer. He told her to pray in her own way, rather than as the rule prescribed, [213] encouraged her in her devotion to the Eucharist, and most importantly, assured her that "a certain union with our Lord I was afraid was a delusion, was not."[214] But if Lambert supported Potter's religious development, he was also becoming convinced that her call to religious life, while genuine, was not to the Sisters of Mercy. This was also a decision reached independently by Mother Louis, who, by the end of 1869, had become convinced that Potter's call was to a contemplative community. She raised the issue with her novice, suggesting that she was more suited to a contemplative order, one that would offer her scope for a life centred upon prayer.[215] Potter's response was that she feared such a move, that she "might have to have high states of prayer and I did not want to. I have had such a dislike to anything out of the ordinary way."[216] Willing to wait until Potter came to some personal determination about her life direction, yet anxious for her charge to have the spiritual supports necessary to her, Mother Louis took the unusual step of requesting permission for Potter to receive Communion more often.[217] It was a request that was denied by the new superior of the House, Mother Joseph Barrington, who, rather than permit Potter more frequent reception of communion, actually withheld her from it.[218]

Barrington's decision to restrict Potter's reception of the sacrament is an anomaly considering the Mercy rule. The constitutions provided a support for a strong devotion to the Eucharist. Sisters were admonished to "cherish in their hearts the tenderest and most affectionate devotion to this Adorable Sacrament,"[219] to attend daily Mass "and approach the Holy Communion with lively faith, profound humility and the utmost purity, as often as their spiritual director may permit."[220] However, a clause forbade the reception of communion three days in succession "without permission from the Mother Superior."[221] In denying Potter the right to receive communion more frequently, against the recommendations of her novice mistress, Mother Louis, and her confessor, Father Lambert SJ, Mother Joseph Barrington was acting with a degree of autonomy contrary to the perception of the church and the spirit of the rule. Though charged with the spiritual care of those under her,[222] she was, as superior, still under the canonical requirement of the church. Her refusal to permit Potter to receive communion with greater frequency and at times, to forbid her to approach the sacrament contravened the discretion of the superior's office. [223] Unfortunately for Potter, Barrington did not consider her a worthy candidate for the Mercy community, as later events demonstrated, and her assessment of the novice was that "her mind was weak and she was nervous and imaginative, and this most probably would have increased in her."[224]

From the end of 1869, a growing tension surrounded Potter, and her future within the Brighton community was becoming even more tenuous. While there was consensus between Mother Louis and Father Lambert regarding the reality of Potter's religious vocation, there was a lack of agreement about where that vocation would find its fulfilment. Mother Louis maintained her belief that Potter's vocation lay within the contemplative community of Carmel, while Father Lambert was equally convinced that she would find a fulfilling role with the semi-enclosed community of the Sisters of the Assumption, also known as the Order of Perpetual Adoration, in Kensington.

Lambert's selection of the Sisters of the Assumption for Potter gives some indication of his own belief regarding the spirituality of the woman he was directing. Eschewing the Carmelite life of prayer and penance, he had selected an order in which the contemplative life was blended with Eucharistic adoration and apostolic activity. Founded in 1839 by Eugénie Milleret de Brou as an outcome of the revival of religious life in France,[225] the congregation of the Assumption had as its aim the "contemplation and study of divine things as the source of an active life of apostolate."[226] According to Steele, it was a truly "mixed" congregation. It united the monastic life of the old orders with an apostolate of education.[227] Recitation of the Divine Office and adoration of the Blessed Sacrament were fundamental aspects of the inner life of the community, and Lambert was convinced that this more monastic community could provide an environment in which Potter's desire to live for God alone would flourish. He discussed the issue with Potter and suggested that he make enquiries of the superior of the Assumptionist community regarding a transfer.[228] In the meantime, she was to leave the issue in his hands and continue her novitiate.[229] He did not discuss the issue with Mother Louis or Mother Joseph, apparently believing that time was not of the essence and that there was no concern within the Mercy community regarding Potter's continuance as a novice of the order.

Problematically, however, tensions between Mother Louis, Father Lambert, and Mother Joseph continued, and were further exacerbated by Mother Louis' control of the spiritual life of her charge. She remained convinced that life as a Carmelite would satisfy and make

sense of Potter's contemplative nature, and continued to suggest that Potter consider trans-
ferring to such a community. Potter continued to vacillate. While the Carmelite order
appealed, she feared the consequences of an intense prayer life. Unable to make up her
mind, torn by the conflicting advice she was receiving from her two spiritual advisers, she
began to suffer in health.

Mother Joseph, now convinced that Potter's response to the suggestions made by
Mother Louis was stubbornness,[230] held to her belief that the young woman was no fit
subject for religious life in general and the Mercy congregation in particular. As Potter's
health deteriorated, she began to suggest to the novice that her illness, manifested by faint-
ing in church and general debility, "was a difficulty in the way of perseverance."[231] In spite
of Mother Louis's concern to allow time for Potter to accept her vocation to a contemplative life, Mother Joseph continued to pressure Potter to leave the community. Still using
the pretext of Potter's health as the issue of concern, but apparently reluctant to actually
dismiss her, she told Potter that while she had "full leave to stay… she thought I had better go, on purpose to make it easier for me to obtain permission in another convent."[232]
Potter was now even more confused. Her confessor was advising her to continue her novitiate while he explored the potential for transfer to an order, which, he believed, would
lead Potter into the contemplative life to which she was drawn. At the same time, Mother
Louis was advocating a move to a contemplative house, namely the Carmelites. Now
Mother Joseph's intervention provided another alternative – she could stay, but if she did
she may not get accepted for profession due to her health, and her continuance with the
Sisters of Mercy could jeopardise her chances to enter another order.

The conflict between superior, confessor and novice director became increasingly obvious in the early months of 1870, yet Potter remained uncertain about what path to take.
Tensions became more overt when Mother Louis refused to permit Potter to make a general confession to Lambert, and even Potter became aware of the difficulties between priest
and community leaders, stating that:

> though I was a child and knew nothing about the sometimes difficulties between nuns
> and priests, I instinctively felt he would not be pleased with the interference and there-
> fore let him think I had changed my mind rather than let him be put out with the
> Convent.[233]

The young woman remained unable to make a decision. Believing she had a religious
vocation, though now aware that it was not to the Mercy order, she still sought to abide
by the advice of her spiritual director and her novice mistress. Neither had advocated leaving the community, and Lambert's instructions were quite specific: she was to continue
her novitiate and leave the matter of a transfer to the Sisters of the Assumption to him.
Accounts of the pressure being applied to Potter by Mother Joseph were conveyed to
Lambert, who reacted with great displeasure.[234] He suggested that time be given to allow
discernment to take place. Under his direction, Potter wrote to the Superior of the

Assumption Sisters, requesting a transfer. The superior accepted this, but due to a number of refugees from France needing accommodation, the community could not admit Potter for some months.[235] An uneasy time of waiting commenced. The matter was finally resolved in the June of 1870, when Potter suffered a complete breakdown in health. Mother Joseph, concerned by the apparent severity of the collapse, immediately wrote to Thomas Potter, and informed him of his sister's illness. Mrs. Potter was distraught at the news, and directed Thomas to write to Mother Joseph suggesting that Mary should return home. Mother Joseph replied by return post. "I cannot demur to your sister's return," she told Thomas, "as I am convinced that she has neither health nor capacities for a religious life."[236]

In spite of believing that Mother Joseph's assessment of Potter was erroneous,[237] her family responded to her letter with immediate action. On June 23, 1870 Mary's mother and brother came to collect her and her departure from the community was as odd as her entry. On her mother's arrival at the convent in Brighton, Potter informed her family of the temporary nature of her return home, and of her decision to transfer to the Sisters of the Assumption. Mrs. Potter responded with an immediate, passionate outburst. Her daughter – whom she had permitted to try her vocation as a Sister of Mercy only after Bishop Grant's intervention – would not be permitted to leave home ever again. The outburst shocked the gathered sisters. Mother Joseph, according to Potter, "tried to get my mother to promise that when I got well she would let me go to the convent Fr. Lambert had chosen for me,"[238] and went so far as to suggest that should Mrs. Potter persist in refusing to consider her daughter's return to religious life (though not to the Sisters of Mercy), Potter could do her convalescence at the Brighton convent.[239] In the face of such pressure, Mrs. Potter offered a grudging assent, but neither she nor her daughter knew that Potter's future was to be shaped by other circumstances, and that her proposed plan to enter the Sisters of the Assumption would never be realised.

On Thursday, June 23, 1870 Mary Potter returned home to Southsea with her mother and brother. The convent annals give some indication of the complex issues and the confusion surrounding her departure:

> It was found impossible that Sr. M. Aloysius Potter should remain, her health continued so delicate. She was exceedingly good and holy, but quite unable for the duties, besides which, her mind was weak and she was nervous and imaginative, and this most probably would have increased in her. Father Lambert, the Jesuit was quite grieved at the decision of the community, and applied to the Assumption nuns to receive her. She went to the convent and was introduced to the Superior, but she was afraid of receiving her. She returned home to her mother and has since founded an Order of her own.[240]

Two days after her departure, Mother Joseph wrote to the Vicar General of the Southwark diocese notifying him that Sister Aloysius Potter had left the institute. Absolving herself of any interference in the decision, she merely remarked that Potter left because "her Mama, fearing that a longer trial here might increase her disease, thought it better to take her home immediately."[241] Broken in health and spiritually depleted Potter returned to her family home. In many respects, her illness could have been anticipated, for life within the community of the Sisters of Mercy was hard for an aspirant, and the daily round of prayer and manual labour took their toll on Potter's already frail constitution. But was there a deeper reason for the sudden physical collapse?

Above all things else, religious life is a process of asceticism historically grounded in the quest to lose all things in order to gain God.[242] Through the process of formation a novice was thrust into disciplines of service, self-abnegation, and prayer in order to create the conditions necessary for a shifting of consciousness, a potentiality for mystical experience, and the acquisition of that spiritual or inner freedom which would consolidate spiritual power and authority.[243] Lambert's belief in Potter's religious experiences offers support for the fact she was already being drawn into some form of union with God. Her fear of "delusion," arising from the para-mystical "symptoms" of her prayer – a heightened sensitivity and a sense of taste and touch particularly after reception of communion[244] – was understandable, as was her fear of the further consequences of such a prayer life. Though delighted to know that she was not suffering from any delusion regarding to the experiences she had related to Father Lambert, she remained ambivalent about their meaning. Her response to her director's belief that she was called to a contemplative life was that she did not want to have "high states of prayer,"[245] disliked "anything out of the ordinary way,"[246] and sought only a simple life.[247] Indicating both an unwillingness to venture out of comfortable patterns of piety and a fear of becoming something "other" than what she considered herself to be, her resistance to her director's insight must be placed against the cultural determinants that maintained women as a subjugated species throughout the nineteenth century.

Prescriptive and material reality combined to impose upon women a lifestyle and pattern of behaviour that shaped their responses to life and their own creativity.[248] Considered a member of the second sex, a "helpmeet" to man, with limited capacity for self-realisation or self-direction, women had roles which were clearly defined and stringently enforced.[249] To welcome any movement towards personal autonomy or self-realisation was to enter ambiguity, for it required a self-definition unconfined by received tradition or the surrounding culture.[250] It was a daunting process for any woman, including Mary Potter, for it required the capacity to imagine a life beyond the confines of conditioning. Potter needed the courage to grasp the power of self-identification, the power to be:

> imaginative – to outline their own lives. And by this, I mean the power of marking out distinctly the channels into which one's energies should flow, and for which they should be reserved. People are but too ready to make demands on time and strength not obviously appropriated; and without a distinct outline in one's own mind, it is doubly hard not to yield to such demands.[251]

There was a price to be paid for that acknowledgment. The movement to inner freedom that had begun in Potter, asked the willingness to move beyond social stereotypes, even the stereotypical forms of what constituted a "good" religious or what it meant to be "holy." Potter's resistance to "high states of prayer" was not simply a pious humility (though undoubtedly part of it), but a very real fear of the demands such a life would make upon her. Lacking the imagination to "see" herself within the contemplative path, yet by nature and inclination drawn to it, she fell into confusion and resistance. Perhaps too, Potter partially recognised the consequences of the mystical life. In her persistent rejection of "high states of prayer," she also rejected the loss of ego boundaries, the radical aloneness and the new realisation of self that the journey to the mystical life demanded.[252] It would be some years before a "liberty of spirit" would take root in Potter, and prior to its fulfilment, she would experience physical breakdown and psychological turmoil as her inner life developed. Symptoms of inner pressure and stress, her illnesses and fragility were not helped by her rapid and pressured exit from the Mercy community or the restraints again imposed by her home life. If Potter was to achieve self realisation, then she had to face and overcome the strong biological and religious arguments regarding women's nature and their role within society, which continually placed women in the position of "being little capable of reasoning, feeble and timid, requir[ing] protection."[253]

According to society, good women were "to dwell in homes, amongst a few friends; to exercise a noiseless influence, to be submissive and retiring."[254] Those who did not conform, who asserted their rights and their competence to enter the professions or engage in social reform with its implicit criticism of the male conduct of public affairs, were deeply troubling in the nineteenth century, as their independent lives appeared iconoclastic to many of their peers. They were also deeply troubling to themselves as they sought to make sense of the inner imperative that drove them, and they adopted various mechanisms for coping with the relentless demands of family and culture.[255] Problematically, the choices were limited, and when they resulted in the adoption of a career, entry into a convent, or the embracing of social or religious causes, women were ridiculed, criticised and, at times, alleged to be mad.[256] Such accusation would follow Potter as she moved back into the family home and sought to come to terms with the changes in her life. Her slow growth to self-realisation confronted the extraordinarily sensitive issues of self-esteem and culturally determined "otherness" of being.

The journeys begun through a spiritual process, now demanded Potter choose her life direction. She could either decline into being a genteel, useful female drudge within her brother's home – or assent to the "glimpse of consciousness divine" she had experienced, however dimly, within the Mercy community. To accept the first was to remain in a condition of subservience, to accept the second was to accept that she was central to the process and that a degree of independence and pro-activity was needed. What she did not know, nor could know, was that the next six years of her life were to be years of transition as her spiritual odyssey drew her to a new understanding of herself, her God and her ultimate vocation. The spiritual formation she had received with the Mercy community continued to provide the basis of her life of prayer. She now knew, experientially and intellectually – though still within certain limits – the meaning and call of the spiritual life. To live for God alone was a reality for which she longed. She kept herself focused on her goal to live the life of a religious, for she now believed that was truly where she belonged. At the same time, however, her lack of desire for what she called "high states of prayer" remained. Paradoxical as it may seem, this very lack of desire may have been the reason that over the following years, Mary would experience both the joy and the suffering of the contemplative life.

SECTION 2

Transitions (1870–1877)

Transitions (1870–1877)

When Potter entered the Brighton community of the Sisters of Mercy, she was an emotionally charged, religiously enthused twenty-one year old. By the time she left the community in 1870, her understanding of the spiritual life and her view of her place in the world had undergone a subtle, if not monumental, shift.

Both the discipline and the activity of religious life had broadened Potter's world view. The next seven years would see a further shift in consciousness as she struggled against the narrow confines of home and the social constructs, which placed her in a role of dependency, submission, and domesticated virtue. Religion continued to play an important part in her life, and through the adoption of a way of spirituality that encouraged deep asceticism, meditation, a penitential life style and openness to revelatory experiences, Potter came to a new depth of understanding of herself and her world.

As this section illustrates, her growth and development were essentially linked to her adoption of another way of knowing, which brought with it the ability to reach beyond the confines of studied ignorance and intellectual dependency to which women of her class and time were condemned. As she entered the practice of a spiritual path, which had as its end mystic union with God, she not only realised herself in new definition, but also became convinced that she had a call from God to initiate a new religious order within the Catholic church. Influenced by an apocalyptic sense of the need for change and renewal within the church, Potter backed her claims for her mission and her vision on experiences of God. These shaped and patterned her responses to her church and world and, as this section will illustrate, became a source of power and creativity.

Convinced that her experiences gave their own veridicality, Potter began to construct a theology of religious life. Her view that religious life did not exist in the church simply as a means for personal holiness or for the provision of social welfare services, found few supporters, but she continued to seek acceptance for her belief that religious orders were prophetic "gifts" of the Spirit, brought into being for the renewal of the church. In a world in which theological thought and creative vision were denied to women, she found small welcome. Her emerging theological acumen drew her into conflict with ecclesial authorities, as did her conviction that there was a need for reform and renewal in the church.

In spite of the opposition ranged against her, Potter's journey over the years 1870–1876 was one of personal and spiritual growth. It was, however, a journey marked by suffering and contradiction, as the woman became the mystic and visionary that she believed she was called to be.

Transitions 1870–1872

Mary Potter returned to her family home in the July of 1870, broken in health and spiritually depleted. Her congenital heart condition, aggravated by the emotional and spiritual intensity of life within the convent, had brought a great physical debility that left her an invalid for the remainder of 1870 and the first half of 1871. In the solitude of her room at the top of her brother's house in Southsea, Potter vacillated between hope and despair. Now isolated from the support of her novice mistress, Mother Louis, and her spiritual director, Father Lambert, her struggle was to regain her health in order to enter the convent of the Sisters of the Assumption. As her strength improved, however, she found herself again at odds with the petty tyrannies of her mother's care. She was unable to go out without her mother's consent or approval, and the tension between mother and daughter mounted.[1]

In spite of her promise to Mother Joseph on the day of Potter's departure from the Mercy community, by 1871 Mrs. Potter was obdurate in her refusal to consider her daughter's re-entrance to a religious community. In her eyes, Mary's return to the family home was an act of God. "[T]he good Lord restored her to [me] even as He did the young Isaac to Abraham" she wrote to a priest supportive of her daughter's wishes, "[and] I consider she was given back to me, so God helping me, not again will I part from her."[2] Potter, however, believed that she "had broken with home and all ties and was only remaining from necessity, intending to enter a convent again."[3] The disparate views between mother and daughter became fertile ground for tension, and though Potter maintained a dutiful presence within the home, the continued possessiveness of her mother rankled.[4] Frustrated by the lack of opportunity to practice the skills "to nurse, teach, write etc., even housekeep and cook"[5] she had learned in the Mercy convent, she began works of philanthropy in the Southsea and Portsmouth districts visiting cases recommended to her by her parish priest, Father Horan.[6]

Such activity not only gave Potter an outlet from the confines of her home environment, it also provided opportunity to practice the virtues of the spiritual life – active charity, self-denial, and the scope to demonstrate love of neighbour. The pattern of prayer established in the Mercy novitiate continued, but as her rounds of visitation to the poor and sick continued, she found herself drawn to pray particularly for the dying.[7]

Of itself, Potter's interest and involvement in prayer of intercession for the dying was not unusual. As historians Michael Wheeler and Pat Jalland both suggest, theological shifts created complex questions regarding death, dying, heaven and hell, for the Victorians,[8] and if the English Catholic experience of death and dying lay in a more ambiguous relationship to its cultural surrounds, Catholic tradition shaped the concerns of its members.[9] Fed by missions and fuelled by fear, prayers for "a happy death" were part and parcel of every Catholic's private devotion.[10] Potter's concern for those "at the hour of death," expressed itself through her prayer for those souls "in danger of eternal separation from [God],"[11] and was consistent with a theology in which the fires of hell were deflected by contrition for sins committed in life. Prayer for the dying was prayer for the grace of repentance, for a good death was one in which repentance for sin (whether through fear of hell or love of God) took place. If heaven were not at once accomplished, the doctrine of Purgatory, that state of purgation between heaven and hell, provided a solace, for in that ambiguous state lay ultimate purification with heaven at its end.[12]

Death and dying were to become more important for Mary Potter. By 1872, this concern to pray for the dying became more focused and intense. A vague sense of "being called" to this particular "work" for those dying grew to a tentative belief she might be being called to a religious order in which prayer for the dying was a priority. As the year progressed, as her spiritual life brought her to new level of awareness, this vague sense deepened and changed. It was a process aided by her deliberate entry into a path of spirituality promoted by Louis Grignon de Montfort (1673–1716) a disciple of Pierre Bèrulle (1575–1629),[13] and possibly the last of the great teachers of his doctrine.[14]

Mary Potter and the French School of Spirituality

A detailed analysis of the depth and integrity of the spiritual teaching of Bèrulle and the "French School" of spirituality is beyond the scope of this thesis. What must be said, however, is that it was a spirituality marked by a strongly contemplative, incarnation and missionary spirit.[15] Bèrulle's spirituality was theocentric. It rested in the belief that the human person exists for no other purpose than to give glory to God, and that God who is the Creator of all things remains the source and centre, energy and power of the human soul. Theologically distinct from other spiritualities in which God is the end of the human condition, to be "won" by the practice of the virtuous life, Bèrulle's teaching was radically simple. God was the first principle, the source, the originator, and the sustainer of human life. Linked to humanity by an endless communication of creative power, God was always the "ground of being" of the human soul and the path to holiness for the human person rested in surrender to the Divine Essence, in a willing dependence of the creature on its Creator.[16]

United to humanity through the second person of the Trinity, and through the mystery of the Incarnation, in Bèrulle's theological thought, God provided the power or grace necessary for such union to be accomplished. Solidly grounded in an incarnational theology, it was Jesus, the Word of God, who, having assumed humanity to himself, and in the active power of redemption incorporates humanity into Divinity.

Symbolically represented in the sacrament of Baptism, the saving act of redemption unites humanity to God, for humanity is "appropriated to Jesus, existing in Jesus, grafted on Jesus, living, working and bearing fruit in Jesus."[17] It was a union with God in Jesus through the power of the spirit, and one which Bèrulle and his followers found most perfectly expressed in the person of the Virgin Mary. For the followers of the French school, she represented humanity most truly aligned to God – through the surrender of herself to the over-arching power of Divinity who filled her with the grace that was Jesus.[18]

This Marian element of the spirituality of the French school was the focus of De Montfort's treatise *On True Devotion: Preparation for the reign of Jesus Christ.* In this small work, which had been translated by Father Faber in 1862, De Montfort proposed a way of living the Christian life according to the Bèrullian doctrine. His contemplation of the mystery of Redemption drew him to reflect on the manner in which God chose to draw humanity to union with the Divine by entering the human condition with the co-operation and self-willed surrender of the Virgin Mary.[19] The Virgin, for De Montfort, was the truest expression of human divinisation and discipleship. She was the person who, responding to the Spirit, received the Word in faith, put herself totally at its service, and allowed Jesus to be formed in her and given to the world.

In De Montfort's eyes, the Virgin Mary was the exemplar of the Christian life. As Mary co-operated with the Spirit in the formation of Christ – named "Wisdom" by De Montfort – so the Christian was called to co-operate with the Spirit in order to allow Christ to be formed in them.[20] The "easy" way for this to be achieved, according to De Montfort, was to live in the docility of the Holy Spirit, with the welcoming of the Virgin and in union with the church. If a Christian could live with "the spirit of Mary," then that spirit would become the operative and creative means of becoming a "real Christian," one whose life is wrapped in God and totally committed to God's will being done in both self and in the world.

For De Montfort, living "in imitation of Mary," did not demand a subordinate state, or an introspective spirituality, it required an active and responsible participation in the redemptive mission of Jesus. The practical steps of the devotion were simple. The devotee of this path of spirituality would strive to become a "pure capacity for God." Again following Bèrulle, De Montfort saw the Christian life in terms of "Jesus living in us." [21] In order to be filled with God, the soul had to be empty of all save the desire for God. The Virgin Mary made visible the model of the human person, redeemed and graced with the indwelling presence of Jesus.[22] In the somewhat harsh language of the French School, she was "*le néant capable de Dieu*" (the nothing capable of God),[23] because she had "surrendered" to the Word. Those who sought to live a truly Christian life would emulate her attitude of self-emptying. They would 'learn of Mary', the secret of being imbued with God, and thus become filled – as Scripture promised – with the fullness of God. It was a process summed up in De Montfort's work *The Secret of Mary*[24], in which he wrote the following prayer to the Virgin:

> Grant, if it be possible, that I may have no other spirit but yours to know Jesus and his divine will. May I have no soul but yours to praise and glorify the Lord. May I have no heart but yours to love God purely and ardently as you love him. I do not ask for visions or revelations, for sensible devotion or even spiritual pleasures … I wish only to have

... [a] simple faith without seeing or tasting, to suffer joyfully without the consolations of men, to die daily to myself without flinching, to work gallantly for you even until death without any self-interest.[25]

In this spiritual pathway, Potter found a real direction. It suited her affective nature, her desire for holiness and had the added attraction of being strongly "Marian." The emphasis it laid upon the benefit of small mortifications, both interior and exterior also appealed,[26] as did the centrality of the doctrine of living for God alone. What she did not expect, however, was that this spiritual process would ultimately lead her into a relationship with God which would transform her life and extend the process of self-realisation that had been begun in her formation as a Mercy novice. She had not entered the path of De Montfortian spirituality with the understanding that it was directed towards the creation of "apostles of the end times,"[27] women and men whose spiritual consciousness was illuminated by an inner knowledge of God. Such men and women, De Montfort believed, would be agents of the Spirit in building up the "New Jerusalem." Their task was to "kindle the fire of divine love throughout the world, to renew the face of the earth and reform the church."[28] However, as Potter grew into a spiritual consciousness, the same missionary zeal that had fired De Montfort, began to burn within her own life. It was to create significant difficulty.

Potter set about following the pattern of prayer she believed the *Treatise* demanded. She focused on trying to live according to the "spirit of Mary" which she defined as "as clear and calm sense of her position as a creature to God her creator,"[29] which sought to do nothing more than "give God the glory by living for him alone."[30] She commenced by walking the precarious paths of spiritual asceticism. She practised physical mortification, made various spiritual exercises, and continued the practice of the presence of God learned in the Mercy novitiate. Slowly the impact of the growing intensity of her prayer life began to be felt and Potter, believing she could benefit from the guidance of a spiritual director, sought help from a newly arrived priest in the area, Monsignor John Virtue (1826 – 1900).[31] It was to prove a critical step, one which brought with it conflict, antagonism towards and, ultimately, condemnation of her spiritual life.

The newly appointed chaplain, to whom Mary turned for assistance, was an unusual cleric. Entering the English College in Rome in 1848, he had been ordained priest in 1851 and was appointed secretary to the Papal Nuncio of Brazil. Returning to England in 1854, he was given the rank of Monsignor, and in 1855, was one of the first chaplains appointed to the army and navy by Lord Peel. He served as a chaplain at Aldershot (1856–61), Bermuda (1862–4), Colchester (1866–71), and came to Portsmouth in 1872.[32] Taking up residence in the village of Southsea, he would remain as chaplain to the army until his appointment to Malta in 1876. Destined to become the first bishop of Portsmouth, he exemplified a form of English Catholicity Edward Norman views as most common among "old" Catholics, namely the devotion of Richard Challoner and an interior life that was restrained, sober, and focused on living according to the truths of the faith.[33] Editor of a version of Challoner's *Garden of the Soul*,[34] his life reflected his devotional outlook, and he was remembered by those who knew him as "a strong kind man, a strict and conscientious officer, a prelate cultured and refined, a priest who lived in the presence of his God."[35]

Articulate, educated and refined, Virtue was an antiquarian and bibliophile.[36] A Fellow of the Society of Antiquaries, he loved to surround himself with the "exquisite medieval paintings" he collected.[37] And, if considered by some to be "a society priest [one] invariably to be found at social functions,"[38] he was also known for his commitment and zeal in working for the good of those given to his care.[39]

According to custom of the day, Monsignor Virtue did not live within the Portsmouth garrison, but in a private residence. In a small terrace house in Southsea, he maintained an oratory to which local Catholics were invited to attend Mass and various devotions including Benediction and Confessions.[40] In 1872, sometime after the priest's arrival in the district, Potter used the opportunity offered by the confessional to consult with Monsignor Virtue, and through this means, as well as by letter, she sought his advice regarding her devotion, her spiritual life and her continued desire to re-enter the convent. As 1872 moved into 1873, that prospect seemed no closer to fulfilment. In the face of on-going bouts of ill health, Virtue counselled Potter to patience, but nonetheless gave her encouragement in her spiritual life. On December 8, 1872 he permitted her to make an act of consecration according to the rite elaborated in the De Montfort's *Treatise*, and by that consecration, Potter committed herself to live according to her baptismal promises and within the De Montfortian understanding of "the spirit of Mary."[41]

By the end of 1873, however, the relationship between Potter and her confessor-cum-spiritual director had grown somewhat tense. She told him of her increasing awareness of a call to "help save souls in their last hour and a certain vague belief that a new religious order was being called for within the church – one that had Calvary as its model."[42] Virtue was quick to refute this latter notion, telling Potter not to think she had been given a revelation. Rather than fritter her time away on such useless speculation, she was to concentrate on her everyday life and not be so invested in her prayer.[43] His admonitions to pay less attention to her prayer life and more to the ordinary business of daily life became stronger as Potter began to relate experiences that she claimed were direct communications from God. As will be seen, these were significant enough to draw her to a new sense of herself, and to an independence of spiritual thought and action.

Mysticism in Nineteenth-century England

David Knowles points out that a general interest in mysticism was absent from the Catholic church for "some two centuries before the twentieth." The reasons for this appear varied; some resting in the turmoil of the heresies that emerged from the seventeenth century, others in the conflict with the traditional and reformed influences within the church. The dark and pessimistic spirituality of Jansenism had a far-reaching influence, stressing the alienation of humanity from God. Equally destructive was the quietism that had brought the intrinsic mysticism of the French School into disrepute.[44] By the nineteenth century however political exigencies in Europe brought a revival of things mystical, visionary and prophetic. These were encouraged by European Catholicism as a means of propping up a faith brought to doubt by the heady advances of scientific thought and by defending itself against the encroaching tide of rationalism.[45] But if European Catholicism of the nineteenth century was awash with apparitions and visionaries, they had little effect within the emergent Catholic community of England. There, men like Virtue, schooled in the sturdy spirituality of Challoner, repudiated the emotionalism of continental pieties and emotional excesses. The robust common sense and virile rationality of the British character forswore mysticism and mystical leanings as something repugnant to its essence, to be spoken of in lightly contemptuous terms.[46] "Manly" English devotion promulgated a healthy, socially-committed and domestically-idealised Christianity in which duty and social service held higher value that any Manichean flight from the world.[47] In practice, it was a religious outlook in which drains were as important as dreams – however spiritual the latter may be – and its emphasis on duty and good works influenced much of English religious belief and practice as the century progressed.

But Catholic revivalism drew upon emotion and some degree of religious enthusiasm. It was not a revival based upon arcane or esoteric understandings of the spiritual life as such, but upon the need to promote and sustain a piety (however vulgar), which would help dam leakage from the flock. The English Catholic revival encouraged the development of a bright, gaudy and emotional piety.[48] Pragmatism may well have determined its strategies, as Phillip Hughes suggests,[49] but the reality was, that within the sacramental system of the church, the belief in the "real" presence of Jesus in the Eucharist, and in the upsurge of affective devotion over the entire period of the nineteenth century, a culture was created which was not antithetical to the emergence of mystic consciousness. In the practices of "humble and affective worship" such as Benediction of the Blessed Sacrament, *Quarant Ore,*[50] the Stations of the Cross, or the Rosary, love was both evoked and expressed.[51] Women in particular were drawn to the warmth of such piety. Statues and candles, devotions and incense combined, in Gilley's terms, to a "popular continental ultramontanism" a "thoroughly vulgar religious culture".[52] The fact remains however, that such "vulgar piety", when fed by devotional handbooks containing prayers of passionate desire, stirred the imagination and put words on the longing to love and to be loved, and women were drawn to its incipient mysticism, and contributed to its overarching sensory impact.[53]

For the young Anglican Annie Besant, Catholic places and Catholic prayer represented the power of liturgical practice to dignify aesthetic emotion with the garb of piety.[54] Many such prayers were focused on the sensual delights of union with a Jesus, who was "fairer than the sons of men" and who could "transfix the affections of …[the]…soul with that most joyous and healthy wound of … love."[55] Deliberately invoking desire "that my soul may ever languish and melt with entire love and longing for Thee," such prayers and devotions captured the imagination and stirred the heart to passionate love of and longing for the Saviour.[56] Their power cannot be underestimated in the creation of a mystical consciousness. And for many women within the nineteenth century, Jesus was the perfect Lover of the soul, a potent symbol of the power of transformatory love,[57] a gateway through which women could walk into a keen sense of God's abiding presence.[58]

As Aldous Huxley points out, culture can either inhibit or facilitate the actualisation of mystical and pre-mystical potentiality.[59] For nineteenth-century women, the cultural exploitation of religion as a vehicle for channelling them into pre-defined roles may well have maintained in them "the dreamy tendency of the child, that on its worldly side is fancy, imagination, on its religious side, is the germ of mysticism."[60] According to the cultural norms of the period, women were the natural heirs to the spirit of contemplation and reflection on the mysteries of life. Their conditioning to be attentive to the needs of spouse and children, or, if unmarried, to the vast needs of humankind, combined with the emphatic realisation of religion as "woman's role," almost guaranteed that some among them would take the call seriously and apply themselves to their spiritual journey. At the same time, however, if they laid claim to spiritual experience, at least within the Catholic tradition, there was a certain suspicion that all was not well. Bishop Ullathorne was quick to warn others about the weaknesses of women in the spiritual life. When asked to investigate the experience of an alleged visionary and miracle worker, Teresa Higginson (1804–1905), he refused, claiming pressure of work, but urged "extremest caution with respect to females, who are liable to mistake imagination for revelations."[61] No exception to a past which negated women's experience as unworthy of note as an "exemplar of the life leading to salvation,"[62] the Victorian era swept aside women of religious insight. Particularly suspect were those women who claimed a direct knowledge of God's love, spoke or taught from their prophetic insight or used the leading of the Spirit to criticise and call to renewal the behaviour and institutes of men.[63]

Mysticism or madness? A time of trial

In September 1874, Potter's relationship with Monsignor Virtue deteriorated when she began to speak with her confessor about her inner life of prayer. The tension that had been apparent when she had told him of her belief that God desired a new religious order to be brought into being within the church was amplified by her disclosure of a sense that God had in someway taken possession of her soul. As she expressed it to her confessor, she now felt that she lived in an inner union with Jesus and Mary.[64] This sense of unity, she informed her director, was accompanied by feeling "united to the Most Holy Trinity in an unspeakable way … being joined in wonderful union with the All Holy God and feeling that it was His will that you should be one with him."[65]

Virtue was singularly unimpressed by this disclosure. He was even less impressed with Potter's belief that she believed God "had given me a great grace, which led me to believe he would have the Precious Blood specially honoured."[66] Virtue was dismissive of the claim, but Potter's experience would not be denied. The insight had come at prayer, she explained, where she felt "penetrated, suffused with the Precious Blood, and our dear Lord speaking to me, telling me He had given me his treasure, his life."[67] Following the experience, she believed she had heard the words "Honour my Precious Blood, Offer my Precious Blood." This, she told Virtue, was a prophetic word given by God that the church pay more attention to the meaning and the grace of Calvary where Jesus gave his blood for the salvation of the world.[68]

Understandably perhaps, Virtue was horrified by Potter's disclosure. His reaction was swift and to the point. She was to "stop prophesying," cut down on her prayer, and under pain of mortal sin, stop entertaining such blasphemous and ridiculous thoughts. Her "inspirations" he declared, were delusions brought to consciousness by what he appears to have considered a pious but neurotic mind.[69] The interdict placed upon Potter was deeply troubling, and brought "a fearful anguish of soul."[70] In Potter's eyes, the priest held absolute authority in matters of sin. She struggled with the thought that he had condemned her experiences and named them as delusion:

> I do not think it could be understood how literally I took what was said to me in confession. The words were so impressed upon me 'he that heareth you, heareth me', and I did my best, but I could not succeed…. I trusted my confessor so implicitly, the thought was intolerable – if this [was] not our dear Lord within me then I must be possessed. Then I would think, is this how the heretics feel when they believe wrong doctrine – they feel they cannot help it? [71]

In spite of the difficulty of withstanding Monsignor Virtue's brusque responses, Potter was unwilling to simply accept his decisions. In the November of 1874, she sought clarification regarding the two issues he had condemned – her practice of the spiritual path of *True Devotion*, and her emerging spiritual insights. Believing Virtue's objections to *True Devotion* to be illogical and bred from an ignorance of the work itself, she pressured her confessor to give her more cogent reasons for his disapproval. If he did not understand that the aim of the devotion was union with God, she suggested, perhaps he should read the book on the devotion she had given him some two years before, when he gave her permission to make her consecration to follow its path.[72] Furthermore, she asked for clarification regarding the penalty he had imposed upon her:

> The second thing I want to know is about the obedience you put me under, mortal sin. I suffered so much when I laid for about a month in the fear of being out of God's grace, not knowing whether my prayers or sufferings could help others too… I want to know whether I were to say to myself, "It is the will of God I should do as I am told at the present but hereafter I shall be told differently." Would that be disobedience? I could at all times say as though you told me to call white black. It appears to me white, but I will say it black if I am told, but to force myself to think what something superior to myself seems to force me not to think, I do not know what to do. I know this: that

when I do think it is all delusion, that thought comes as others, such as scruples etc., and cause [sic] disquiet, whereas the other thoughts bring peace.[73]

Potter was, in fact, following the instructions she had received from Lambert within the Mercy novitiate and was applying a primitive "discernment of spirits" to her experiences, and those rules of discernment proposed that spiritual consolation or peace was to be identified when:

> Some interior movement in the soul comes to be inflamed with love of its Creator and Lord; and when it can in consequence love no created thing on the face of the earth itself, but in the Creator of them all. Likewise, when it sheds tears that move to love of its Lord, whether out of sorrow for one's sins, or for the Passion of Christ our Lord, or because of other things directly connected with His service and praise. Finally, I call consolation every increase of hope, faith and charity, and all interior joy, which calls and attracts to heavenly things and to the salvation of one's soul, quieting it and giving it peace in its Creator and Lord.[74]

Desolation, which Potter identified with disquiet and agitation, was seen by Ignatius as "not of God," when it led to "a want of confidence, without hope, without love, when one finds oneself all lazy, tepid, sad, and as if separated from his Creator and Lord."[75] It was her belief that the obedience placed upon her by Virtue was a source of such desolation. When she sought to move away from her prayer, to deny her sense of the presence of God, she experienced great distress of soul, and an agitation that seemed to indicate that it was in opposition to God's will for her.

Virtue, however, remained convinced that Potter was suffering from delusion and confirmed the interdict he had placed upon her. In spite of her fear of committing mortal sin, and unwilling to walk away from her confessor, Potter sought to make sense of his reactions and the experiences which continued to press upon her. She wrote again to Virtue and told him of the uselessness of the effort and of the thoughts that kept occurring. Again she spoke of her conviction that the idea of Calvary, and the need for a new religious order was somehow coming from God:

> A train of thought can come so quickly. I was afraid of committing mortal sin this afternoon and did not know how to distract myself. All at once I thought, the Church, the spouse of our Lord, represents his life. Communities arose representing his hidden life, witness those of Egypt and others, then followed more active orders, the preachers devoted to acts of charity, etc, representing our Lord's public life... Oh Father, if you know how difficult it is to put away the thought: Calvary will be next...Your telling me "to put it all away, nothing will come of <u>that</u>" has made it so difficult to think as you wished. You seemed to think if I was wrong in one thing, I must be wrong in all...I know so well that even Saints who worked miracles [have] been deceived and Father Maher told me so too. It does likewise seem to me that an order devoted or with the spirit of Calvary [is] peculiarly applicable to these times. Is not the Church being now mystically crucified with her Lord?[76]

Monsignor Virtue remained obdurate in his resistance to Potter's originality and insight regarding the nature and purpose of religious life and to her claim that it was God's will such an institute be established. Her conviction, that religious orders were "raised up in the Church" to represent different elements or states of Christ's life, was too extraordinary to be contemplated. He, like most of the Roman church of the period, saw religious life as a "state of perfection" to which members of the Church were called in order to live their individual lives in closer union with Christ. Potter's premise was that religious orders were brought into being by the grace of God, that their purpose was to reflect particular elements of the Christian life to the world, was simply not within the bounds of his imagination.[77] It smacked of prophecy and temerity, the more so as Potter made her claim that such an order was needed by the church undergoing a crucifixion of its own, and needing to be called into fidelity.

Virtue's resistance to Potter's spiritual and theological insights must be seen in relation to his own times and is hardly surprising in a climate Julie Melnyk identifies as hostile to women's independent theological thought.[78] If the Bible was remarkably egalitarian on the issue, illustrating that the Holy Spirit did indeed descend upon women[79] that women's prophecy did speak truth[80] and that the God of Israel discriminated against no one when it came to spiritual gifts, particularly those gifts of prophetic insight,[81] the nineteenth-century society was not. As Flamming, Lang and Marina Warner have each pointed out, the historic tradition of the Christian churches was that women of religious insight and spiritual virtuosity, who based their claims to spiritual authority on inner voices or mystical experiences, faced enormous difficulty.[82] Their experiences could not be proven but only accepted or rejected. Faced with such choice, the tendency on the part of the Catholic church was to reject such religious virtuosity, preferring to suspect female experience of "the inner light". As the late Herbert Thurston SJ was quick to establish in his work on *Suprising Mystics*.[83] In this text, he was quick to point out that:

> In these studies of deeply religious women, I have had no thought of directing a campaign against mysticism itself. They were all courageous, generous and most mortified servants of God who did immense good and made a profound impression upon all who came in contact with them. But if anyone, on the grounds of their ardent aspirations and high standard and self-conquest regards their alleged communications with the next world as warranting belief in a divine guidance and supernatural knowledge imparted to such souls, it seems to me that his conclusion is a rash one. The area of mental health has to be considered, and hysteria, while it is itself no bar to sanctity and may not involve any form of self-seeking, is singularly apt to lend itself to exaggerations and pervert the sober judgement.[84]

There is little doubt that in Virtue's "sober" and, one must add, "masculine" judgement, Potter was being deceived in her beliefs,[85] and there was little she could do to alter his opinion. Against his accusations that her mind was not in keeping with that of the church, she protested her right to live "in imitation of our Lord and save souls."[86] To his accusations of pride and arrogance she responded that whilst it was true that she believed God was giving her great graces, there was a corresponding realisation of her unworthiness:

> God gives me great graces but at the same time shows me myself… I think when God shows himself to any soul in a certain way, it must be, so to speak, crushed and prostrate with the sight of itself in the light of God and must hunger as I do to manifest exteriorly its interior contempt and hatred of itself… This is my continual feeling, a constant sorrow, a deep, deep sorrow for my sins.[87]

This sorrow for sin she perceived as a gift, one that she relied on more than "all the spiritual consolations God gives me."[88] It kept her humbled and focused on her own need for God. Nonetheless, she also believed that the insights she received, and which drew her to a greater love of God were to be somehow transferred to be made more real for others, and this became an even greater imperative as her experiences of God became more overwhelming. Virtue, however, remained resolute in his condemnation of her beliefs.

By December 1874 Potter had come to realise that she had to be true to her own experience, but that she also needed to communicate with a director in order to keep her balance under what she perceived as the intimate communications from God. In the absence of any other priest in the local area of Southsea, Potter made the decision to remain under the direction of Virtue. It was a risk, but if she was to discover where these spiritual insights were leading her, she needed a listening ear. She could only be open with her director, and "let God do with me as best pleaseth him."[89]

Early in 1875, Potter communicated again with her director. It was a reluctant communication. "What I tell you now, I must," she said, and continued on to reveal a moment of deep psychological and spiritual awareness which gave her a sense of inner authority and self-identity that she had never before experienced.

The moment began with an initial impression "on the eyes of my soul" of Jesus Crucified. It came "silent and sudden," whilst she was at prayer, and made an indelible impression.[90] Brief, but powerful, Potter recorded it as "the moment God brought me back to himself."[91] Not long after, whilst kneeling at prayer at the altar in her room she had an overwhelming sense of the presence of God:

> [I] suddenly felt the Presence of God. …. I know not what I did till I found the words rising up, "Who art Thou, Lord?" In my heart seemed to echo "The Blessed Trinity who made thee." "I have chosen thee that thou shouldst go and should bring forth fruit, and that thy fruit should remain." "Why to me?" rose up the thought within me, and the same echo within, "The weak things of this earth have I chosen." I do not remember exactly what followed, nor the answer which I made…I remember turning to our Lady, making a Spiritual Communion. I was so afraid of being deluded…I know not how long I remained but I rose up with a feeling of inexpressible peace. I went through the devotion of the Stations, which I had been about commencing with an indulgenced Crucifix, and at every Gloria Patri; I was bowing to the Presence of God in my room with me.[92]

Regardless of what Virtue would think, the experience for Potter was one of empowerment. The appropriation of the authority of scripture to validate the divine election to "to
go and bear fruit that will remain" highly significant.[93] God had called her, and if that call
had been addressed to a "mere woman," it was justified by God's own predilection for
choosing the weak things of the earth as instruments of salvation.[94] Like the apostle Paul,
she could glory in her weakness, for God's power was made more visible by it.[95]
Historically, as Gerda Lerner states, such a transformation was a common phenomenon
for women who were forced to justify divine communication, and Potter was no exception to the pattern by which:

> they transformed this imputed weakness of the femaleness into strength. It was precisely
> because they were weak, uneducated and simple, and because they were excluded from
> the great privilege of priesthood, that God had chosen them as His instrument of sal-
> vation. This argument recurs throughout the centuries [96]

The self-validation given by the experience was of utmost importance to Potter. It filled
her with a sense of personal certitude – a profound conviction of the rightness of her
course. Claimed by none other than the Trinity, she was now under a higher authority,
which weakened, though did not yet displace, the need for institutional authorisation or
approval. Potter found in her "revelations" a moment of liberation. It was one that Woods,
Petroff and Jantzen have each noted in their studies of mysticism, as being significant for
the evolution of self-direction and a relative autonomy in the spiritual life.[97]

Whatever one might think of the veridicality of the experience, for Potter it was powerful, personal and affirming. Whilst her experience may well be questioned for its psychological soundness, or – as by Virtue – even denied,[98] the fact was that nothing could
take away Potter's realisation of herself as creature sprung from the divine creativity of
God, called and chosen to act as God's own agent in the world. It was an experience apparently confirmed the following morning, when she again heard the words "I have chosen
you," and "it is my will that you do this work." But what was the work? Again it centred
around the emergence of a new religious order within the church, one which would model
Calvary, and have as its main work the saving of sinners, particularly those who were "in
their last hours."[99]

The impact of the experience changed Potter. It was "rapturous," giving a great joy, and
brought with it a changed consciousness of the world in which she lived:

> It could not be explained, the union with God, the joy. The world seemed another
> world and to breathe of God. I would wonder whether it was not a return almost to the
> original joy of the unfallen. I went about my few duties the same, making home happy,
> entertaining my mother and brothers, but I had many hours to myself.[100]

She struggled with trying to convey her meaning. Seemingly taken up into God, the
aftershock of the experience held her in its thrall:

I cannot describe it. I almost seem to cease being aware of my own existence. God seems to have such entire possession of me. If I was to sit and meditate as some books advise, to think for instance, there was a time, when I did not exist, it would be but a distraction. I love to think of creation, and yet I seem to have been with God creating, but my meaning may be misunderstood. Those whom God enfolds in a similar manner alone could understand me[101]

With this profound recognition of God as both the centre of creation and source of all creativity, came the recognition of the universality of God's creative power and presence. Creation, she now saw as "an echo" of God, having the task or the duty "to reflect him, to mirror his beauty to reflect the light, the radiant loveliness of the Divinity."[102] The world was "one of the glories of the universe… [and]… if you could rise out of it and [be] in some [other] part of the universe, you would see a radiant orb, reflecting uncreated Beauty, brilliantly radiant with rays of Divine Light …The Attributes of God reflected from all parts."[103]

This recognition of and love for created beauty and its accompanying awareness of the intrinsic loveliness of all created beings brought an unremitting joy and was received by Potter as an illumination of the Divine, rooted and grounded in what Underhill called a "joyous apprehension of the Absolute."[104] It led her to a sense of God's presence within all things, a wonder and joy at Creation and creativity. Child of her own era, her mystical vision also empowered her to find God in the wonder of the age of the machine. She now had:

pleasure in all around, a pleasure from sights and sounds. How to express it is difficult. Many rise to the song of a bird, and to sweet music, but my soul rejoices as I look upon a poor workman, as I hear the singing of a machine.[105]

Almost exultant, she told Virtue she felt that:

He [God] has filled me with his love. He has poured forth His Holy Spirit upon me, and told me to live by it, and now I live no longer in myself, but He my Lord and God liveth in me. Loving him I must love those whom he has made, not with my own poor heart but from the Heart of Jesus that poured forth its priceless Treasure of Precious Blood to save them, from the Mother heart of Mary that was pierced and broken for them.[106]

The claim to be filled with God's love and to be led by that love to love others is not uncommon among the pantheon of mystics within spiritual traditions. As Underhill, Woods, Ghose and Jantzen, among others, have indicated, the mystic experience is not a "private" phenomenon, but a drawing out to achieve liberation for others.[107] Potter had come to realise the truth of that which other mystics wrote, namely the effect of union with God on human consciousness. Jesus had told St. Catherine of Genoa that "he who loves Me, loves all that I love,"[108] and Potter's experience echoed the words and the belief in the "power" given to effect change in the world, either through prayer or direct social action. She tried to explain it to her confessor:

> I felt … and know God has given me a great power of impetration. I must use it. There
> is a sense of responsibility in it. Souls are dying, souls made to the likeness of the Blessed
> Trinity are being lost. It seems as though they belonged to me and I could not bear they
> should be taken from me any more than a mother could bear her children to be torn
> from her. It would be terrible, (realising in the way I do and in a way which I …could
> [not] bear unless God supported me, what a fearful thing it is for a soul to lose God for
> ever) if I could not help them, but I can by the help of God … Those whom you would
> help are made like to Jesus. It is God's Will they should be prayed for.[109]

Virtue's verdict on what Potter revealed to him of her sense of union with God and growing love for humanity was simply that she was quite mad, and her experiences nothing more than the overworked imagination of a fevered brain.[110] Yet Potter remained convinced that her director was misguided in his direction, particularly as her experiences continued to make a profound change in her perception of herself, her God and her world. It was a conviction made stronger by yet another experience of being drawn by God to a union of close intimacy.

In the January or February of 1875 when Potter was meditating on the crucifixion, and physically present before a crucifix in her room, she was suddenly aware of a sense of being united to Christ in a new way:

> Last Friday, during the three hours, I seemed raised upon the Cross and our Blessed
> Lord seemed to tell me He espoused me, but I took not much notice…I got up and
> stood before the Crucifix where I have told you Almighty God brought me back to
> Himself … And with the thought of our Lord hanging upon the Cross, I felt He was
> binding me to Himself, by a new title, as His Spouse … let the work of God be done
> in me and it has made a revolution in me. …My prayer finished in peace and thanks-
> giving, the sign of its being from God.[111]

As she experienced it, this was a moment of "wonderful union, standing before that Crucifix. 'Thou art my spouse… Spouse of Jesus Crucified' was the chant of angels, washed by the Precious Blood, enfolded in the embrace of the Holy Spirit."[112] The sense of being irrevocably wed to Christ and the cross brought Potter into a depth of relationship that was at once sacramental and sustaining. Amplified by a sense of being taken into the wounded side of Christ, and there "fed" on the blood of Christ, she was transformed by a new dimension of relationship. In the "calm sanctuary of [the] wounded side [the] spouse sucks sweetness … and loves all his loves,"[113] she wrote. And the image coalesced and feminised the figure of Jesus to one of maternal care and solicitude, and whether one accepts the veridicality of the experience or not, the moment gave Potter a new and authoritative voice.

Just as other women mystics had found wisdom from drinking from the wounded side of Christ and had been brought to their own sense of their divinity in that experience, so did Potter.[114] Jesus had drawn her to himself, bound her as "spouse," filled her with wisdom, and made her a bearer of his divine life. Reflection on the experience and its meaning in her life, brought a conflation between the recognition of the "maternal love of the Good Shepherd" and her own culturally determined identity as woman. Far from being confined to the limits of home and family, she was called to emulate the "mother love of the Good Shepherd who laid down his life for his sheep."[115] This identification with the maternal role of Jesus meant that she – and other women – were to participate in the missionary activity of the church. They were to "tell the tale of Jesus' pity to save souls…[to] rise up in power and preach the wonders of the pity of the Sacred Heart…[and] draw to this source of strength, the weak, the sinful."[116] Whether spiritual or physical, motherhood was, in Potter's eyes, a "grand office … [an] exemplification of God himself,"[117] and "the highest form of love known among men."[118] By virtue of their likeness to Jesus, women were called by the gospel to lay down their lives to bring to birth spiritual children. "You must be true mothers," she would write to her first companions in 1877, "mothers by suffering, even unto death. Offer your life to give birth to children in the spirit of the Mother-like Shepherd who tells us 'I lay down my life for my sheep'."[119]

In Potter's growing theological insight, women were called to assume their maternal authority and use it for the redemption of the world. Backed by the authority of her spiritual experiences, and her eccentric understanding of Calvary, not as a process of expiation or atonement, but as the place of self-giving love, she drew together the cultural constructs of "mother," "woman" and "spiritual authority." Claiming maternal love as the most complete expression of Jesus' love for humanity, she expanded the role of women, but to a limited degree and for a distinctive purpose, to renew the church in a time of increasing peril.

There was a sense of urgency in the task, fuelled by an apocalyptic sense of doom. "Terrible times [were] dawning" which Potter saw reflected in the world around her by the "signs of the times." These were represented by:

> temptation that may deceive even the elect, distress among the nations, troubles and deceptions even within the church of God. God may almost seem to have forsaken his own; the church may appear a derelict; its members, trembling, may exclaim with their Master: "My God, my God, why hast thou forsaken me?" But courage! It is the Passion, the Crucifixion.[120]

It was a tension shared by other women. The historical enquiries of Barbara Taylor, Robert Kachur and Catherine Keller have each explored the importance of the apocalyptic allegory for women and the use they made of it as a resource for the critiquing of gender ideology.[121] Their suggestions that the allegory provided women with glimpses of a utopian "New Jerusalem" which justified their vision of a more egalitarian community cannot be dismissed.[122] The terrors of the times – the result of the major reconstruction that was the Victorian era – provided a vehicle for this vision of a "new society" to grow and develop, and for women to have a role in its formation.

The great 19th century reformer Josephine Butler shared in this visionary sensitivity. Her initiating insight was, like Potter's, grounded in and emerged from her experiences of

God. "God has bound me His captive for ever," Butler wrote, and explained that "the utmost heights and depths of human passion, in all its beauty, its sweetness, its self-abandonment, are to this love as the feeble flicker of a rush-light compared with the mid-day sun."[123] Her sense of "apocalypse now" echoed Potter's. In *The Hour Before Dawn* (1876), she wrote:

> We see the beginning only, not the end, or nearly the end of the horrors, which are yet to be revealed. It would appear as if the powers of evil were about to combine at the hour before dawn for one last gigantic effort to turn God's dear earth into hell.[124]

Where Butler's vision of the terrors of the times drew her to political activism and attacks against the sexual double standard, Potter's apocalypticism drew her to a critical assessment of the church's spiritual life. Within the church, "many of our Lord's own have fallen away, and throughout the church, there is considerable distress of soul and body,"[125] which Potter believed needed care and solicitude. The church, in failing to recognise the signs of the times, left its members in a conflict they might not be able to withstand. There was a need to understand that:

> We live in perilous times; we are thoughtless and careless. We do not fear for others till we see them fall: but we are not wise. Did our Lord not fear for us? We should be wiser is we did fear more and wonder less.[126]

Potter's perception of the world in apocalyptic disruption was balanced by a belief that God sought to exercise his mercy in "these latter times… as a last stretch of his compassion." That mercy was expressed and shown forth to the world "by raising up an order in his church devoted to the work of rescuing sinners (the souls he loves, for whom he died)."[127] This, Potter claimed, was God's will. Such an order, centred in the maternal self-giving love of Calvary, would preach its word of prophecy by being prepared to "do violence for the sake of others who are threatened with losing their immortal souls." In imitation of the mother love of Jesus, they would "go out into the battlefield [to] pick up the wounded and anoint them…bring to them the treasures of the Precious Blood."[128]

Implicit within the statement was the suggestion that God was choosing to provide a sign to the church, a prophetic "word," reflected in a religious order. This order was to be for the church what the Virgin had been for the Apostle John on Calvary, a strong support, a maternal authority, and in this time of great peril, a source of strength and fidelity.[129] This was the "spirit" or the "charism" of the institute. It was apostolic, and yet contemplative, drawn to action by the trials and the suffering of a world unable to heal itself. It was a belief very much in accord with the apocalyptic vision of De Montfort, in which, as Gaffney states, "apostles of the end times [were] to establish the reign of Christ."[130] Again, Potter shared her vision with Monsignor Virtue, and again he refuted her claims.[131]

Notwithstanding the opposition exhibited by her confessor, Potter maintained her belief in the authority and insights given her by God. As she sought to make clear to him the distinct call she believed she had received, her claims of divine intervention and spiritual insight became significantly centred in the notion of divine appointment and election. Towards the end of 1875, she wrote again to her director, this time making the claim that her election to spiritual authority came directly from the Holy Spirit. While recognising her own unworthiness, the fact remained that God had bound her to his will and service and, in spite of Virtue's opposition, she had been anointed and appointed to dispense the gifts of God. "God has put his Holy Spirit upon me" she told Virtue:

> The Holy Trinity overshadowed me and communicating to my understanding, darkly it is true, but still with a clearer knowledge than heretofore, how the Holy Spirit, proceeding from the Father and the Son is the link of the Father and Son, the Breath of Life, that Breath was breathed into me and I was told henceforth I must live by It. I am bound to God by his Holy Spirit, in some faint way resembling the Act of the Holy Ghost in the Godhead and may the Spirit of my God now guide me to show you as in the deepest humility I acknowledge my utter unworthiness to speak of this aweful mystery...
>
> The Holy Ghost is the Indissoluble Bond, the Limit of the Godhead and we are filled with his Holy Spirit and espoused to him for ever more. The strong right arm of the Eternal Father hath upholden me. His hand, that Hand that lavished blessings upon mankind is put into my hand and speaking He has said, "Thou shalt dispense my gifts for my name's sake...".[132]

Convinced that her experiences had given her a glimpse into the heart of God who longed for his people to know his mother-love, she claimed her right to obey God's will. From the perspective of a patriarchal church, the implication was clear and again subversive. If the spirit of the Lord had been poured upon her as a woman (an image that is directly related to the scriptural definition Christ's prophetic role),[133] then she must act in relation to that call and proclaim the message given. Regardless of male discourse regarding women's role within church and world, God alone anointed his prophets.

But there was a conflict for Potter, for all the assertions of election. Even if God *had* appointed her prophet to the church, and even if her insights into the real meaning of religious orders *were* correct, no implementation of the vision could take place without clerical or ecclesiastical approval. For Potter, a loyal daughter of the church, this posed a significant problem. Aware that any alleged spiritual insights had to be tested by the church, and worn out by Virtue's continued resistance to her insights and experiences, Potter requested that he get a second opinion on the subject.[134] It was a request that followed his direct accusation that she was "no longer of one mind with the church."[135] Potter had had enough. Virtue's accusations of delusion merely exacerbated "the old temptation I have had since a little child – to think I am altogether in a wrong way."[136] She informed him of the anguish he had caused her when "only last week" he told her she was possessed of an evil spirit which could not have come from God, for it distracted rather than focused her on prayer.[137] However, in spite of all Virtue's condemnation, God was still present to her and if Virtue could not see the truth of her claims, then he was blind:

God is present to me, not in his usual way. He has replenished me with His grace. He has filled me with His love. He has poured forth His Holy Spirit upon me and told me to live by it, and now I live no longer in myself but He, [the] Lord God, liveth in me. Loving Him I must love those whom He has made, not with my own poor heart but from the Heart of Jesus that poured forth Its priceless Treasure of Precious Blood to save them, from the Mother Heart of Mary that was pierced and broken for them. My own heart has seemed ready to break, but our Lady helped me so that I could ask Almighty God not to ease me, if my grief could help a soul in agony. Strange if the spirits of light and darkness could be in the same place at once. Strange if an evil spirit has deluded me that every grace has increased within me. Strange that sorrowful as I have been made I was never happier or more peaceful in my life. Strange that I should see more and more my own sinfulness and nothingness, and grieve over my sins…

A great load seemed lifted off my mind as it occurred to me, perhaps I had never committed a mortal sin. Oh, if I could but think that, but of course I would not allow it to remain. It would be a wondrous happiness, but however, as I believed God said some weeks ago to me, as I was before the Crucifix, "I will show forth my Mercy in thee, I will show forth my Mercy by thee." It was a accompanied by the usual feeling of happiness and content, (as I have told you, the inner voice brings peace, when I do not believe or am doubtful I am distressed), so now my very sins in a certain way minister to God.

Why does God permit evil? There are things thought so difficult, and yet there seems an easy answer. Might we not say that one reason or give one explanation – how could the divine Attribute of Mercy shine as it does if evil had not been permitted? It is that Divine Attribute of God that I devote my whole life, and what is the visible form… how does God show his mercy? Jesus with arms outstretched shedding his Blood, his Life. I had perhaps better say no more…

Before finishing this I must excuse myself concerning what you said [about] my mind not being in conformity with the Church. It is not true. All my thoughts, my whole will is centred in the Church. If I could but shed my blood for it…

The devotions of the church accord with the times, and now I must say it again, Jesus shows Himself in these perilous times as giving His greatest proof of love, shedding Blood… I must indeed be self-willed as you say, if my thoughts are not from God, but I could almost say to you what Balaam's ass said to him…."[138]

The reference to Balaam and his ass is from the Book of Numbers 22: 28–30, and was a particularly pertinent thrust at the blindness Potter perceived in Virtue's attitude. Balaam's life is saved from the sword of the avenging angel by his donkey, which sees the angel of the Lord and turns aside three times to save his master's life. Balaam, who does not see the angel, vents his anger upon the ass, which finally says to its master: "What have I done to you, that you have struck me these three times?" Potter's use of the reference was a direct rebuke of Virtue and a condemnation. She claims the veracity of her inner vision. Like Balaam's ass, she can see the Lord then she makes the stinging point that Virtue, like Balaam, is blind to what it is she sees, and out of ignorance, strikes back at her with accusations which wound and pain. Virtue was not amused, and the relationship between the two was not assisted by the fact that Potter now decided to promulgate the spirituality she practised.

Encouraged by a correspondence with the highly influential Sister Clare of Kenmare,[139] Potter had written a small theological treatise on the meaning of De Montfort's *True Devotion*, which she called the *Path of Mary*. It was a manuscript which began with the apocalyptic belief that the times were perilous and that there was an inner desolation at the heart of the church. Renewal was necessary, all were to live for the "end for which [they] were created, God."[140]

Potter's experience of *True Devotion* was that it was a simple way of leading the soul to a bond of loving union with God. Having become convinced that the mystical life of grace was the birthright of all, she sought to popularise it. Union with God would bring as its fruit a "true liberty of spirit...a delightful, holy liberty [in God]."[141] Theologically, her claim was that such liberty of spirit came from the soul's union with its Creator – a mystical union with Jesus already given in Baptism.[142] This was the union that led to the voluntary self-oblation of the disciple which echoed the self-oblation of Jesus on the Cross. And it was this willed offering of life for life that Potter believed would bring new outpourings of grace "upon the church in general, upon ourselves, and upon the whole world."[143] Facilitated by the presence of the Virgin it was a pathway to the richness of intimacy and was a means of bringing the whole church to renewal.[144]

It was a simple yet profound theological treatise, which utilised and integrated material from De Montfort's thesis and Potter's own experiences of the spiritual journey. Implicitly and explicitly, it sought to raise the consciousness of members of the church – including its clerical members – to the need for fidelity and a strong internal life of prayer.[145] In a church and society in which women were barred from university and pulpit, and forbidden to attempt to write in the traditionally male genres of theology, treatise or sermon,[146] the work was received by her confessor as originating from a weak and possibly possessed mind. Potter did not accept the criticism lightly. "I want to ask you if I am obliged to think that what I have written to you must necessarily be the work of an evil spirit" she wrote to Virtue, and noted with some asperity, "I cannot say that I feel my mind is at all weakened," she wrote. "It seems rather to have opened and that is not alone my own thought." [147]

As the year 1875 drew towards its close Potter concluded that Virtue's continued negation of her person was simply not helpful. Her expectation of him had been that, as a priest, he would be an appropriate spiritual guide. By the end of the year, her somewhat ascerbic assessment was that Monsignor Virtue was "a priest ...whose duty it is to live in the world and from duty go to parties, dinners, etc. and visit a good deal, [one who cannot] be expected to have the same light as a religious [priest]."[148] Accordingly, she sought to find someone "who lived more secluded from the world,"[149] and who might, perhaps, be of a more spiritual nature. Ever hopeful, she sought her confessor's assistance in finding a new director, but to no avail. As the year ended, she had come to understand that to maintain the relationship with Virtue was positively dangerous for her, and in January 1876, wrote to him, terminating their relationship, and telling him bluntly of the effect he had had on her. "This will be the last letter I think I shall trouble you with, at any rate for a long time," she told him, and continued on to explain just how much pain his counsel had caused her. Whilst allowing his good intent, his words:

> had nevertheless, broke[en] my heart, … what you said to me, chiming in with my own besetting temptation to despair, made me think and feel almost as though I were already in hell…[and] if it will not be wrong to say it to you, I would say, if ever you have to say such things to anyone else, mollify it, encourage them at the same time, for it is dangerous.[150]

Potter's understanding of her weakness and ability to be manipulated by instruction that fed into her own capacity for despair, underscores the growth that had taken place within her. The woman she had become was now far more capable of self-determination and self-understanding and, by the beginning of 1876, she knew that if her vision was to come to any kind of reality, she had to find someone within the church who would support the undertaking. Whilst Virtue remained in Southsea, he would be her confessor and director but she knew that if her vision was to come to fruition, she needed to find another director, and above all, to gain ecclesiastical approval.

Family Conflicts

Over the years of her direction with Virtue, Potter had maintained her own counsel regarding the developments of her inner life. No family member was privy to either the pain or the joy of the spiritual journey she had undertaken, or to the growing belief that she had been called to bring into being a new religious order. To all intents and purposes, her life continued its round of housekeeping, family walks, some philanthropic visiting, and as a means of making money, music lessons to private pupils.[151] Neither her brother nor her mother "press[ed] for my confidence, never alluded [if they] noticed anything."[152] In spite of the difficulties and the anguish she at times experienced, Potter:

> bore without showing [my anguish of soul] and did my few duties…going out for walks with my mother and brothers, listening to them, singing and playing, mending their socks and so on, so I had hours to myself in the day, and used to come down from my room, as if nothing was going on within me…My room was a sanctuary, and I spent hours in prayer when those of the house were out at High Mass or Benediction, which I was considered too delicate to attend.[153]

Isolated from the surrounding community by Mrs. Potter's determination that her daughter held invalid status, Potter found some companionship in the person of the young woman employed by her mother as maid-of-all-work.

Mary Fulker, daughter of Sarah Fulker, shopkeeper and "Catholic bookseller," of Prince George's Street, Portsmouth[154] had been employed by Mrs. Potter sometime in 1874, and though considered by her employer as lazy and ill-tempered,[155] Fulker had forged bonds of affection with the daughter of the house. In the absence of any other confidant, Fulker became a support to Potter who shared some of her aspirations with the young woman.

Herself a Catholic with an overtly religious bent, Fulker spoke with Potter about some priests she believed could provide Potter with the direction she needed.[156] Mrs. Potter, more concerned with the propriety of social relations with subordinate subjects,[157] disapproved of the relationship between the two young women, and following Fulker's dismissal from the Potter home in 1875 for a display of temper and insubordination, forbade her daughter to have any more to do with her ex-servant.[158]

Ignoring the prohibition placed upon their friendship, which in Potter's words "was crossed, but I do not think forever, [for] you wound yourself strangely around my heart,"[159] the two young women maintained contact. Fulker moved to London to seek work in the clothing factories around Spitalfields, and at St. Anne's church, Spitalfields, met a Marist priest, Father Edward Selley. This priest, she enthused, was a true spiritual guide. She had taken the liberty of informing Selley about Potter, and, she informed Potter, he was willing to meet with her.

Potter responded to Fulker's information in somewhat guarded fashion. She had shared some of her spiritual thought with her friend, and told her some of her aspirations regarding a religious order. She was, however, still under the direction of Monsignor Virtue, and though looking for a new director, had not yet cut her ties with him. There was also the fact that Monsignor Virtue had spoken with her parish priest, Father Horan, who had decided that something needed to be done about the young woman and her desire to found a religious order. Writing to Fulker, Potter told her of the current situation:

> At the present time, I must keep quiet upon the matter or should really feel inclined to write to your kind Father. I may tell you however…Father Horan now knows about it and wishes it settled one way or another, and either has already or is going to lay it all before the Bishop, so it may be under discussion at the present time – therefore you must pray, for though of course we believe Divine Providence overrules everything, we must do our part and likewise you must pray that when I have an interview with the Bishop I may speak as God wishes me, but you know I am not like you, and have a dislike to talking to priests etc.[160]

Potter was not to see the bishop until 1876, and her reluctance to make contact with Father Selley ended as family pressures began to mount.

In the years since leaving the Mercy novitiate, the relationship between Potter and her mother had remained ambivalent. Although Mrs Potter's resistance to her daughter's desire to re-enter religious life had persisted, and, according to family members, grown more intense as her own health deteriorated and deafness made life difficult,[161] her brother Thomas was supportive. His life had taken a new turn upon meeting Marguerite Faveraux, a young French governess his sister had befriended early in 1875. A growing intimacy developed between Thomas and Marguerite, and Mrs. Potter, unused to the ways of the younger generation, found herself dismayed by the displays of intimacy that were now seen within the home, whilst her daughter found delight in narrating their idiosyncratic behaviour to her friend Mary Fulker:

> They are a funny couple, one of their idiosyncrasies being that it is essential to their
> happiness to sit on one chair. Poor Mama watches their entry into her room with dread,
> trembling for the springs of her chair. Regarding the number of chairs they have bro-
> ken (ours not being the strongest you can find), I should really be afraid to say. Mama's
> old-fashioned ideas quite put to the rout [as] you may imagine. "Your Papa and I, Mary,
> never took any notice of one another in company."[162]

Thomas and Marguerite married in October 1875, in the small town of Portsea where
Marguerite worked as a teacher. It was, Potter noted to Fulker "one of the grandest [wed-
dings] seen for some time":

> Father Corbett rode home in the same carriage with the bride and bridegroom, my
> brother amused at a voice from the crowd, "She's gone and done it now." Breakfast was
> at the school – Champagne etc. Wedding supper at our house after the honeymoon,
> some company. I made Matrimony pudding, which Fr. Horan in his dry way opined he
> and Fr. Corbett had better not touch.[163]

The addition of Marguerite to the home in Norfolk St. Southsea proved to be a positive factor in Potter's life, for she became the dutiful daughter-in-law, and as "Madame
Potter," took over the management of the home. Perhaps fortunately for her relationship
with her mother-in-law, she was not particularly skilled in domestic routine. According to
her new sister-in-law, she was "very delicate…she does remarkably well as regards housekeeping considering she was never used [to it], but is not fit for doing much herself."[164]
She did bring to the home her skill as teacher, and in the months following her marriage
to Thomas, she joined Potter and Mrs. Potter in commencing a small school within the
family home. There they received "a few Catholic boys for a few hours of school-
ing…[Marguerite] teaching French and [Potter] teaching Music and English helped by
'Granny' [Mrs. Potter]."[165] The venture had its difficulties, mainly because Potter herself
fell ill, and could not take the classes as arranged.[166] But the women struggled on.

By April 1876, however, Potter's hopes for the establishment of a religious community
were no closer to fulfilment. Father Horan had done nothing and Monsignor Virtue, who
had received his transfer to Malta in November 1875, was preparing to leave the area. If
anything was to happen, it seemed that she would have to take her own initiative. Thus,
in May 1876, against the advice of Virtue, who told her that the bishop of Southwark,
James Danell,[167] was in total opposition to any new order being established in his diocese,[168] Potter made an appointment to see Danell and place before him her hopes and
vision.

To her surprise, Danell not only welcomed her courteously, but also gave a guarded
assent to the establishment of a pious guild of women who could gather, hold meetings,
and pray for the dying. With the consent of the parish priest, they could visit cases pointed
out to them, and if desired, even live together under a rule. They were not, however, to
call themselves a religious order. Potter wrote to Fulker of her reception:

…[T]he Bishop …was very kind to me and said I might influence others to join me in devotion to the dying, that we might hold meetings, we might even take a house and live together under a rule, visiting cases pointed out to us. He told me the prayers we might use, mentioning one he himself said every day, and he said we might see him again. One thing he distinctly said, and that was the word "Order" was not to be mentioned among us. He gave his blessing to my school. He first refused to allow me to have Mass, and then said the demand must come from Fr. Horan.[169]

Mary was pleased with the positive outcome of her interview. Even if Danell had forbidden her to speak of this pious association as religious order, his agreement to the formation of a group of women, who could live in community, under a simple rule of life and engaged in works of Christian charity, was a beginning. His support for a small Catholic school was a bonus, as was his agreement to practical work within the parish. What mattered was that the bishop had given his consent, and time would sort out the rest. Cheered by this success, she also took the step of making contact with the priest Mary Fulker had recommended to her, Father Edward Selley SM, "in the hope of obtaining a friend to a work of God now in its infancy."[170]

Edward Selley was born in Pimlico, on March 23, 1843,[171] the son of highly respectable and wealthy Anglican stock. Disowned and disinherited by his family after converting to Catholicism in 1863,[172] he entered the Dublin novitiate of the Marist Fathers in 1865.[173] Moving from Dublin to the United States in 1870, he was ordained in 1872 and returned to England as a curate at St. Anne's, Spitalfields in 1874. There his fame as a confessor became widely known – perhaps because he was one of the few English-speaking priests in the parish, the rest being French.[174]

The correspondence initiated between Potter and Selley commenced in June 1876. Potter told the priest of her encounters with Monsignor Virtue,[175] and of her belief that a new religious order was to be founded in the church.[176] She told Selley of her need to find a new director, and of her current insecurity, with Virtue still in the Portsmouth district and still opposing what she termed her revelations.[177] On June 13, she informed him of her meeting with Bishop Danell, and of the cautious acceptance, not of a religious order, but of a pious guild of women dedicated to prayer for the dying. Still hoping to gain patronage and help to establish a religious community, she sent him a manuscript containing an outline of the proposed order. [178] It was a document that contained some novel elements.

As the historian Susan O'Brien recognised, Potter's idea for her religious community did not fit the model established by other English religious communities founded in the nineteenth century,[179] nor did it build upon "models provided by the Daughters of Charity, the Ursulines and enclosed teaching orders."[180] Lacking a clear social or utilitarian purpose, its principal focus was on incarnating a particular element of Christ's life, and of prayer for, and where possible, care of the dying. Its spirit, as she had clearly enunciated to Virtue, was to be that of Calvary.

For followers of the French School, the "spirit" or "states" (*états*) of the mysteries of the life of Jesus were of vital importance. According to the teaching of the French school, true Christian living was perceived as a specific, personal and deep identification with Jesus and the church, which was realised by the action of the Spirit within the believer. This "life of Jesus in us" began at Baptism and was to be nourished by participation in the Eucharist and through contemplation, the latter being seen as "non-sacramental" communion.[181] For De Montfort, and his new disciple Mary Potter, the central mystery of Jesus was the Cross. It was the culminating point of God's love for humanity. To contemplate the Cross, and to be united to it, was to enter the paradox of self-emptying and self-transcendence. Only in this manner could unconditional service be given to the world. In keeping with the apocalyptic vision of a world in need of redemption, Potter's belief was that the institute was to give witness to the value of and need for such unconditional love. It was the charism or the gift to be brought into being. Fundamental to the integrity of the institute it would, however, become a source of much difficulty. It presumed both the willingness of the members to be formed in the contemplative life such a focus demanded, and that church authority would permit them to be so formed. In contradistinction to religious orders that emerged in response to direct social need, or as a means of doing good work under church control,[182] Potter's institute was to be filled with the apostolic zeal of Jesus. This "apostolic zeal" Potter transcribed and identified as "the mother-love" of the Good Shepherd and it was this that was to be the source of all of the works that the members might perform.

Forming one body, the members of this institute were to unite the active to the contemplative life. The community was not to be enclosed, nor were there to be lay sisters. The only distinction was of the choice of the members for the active or contemplative life:

> The order in question would not consist, as many others, of lay sisters and choir sisters. No! Like the Sisters of Charity, there would be no lay sisters in it, the only distinction, it may be called, being that there would be working members, and for two reasons: Firstly, an order whose spirit is to be the spirit of Calvary and has Calvary as its model, must practice poverty in its integrity, and therefore the members, like poor people, must earn their living. Secondly, there may be many, who, anxious to join this work of Mary, yet might be afraid to join an Order completely devoted to Calvary, as requiring too much of them, and most certainly, no one could devote themselves to the mystery of Calvary without aspiring to the highest perfection, and if they are faithful, attaining it.[183]

Perhaps shaped by her own experience within the Mercy community, the outline of the congregation offered a solution to those who might not be sure to what life they were called: "[T]here would be less danger of mistake in such an order as this" she wrote in her plan, "than in one purely contemplative or active, for they would find both, and be able to choose, even if they had entered only as a working member."[184]

The pure pragmatism of the idea held merit. But there was a deeper importance to the words. Potter had been unable to follow her natural inclination to enter a contemplative community because of her class and financial inability to pay the dowry. Her view now was that "no one seeking admittance is required or asked to bring either dowry or pension, and neither would a large dower be accepted."[185] This determination opened the doors of this community to women of any class or circumstance, and meant that the contemplative life was available to women of all classes,[186] including working-class women such as Fulker.[187]

The twin branches of the congregation, Potter believed, also answered the needs of those who were "afraid that too much would be required of them, and therefore prudently afraid of pledging themselves to what they might not be able to perform."[188] Fear of the discipline or the prayer life of the community, she believed, would be overcome by a gradual assimilation of the spirituality of the congregation, and "the Holy Spirit [who] forms the saint at will," would lead each to her particular expression of the active or contemplative vocation of the sisterhood.[189]

Conformity to the Calvary spirit affected the ordinary life of the community. "The order being strictly devoted to poverty, must not be possessed of funds, but…must support itself by labour" Potter's manuscript stated.[190] Work such as "teaching, laundry work, needlework, writing, etc., might in turn be collectively required"[191] if the houses were to support themselves, but the kind of works performed was left open, for in Potter's view "[a] foundation would have to work according to the people and place they were in."[192] In what appears as an attempt to ward off contemporary criticism that the works of religious sisterhoods undermined the work of unmarried women, Potter stated that in her view:

> the trite objection of monopolising the various works to which single women are obliged to resort to support themselves cannot apply to this order (if indeed it can apply to any), since so many single young women will be, by this means, provided for.[193]

Potter's religious experiences were seminal to her understanding of religious life. These had convinced her that the nature and purpose of religious life was not primarily to perform works of social action, but to reflect particular "states" of Christ's life and secondly that those states could only be realised through the prayer life of the each member of the community. Missionary activity followed prayer as naturally as night followed day, but it was activity generated from an interior union with God. Whether active or contemplative, the life demanded a willed offering of self. If the members of the institute were bound to Christ on the Cross, by a mystical union such as she herself had experienced, Potter was convinced that their world view would be altered and patterned after the world view of Jesus who died for the whole world. The important thing was that each member was willing to "lay down her life":

> Those who have to show a way, may first have to go through it. Those who join this work of Calvary may be required, as it were to die daily, to lead a dying life, to be constantly offering up their lives, to show their willingness to lay them down if required, if their life, for instance could be taken instead of another not prepared. The constant acts

they could thus make might be accepted by God, for the assistance of others without such… It may be simply that God might wish me to possess and make known to others this spirit – to be constantly offering their death to Him and yet not die, like our Lady on Calvary…[194]

None would be barred from this call by virtue of class or financial ability. All shared the one mission, and the primary ministry was prayer that "none may be lost." The members would watch before the Blessed Sacrament as Mary watched by the foot of the Cross.[195] Some would be engaged in perpetual intercession for the dying, others in varieties of service.[196] Those called to live the contemplative life with greater intensity would live a more structured life of prayer, while those for whom a life of active service was more in keeping, would be engaged in whatever was needed for the building up of the community and the church.[197] All, however, would live the same sacrificial interior life.

Following the bishop's directions that the word "order" was not to be used with reference to the group Potter clarified her position regarding the initial gathering of a community with Selley:

> You must understand, my plan is simply this to those I shall ask. I am going to establish a larger school than the one I have at present. I hope likewise to have a chapel in the house. We shall unite out prayers and visit the cases Father Horan points out to us…Our plan of life will be very simple. Until I myself have a guide to consult upon the penances, exterior practices etc., I think it would be better to confine ourselves to forming the interior spirit which will be that of our Lady. God has not left me in ignorance of what he expects from me, but as I cannot even tell those who join what will follow, I shall content myself with striving, by God's help to induce them to have a devotion to Our Lady that they may never have had before…[this]…devotion would make them saints in the world…I have practised it for years and now it is a part of me…I have such confidence in the devotion that give me a soul that is willing to embrace it (I do not say even like it…) no matter what may be the defects of that soul it will be entirely changed. It is some years since Sr. Clare (the nun from Kenmare) urged me to write a book about it, she said make it "Practically instructive" and the great good I should do, I had many letters from Kenmare about it…[198]

Selley was swift in his response to Potter's letters. He had no conflict with her Marian devotion[199] and not only believed her experiences, but was prepared to help her establish her community. Willing to act as her director, he also advised her that he knew of some women who would be interested in her project, and suggested that she come to London and meet with him. Potter was overjoyed at finding a priest who seemed to understand the mission she believed entrusted to her. With the bishop's permission, a supportive director, and prospective candidates, the way seemed clear to commence the venture. It was a short-lived happiness. By the end of June, Potter was at odds with her family.

The source of the new conflict lay with Potter herself. Enthused by the bishop's vague consent, Selley's support and his promise of candidates, Potter decided she now needed to find a house in which to commence the venture. Father Horan had been placed in charge of any developments and the venture seemed assured of a good beginning in Portsmouth. A grand idea presented itself to her. If her brother and sister-in-law could be persuaded to buy another property, they could give her possession of the residence at Southsea. She wrote to Mary Fulker of her brave new idea:

> I hope within a month or two to have this house as my own to open a school on a larger scale than I can at present, and with others to live together under a certain rule, the principal [sic] of which will be to honour the Maternal Heart of our Lady, to work, pray and suffer in union with it, and to assist the dying. I hope likewise that I may have a chapel in the house…. I am praying now that we may have this house, that my Mother, sister and brother may move, which at present they have no intention of. Then that Fr. Horan may accept my offer of either the ground floor or drawing room for a chapel and that all the necessary arrangements may be concluded by the time Monsignor leaves, which I understand is July.[200]

Potter's single-minded passion to follow what she believed was God's call made it all seem perfectly sensible. Thomas was married. The house was already small with four adults in it, and when her brothers George, Henry, or William came to visit, it was positively overcrowded. Once children were born to her brother and his wife, a larger house would become a necessity, so why not now? Oddly enough, Thomas and Marguerite appear to have humoured Potter in her desire, but she would have to prove to her brother that she could take financial responsibility for the home. It was hardly a risk as Potter had no finances, and her hope to establish a larger school had no basis in reality without community members who could teach. But, undaunted by the difficulty of the proposition set by her brother, Potter wrote to Mary Fulker, crowing her delight. "They will move," she wrote, "if I can show my brother on paper that I can, without great risk, take the house."[201] Convinced that all was now well, she invited Fulker to join the new community, assuring her that in this utopian venture, all were equal, and there was no division of class:

> Understand distinctly, if you come, you come on equality with all the others. We are simply poor women devoting ourselves to a good work, but still like poor women, we must earn our living. It was your favourite, St. Paul, who put that idea into my mind. The school is not part of the idea; it is our means of living. In another town, we might have something different to do, but it so happens schools are sadly wanted for the middle-classes here. We shall have no fine ladylike ways. We must have our meals in the kitchen. You will understand you will not come as anything different from a grand lady, if she wished to join us. We shall all be equal and as regards your slaving away at all kinds of things you have not the strength for, I should think it really wrong of you. As there may be two or three of us to begin with, we shall have to be employed a good deal in school.[202]

In terms of Potter's own times and family background, the egalitarian aspect of the society was unusual. As O'Brien and Thompson have pointed out, few congregations were founded on such principles, class distinctions within convents tending to echo those of the surrounding society.[203] Such distinctions were inconceivable to Potter whose worldview had been altered by her spiritual insight into God's all pervading presence. All persons are made in the image of God – there could be no separation into classes within the community she envisaged. If Fulker wished to join the infant community, then it was as one among many. Unfortunately for both Fulker and Potter, the proposed gathering of the community was postponed by the reaction of Mrs. Potter to the news of her daughter's proposal that she and her son and daughter-in-law move house to enable a religious community to take residence. Angry at the apparent lack of concern for herself and for the family, she refused to consider any such move on the part of the family. She had become ill in June of 1876, and though cared for by her daughter-in-law and son, demanded that Potter give up all idea of entering a religious community. Potter was angered by the response, but again caught in a moral dilemma.

It is not hard to find examples of Victorian daughters who renounced any life of their own to nurse aged or ailing parents.[204] The expectation placed upon Potter was no more or less than that placed by the filial piety promulgated by the period upon any other dutiful and unmarried daughter. Mrs. Potter's own stern notions of duty and filial respect combined with the power of her maternal control almost guaranteed that the relationship with her daughter would lead to ambiguity. Potter's conviction was that her obligations to her mother could not stand in the way of her vocation. Mrs. Potter was equally convinced that God had returned her daughter to her. If marriage were not to be her lot then nothing would remove her from the family home again. The relationship between the indomitable Mrs. Potter and her female offspring faltered as two strong wills clashed. Quite simply, her mother's demands irritated Potter. If her spiritual experiences had drawn her into a deep and loving relationship with her God, they had not and would not destroy the capacity for irritation and anger that Potter could and did feel towards her demanding, "peculiar"[205] and overbearing parent. In a surprising admission of the depth of anguish and anger towards her mother, Potter wrote to Father Selley:

> [this] evening [there was] a most painful scene with my Mother who is ill. (I could almost pray God to give her a happy death, if it were right). She thinks me so cold-hearted and cruel to her. I hear her coughing now and know she is awake and full of sad thoughts. She has had so many trials; she told me she would oppose it all she could, that I cannot go without her consent, which is true.[206]

Less than a week later, she again wrote to Selley, informing him that the proposed community was in abeyance, and that her mother's opposition had strengthened still further:

> As regards the person you would kindly send me, I can do nothing much until I get my mother's consent. I did not expect such strong opposition. She seems to think she has done all that could be expected of her by giving me up before and that I was given back to her like Isaac. She has said that she would appeal to the Holy Father sooner than let

me go. When I have her consent, I should be very glad of the one you mention. I shall commence praying for her now.[207]

Selley responded to the letter and manuscript with words of encouragement, and continued to press for a meeting. At his instigation, a correspondence was initiated between Potter and Selley's candidate for her community, Elizabeth Bryan.[208] A friendship began to grow between the two women as Potter shared her hopes for the new community. Maintaining her contact with Selley, Potter told him of the manuscript she had prepared on De Montfort's spirituality, and, to her delight, the priest offered to revise the manuscript and prepare it for publication.[209] Publication of *The Path of Mary* would help the community come to fruition, for it would be "a help to our income and bring in money,"[210] and, it must be said, find them some independence.

Mrs Potter's continual resistance to and annoyance with her daughter's plans began to impact upon other family members. Thomas, resenting the disquiet the conflict between his sister and mother was bringing to his connubial bliss, began to agitate that she give up her own ideas, settle down and do what her mother requested. Not at all dismayed by the turn of events, and not above using deception to gain her mother's consent, Potter began to plan a trip to London to see Father Selley. She told her mother of the possibility of becoming published and of the need to see a publisher about her manuscript. She would stay with her brother William and get her business organised. Mrs. Potter finally gave her permission to go and on June 29, Potter advised Selley of her impending arrival in London.

Potter left Portsmouth on June 30, 1876 and, upon her arrival in London, made immediate contact with her new director. He organised for her to meet with members of his women's guild, and made the suggestion that she stay in London and make a retreat under his direction. Potter agreed with the idea, and wrote home, informing her mother that she was following the advice of the priest and would be staying in London longer than first thought in order to make a retreat and consider her future.

At first, Mrs. Potter made no comment about her daughter's duplicity, or her decision to remain in London. Her ire was stirred however, when she discovered that her daughter was staying with Mary Fulker in a squalid little room in Spitalfields, and also by a letter she received from Father Selley. He informed her plainly that he believed her wrong to refuse her consent to her daughter's obvious calling, and that she and the family should make amends by giving Potter the family home to enable the community to commence. Mrs. Potter was furious. She wrote to Selley telling him that she did not want him directing her daughter, that the venture was impossible from a financial point of view, and that she could not, would not and did not want to be separated from her daughter.[211]

Mrs. Potter was not simply dismayed at Selley's support of Potter's ideas; she was also in distress by the way her daughter was dragging down the family name. The thought that Potter was sharing lodgings in the working class area of Spitalfields was anathema. That the person she was sharing with was an ex-servant of the Potter house "whose violent temper rendered her immediate dismissal requisite"[212] only made the situation worse. Mrs Potter wrote to her only daughter accusing her of creating a scandal that placed her entire family in an odious situation, and of abandoning her in her old age and infirmity.[213] Condemning the unusual and unseemly behaviour her daughter was demonstrating by being in London "without a protector," she sought to get Selley to believe that Potter was suffering a "mental weakness, caused by keeping to reading and writing on one subject."[214] Moreover, the scandal of her remaining in London was a mischief to other members of the family notably one George Saul, who was in the "literary world, as are his connections [and] it [was] by no means unlikely the affair, with comments by the Press… [would]… become public."[215] Furthermore, Selley should know that she believed that her daughter's instability would inevitably lead to problems if she was allowed to commence a community, the more so if it required financial acumen:

> my daughter has a singular inaptitude for managing even small financial matters. Soon would a community, which she managed, be in pecuniary embarrassment. She is a large hearted, generous girl, and of such a confiding disposition that the objects of her charity have imposed sadly on her, and been of the worst sort themselves, a real scandal to religion.[216]

All Mrs. Potter's attempts to gain Selley's support in returning Mary to her home failed. Potter followed the priest's direction. In spite of a plea from her mother to "come home and be my comfort,"[217] and criticism from her aunts and uncles that she was "setting up an idol she called duty; and filial affection common sense and reason must all bow to it,"[218] she remained in London. To placate some of the tensions, however, she removed herself from Fulker's boarding house, and went to stay with her brother Henry in Southwark. Henry, though accommodating, was unimpressed with her determination not to go home until she had resolved the situation. Undismayed by such lack of support and with Selley's assistance, Potter gained an interview with Cardinal Manning (1808–1892),[219] and also made arrangements to see Lady Georgiana Fullerton (1812–1885), whose reputation for assisting in the establishment and support of religious orders was legendary.[220] Neither interview was to prove satisfactory.

Henry Edward Cardinal Manning was not unfamiliar with the potential offered to women by religious life, or of women's capacity to initiate and establish religious communities.[221] As the Archdeacon of Chichester, he had been directly involved in the founding of the Anglican community of St. Mary the Virgin at Wantage, had encouraged Miss Elizabeth Crawford Lockhardt to join it, and recommended her to the vicar of Wantage, as its superior.[222] She had become a Catholic in 1850, and, following his own conversion in 1851, Manning had maintained his interest in women's communities of service. Directly involved with the establishment of the Franciscan community founded by Lockhardt in 1857, he was also instrumental in the foundation of the Poor Servants of the Mother of God, undertaken by Lady Georgiana Fullerton and her friend Fanny Taylor in 1869.[223]

Ascetic, severe and believing passionately in the life of the Spirit as central to the Christian life,[224] Manning gave an initial, cautious encouragement to Potter. He was a man noted by his friends for a passionate concern for the suffering, and the suffering of women touched him as deeply as that of his beloved poor. Lady Dilke, writing to Mr. Bodley after his publication of an essay on Manning, stated that:

> 'Misery and suffering', you say, 'caused him always the acutest anguish.' This was true in a degree that I have known in hardly any other man. I have heard him speak with a sound in his voice and a light in his eyes which meant depths of restrained passion. 'Give all yourself to London, it is the abomination of desolations' or 'No one knows the depth of the sufferings of women save the doctor or the priest.' That he was so pained by your pain was the chief cause of his great power.[225]

He was, however, a man who also valued the virtues of family life. When informed by priests of his own deanery[226] of Mrs Potter's alleged need of her daughter's care and support, he withdrew his approval. Potter received a message that simply stated his belief that "if this [the foundation] is of the Holy Ghost – and I am not saying it is not – it will be …[brought to realisation] … but let Miss Potter go home to her mother now."[227]

Despite the Cardinal's injunction to return home to her mother, Potter delayed her return until she had seen and sought advice from Lady Georgiana Fullerton and Fanny Taylor, now Mother Magdalen of the Poor Servants of the Mother of God. Lady Georgiana, who had been so instrumental in assisting Fanny Taylor in her foundation, received Mary kindly,[228] but made no commitment to assisting the new venture. Rather than commence a new religious order, she suggested it might be better for Potter to explore amalgamation with another community, and told her of a group in Lyon, dedicated to prayer for the Holy Souls.[229] It was the same principle that had influenced her in the foundation of the Poor Servants of the Mother of God, [230] but it failed to impress Potter. She tried to explain the difference she believed existed between religious orders,[231] and the need for each to live according to its founding spirit.[232] Fullerton failed to understand, and in dismissing the young woman suggested that perhaps it would be best if she did as Bishop Danell suggested and begin by an Association of Prayers.[233] With that advice, and a vague promise of support should anything come of the idea, Potter had to be content.[234]

Potter returned home on July 29, 1876. Regardless of the instruction given her by Manning, her inner conviction remained unchanged. Opposition again surrounded her. On August 10, she wrote to Selley of a new outburst of anger from her family and friends:

> My movements are well known I believe. To my surprise, on visiting some Protestant relatives in London I was told about being a visionary, wanting to found an Order in opposition to my Bishop and Monsignor etc. I have been very careful about only mentioning under confidence and to a very few, but it was made known to my brother by Father Horan.[235]

The gossip gathered intensity. A priest from a neighbouring town called upon the family and "began talking so pointedly about religious mania etc. that I thought – he has heard of my plans, he is talking of me, and it seemed to me to be the beginning of what was coming."[236] But, in spite of the mounting public criticism, Potter held herself in peace. She continued planning for the new venture, seeking for ways to enable it to be self-supporting, and how it could expand knowledge of God among the people it served:

> I once thought of learning Latin on purpose to translate the Latin works of the Fathers, but I was told it would be too much for me, but I hope in course of time, when the little Society is joined together, someone may carry out that idea. Such books it seems to me would show how orderly, I know no other word, God is in all he does…

> Do you not think that working members [of the society] might go out as governesses? … It would be a good source of income. I know a lady who, I have heard, has no accomplishment even such as French or music, who has been all her life a governess. She received a salary of one hundred pounds and more. Grand families would not mind paying a large sum, of course, to secure the advantage of a religious to bring up their children, besides, they would save at a high salary, considering what they would pay at the higher class convents. I myself would gladly go out for a time and earn money that way, if I had the power.[237]

However naïve the thoughts, the reality of Potter's situation was that finances were needed if the venture was to succeed. The publication of the manuscript of *The Path of Mary* was taking some time to organise and sales of that would not provide sufficient to establish any convent or support a group of women. Without some kind of patronage or a definite employment of at least some of the members, nothing could be achieved. Before any further speculation could take place however, the Potter household erupted. Bishop Danell withdrew his support for the society, Selley was informed that any co-operation he gave to Potter in founding an order would be a deliberate disobedience not only to Bishop Danell, but to the Cardinal Archbishop, Manning himself. Moreover, any thought of Miss Potter publishing a book on Catholic doctrine or devotion was seriously doubtful.[238]

The source of much of this dissent lay with Potter's brothers. Thomas, a well-known figure within the Catholic community,[239] had written to Bishop Danell of the family turmoil over Potter's beliefs, and with this missive, any hope of Potter's commencement in the diocese of Southwark vanished.[240] Danell, already embroiled in difficulties with women religious, was unwilling to have any other disturbance within his diocese.[241] Once notified of the crisis in the household and of the support for the establishment of a religious order being given by Father Selley, Danell acted immediately. Potter was advised that she was forbidden to found a religious order in the Diocese of Southwark, and that she had utterly disobeyed the direct instruction of Danell that the word "order" not be used with regard to the pious association to which he had agreed. A terse note from Danell summed up the situation:

My dear Miss Potter,

In the most positive and decisive manner possible I forbid you to found any religious society or order in my Diocese. I am surprised after my clear prohibition when you called some little time ago, you should have so soon disobeyed me. You may tell your confessor, Father Selley, he may call on me next Monday morning at 12.

Blessing you, Yours Faithfully, James Danell.[242]

Selley responded to the summons accompanied by his superior Father Chaurain. He was advised by Danell to offer no further assistance to Miss Potter or her ideas of founding a religious order.[243] Selley's Marist superiors imposed their own constraints. He was forbidden to carry on "spiritual direction by letter," ordered to confine his activities to his work within the confessional, and told to having nothing more to do with Mary Potter.[244] It was a distressing situation for both, but with the agreement of Elizabeth Bryan, and Mary Fulker, members of Selley's small group, correspondence was continued. On the home front, things were equally distressing. Thomas, resenting the disruption of the family home "seemed positively to insist I must go away, that it was causing uncomfortableness [sic] and dissension in the house."[245] George, whose gossip amongst his priest friends had led to Manning's initial rejection of Potter's community, made the suggestion that she should "go and stay in a Convent and that he would pay the board."[246] Potter was puzzled by the sudden and complete rejection:

It is not that I have been, so to speak, making a martyr of myself. I have been merry and so on. In fact I have tried to act the same and told my brother I was really very sorry (as I am) to cause him so much bother, but however he feels uncomfortable and said likewise that if I did not go, he and his wife would. It is very strange. What is to be done?[247]

She could do little. Defined and constructed around the central themes of family, species, and property, women's lives were shaped and patterned by the men who guarded them, suffered their fragile sensitivities, and wrote of their virtues, vices and vicissitudes.[248] To break away from the family circle or the dominant ideology was more than aberrative; it was to threaten the social fabric of home and society.[249] Conformity was expected, and when it was not forthcoming, was perceived as obstinacy – a point made to Potter by her uncle to whom she had turned for support:

My dear Mary,

Of course I do not suppose that I am infallible, but I believe I am quite right in distrusting your judgement, and business-like habits when they are directly the reverse of those of your family, to say nothing of Bishops, priests, et.

I am quite sure that did the views of your mother and brothers correspond with your own, they would ready find means to assist you in your plans, and the fact of their opposition shows that you are altogether mistaken…I suppose persistency in your case is a refined species of obstinacy… I hasten to reply that I will be no party to assisting you…

With best wishes for your reformation…[250]

Potter's cardinal sin was to seek to be more than she was in the eyes of her family, the unmarried daughter, whose virtuous charity and chastity would serve the needs of her household.[251] Self-direction and the quest for self-fulfillment not only broke the bonds of security and stability of the Victorian home,[252] but also challenged hard won values, and this, for the Potter family, posed significant threat.

In the flood of disapproval that now surrounded her, Potter remained remarkably calm. Deeply concerned for Father Selley, she wrote assuring him of her own belief that good would prevail from all the fuss that was surrounding the issue.[253] Spiritualising the conflict, she stated that it only made her more convinced of the rightness of her actions, as "the one great sign of its being God's Work [is] the absence of human eagerness and impetuosity about it."[254] Patience appeared to have it own reward, for on August 17, Potter again wrote to Selley to tell him that her brothers, in particular Henry and George, had come to the conclusion that they had been hasty in their judgements of their sister and were now anxious to make amends.[255]

Henry – who had contributed to stirring the bishop's wrath and thus contributed to Selley's receipt of an episcopal correction – was now overcome by repentance, and wrote to both Danell and Manning 'carefully, justly and prudently' in support of his sister and her plans. To the Cardinal Archbishop of Westminster he wrote:

> Your Eminence, I beg to recall to your mind certain interviews and correspondence you have had respecting my sister Miss Potter. I am one of her brothers and wish to express my entire disapprobation of the course of action my dear mother and one of my brothers have taken in her regard. Respecting any new Order to be founded I, as a layman, will not presume to express an opinion. My sister, in her great zeal for the love and service of God, has undoubtedly, from a worldly point of view, done many imprudent things and has been too anxious to have her idea carried out at once, and has thereby raised a storm about her, but that is all. I wish, as a business-like and yet devoted Catholic, writing to you as her brother, to beg your Eminence to believe that my sister has a sound, sensible and powerful mind, that her wish is for the greater glory of God, and that any work that she may be allowed to publish will be, I believe, a welcome addition to our Catholic literature…. I feel bound to write these few words to your Eminence as having received letters from others of her relatives which may leave a wrong impression on the mind of your Eminence: I wish, as far as I am able to counteract that impression…. [256]

For all Henry's good will, Potter was barred from any further activity with regard to commencing a new religious order, and from receiving any assistance from Selley with regard to her congregation. This, however, did not prevent the priest from continuing his work on the publication of the *Path of Mary*, or from encouraging Potter to keep on with her writing. She commenced to write *The Spiritual Exercises of Mary*,[257] a work that, she informed Selley, was to be a retreat for those entering De Montfort's spiritual pathway.[258] At the same time she set her sights on the production of a far more theological tome entitled *The Attributes of God Mirrored in the Perfection of Mary*.[259] Then, on September 4, 1876, Potter received the first bound copy of the *Path*. It was a momentous occasion. She was a "published" author, and she was delighted.

There was to be a standard edition, but some were to be "got up better with the title outside in silver letters and the leaves silvered,"in order to maximise sales, or at least "make an attractive book …for presentations and prizes."[260] Receiving copies from the printer, she immediately started selling the book to family and friends, and on September 18, wrote to inform Selley that she had disposed of all of the copies the printer had supplied and was waiting on two hundred more. She had evolved a novel approach to sales:

> I asked a good old Irish woman to sell one or two, as I did not like asking myself, and now it is "your money or your life" with her. I heard her myself last night, outside the Church. "Come now, put your hand in your pocket and give me a shilling and take this." I wish I had some more books to give her to sell, she sold them so quickly and asked for more.[261]

The publication of the book did much to boost Mary's ego. When it was actually reviewed positively in the *Catholic Times* and the *Weekly Register*,[262] she was delighted, and wrote to Elizabeth Bryan of her success:

> The Path has sold very well and reviewed very well… [I am]… like someone else. I have extraordinary health, and this time of year used to try me so. I must say I enjoy being so well after all these years, and am very grateful that one complaint after another has gone.[263]

For the first time in her life, Potter was experiencing a personal success – a success that allowed her to claim an intellectual and financial authority of her own. Even her mother acknowledged that she had not thought her capable of writing. Potter celebrated this fact with a note to Selley: "She is so pleased about the notice in the 'Register,' …[she] made the remark she did not think her child would have written anything but what was wishy-washy as she was 'all heart and no head'."[264] Her brothers likewise expressed their approval, and even Sister Clare of Kenmare,[265] sent to London for a copy and her response to the work almost frightened Mary with its passionate intensity:

> In the NAME OF GOD [sic], and as you have to answer him at the great Day of Doom I ask you one question. Have you compiled this book from any source or is it your own or rather God's own? I never read anything like it … Believe me dear Mary, I feel deeply there are some lines in this went to my heart about …[sentence indecipherable]
>
> God knows I have had a bitter experience of it, but you write as if all felt alike. This idea of the religious orders replicating the Lord's life on earth is sublime and so manifestly true.[266]

Lady Georgiana Fullerton graciously requested six copies of the book; found it a "very interesting and devout little work,"[267] and promptly forgot to pay for the copies she purchased.[268]

For all the favourable reviews, however, the *Path* drew its own share of criticism, from predominantly clerical critics. Summoned from her prayers in a local church by its parish priest, she was subjected to vigorous criticism which was representative of the way the work was received by members of the clergy:

> [B]eing in a Church the other evening, (not in this town), I was summoned by a Rev. Canon out of the church and told to go and wait in his room. I am getting used to so many things that I was not in the least surprised to hear (after being told I had written of what I did not understand and I should learn to teach before I taught etc.,) that there was an error … He talked a long time, I standing tired and exhausted, and at last when he said to me did I understand, I was obliged to say I really did not…. The simple way in which he said, "If you had asked me I should have advised you not to publish" amused me too. He said he thought it was best to speak openly. I thanked him, and we parted good friends.[269]

However not everyone disdained her work. If there was a general ecclesiastical disapproval, it was softened by the positive responses from others including her family. It was a milestone in Potter's life, giving her a sense of independence, self-confidence, and personal worth. Increased sales gave her the promise of a minute, but important income. With the publication of *The Path of Mary*, Potter joined the ranks of those women for whom devotional writing, either in the form of religious novels, or devotional tracts, provided a source of income, thus relieving what Jane Austen called the "unhappy propensity" spinsters had of being poor.[270] The book also brought her to the attention of a reading public and the varied responses to her achievement led her to reflect that personal success did not take away from her the recognition of her own unworthiness, but that encouragement was something from which she benefited:

> If by one person I am thought almost possessed or out of my mind, and puffed with pride … another time I am spoken of almost as an angel. Thank God I know myself (at least to some degree) and that knowledge really renders me so hateful to myself that I do not fear now as at one time to be praised. I rather feel that I need some encouragement.[271]

This sentiment flowed over into her home environment. Within the confines of her brother's home, she was both boarder and help. When the servant was absent, she cooked the meals,[272] mended clothes,[273] and following the birth of Thomas and Marguerite's child, acted as nanny.[274] The money she earned from running her small school, or brought in by writing or was doled by her brother from the family trust funds, all went towards her board and keep.[275] There was a growing irritation at the waste of time and money such a life was causing her. "It seems such a pity," she wrote to Selley, "to be paying money to live in a style I do not wish to live in,"[276] and for all her piety, it was with a sense of injustice that she complained to Elizabeth Bryan of being ejected from her room when ill, in order to provide a bed for one of her brothers:

> It was a wonder I got well so soon – There I lay in a cold little room, almost part landing (my brother having mine) terribly cold, hungry and comfortless, wanting even light.[277]

For all the love Potter undoubtedly had for her family, the expectation that she surrender herself to its care and to be "useful" from kitchen to nursery was no longer acceptable, as no time was allowed for a life of her own. Tired of playing servant to her family, she wrote to Elizabeth Bryan of the difficulties she encountered:

> Those who read would little think of how I have written, I mean in what distraction, getting up to look to a pudding in the oven, make some gruel, go to the baby, or give music lessons etc. You would be amused, likewise, to see me with hands in my ears, praying before my Crucifix, so that I might not be distracted by the talking (and baby) which the folding doors of one room into another, allow to be heard.[278]

Though now twenty-nine years of age, Potter was without credibility in her own home. In November 1876 her hope for founding her religious order seemed even further away. Father Selley was again facing the ire of his superiors and contact between Potter and himself was through the good offices of Mary Fulker. Immediately following the publication of the *Path*, Selley's superiors had been summoned before Cardinal Manning, and there notified that they were to ensure no contact between Selley and Potter. Again, he was told to confine himself to the duties established for him by his superior Father Chaurain.[279] Selley was furious. His relationship with his French superiors was becoming tense, and though his personal commitment to the priesthood never wavered, his attraction to the Marists was on the wane.[280]

In view of the fact that Selley was no longer to have any contact with Potter, other than through "accidental" encounters in the confessional to which he had been banished, Potter took a rather devious step. She wrote to the superior of the Marist house in Spitalfields and asked Father Chaurain if he would be her director. It was a transparent move. If Chaurain agreed to be her director, she would have reason to visit Spitalfields and thus have access to meetings with Selley. Chaurain, however, responded carefully and quite clearly:

> My dear Miss Potter
>
> I fully understand your present trials and difficulties. You are now in need of a spiritual advisor. I wish I could undertake the task, but were I to assume the same function which brought Father Selley to grief, I would certainly share the same fate.
> The fact is, that the Cardinal Archbishop had just written a letter to our Provincial who had consulted him and from the contents of this letter, as well as from what I have

heard the Bishop of Southwark say on the subject, it is quite evident we cannot [associate] ourselves with your present views and plans.

Please have the kindness to consider these few lines as confidential strictly.

Believe me in Jesus and Mary

Yours very sincerely, Stephen Chaurain.[281]

Things appeared to have come to a sorry pass. Potter was without the support of a spiritual director and friend. She was considered to be a trial to clerics, a misguided female who believed she had a mission from God and a burden to her family. Others, however, were sympathetic to her cause. With the help of Mary Fulker and Elizabeth Bryan, letters and messages continued to flow between Selley and Potter. Neither had given up hope of Potter's vision being brought to reality, and in late November 1876, Potter was able to share some extraordinary news. A benefactor in Lincoln had made an offer to provide a convent and funds for the establishment of a community dedicated to Our Lady. He had read Potter's book and been delighted by the devotion it expounded. He wrote to Potter and without further ado invited her to his parish to begin a community and extend Marian devotion among the people.

Mr. Thomas Arthur Young, KSC,[282] was a wealthy member of the Catholic community in Market Rasen, a village in the diocese of Nottingham. Eccentric and reclusive, Young's contribution to the expansion of Catholicism was to build churches in the surrounding districts of Gainsborough, Spalding, and Crowle. Deeply religious, he was known to choose the subjects of his philanthropic endeavours in a somewhat idiosyncratic fashion, and though his wealth was courted by an often impoverished church, his gifts were given at his own discretion.[283]

Potter was overwhelmed by the offer made to her by Young. But before she could respond, her brother George arrived home for the Christmas vacation, to tell her that he believed she would be able to commence her community in the diocese of Nottingham.[284] A teacher at Radcliffe college, he had many friends within that diocese, and had been informed that the bishop of Nottingham would not be unwelcoming if an approach were made to him. Lincolnshire was part of the Nottingham diocese, and Potter's mind blazed with the possibility of gaining the bishop's approval and the patronage of Mr. Young.

Potter now faced the challenge of gaining her mother's approval. It was steadfastly withheld, and as Christmas came to the Potter household, so did the realisation that if the community were to be established, it would be without the consent or approval of Mrs. Mary Ann Potter. It was to be a time of decision. In the midst of family celebrations that demanded her presence, there was little enough time for reflection, but as Potter's letter to Mary Fulker illustrates, the family Christmas brought its own joys:

I have been so busy: Christmas brought my brother, took up time. Christmas day especially, what with housekeeping in the morning, dinner etc, in the afternoon, cards in the evening – hardly time for prayer, but I got Benediction in this way. Service was to begin at four o'clock. Four o'clock came and we were still at table. Rita {Marguerite

Potter] recollected that Mamma had instructed her that it was the English custom for ladies to leave the gentlemen after dinner (be it known that it was a ruse of Mamma's to get her nap) so she got up, the other's followed. I escaped, seized a shawl and bonnet, and got out into the street. Well, I heard a cab behind me. – I thought what a long way it was and I might lose the blessing. I had got no money, but I hailed the cab. Cabby shook his head and passed. Crossing a place I got up to it again and looked at Cabby. Cabby's guardian angel said to him "take her up." Cabby himself said: "Where do you want to go?" "Portsea." Cab stopped. "I don't know if the old lady will mind," said Cabby, but M.P. did not ask if the old lady would mind, but got in and sat down opposite to old lady (very old fashioned lady she was, never been in a cab before she told me), did not at first enquire the meaning of M.P's entrance but earnestly enquired about windows being shut. Having satisfactorily arranged this I explained why I was there, because Cabby had said if she did not mind I might. "Well," says the old lady a little bit surprised, "I think he must have liked the look of your face."

Not knowing that the old lady was far enough advanced in theology to explain to her the doctrine of guardian angels, I remained quiet and remarked I wanted to get to the church. The good old soul then let me know she often wanted to go to the Catholic Church and she liked to pray to God, that we were all going different ways, but of course I told her there was only one way, one God, one Church, and the old lady herself repeated the word, "One Lord, one Faith, one Baptism." Cab put her down not far from the Church. I got Benediction and ran home in time for tea.[285]

As the New Year of 1877 began, the possibility of commencing in Nottingham received further affirmation. Notified by Potter of the offer of Mr. Young, and of her brother's information regarding Bishop Bagshawe, Father Selley made it his business to speak with the bishop's brother, Mr. John Bagshawe, who lived in London. John Bagshawe assured Selley that he felt his brother would welcome Miss Potter and at least give her a hearing. Now it was up to Potter. Against her mother's continued resistance to her leaving home, Potter had to either make a stand or keep on searching for someone to support her endeavours in the Southwark or Westminster dioceses. Potter made her decision. On January 12, 1877 she went with her sister-in-law to Brighton for a day's outing. When the time came to take the train back to Portsmouth, Potter, with a degree of agitation and hesitation, told Marguerite that she would not be returning to Portsmouth with her, that she had decided to go to Nottingham to see Bishop Bagshawe.[286] She took the train to London and spent the night with her brother Henry. The following morning, having received money for the fare from her brother, she left London for Nottingham. The journey to foundation begun.

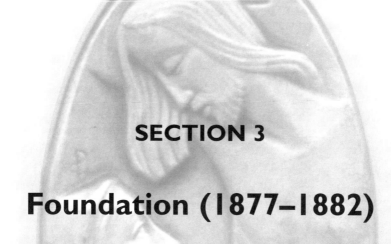

SECTION 3

Foundation (1877–1882)

Foundation (1877–1882)

When Mary Potter stepped off the train into the wintry evening of January 14, 1877, she walked into one of the largest undermanned dioceses within the English Catholic church. Ruled over by the ebullient, self-directed and stubborn bishop of Nottingham, Edward Gilpin Bagshawe,[1] the diocese of Nottingham consisted of the counties of Nottinghamshire, Derbyshire, Leicestershire, Lincolnshire, and Rutlandshire.[2] Each of these counties held its share of tragedy, vice and slum-dwellers. Each sheltered numbers of poor Irish immigrants and these Irish poor were a major source of concern for the bishop, who had taken his place among the hierarchy in 1874. A known social activist and Hibernian politophile, Bagshawe was the only one of the English hierarchy to share in Cardinal Manning's social and political consciousness, and his views sat uncomfortably in a diocese long used to a more benevolent and less politically oriented rule.[3]

Authoritarian and ultramontanist, Bagshawe's governance was vastly different from that of his much-admired predecessor, Richard Roskell.[4] A member of the Oratory, he had been trained by Father Faber, and brought with him a love for pomp, ceremony and all things Roman. His translation of the Italianate renaissance style of the Oratory into Nottingham cathedral[5] along with his attempts to alleviate a shortage of priests by sacrificing quality to quantity earned the censure of many.[6] Yet, for all his faults, Bagshawe was the "closest Episcopal approximation" the Catholic hierarchy had to the social reformers of Anglicanism,[7] and it was perhaps unfortunate that the results of many of his attempts to serve the needs of the poor led to disputes.

Impetuous and overbearing, his poor sense of judgement in his choice of clergy, and his aggressive desire to expand missionary endeavours alienated many, and resentment ultimately led to complaint to Rome about his manner and organisation.[8] The support he first offered to the young woman, who came to see him on the morning of January 15, 1877, did not add to his popularity. Tales had already been carried from Portsmouth and London, and Potter's reputation as an unstable religious "enthusiast," a self-professed "visionary" who showed "an utter want of humility and docility" had preceded her to the diocese.[9] Through a peculiar twist of fate however, the very fact that others had rejected Potter's vision appears to have acted as a positive factor in her dialogue with the bishop. He not only received the young woman, but also actively supported the evolution of the community. Yet, as this section will illustrate, Bagshawe's assistance in founding the congregation was to bring further problems, and conflict erupted between the bishop and the founder, as Potter sought to establish the community according to the specific vision she believed it was to follow.

While Bagshawe's personal eccentricity and authoritarianism were significant factors in the struggles of the new community, more general issues impacted upon the foundation. Religious orders of women were subject to male governance, and as Mary Magray has noted, a general management model had been established at the Council of Trent in 1563 and followed since that date.[10] The significant ruling was that all religious orders and congregations of women were subject to the authority of a male superior, though female religious orders associated with male groupings were traditionally governed by the male wing of the order. Thus, Franciscans governed their Poor Clare sisters, and male Dominicans ruled over their female counterparts. Over the nineteenth century, however, there was an increasing tendency towards episcopal control. Potter, in applying to Bagshawe for permission to commence her institute within the diocese of Nottingham, was placing herself and her community under the direct authority of the bishop. Having the power to accord a community the status of religious of diocesan right, he was directly responsible for it as superior, legislator, and arbitrator. His hegemony was complete. To him belonged the right of approval for women to be received into or dismissed from the congregation, of overseeing the financial status of the community, and of attending to "all weighty matters" put before him by the Mother Superior.[11] Whilst many bishops did not avail themselves of the opportunities for lordship over such communities of women, some, like Bagshawe, did. Following the First Vatican Council in 1870, there was an increasing tendency on the part of bishops throughout the Catholic world to exert greater controls over religious institutes of women.[12] It was a position of power open to abuse, and that such abuse did occur is testified to by the numbers of women's congregations who petitioned Rome for a change in canonical status – or for arbitration in the case of dispute.[13]

Yet the power vested in Bagshawe's role was critical for Mary Potter. If the congregation she believed she was called to found was to be established, it first needed to be accepted and legitimated. As this section indicates, such legitimisation came at a price. Bagshawe, lacking an infrastructure to support welfare services to his increasing flock of poor, grasped the opportunity to further the influence of Catholicity within his diocese. His vision of the relevance of this new religious order was coloured by the needs of his own diocese, and by the commonly held conviction that all religious orders were of essence the same. When he failed to share Potter's conviction that religious orders were to be distinguished by their particular spiritual orientations or charisms, conflict erupted. Potter, though committed to service of those in need, had a different priority. Her conviction regarding the necessity of forming the first members of the community into its spirit and spirituality fell upon deaf ears, and her relationship with the bishop became increasingly strained as she fought against the distortion of her vision.

Fundamental differences lay between Potter and Bagshawe, not the least of which were the perceptions each held regarding women. Bagshawe's paternalism, whilst accepted in part by Potter, was unacceptable in other ways. The "woman question" was an issue over the whole of the nineteenth century, and, as will be seen, Potter's use of the image of the Virgin Mary to determine and justify the role and the ministry of the members of her congregation was significant. Moving away from masculine theological constructs of the position and place of the Virgin Mary in the church – debate over which raged throughout the nineteenth century[14] – Potter's theology emerged from a creative interpretation of her own religious experience. For Potter, the Virgin was not "singular." She was the representation of the woman disciple. In the Virgin's maternity, humanity, union with Christ and commissioning at the Cross, Potter found an exemplification of the "woman's mission" she believed applicable to her congregation.

Deposed as Superior, forbidden to speak with her sisters, enduring physical and psychological abuse from within the community, Potter's suffering over the first five years of foundation was intense. Yet, her belief in her call to found an order which would "renew upon earth the life of Jesus and Mary" continued. Ultimately, obedience to the church – in the person of Bishop Bagshawe – could not prevail over obedience to God. The cumulative effect of the first five troublesome years of the foundation was to force Potter to walk beyond the confines of obedience to her local bishop and to seek papal approbation of the institute, in order to preserve its' charismatic originality.

Foundation

The first meeting between Bagshawe and Mary Potter, took place on the morning of January 15, 1877. It began in some confusion. Mary found the Bishop "rather cold at first," and he appeared to have some difficulty coming to grips with the purpose of Potter's visit.[15] He had received the impression from his London contacts, that the foundation Potter was proposing "must be directed by Marists," and that the yet unformed group "was a branch of the Bon Secours."[16] Potter soon clarified this misunderstanding, but the bishop had further difficulties with the proposal. Practical issues needed addressing if such a request was to be considered. The diocese had too few funds to make a major contribution to founding a convent simply on Potter's belief in her own calling. How would the community support itself? What would they do? What use would they be to the diocese? The practical implications were obvious.

Mary responded to the bishop's concern by informing him of the offer made to her by Mr. Young of Lincolnshire. There was, she told the bishop, a chance that a few could come first and establish a middle-class school in the diocese, using the buildings and support that Mr. Young was only too willing to offer. This information simply made Bagshawe laugh! He told Potter how little love Mr. Young had for his bishop, and suggested that whilst Mr. Young was generous in endowments, they were given at whim, and the old man was easily turned away from his impulses. The idea of a school did appeal however, as there were few such Catholic institutions within the Nottingham diocese.[17] The bishop's caution remained evident in the discussion, and not until Potter told him of the rejection she had already received from Bishop Danell and Cardinal Manning did the ice melt. His response to that information was indicative of the man. He dryly informed her that he, "Bishop Bagshawe could give [her] leave to found an Order (sic) subject to the Holy See, and if [he] wanted to, why shouldn't [he]?"[18] With that almost jocular remark, and the assertion of his own autonomy within the English church, his decision appeared made. In spite of the fact that priests from Portsmouth had already been in contact with the diocese about Potter's alleged vision of her order, the bishop did not dismiss her too lightly,[19] and was prepared to examine both the woman and her vision at greater length. He took the rules Potter had already established for the community, asked how many women would join the group, and planned another meeting.[20]

Buoyed by the positive reception, Potter immediately wrote to her friend Elizabeth Bryan and requested that anyone who was interested in joining the venture now write to the bishop, that he might know of the interest held in the proposal.[21] On January 22, there was yet another meeting with the bishop who was "very kind and interested."[22] He had come to think that such a group of women could well assist in the needs of the diocese, but not in Lincolnshire, where Mr. Young had offered support. If Potter were to commence her institute, it would be in a place where the needs of the diocese were not being met, and where Potter and her vision could be tested.[23] As she explained to Mrs. Bryan:

> The Bishop is very favourably disposed towards the work and we are now discussing the means of setting up in Nottingham [he] told me to devote this week to looking about, mentioned one particular suburb where a school is much needed. He said we might have 40 children if we opened a school…He has not finally consented to our commencing in his Diocese, but he has told me how he approves the work; he has yet to see into much. He has not yet seen the Cardinal or Bishop Danell. I think he intends to do so this week. In the meantime, I must let him know how many I have ready to join me, so I must ask you, dear Sister, to tell me formally if you wish to do so and when you would be able. I do not see any great hurry, only I must naturally have something definite.[24]

Bagshawe sent Potter to visit the district that he now felt would be an appropriate place for such a community to begin their work. The suburb in question was Hyson Green some two miles from Nottingham City. No rural retreat, it was part of the parish of Lenton, and had grown up around the expanding lace and stocking frame manufactories of Nottinghamshire. In 1877, it had its own lace factory, a bobbin and carriage works, and a brass foundry.[25] There were "hundreds of workmen's dwellings lining side streets and back streets" where miners from surrounding collieries lived alongside workers employed in the Nottingham manufactories and general labourers. The town boasted a main road with lots of shops; tiny cottages sharing communal yards as well as better type houses for the well to do, and those riding the boom of the lace trade in Nottingham.[26] Corporation housing for the working class completed the variety of accommodation, and held its own complement of poor, who were "composed principally of Irish and of the labouring classes."[27]

Though baptised, the majority of the Irish inhabitants of Hyson Green were (like their compatriots throughout England) non-practising members of the church.[28] They were also noted for being somewhat rumbustious in their behaviour, "… generally [taking] a little too much on Saturday afternoons, and [keeping] at it until Sunday night. The women are as addicted to the 'little too much' as the men, and often more so… the children want clothes etc., etc."[29] Bagshawe's desire was to reclaim these men and women to the faith of their fathers. That could not be achieved without working among them, and with the shortage of priests the diocese faced, other workers were necessary. In the absence of priests, a committed group of religious could do much. Like Cardinal Manning, Bagshawe was after missionaries for his "beloved poor," and if the model of the community Potter had presented to him did not have such an active focus as other groups of women religious, no matter, he had the power to change that.[30]

In Potter's discussions with Bagshawe, she had carefully enunciated the focus of the group she wanted to found. It was to be comprised of both contemplative and active sisters, united by a common spirituality. Impelled by its Calvary spirit, it was to be evangelically oriented in both its contemplative and active membership, with a mission to draw souls to greater union with God. Its particular ministry was that of prayer for and care of the dying. Hoping to be self-supporting, Potter had proposed that some members work for a wage, and that corporal works of mercy would be according the needs of a given area. Bagshawe, however, was less interested in the specific spiritual focus of the institute than he was in the potential held by a group of committed women under his direction. The diocese was in desperate need. The two communities of women in Nottingham (the Sisters of Mercy and the Sisters of Nazareth) were both tied to institutions and schools.[31] Hyson Green had no church, no school, no sisters and no priest. If such a settlement were made, it would provide a chapel for Mass, a community to chase up recalcitrant Catholics, physical care of the sick and elderly and a means of educating the young in the faith, thus reducing "leakage" from it.[32] It was all most promising. If the community were to be self-supporting, so much the better: It would cost the diocese nothing to establish and staff such a mission. A priest could be provided as chaplain to perform the sacraments, whilst the bulk of the missionary work could be carried out by the sisters.

Bagshawe continued to mull over the idea, and pressed Potter to look in Hyson Green for a place which might prove suitable to rent when and if he gave firm consent to the idea she had proposed to him.

Anxious to see the place the bishop was recommending as a possible place to commence, Potter walked the two or three miles to Hyson Green on a regular basis. In her search for accommodation she finally came to hear of a property to rent which, whilst not palatial, might prove an adequate point of assembly for the surrounding Catholics and provide accommodation for the community. The building in question was a disused stocking factory and adjoining house in Lenton Street, a narrow cobbled passage, "where humble folk dwelt."[33] Inspecting the building, Potter found "it was a tumbled down place … such as I have never seen before or since…everywhere bricks and broken pottery."[34] Two houses knocked into one, with a loft running the length of the building, the Lenton Street property left much to be desired, but it was among the poor, close to shops, and could provide a home, if members were forthcoming and the bishop continued his support.

The bishop made his decision. The community could start in his diocese, and on the January 26, 1877 Potter wrote to Elizabeth Bryan requesting that those who were interested in the community were to now write to the bishop and tell him of their availability. Father Selley responded with a letter to Bishop Bagshawe on behalf of the group. It contained the list of those who were interested and could come immediately notification was given of formal approval:

> To the Right Reverend The Lord Bishop of Nottingham
>
> This is to certify that I the undersigned do sincerely and from my heart desire to belong to "Mary's Own"; and that I am willing to annex myself to the sister-hood in Lincoln, as soon as the Bishop and my director do advise:
>
> 1. *Mary Potter –30 –Contemplative or Active: Accustomed to teach
> 2. *Jane Fuller –25 –Contemplative
> 3. *Madeleine Doyle–19–Contemplative: Accustomed to teach
> 4. Margaret Allen–17–Contemplative or Active
> 5. *Margaret Leery –19–Contemplative or Active
> 6. *Mary Bray–24 –Contemplative or Active
> 7. *Mrs. Elizabeth Bryan–43–Contemplative or Active
> 8. *Mary Eleanor Smith–18–Contemplative or Active. [35]

Further names of those who were interested, but who were not able to come immediately were included.[36] Potter's reaction upon receiving this was to send it back to Selley. It should have been most satisfactory, women willing to enter the community, and more waiting in the wings. Potter, however, was not happy. Two things about the document troubled her:

> Since writing, I have thought it well to send document back. Father Selley will, I hope, not mind, but I have two reasons for thinking it had better be altered. 1stly: The Bishop did not quite approve the title Mary's Own (it has somewhat a pretentious sound). Now, I never meant it to be applied to the Society alone. I meant it for all who walked in the Path of Mary. I used it instead of the word Mary's Slaves. We are Mary's own, but if we apply it to the society it has the appearance that one little Society alone are Mary's own, whereas all, whether in the world or in religion should have the name.
>
> 2ndly. I thought the principle laid down was that those who enter are to leave to their confessor to decide if they are fitted for an active or contemplative life. Of course no confessor would do otherwise than follow their own preference for active or contem-

plative life, that is to say unless he had great reason, therefore it seems better not to put they are indifferent, since if it is one of the rules, there is no occasion. It would in fact look as if there were no rule of the kind. [37]

If Potter was to prove the seriousness of her intent to Bagshawe, it was necessary that those who sought to join the enterprise be aware of what it was they were doing by presenting themselves as postulants to the order. Discernment was vital, "not a light matter" and there could be no "indifference" even regarding the choice of the active or contemplative life in anyone considering a vocation to religious life. Apart from anything else Potter believed that:

> [e]veryone has some particular work to do for God…He desires each one to minister to his glory in some particular way…[and guides] their spirit to some better end (perceived perhaps better by their directors than themselves).[38]

Failure to engage in such a process meant that candidates could come into a community for the wrong motives, seriously marring the tone or quality of the "religious life" of the group, or bringing themselves to unhappiness.[39] Potter's own experience of discernment had led her to believe that she was not called to the active life of a Sister of Mercy, but to a more contemplative life. It was a discernment which had proved true, as her experience within the Mercy community had shown, and it is reasonable to suppose that her experience influenced her view that careful individual discernment and wise direction were important considerations for anyone seeking their path in life. There was also a certain pragmatism behind the religious imperative. Attraction to becoming "sisters of mercy" appealed to women and gave them the freedom to walk the back streets of cities, move among the poor, act with professionalism and competency, and thus gain new independence of thought and action,[40] but the inner life of the community, the spiritual reality it contained, needed to be carefully explored if women were to remain content within it.

Circumscribed by the vows of poverty, chastity, and obedience, the life of women religious was often difficult, and notions of idealised living soon vanished under the regimes of superiors, the restrictions on activities and works. Pettiness and discontent, Potter believed, resulted from a lack of discernment, and those who entered any form of life without adequate discernment of its appropriateness for them, placed themselves at risk. "They will never know why they are not as happy as others," she wrote, "[or] why such difficulties rise round them…seeming to endanger their souls, and, in some cases, not merely seeming, but actually doing so."[41] If women were to come, they were to be free, "unbiased by self-will, self-love or selfish inclinations."[42] No other view was acceptable and indifference to the will of God was neither holy nor wholesome.[43] Unfortunately, the bishop did not hold such beliefs, as later events were to demonstrate, and much tension and turmoil resulted from his use of the community as a refuge and reformatory for some of his own women penitents.

Mary Potter, Sr Cecilia, Mother Philip and Bishop Bagshawe, circa 1903, Florence.

Mary Potter, circa 1890.

*Mother Philip, Mother Cecilia and
Mother Potter, circa 1890.*

On February 4, 1877 Bishop Bagshawe gave formal permission for Potter to commence her small community. It had taken precisely twenty-one days for him to make up his mind, and it was a decision made *inconsulto* – without consultation from his diocesan chapter. These clergy, felt they should have been consulted regarding the project, and did not receive the bishop's decision kindly, finding in such behaviour a representation of the new Catholic identity of the restored hierarchy, whose authority and authoritarianism alienated more liberal clergy used to a more flexible leadership.[44]

In spite of the complaints directed to him about Potter, Bagshawe held to his decision. As Potter had no funds, he offered to pay the annual rent and taxes on the building in Lenton Street, and in order to get the community established more quickly, offered financial help to restore the house to livable proportions. On the February 7, 1877, he leased the tumble-down property for one year, paying the princely sum of £33/12/-.[45] All that remained for Potter to do was to prepare the house for habitation and gather the community. Restoring order to the set of buildings at Hyson Green was a huge challenge for Potter. Her physical capacity for rough, hard work was severely limited by the severity of her heart condition. However, enthusiasm for the task provided its own energy and over the weeks following the bishop's acceptance of the house, she stayed in the disused building, and delighted in a new-found freedom:

> I wonder at the grace God gave to one who certainly over the years of childhood, was still a child – not allowed to go out alone ever at night, ever thought for and kept, as it was said, in a hot house. Here I was, wandering about alone, then sleeping in an old dilapidated place, in the midst of mortar and rubbish of all kinds, with doors that would not fasten, for I remember getting a pickaxe against it to secure it. When the Bishop after some time, came to hear of this he forbade and I had to go to the Tacey's, but when I found I was expected to sleep with one of the girls, I laid on the floor, which by that time I had got quite accustomed to… I, who had been so delicate and being supposed to need meat two or three times a day, often made my dinner on bread and pork dripping. [46]

The house repairs got underway. Determined that the local area be made aware of the new venture rising in their midst Potter nailed together two pieces of wood, painted them red, and erected them on top of the building.[47] Tradesmen were engaged to prepare the building for habitation, and Potter helped in the cleaning up. It was a time of preparation, and she made the best of it, visiting the sick poor and making friends with those in the surrounding district.[48] On March 16 Bagshawe told her to call the first members of the institute to the diocese, and named her as first superior of the group. In order that the establishment of the community be placed on a correct footing, he instructed her to write to those who desired to come advising them to make contact with his lordship, and warning them of the possibility of dismissal. Potter sought to avoid what she saw as "the terrible responsibility" of the superior:

> When our good Bishop told me that I was appointed Reverend Mother… I distinctly told him I could not do it…He was very pained. "My child," he said, "I am undertaking

this work upon your word" and the conversation which followed ended by my taking the reins of Superiority which I knew I was unfit for.[49]

Embarrassed by her appointment as "superior," and perhaps taken aback by his statement regarding dismissal, Potter wrote to the small group in London, who were on retreat at Spitalfields. Though reluctant to assume the position of superior, she would, she assured them, do all she could to support and care for them:

> You must forgive my interrupting, at least perhaps bringing a distraction into your Retreat. I would not wish to bring your thoughts away in the least from the close inter-course you are now holding with our dear Lord, but his Lordship has given me a command to write to you, who are proposing to join me shortly to work in this Diocese, to tell you that he wishes you to come as postulants who may be dismissed if not found suitable and that he has appointed (under obedience) as Superioress my unworthy self … It is with extreme repugnance I write this. Let me add that you will find that, by the grace of God continuing with me to the end, to my last hour I shall be devoted to you with a love our Lady has planted in my heart and that no mother could do more for those under her care.[50]

As an addendum to the letter, she wrote:

> Dear little one's of Mary's heart: do not think I write coldly because of the few lines. I am overwhelmed with business and besides, it was painful to me to write as in obedience to our Bishop and spiritual father, I had to. [51]

If neither Potter's embarrassment nor her protests of unworthiness for the task of superior had any effect on the bishop, he was equally adamant that the first members of the community not include "one of the ordinary servant girls, someone not quite lower class, unless refined too."[52] In light of the women Bagshawe would send to the community the request was odd, but it revealed the underlying class system that existed within and without religious life, as a legacy of its traditional monastic framework. As Margaret Susan Thompson points out: "Class distinctions must be appreciated as integral parts of the traditional structure of religious congregations, whose fundamental design had remained relatively unaltered for over 1000 years… Apostolic communities of women – that is those whose members left their convents to engage in teaching, nursing or other active works – were still something of an aberration."[53]

Inherent in distinction of class was the belief that the lower classes possessed none of the refinement, restraint, education, or gentility of manner expected of women religious. Such virtues were the prerogative of ladies, those more or less respectable members of the upper and middle-classes of society. Potter's congregation would never attract membership from the upper classes, and few of those who joined were from the wealthier middle-classes. From the outset, it was a congregation of lower middle- and working-class women, and that characteristic would be heightened by an increasing number of Irish postulants. By demanding no dowry, Potter offered women from all ranks of society a place within her congregation, and her insistence upon the basic equality of all members gave opportunity to those whose class or financial impecunity barred them from entry into other congregations except as lay sisters.[54] Her personal belief in the equality of all had emerged from her particular experiences of God, and whilst it reflected the rising democratic inclinations of the mid-nineteenth century, her fundamental perception was that intrinsic equality of every human being rested in their creation as *imagio dei*. Thus, it was inconceivable to Potter that distinctions of class would dictate either entry into religious life or service of humanity.

Potter was not alone in her hopes to achieve an egalitarian membership. Other English founders held the same vision. Alice Ingham (1830–1890), founder of the basically working-class congregation of the Franciscan Missionary Sisters of St. Joseph, shared a similar structure to Potter, in as much as the distinctions within the congregation were simple, based on stages of formation – postulant, novice, temporary and finally professed.[55] Elizabeth Prout (1820–1864), founder of the Sisters of the Cross and Passion in Manchester likewise shared the egalitarian view, and accepted (as did Potter), illiterate candidates.[56] As O'Brien suggests in relation to the Franciscan Missionaries of St. Joseph, the characteristics of life in an undivided congregation enabled "a wider and more self-determined expression" in relation to vocation.[57] Their betters did not shape their lives, nor were spiritual exercises distinctive.[58] Ingham, like Potter, viewed all members of the community equally, and all shared in the spiritual and material works of the congregation on an equal footing. If some were skilled in some areas more than others, so much the better for the works of the congregation. There was, however, a disadvantage suggested by O'Brien and experienced by Potter: that of the relationships between such institutions and the hierarchy.[59]

Realistically, class mattered in Victorian society, and it mattered for women in religious life in terms of their relationship with clergy. As Magray indicates, the early founders of Irish communities, such as Nano Nagle, Catherine McAuley, or leaders such as Mother Vincent Whitty or Theresa Ball, while cognisant of episcopal authority, were not afraid to confront it. Wealth brought its own privileges and gave women a voice, even if it did not prevent conflict or dissension. Bishops and clergy were as class bound as the society in which they lived, and there is little doubt that Potter's reception by Monsignor Virtue, or Cardinal Manning would have been significantly different had her class and connections been higher. Without rank or status, women of the lower orders were far less likely to confront authority. Humility, subservience, and obedience were not only expected of them by their "betters," whether male or female, but were also the more likely responses.[60]

However, as Magray succinctly points out, class does not determine character,[61] and for Potter the subservience of learned obedience would give way before the imperative of a stubborn belief in her call and a strong sense of an inner authority. Others of her community, less driven by the founding vision, were also less likely to confront ecclesial powers. As shall be seen, this resulted in a period of great turmoil. Later erosion of the strong visionary and missionary thrust of the institute must be related to the inability of those within the institute to withstand the dominance of episcopal control and the emergence of the ideal of the "good sister" as meek, subservient, and above all acquiescent.[62]

The Community Gathers

In response to the bishop's request, Elizabeth Bryan, a widow, who had held a "responsible position" in an upper-class establishment in London and Mary Bray, who worked as a domestic at the convent of the Carmelite Sisters in North End, Fulham, made their decision to join Potter in establishing the community. The foundation now appeared secure, and on March 17, 1877 Bryan and Mary Bray arrived in Nottingham.[63] The three women took up lodging with the Tacey family, and continued the work of supervising repairs, cleaning up the community house and extending visitation of the sick and poor in the local area. Potter rejoiced in the camaraderie, but the two other women found the work hard. A week later, on March 25, Potter reported the effects of exertion to Selley: Mary Bray had succumbed to a cold and Elizabeth Bryan to tiredness, both had taken to their beds to recover. The renovations, she was glad to report, were moving along at a good pace, at least in the chapel.[64]

Financial and material support for the proposed community was slow to appear. Elizabeth Bryan contributed some of her personal resources, as did Mary Potter. However, one gift to the community was of real significance to the group identity. A donation of a statue of the Virgin for the new convent was made, and Potter, wanting to provide a symbolic focus for the spirit of the community, accepted the gift. Receiving a note that the statue could be selected from the shop of an Italian artisan in the East End of London, she made the journey. Like much of what was happening to her, it proved to be an adventure, one that she recorded in detail:

> I went off to a part of London new to me. I was never allowed out at dark alone and I shrank into myself as I went through streets crowded with yelling people who seemed to be cutting up meat in the middle of the road by the light of flaring torches. At last I arrived at the little shop where an Italian man showed me the statue, which I did not like. Pointing to another I said, "Put a heart on that." "But," objected the man, "how can I put a heart on an Immaculate Conception?" I did not understand art, so settled the difficulty by letting him know that if he wanted to sell the statue, he must put the heart, and according to my directions my idea being that the Immaculate Heart of Mary has only the lily, but the Maternal Heart must have the sword of sorrow through it. I believe I helped to make that man's fortune for, after sending these statues all over the world, he has retired to his own country, Italy. The first statue arrived at its destination in time for the opening…[65]

Potter's determination to create an image reflecting the Maternal Heart of Mary rather than the abstract purity of the Immaculate Heart is interesting, given the contentious position the Virgin held within Victorian England.[66] Roman Catholic veneration of Mary had reached to new heights with the promulgation by Pius IX of *Ineffabilis Deus* – the decree that proclaimed that the Virgin Mary had been conceived without any stain of original sin.[67] It was a doctrine which served to give the Virgin an ascendant position within the

Catholic church, and spoke of "mariolatory" and even goddess-worship to non-Roman Catholics.[68] The decree brought with it ornate claims for the power and the glory of Mary which threw into relief not only the very real differences between Catholic and Protestant of all persuasions, but also the anxiety felt by Anglicans regarding their own identity.[69] For all the political and religious conflict and discussion generated by the use of images, visions and statements regarding the nature of "the Woman," and her power and privileges, a more fundamental discourse regarding the Virgin Mary was taking place amongst women of all religious persuasions.

From the middle of the nineteenth century, women drew upon the same images of the Virgin that men argued over, in order to construct, validate and affirm women's rights and roles within their culture. Women of such disparate religious persuasions as Anna Jameson (1794–1860), Frances Power Cobbe (1822–1904), and Margaret Fuller (1810–1850), contributed to the discussion by using their favourite image of the Virgin. Icons of the mother of Jesus presented a new vision. For Anna Jameson, such portrayals allowed women to find within them "some great elemental truths interwoven with our human nature, and to be evolved perhaps with our future destiny."[70] In her consideration of the heroic or mythic possibilities for women, Margaret Fuller likewise drew upon the image of the Virgin, and concluded that if a woman lived:

> first for God's sake, she will not make an imperfect man her god, and thus sink into idolatry…would she but assume her inheritance, Mary would not be the only virgin mother.[71]

In Fuller's vision, "the virgin mother is a pure, independent woman, whose maternal love and spiritual gifts, joined to a developed intellect, make her not only the perfected woman, but model and instrument of a perfected humanity."[72] It was a view shared by Anna Jameson whose liberal Anglican interest in the Virgin was informed by what she perceived as the "true" portrait of the woman of Nazareth, forwarded by Luke's gospel.[73] According to Jameson, the gospel portrait of the Virgin showed the blended virtues of humility, self-sacrifice, a capacity for decision and prudence; an "unusual promptitude and energy of disposition," intellectual power, maternal devotion, sublime fortitude and a contemplative spirit. The Virgin was the "most perfect moral type of the intellectual, tender, simple and heroic woman that ever was placed before us for our edification and example." Woman majestic, she was to be imitated. Woman of power, she was to be given deference.[74] As the Mother of Pity, a being of "divine compassion…" the Madonna was utterly worthy of emulation.[75] If portraits of the Virgin provided Jameson with a portrait of the ideal woman, they provided other women with opportunity to critique overtly masculine and judgmental elements within the religious ethos, and to propose a feminising principle.

Frances Power Cobbe, disciple of Jameson, and an extraordinary, complex figure in the constellation of leaders within the nineteenth-century women's movement, found in the image of the Virgin, a lesson for all men and women. Cobbe believed that it was time:

we gain something from woman of her Religious nature! And we want her Moral intuition also. We want her sense of the law of love to complete man's sense of the law of justice. We want her influence inspiring virtue by gentle prompting from within to complete man's external legislation of morality. And, then, we want women's practical service. We want her genius for detail, her tenderness for age and suffering, her comprehension of the wants of childhood to complete man's gigantic charities and nobly planned hospitals and orphanages. [76]

Less involved in activism than in developing a range of arguments for the liberation of women, Cobbe's fundamental stance on feminist issues was that women were not adjectives, dependent upon others for their existence, but rather nouns, persons in their own right.[77] Never questioning, but rather underscoring the maternal nature of women, Cobbe articulated the moral autonomy of women, their responsibility for their own conscience and their rights both within and without marriage.[78] In the icon of the Madonna, she found the personification of:

goodness, mildness, pity – in a word, Motherly Tenderness. She is the representative of all the feminine virtues and perfection, Purity, Simplicity, Humility; but above these and in pre-eminent degree, of Maternal love.[79]

In Cobbe's understanding, maternal love would benefit man's complex undertakings, by bringing to them female wisdom and tenderness. This was necessary because "the heart of humanity longs to rest itself on the Compassion of its Creator," and had had enough of the terrors of the Lord.[80] She believed her world was:

sick of such nightmare horrors and turns away with disgust from the religious systems in which they lie embedded. We crave one and all of us, for a God whom we can perfectly, spontaneously, absolutely adore. That God is he and he alone, who unites in one the Father's justice and the Mother's love.[81]

In the image of the Virgin, Cobbe believed the Catholic church was actually portraying that tenderness and compassion which were the feminine dimensions of a creator, whose mercy tempered justice and whose gentleness nurtured life.

Potter's view was similar to that expressed by Cobbe. She too saw God's attributes reflected in the Madonna. Within God lay justice, power, might *and* the gentleness of maternal care and tenderness. Woman, as reflected in the person of the mother of Jesus, imaged forth the Divinity in her physical and spiritual maternity. With the mother of Jesus, all women reflected God to the world, and were the instruments made use of by God to reveal both Mercy and Providence.[82] With Mary on Calvary, all women receive a divine commissioning to "behold your son,"[83] and in the acceptance of that maternal role towards church and world, "adumbrate the office of God…God who is our Mother."[84] "God's love is Mother-love," Potter argued and the "grand office of a mother is [an] exemplification of God himself." [85]

This use of society's dominant, potent and controlling maternal image of woman subverted and attacked the inequality of women in society, whilst adjuring abstract theological debate. For Potter, the mother of Jesus was a model of womanhood, which was liberating and empowering precisely because she was woman in relation to the Divine. Her "mind was strong" because it was "strengthened by the All Powerful."[86] In the Virgin Mother, the virtues of purity of mind and heart combined with a maternal wisdom that sprang from the willingness to suffer the "wounding of love" maternity brought with it. It was a view consistent with Potter's own religious experience and an expression of a devotional revolution that had been gaining momentum over the century. It was a revolution focused on the warmth of an affective and popular piety.[87]

Redolent with metaphor and images, this devotional change had its origins within the seventeenth and eighteenth centuries, and emphasised and insisted upon "the heart, the human will and the affections" as the crucial links between divinity and humanity.[88] It was a shift from the stern determination of objective truth based upon scripture or tradition and the dogmatism of the post-reformation churches. Dangerous in its capacity to enthuse its adherents, it sought to bridge the distance between personal experience and the power structures of sacramental systems, and it fed the spiritual hunger of those emerging from Enlightenment rationalism. It was a piety that found a particular home in the hearts of women, providing them with a way to assume leadership by the development of new expressions of spiritual realities.[89] In the context of nineteenth-century England, as Susan O'Brien points out, other women founders of religious orders facilitated this devotional revolution. Margaret Hallahan, Cornelia Connolly, and Fanny Taylor all promulgated affective devotions and became patrons and distributors of emotive imagery.[90] Other women also participated in the evolution of affective piety, as O'Brien illustrates, and the effect of their work in popularising Marian devotions and promoting devotion to female saints, was to valorise women and feminine attributes.[91] It was a process that showed a remarkable synchronicity with elements of the debates on the "Woman Question" that raged throughout the century.[92] These devotions, and their feminising components also pointed to another issue which was central to Potter's own understanding of the charism she was called to express within the church, which also centred on devotion to and emulation of the Maternal Heart of Mary.

The Maternal Heart of Mary and Spiritual Maternity

Following her experiences of 1872–1875, Mary Potter had become convinced that part of the task given to her by God was to encourage a new awareness of the maternal role of Mary within the church. The congregation, having its spirit and spirituality grounded in the Cross, was to reflect back to the church its own role in nurturing its members who constituted "the body of Christ." In Potter's eyes, Calvary marked a new commissioning of the mother of Jesus. In Jesus' words, "Woman, behold your Son," the Virgin was given a new motherhood – "mother of the church" – which had its corresponding relationship in Jesus' statement to John, "Son, behold your Mother."[93] The maternal heart of Mary, iconised at the foot of the Cross, and given a "universal motherhood," was a recognised tradition for both Anglican and Catholic in the nineteenth century.[94] But Potter manipulated this image, applying it to both women and the church.

For the women of the community, devotion to the Maternal Heart of Mary was to be more than a simple piety. The statue that Potter brought back to the community at the end of March 1877 gave representation to the mission Potter believed her community held. Maternal solicitude and compassion were the hallmarks of Jesus' love for humanity and were expressed most vividly in the discipleship of his mother. She, who was mother of Jesus, was made mother of the church, by divine commissioning, and that commission pointed not only to the maternal nature of the church, but also the role of women within it. Women, with Mary the mother of Jesus, shared the divine commissioning from the cross. Called to live their "religious nature" through an intimate union with God, women were to be prophets, speaking by their lives and works, the dangerous memory of the maternal leadership of the mother of Jesus.[95] Why? To raise the church to new consciousness of its role and function in the world and times it lived within. In Potter's thinking, a new pedagogy was called for; one in which Petrine authority was tempered by Marian solicitude. There was a need, she believed, for a church that was more "maternal in its long-suffering, its untiring patience."[96] Those who served the church as priests were to have "the heart of [a] mother" and be willing to "take the sheep to himself, to wash, purify and heal the wounds and feed with Jesus' body and blood."[97] They were to preach and practise holiness, they were to "go forth … the whole world [was their domain]… [they were to]…go forth teach all nations – the one grand object of their creation: to mirror God." [98]

For Potter nurture, not penalty, was the hallmark of a maternal church, and its task was to "lead others to God." [99] Far more than simple iconography, the image of the maternal heart of Mary called the community and the church to its mission, just as much as the red cross that surmounted the building shouted its commitment.

Beginning the Mission

With the completion of the rough chapel area on the second storey of the building, Bishop Bagshawe determined to open the mission – regardless of the fact that the building's living quarters were not yet completed. Canon Douglas of the Nottingham diocese contributed a chalice, ciborium and vestments, while the superior of the Sisters of Nazareth helped with the purchase of other necessary items.[100] On March 29 Potter wrote to Mary Eleanor Smith, telling of the preparations and of the support given by Protestant friends and supporters.[101] A non-Catholic lent an organ for the celebration; another volunteered to make the garden ready, yet another provided roses for the chapel.[102] The daughter of the local Anglican vicar came to help with the decorations for the opening, held on Easter Monday, April 2, 1877.

It was a splendid occasion in poor surrounds. Greenery framed the pictures of the Stations of the Cross, the new statue stood proudly in place, and the tiny chapel crowded with members of the local citizenry. Pomp and circumstance played their part with Bagshawe, assisted by Potter on the borrowed organ and members of the choir from St. Barnabas' Cathedral, [103] singing a *missa cantata*.[104] At Potter's request, the chapel and mission were dedicated to the Maternal Heart, and, following the celebration of Mass, Exposition of the Blessed Sacrament went on throughout the day, followed by Benediction in the late afternoon.[105] To Potter's surprise and joy, the bishop went home after Benediction, leaving the Blessed Sacrament enclosed in what served as a tabernacle – a walnut sewing box lined with white silk, which Potter had brought with her from home.[106] As there were no locks on any doors and no furniture throughout the rest of the building, the three women made a decision to "protect" the reserved sacrament by moving into the chapel to sleep. Beds were improvised, Potter sleeping on a straw sack on the floor, whilst the others made their beds on rough-hewn benches borrowed from the Cathedral for the opening. The mission and the sisterhood had begun.

News of the foundation spread through the diocese, and Bagshawe himself encouraged aspirants. Within a short time, another candidate for religious life, a Miss Mary Thompson, joined the little group. A woman noted by the community annalist as being "not too young and in many ways queer," she would remain for only two years.[107] A young priest, Father Burns, ordained the day before the opening of the chapel, was appointed to the mission as its chaplain. Inexperienced and untried, he was also delegated by the bishop as "superior" of the community. It was to prove a difficult appointment for the women under his charge.

Absent from the opening of the mission was Father Edward Selley. While Potter had been entering into her negotiations with the bishop, he had been working quietly in the background, assisting those who were thinking about joining the institute, giving them retreats and spiritual counsel. His interest in the formation of the community, and his desire to continue his participation began to antagonise Bagshawe.

Selley had hoped to participate in the community as its chaplain or spiritual guide. His own superiors however, had instructed him that he was to have nothing more to do with "that mad woman," Mary Potter.[108] It was an injunction that irritated the priest, and contributed to his growing antipathy towards the French, their customs and the very traditions of his Marist community.[109] Hoping to gain the support of Bagshawe, he wrote requesting that he be appointed chaplain for the community. Bagshawe, reluctant to share control of any group within his diocese and unwilling to embroil himself in a situation in which he was seen as "enticing, as it were, a religious from his Order into his own diocese" offered no encouragement.[110] Selley persisted in his requests, and the situation dragged on until the priest's superiors wrote to Bagshawe asking him to cease any dealings he was having with the priest. The bishop replied by taking the high moral ground, indicating that *he* had in fact refused all correspondence with Selley unless it was with the knowledge and consent of his Marist superiors.[111]

In an attempt to bring Selley's involvement with the community to closure, Bagshawe again wrote to him on April 4, 1877. He told Selley that as he (Bagshawe) was to be the legitimate superior of the community, wisdom suggested that the Marist's continued association with the group was no longer necessary.[112] It was a difficult situation, as Selley continued to support those who were interested in joining Potter's small band, and maintained correspondence with them. In May 1877, he gave a pre-entry retreat to Miss Mary Eleanor Smith, Potter's young friend from Portsmouth. On May 24, Smith left London and made the trip to Nottingham to commence her life as a member of Potter's new institute, now known as the Little Company of Mary.[113]

Eighteen years old, full of vitality, and completely unsure of what it was all about, Mary Eleanor Smith determined that she had a vocation to religious life. She set out from Euston with hopes high. Potter had written to her of the opening of the mission and of the need there was for others willing to join the works of the community. She included instructions on the dress that was expected of those who came to the community:

> I am sorry you were not here for the opening of the first sanctuary dedicated to our Lady's Maternal Heart in the world. His Lordship the Bishop of Nottingham came on April 1st, Easter Monday, said Mass and blessed the little chapel. We are full of work, and only Mother Elizabeth, M. Agnes [and] Sister Joseph to do everything. I am out a good deal among the people, looking up Catholics who have left the church, for many years etc. We want help, so come as soon as you can, but be sure you are here by the 24th, the Feast of Our Lady Help of Christians. Also, come dressed in black and wear a black bonnet.[114]

The last request was a problem. Mary Eleanor Smith was young and fashionable. The request that she dress in black, and more particularly wear a black bonnet, led to her first encounter with the expectation Potter had that religious life also meant obedience. Smith could not bring herself to purchase an "appropriate" hat:

> Here was the difficulty, nothing could be found but the Salvation Army Lassies (sic) poked bonnet. This I would not wear, and both my friend and Father Selley said to go in my own hat, which was black, but a bit fashionable I had however, to pay for my vanity and first act of disobedience in the spiritual life. Mother Angela [Potter] met me at the Nottingham station, she received me in her own sweet manner but at once said: "Why did you not come in a bonnet?" Of course I made some excuse about the difficulty of finding this ungainly article, but she had told me to come in a bonnet… We reached the convent in a country-sort of van – and after dinner Mother Angela took me down to see the Bishop. My fashionable hat was transformed into the ugliest poke bonnet, front and back was poke – with just one broad ribbon, on the crown, the strings of the same under my chin. Then an old lady's three cornered black shawl – …Mother Angela handed me a blue checked handkerchief and told me not to wear gloves, they were not religious. Eh! I shall never forget that first walk in Nottingham and having to appear before the Bishop in this guise.[115]

Smith's ability to see humour in the situation was to stand her in good stead as Potter took the young woman under her wing, and introduced her to the tasks of the community.

It was a rather rude awakening and Mary Smith was alternatively warmed and horrified by what she was expected to do:

> After a good night's rest, I arose, had Mass and Holy Communion, then later on in the day, Mother [Potter] whose zeal knew no bounds, took me round the village to make the acquaintance of a lot of poor sick people…[She] took with her food for the poorest and a big apron which she put on and began our first district nursing. I looked on in amazement; "Mother" was delicate, but her love for God's poor made her strong. First she washed a poor sick mother, gave her some nourishment, then washed the children and gave them their breakfast and sent them off to school, then there was the husband's dinner to prepare (generally these men were colliers). She swept the kitchen and left all ready on the stove for the poor man's dinner…I wondered how I would get on when she sent me off to do the same…these people were nearly all protestants, but through her loving kindness, many were converted and became splendid Catholics. [116]

If Potter succeeded in amazing the young Mary Eleanor Smith with her housekeeping skills, she shocked her with her complete lack of embarrassment in tending to the bodily needs of others, and nowhere more than in her complete lack of self-consciousness in improvising care for a young nursing mother. As Smith noted in her diary:

> We had just arrived in a very poor alley, when a woman met us (she was Irish, but had neglected her religion). "For God's sake, Sisters," she said, "do go to Mrs. N… she is suffering so much. She is a Protestant but I am sure she will be glad to see you." We went up one flight of stairs, where we found a young woman weeping, with a new-born infant crying. The woman and her poor room were spotlessly clean, but she said, at once, what her trouble was, how the baby was too weak to draw milk from her and would surely die from starvation. Neighbours had said, "Why not get a breast pump" but she said it cost too much and her husband was only a poor labouring man. I was only 18, and stood listening, but Mother went to work, first rubbing very gently the breasts and then to my astonishment, she bent down and sucked that poor woman's breast till the milk came. The baby was put at once to its fount of life and both mother and child were happy and contented. I looked at Mother in wonderment, but felt I could never do such an act.[117]

The intimacy of Potter's actions is revealing, and represents a major shift of consciousness. The child who had been ashamed of wearing a low cut gown on the day of her reception as a novice in the Sisters of Mercy had grown into a woman unafraid of breaking through conventional moralities to serve another. It was this liberty of spirit, this unconcern with other people's notions of respectable behaviour that she demanded of those who would be members of her own institute. Yet it was an attitude of mind and heart, which could only come about from strong convictions – and such convictions and liberty of spirit, she believed, were the result of a deep inner life of intimacy with God. The necessity of formation in such a life of prayer was to be a major source of difficulty as the infant congregation took shape.

Attempting to live out of her belief that perfect love cast out fear, Potter took on the more difficult, or challenging cases presented to the community. Conscious of her own limitations, and in particular her lack of nursing skills, she often resorted to prayer and pure ingenuity. Humour saved many situations. When forced to take the care of a rather large and violent woman suffering from *delirium tremens* (because other members of the sisterhood refused the task, due to the woman's violence and profanity), she doused her with holy water to prevent her swearing – an action which, according to Potter, "kept her from saying anything worse than that I was 'a lazy slut'."[118] To young Mary Smith, Potter seemed drawn to the least lovable and believed that "she loved especially those whom no one seemed to care for…she just saw God in all His creatures."[119] A warm and deep affection grew between Smith and Potter, which was to last over the latter's lifetime. Smith's loyalty and support were to prove important as the community staggered through its growing pains.

The works the four women undertook were varied and draining. Without funding or charitable donation, they were often dependent upon the charity of the poor they served. The Tacey family provided food in the form of eggs and other produce, and though the women lived poor, and worked hard, the five pioneers, Potter, Bryan, Smith, Thompson and Agnes Bray survived the first months of the foundation. Potter used their little spare time to try and give some pointers on the religious life, as the young Mary Smith, recalled:

> Mother took great pains to teach … the correct pronunciation of the Latin for the Office, and gave us many a lesson on religious decorum…Then she taught me to play the harmonium that it might be necessary in some Mission to play a Benediction Service. How many times I went over and over Webb's. [120]

Though not yet established as a religious community, they adopted a timetable of prayer that had been established for them by the bishop. As recorded by Smith, it too was a gruelling schedule:

> Every hour of the day had its appointed duty, commencing with morning prayers, meditation and Holy Mass. After breakfast, during which the Imitation and a life of a Saint was read, we went about our works, after the house was put in order, there were the sick of the village to visit and tend, the school and the mission work, hunting up bad Catholics etc.

> We returned to dinner at which there was Spiritual reading, then after the visit to the Blessed Sacrament, there was Recreation. Then followed the Particular Examen, Prayers for the Dying and Vespers and Compline and then work again … two or three evenings in the week we had Benediction of the Blessed Sacrament, but on other days, after Matins and Lauds, we made half an hour's meditation … on most evenings there were classes for the grown-up people, some to learn lessons, others to read, write etc., others to be instructed in preparation to reception into the church, and often our evening recreation was very short…From 9 p.m. there was strict silence.[121]

The school was a challenge. Elizabeth Bryan, given charge of the infants' class, failed miserably, though Mary Smith, "set about it boldly and fearlessly," with some success.[122] It was a hard schedule and "the duties of the day, with its multifarious occupations left little time for anything unnecessary."[123] When all was done, the members of the community retired to their "cells" freshly renovated rooms that had "three beds in each, with white curtains round each bed. The walls were painted blue, the floor was of stone, and there were three-legged washstands, with little tin basins."[124] Potter, however, slept in "a little dark room" under the stairs. In the privacy the closet offered she continued her life of intense prayer. There too, as the rest of the community slept, she continued her writing. The bishop encouraged her to write and to publish her books as a means of providing income for the community, and had promised his imprimatur.[125] There were two works in progress in the early months of 1877: a retreat in preparation for undertaking the De Montfortian way of life, entitled *The Spiritual Exercises of Mary*, and *The Attributes of God as Reflected in the person of Mary*. Selley was still working with Potter on manuscripts and maintained his contact with her through letters to Elizabeth Bryan, Mary Bray, and Mary Smith. The bishop soon ended that situation.

In early June 1877, Bagshawe received a further communication from Father Selley in London regarding suggestions for how the society could be governed and who should be its leader.[126] Although the bishop had written and suggested that his work with the group be now finished Selley could not let go. Bagshawe was not impressed with Selley's continued intrusion. On June 13 he wrote an abrupt note to the Marist, which effectively ended Selley's role with the institute, though it did not prevent his continued interest or friendship:[127]

> I hope that the clothing of the Sisters will take place soon. I am afraid that I cannot ask your Reverence to assist at it, as I have reason to believe that it would not be agreeable to your Superiors. You will I am sure help them with your prayers. Another Sister from London is coming to join them shortly. The house will then be full and I shall not be able to receive more just at present. If after a while you have anymore penitents whom you judge to have a vocation, and can conscientiously recommend to come to the little company, please let them apply to me, or do you apply to me for them as you like, in the first instance, and I will take the votes of the Community and let you know whether they can be received. For the reason given above viz., the wish of your superiors it will be best that your Reverence should not any longer write letters of direction and advice to the Sisters now at Nottingham, not even to Sister Mary. I observe that you speak of writing to them all and of their writing to you. You will remember I had already suggested to you the evil that could not fail to arise from anything like a divided direction, and a regular correspondence must necessarily involve this. You must not think me unkind therefore if I concur with your superiors in desiring that this should cease…I can well understand your anxiety for the Spiritual welfare of those whom you have trained with so much labour, but I am afraid there is no help for it. You must let them run alone, or rather entrust them to another's Keeping. [128]

If Selley had some doubts about the capacity of the group to "run alone," he could do nothing but leave them to Bagshawe's care. As Potter soon found out, the working relationship she had enjoyed with Selley was not possible with the new "father and director" of the institute. In June 1877, Edith Coleridge a large, robust woman with an iron will, a tendency towards jealousy and an irascible temper, joined the community.[129] Coleridge, one of Bagshawe's protégées, was born in London in 1847. Trained as a nurse at St. George's hospital in London, she had been received into the Catholic church by the then Father Bagshawe at the Brompton Oratory. With her arrival, the bishop decided that he had the numbers to enable a formal inauguration of the institute. The members of the sisterhood would be received as novices of the new congregation at a public ceremony of clothing in the religious habit.[130] Much debate centred on the name of the group. Father Selley had expressed his belief that the community should be called "Mary's Own," but the bishop rejected this, and Potter's recommendation that the infant congregation be called the Little Company of Mary was accepted.

That decision hastened another: what would the community wear as its formal religious garb? Mary Eleanor Smith, being the youngest of the group was called upon to model variously designed articles of clothing. A final decision was made in favour of a black dress with a leather cincture, and a pale blue veil. This became the community habit. The clothing day fixed for the Feast of the Precious Blood, July 2, 1877, preparations began. It was to be a simple and discreet ceremony. No fine wedding gowns were worn to nominate these women as "brides of Christ," nor did Potter permit the use of a pall to cover the sisters as a symbol of their "dying to the world." In most congregations of Catholic sisters, as Margaret Susan Thompson points out, this "shrouding" of either newly-received or newly-professed sisters was a significant issue. It marked not merely a dying to self and to the world, but incorporation into Christ.[131] Potter's decision to abjure the use of the pall reflected her theological stance. The commitment the members of her institute took was not to die to life or the world, but to become immersed within it. The world was the place where God was to be encountered, it was alive with God's presence, and was the "cloister" in which all men and women were called to live out their intrinsic holiness of life.

With Bagshawe's agreement to Potter's decisions regarding the ceremony the planning continued. As a preparation, Potter gave a retreat to the sisters according to a program developed by the newly-ordained priest, Father Burns.[132] The young man's enthusiasm appears to have outrun his common sense in the timetable he prepared for the small community. Each half-hour of the day was accounted for, including time for the sisters to recreate "in silence and separately."[133] Following the retreat, the preparations for the ceremony continued. Again the mission chapel was decorated and borrowed organ was installed. On Sunday July 2 at 4 p.m., the seats inside the little chapel were filled, and outside, curious crowds gathered for the momentous occasion:

> It took place in the afternoon; the Bishop performed the ceremony. He preached and then gave Benediction. We were not attired in fine white garments for that first clothing, but just as postulants, in black, with a white tulle veil on our heads. The little chapel was crowded but that was nothing to the curious crude crowd that was waiting down in the

street to see the transformation which had taken place in us. We received the blue veil from the first…Six sisters of Nazareth came to help us and settle us in our new habit. There were 6 of us, Mother, M. Elizabeth afterwards called Magdalen, M.Philip, M. Agnes, a Sister Joseph, who did not remain with us and myself, M. Cecilia…The little chapel was packed. A good harmonium had been lent us and the congregation did the singing. The altar looked a picture and we newly-clothed were so happy.[134]

To the chagrin of at least the youngest member, Cecilia Smith, the newly-clothed novices could not share the feast prepared for the occasion by Mother Philip:

We newly clothed had had a very hard week, previous to the ceremony. M. Agnes and myself especially, whilst M. Philip had taken great care to prepare some very nice things; custards and jellies etc. So that when all was over, we could sit down and have a nice meal. But alas, His Lordship invited some of his cathedral ladies, generally called his pets, and into our little refectory he invited them, and very soon those pets ate everything. I can see now in my mind's eye poor M. Philip's indignation, and in a quiet corner of the house, she told the Bishop all she thought. Then Himself and those ladies said goodbye, in letting them out, there were crowds in the street, curious to see how we looked in our new clothes. Meanwhile M. Philip made us a cup of tea, and then, being very tired we retired to our beds after a short night prayer. We were just in our first sleep, when dear Mother thinking we were hungry, appeared on the scene with a tray on which were five glasses of delicious egg flip.[135]

The happiness of the reception and inauguration of the community was not to last. Almost immediately tensions emerged as Potter sought to begin a process of formation for her sisters and the bishop began to interfere more and more in the shape and direction of the institute. It was a tension born of two very different concepts of religious life and the problematic nature of religious virtuosity in the church.

Conflicts and Contradictions

From the outset, Mary Potter believed she was to work to establish a religious community that had a distinctive shape and spiritual identity. She had shared her view of the institute with Bagshawe, and had assumed, gained his acceptance of her idea. Potter's unchanging view of the community was that it was not an agency of social welfare, nor a simple association of women banded together to live a good and holy life:

A number of kind hearted women, living together doing acts of charity with a very good will, anxious to please and ever willing to do something kind is indeed a good work, and such a sisterhood would deserve the esteem of men, but it would not be esteemed by God if it had been founded by him to be a religious order – that is, a body of people bound. A body of people who have given up their own will, their own way to live according to the will of another.[136]

As previously stated, Potter's theological view was that religious orders were born in the church by the action of the Holy Spirit. Archetypes or expressions of a particular element of Christ's life, the different orders modelled the appropriate attitudes and spiritual focus historical circumstance demanded of all Christians. If the wider church was to learn how to clothe itself more fully in the virtues of Christ, each order had to live according to its own particular spirit. The Little Company of Mary, with its call to emulate the maternal love of Jesus Crucified, had to form, and be formed by, its inner spiritual reality. Only with this accomplished could it become a "living memory of the hour of following Jesus."[137] It pursued the "way of Mary" who: "…on Calvary, came forward more prominently than at any other time in her life."[138] The effectiveness of the mission of the community did not depend on the works it did, but according to Potter's insight, on an experiential under-standing of the meaning of what she termed the "Calvary spirit":

> [those] who have been vowed and united to Jesus on the Cross will henceforth live in a constant union with him – a union of thought, desire and feeling. That is to say, his thoughts during those three hours, his desires, his feelings will be theirs for the remain-der of their lives…those who have received this grace cannot be too careful to corre-spond with it, and by daily more and more studying the interior dispositions of our Lord and his mother (though these two are really one), will, day by day, enter more fully into the spirit of their institute. [139]

To achieve such conformity to the spirit of the institute, a deep inner life of prayer was necessary. If the institute was to be true to its founding vision, the women who formed the infant community had to be enabled to live such a life. In order to achieve that, Potter believed formation in particular spiritual practices of prayer and asceticism was vital. It would provide the structure through which the spirituality of the institute would grow. It was not a side issue. "I intend True Devotion should form the spirit of our Little Society," she wrote to her brother Henry, "so that we might all have one spirit among us." It was non-negotiable, as "anyone who did not like this devotion, and would not adopt it should not remain."[140] Because Potter had found in the spirituality of De Montfort an "easy way" to such asceticism and inner union with God, she determined that the spirituality she found so beneficial, should become the spirituality of the infant community.

Believing that instruction in the spiritual path of De Montfort would lead to a common vision and a common commitment to the evangelising mission of the group, Potter began to press for a greater emphasis on the spiritual development of the sisters. If they were to "rise up in power and preach the wonders of the pity of the Sacred Heart," time had to be made for their formation in the things of the spirit.[141]

Unfortunately, this was not a view shared by the bishop, who, by virtue of his accept-ance of Potter into his diocese, now viewed himself as the superior and the father/director of the institute. Potter may well have been graced by God to be the "founder" of the insti-tute, but the fact that Bagshawe had permitted and facilitated its foundation now meant that he assumed control over it. Potter, like any other member of her community, was now under his authority as bishop, and bound by obedience to his demands.[142] In the days following the clothing of the sisters, there was a growing discord between the bishop as "superior" of the institute and Potter as its "founder." It was a situation that led to much pain and confusion for all concerned.

Necessary to any understanding of the conflict that was generated by Potter's initial founding vision and the control the bishop sought to exercise over the members of the new institute is the fact that however virtuous, enlightened or prophetic, Potter was a woman. This basic reality, when combined with the normative cultural values of Victorian England and the Roman Catholic church, placed her in a position of vulnerability to and dependency upon masculine authority. As a woman, she had no legitimating personal authority upon which to base her right to act outside of the roles assigned to her by the dominant culture.[143] Women's legitimisation came from the offices assigned to them as daughter, wife, or mother. To push back those barriers by independent thought or action was to create a threatening tension in the ordered world of the Victorians.[144]

In terms of religious "virtuosity," the same reality applied. Whilst women's roles were traditionally defined to include religion as the "women's sphere," religious virtuosity was as suspect as any other form of independence.[145] Potter's mystical experience had already brought her to disrepute, as had her claim to theological insight. If authorisation for, and implementation of, her visionary perception regarding religious life were to be legitimised, such legitimisation could only come through the male hegemony of the church. To act independently of such authority was to risk one or all of the charges of stupidity, heresy, or madness. However, the cost of such legitimisation also ran high. Without ecclesiastical authority in their own right, women religious were at the mercy of male authorities, who believed they had not only the right, but also the duty to "test" the virtue of women religious. As Catriona Clear notes, the petty tyrannies Bagshawe exerted over Mary Potter, in order to test her veracity as founder, not only illustrate the weak position women held within the ecclesiastical structure, but also the degree to which independent initiatives undertaken by women were suspect, and subject to clerical interference.[146]

Potter knew that acceptance of her institute as part of the charismatic nature and structure of the church, required a legitimating authority. She also knew that such authority rested in the hands of the hierarchy of the Roman Catholic church, its clerics, bishops, and ultimately the papacy. Monsignor Virtue, Bishop Danell and Cardinal Manning had already refused such legitimisation. Bagshawe, by his acceptance of Potter and her society into the diocese of Nottingham, and by the action of receiving novices, had begun just such a process. It was both fortunate and unfortunate for Potter. Whilst it brought her institution into a form of canonical status as a diocesan congregation, thus providing an umbrella under which it might take root and flourish, it offered no promise of continuance, and carried enormous risk.[147] The subjection of women's institutes of religious life to episcopal direction often damaged the integrity of their founding aims and objectives, as Clear has pointed out, and such damage usually related to the imposition of structures that did not support the fundamental orientation and vision of many of the foundations.[148]

Usually such damage related to the imposition of structures that did not support an institute's philanthropic motivation.[149] Potter's problem, however, was the direct opposite. Her institute would suffer from the imposition of a way of life destructive of its inner, contemplative dimension. Bagshawe, driven by his own concerns to provide welfare services to the poor of his diocese, would neither permit nor encourage the contemplative dimension of the institute, and imposed his own perception of the role of these women within his diocese. Potter quickly came to realise that legitimisation was dependent upon the degree to which the expectations and demands of the local ordinary were met. His concerns, she discovered, were those of his immediate diocese, and, like most other legitimising agents within the nineteenth century, Bagshawe worked from a basis of utility.[150]

As Michael Hill points out, the most common means of legitimisation of women's religious orders in the nineteenth century rested on the ability of any new institutes to demonstrate pragmatic and utilitarian characteristics.[151] An impulse of pious benevolence and a clear social purpose were of enormous importance to the nineteenth-century church, and women who could demonstrate their religious zeal and willingness to undertake the multifarious duties of social support were encouraged in their endeavours.[152] Active sisterhoods within the Catholic communion were lauded in the secular press, held as models for others to emulate, and praised for the works they carried out. The *London Review* of 1865 was fulsome in praise of the works of Catholic women religious. "Opposed as we are to their creed on doctrinal points, it would be unjust to withhold our meed of praise," it stated. The educative work of nuns was noted as a "perfect model of what institutions of the kind ought to be," their reformatories were models of their kind and their care of the sick "worthy of the highest praise… [for] their attention and kindness to those under their charge might serve as a model to many of our Protestant institutions of a similar character."[153] Leaven in the lump of the sprawling mass of a predominantly poor, urban church, new women's religious orders proved themselves by the services they provided. And serve they did. Religious communities of women initiated and maintained institutions, built and staffed schools, colleges, hospitals, asylums, and orphanages on an immense scale.[154] They were the "unpaid servants of the poor of Christ"; whose works "entailed no heavy staff expenses."[155] The simple truth of it all was that without such willing zeal on the part of women, it would have been both financially and physically impossible for the post-restoration Roman Catholic church to carry out its educational and pastoral policies.[156]

Bagshawe, faced with the pastoral needs of his own diocese, had readily accepted Potter and her congregation on the grounds of their social utility, and indeed capitalised on the zeal of the woman who had appeared on his doorstep six months previously. His evangelical love of the poor was well served by the conviction he appears to have shared with his former novice master, Faber, that "all religious methods were right and good which won souls lost in the spiritual destitution of the great English cities."[157] The spiritual destitution of the Irish immigrant and the endemic poverty in which they lived,[158] had prompted his acceptance of Potter's community, and the sisters' work amongst the poor had already shown the value such an institute could play in evangelisation and increasing commitment to the church.

Statistically, the parish of Hyson Green and its surrounds had seen an increase in the numbers attending Mass and the sacraments, children were receiving an education, the sick were being tended, and numbers of people converted.[159] It was all most satisfactory in terms of a numeric increase, and Bagshawe's support for the work of the sisterhood would not be withdrawn whilst that continued. However, what the bishop was not prepared to support was Potter's belief that the institute was not simply a philanthropic enterprise, but a religious order, whose significance to the church was not dependent upon the works it performed.[160] Writing to Elizabeth Bryan in 1876, she had shared her belief that the congregation would:

> [fulfil] the wish of the Church …[and] be a drawing together, uniting the contemplative and active, teaching etc. The one thing required by all would be their being Mary's Own, imbued with "True Devotion." This would be absolutely requisite.[161]

It was a view that Bagshawe did not share. Despite Potter's anxiety that the spiritual life, so central to her concept of the dual focus of the institute, was being crushed by activism, her continued requests for a greater depth of formation were denied. The bishop had provided a timetable and a structure, which made room for prayer, facilitated work and provided a half-hour's instruction in nursing each day. He believed the daily *orario* [prayers], would supply the spiritual needs of the sisters, and "special exercises may be allowed here and there to supersede [it]."[162] As superior of the house, Potter could "at the Weekly Chapter add any extra reading or instruction or correction … ask any advises [sic] or opinions, say any prayers etc, you like."[163] Any further formation was out of the question. The sisters could not be spared from the works, and besides, in the opinion of the bishop, the activities of the mission provided considerable opportunity for practising virtue.[164]

Lacking any understanding of the twin focus of the institute, Bagshawe merely laid it aside. Such denial Potter found hard to accept. It obviated the primacy of the spirituality of the institute, and denied the right of members to follow their own spiritual leadings. The contemplative members of the community were necessary to the vocation of the whole. They were to intercede before the Blessed Sacrament on behalf of the dying. Their ministry of prayer was complementary to the works of the active members. In a note penned prior to her leaving the diocese for Rome in 1882, she wrote:

> There is an omission in the present rule of an important part of the original idea, to which the Bishop agreed at the commencement, viz. that part of the sisters should be contemplative, that is to say they should not be required to leave the convent for active works. They would have the same spirit [as] Our Lady on Calvary and would watch in choir praying for the dying whilst other sisters are engaged in personally assisting them. They would also be employed in all the … work of the convent, thus saving the time

of the sisters engaged in nursing or mission-work. The contemplatives would be chosen when found more fitted either from spiritual reasons, or bodily. There are no lay sisters, we are all one. [165]

Bagshawe still could not accept the double focus of the institute. His major concern was the immediate need of his own diocese, and to all else he was blind. His view was not extraordinary, for as Tillard notes:

> Councils, popes and bishops have been led by circumstances to regard the great variety of congregations mainly – if not almost exclusively – as a providential source of apostolic manpower generously placed at the service of the Christian mission.[166]

Potter's understanding of religious life, however, was not focused on its pragmatic functionalism. In her view, religious orders were not primarily *useful*, or founded *in order to serve* local needs. According to her originating insight, religious orders were to reconstitute particular values of Jesus in the world. The community disclosure of a particular trait of Jesus (reflected in lifestyle, orientation, attitudes and actions), would challenge and revitalise the surrounding culture.[167] However, the ability of the community to express the totality of its charismatic nature depended on a rule, which guided and established the path of virtue, asceticism and moral conduct necessary to the particular experience it held.[168] Such a rule needed flexibility *and* focus. In her institute the individual life style of sisters was to be governed by the leading of the Holy Spirit, and the single imperative was to live according to the will of God.[169] Thus some would be drawn to a more contemplative expression of the self-giving love of Jesus, through pouring themselves out in prayers of intercession, while others would be called to express that same reality through their practical care of the world in which they lived. What was of utmost importance, however, was that each lived according to the grace given her,[170] and that would be determined by God's election, spiritual readiness, and personality.[171]

Considered against the sweep of history a variety of influences may be seen in Potter's perception of a blended community. Like the Brethren of the Common life, and the exponents of the *devotio moderna*,[172] her personal spirituality centred on the primacy of the inner life over the material. Reflecting the simplicity of an imitation of Christ, which cut across sterile intellectual debate on the nature of God or overwhelming and elitist understandings of the meaning of holiness,[173] her commitment was to lead people to their Christian vocation. This vocation she saw as an intimate union with God, which brought with it the gift of autonomy or liberty of spirit, and gave power for real apostolic effectiveness. Her vision of a religious community in which lifestyle (active or contemplative) was determined by God's election, stood apart from the legalities which surrounded and curtailed women's religious communities, and it was a threatening concept. As theologian Dorothee Soelle points out, the mystical tradition is based upon experience rather than authority, and women in particular found it empowering and liberating.[174] This, as

McLaughlin has also noted, was unacceptable for women within a patriarchal church, for even as it focused women's actions and directed their mission and service, it also embraced a fullness of possibility beyond social stereotyping.[175] Thus, mysticism and contemplation, while acceptable in principle within the traditions of the Catholic church, posed significant difficulties when embraced by its women members, and Potter continued to find difficulty gaining acceptance for her views on the meaning of the spiritual life and religious communities. More importantly, the suspicion which surrounded women's religious virtuosity, and the blended lifestyle of medieval communities,[176] had led to a series of regulations regarding women and religious life. These now became a stumbling block for Potter as she sought to gain acceptance of her rule and her particular understanding of the charismatic nature of religious life.[177]

Canon law and women's religious communities in the mind of the church

By the thirteenth century, in an ever-increasing pluralist society, the Catholic church was faced with countering a growing diversity of religious expression. In 1215 the Fourth Lateran Council sought to control what it saw as dangerous trends.[178] A rapid proliferation of new forms of religious life were "causing serious confusion in the church of God" and to abate the growing popularity of new forms of community life, Canon 13 of the Council legislated that no new Religious Orders could be established within the church.[179]

The decree meant that anyone desiring *to enter* the religious state had to assume one of the approved forms, and anyone desiring *to found* a new religious order was to accept an approved rule. Following this regulation, religious life was canonically defined by four major "signs": 1) the profession of the evangelical counsels of Poverty Chastity and Obedience; 2) perpetual and solemn vows; 3) in a legitimate, papally approved institute; 4) under a recognised rule.

In 1298, following the decree *Periculoso* of Boniface VIII (1294–1303) the "closing off" or "enclosure" (*clausura*) of women's religious orders became mandatory, and was a means of curtailing and controlling an explosion of women's religious virtuosity. In the words of Elizabeth Makowski, this document:

> transformed pious counsels to nuns – women bound by solemn profession of the three vows of poverty, chastity, and obedience, and living under an accepted monastic rule – into universal church law.[180]

It was a decree that persisted to entertain the interest of canonists, and with its re-enactment at the Council of Trent (1545–6), new and stern penalties were added to the prescriptions of *Periculoso*, which according to its later historians, became a watershed in the history of religious life.[181] Following the decree *Periculoso*, enclosure became the fifth sign of all canonically approved forms of religious life for women. Lay associations of "pious women" were acceptable, but lacked recognition as religious orders.

By the time of the Council of Trent, however, to counter a growing move away from solemn vows and enclosure the decree *Periculoso* was affirmed, and new restrictions applied. All women religious were enjoined to keep their rules faithfully: they were not to work outside their monasteries and they were to keep strict enclosure unless for lawful reasons and with the permission of the bishop.[182] In 1566, Pius V promulgated the decree *Circa pastoralis*. The document again sought to regulate the canonical definition of "nuns" (*moniales*). It affirmed that all groups of women who claimed to be "religious" were to preserve the decisions of *Periculoso* and the Council of Trent. All women who took solemn (public) vows were now subject to enclosure. In addition, no monastery could admit more numbers than could be supported by its own resources – effectively prohibiting mendicancy. It established the principle that no local bishop could give ecclesiastical approval to women religious ("nuns") doing charitable works.[183] Bishops could, however, approve groups of pious association, as long as they were not living in community, nor wearing distinctive garb. If such a group assumed either of these attributes of religious life, they were to assume all, including canonical enclosure.

The effect of *Circa Pastoralis* and its companion document *Decori* (1570),[184] removed women from all external apostolates, such as teaching, caring for the sick or looking after the poor. If a woman had a religious vocation, it was now, by definition, to the contemplative life, and a contemplative life removed from its natural extension of social action.

Fundamentally of course, all the discourse and legalism had little effect upon those women who believed in their own religious virtuosity. Law could not prevent on-going movements of spiritual renewal sweeping across Europe from the fourteenth to the sixteenth centuries. Stirred by the needs of their own period, and the desire to have a role in the ever-emergent church, women such as Catherine of Sienna (1347–1380), Angela Merici (1470–1540), and Mary Ward (1585–1645), proposed and initiated new expressions of religious life.[185] Nor could the law contain the religious ingenuity that, in the seventeenth century, saw the rise of the *filles séculières*.[186] Their successful forays into health, education, and other forms of social action led to a form of canonical approval of institutes of apostolic religious life.[187] In 1749 Benedict XIV's *Quamvis Iusto* set a precedent and gave canonical legitimacy to women who did not preserve perpetual cloister.[188] However, the cost of such legitimacy was that all new communities had to assume one of the four or five great "rules" of the monastic or mendicant Religious Orders "with adaptations" for women, and this was a process guaranteed to undercut charismatic originality.[189]

Furthermore, legitimisation according to the norms laid down by canon law, perpetuated the distinction between contemplation and action. What was forgotten in the application of the rules of Augustine, Francis or Ignatius, "with adaptation", was that these rules were themselves the product of a charismatic vision, and were linked to a specific form of spirituality. As Anson notes, this was not a consideration given to the application or adaptation of these rules.[190] The result was that the distinctive spirituality of the Ignatian, Augustinian,

Franciscan or Benedictine way of life – which the rule was supposed to nourish and protect – was either ignored or transmuted into a formal piety more easily accommodating of the social activity the group performed.[191] In what must surely stand as a triumph of the letter over the spirit of the law, all that was pertinent to the hierarchical church, was that the new religious communities had an already recognised and approved rule. It was a determination that had the effect of forcing modification of the original vision of new congregations, or distorting their charism, in order to conform to Roman ideals of religious life, and thus gain papal approval.[192] In real terms, whilst Rome may have approved the rules and constitutions, it merely tolerated the new congregations that held them.[193]

By 1800, the European explosion of active women's congregations was well begun. By the last quarter of the nineteenth century, aided by a growing evangelicalism within the Catholic church and the continued redefinition of the roles of middle-class women within society, active apostolic life for women was the norm, rather than the exception.[194] They were, however, still not "true nuns." The legislation of the past centuries remained in place, as did the belief that no new Religious Orders could come to existence within the church. More importantly for Potter, the most devastating effect of the legislation was the acceptance by the church that the charisms of new founders were ignored, for the church had given a final and complete legal definition to religious life for women.[195]

Potter's vision of the religious orders as being charismatic expressions of grace for the wider community did not fit the definition of the church. Nor did it fit the understanding of her bishop. If his concept of this new group of religious women was based upon notions of utility, hers remained linked to a blended structure, in which the spiritual life dominated and focused the energies of the group. Neither "religious in the sense which the world generally understands the term, [n]or in the secondary sense of the word," not "a very perfect form of monastic or conventual life,"[196] it was a life that sought to unite the deeply meditative love of a Mary with the active charity of a Martha.[197]

Bound by rituals of community, a shared spirituality, a deep spirit of asceticism, and a common commitment to the mystical life, the community needed no enclosure. Whether contemplative or active in lifestyle, the task of all members was to enter into "a constant union with Jesus on the Cross – a union of thought desire and feeling."[198] Whether given over to a life of prayer or a life of service, the women of the institute were called to offer their lives in union with Jesus who "went about everywhere doing good,"[199] so that "the Holy Spirit might speak and live in the hearts of those whose nature he had assumed, and to whom he made himself a brother."[200]

Potter's understanding of the reciprocal dependence between contemplation and action for the mission of the congregation was lost on Bagshawe. Nor did he understand her vision of alternative structures for women within the same institute. However, there were those among the community whose expectations of religious life did not include a serious commitment to living "in imitation of the Incarnate One,"[201] or to a conventual life such as Potter presented. For these women, her ideal of religious life was both harsh and unreasonable. Complaints flowed to the bishop from Sister Joseph Thompson and Sister Elizabeth Bryan. Whilst possessed of an undoubted commitment to caring for the physical needs of the people of God, neither shared Potter's wider vision of the nature of the community. Nor were they invested in its underlying spirituality, yet this was of primary concern if the foundation was to remain true to its original inspiration. The bishop, focused on the needs of his diocese, saw the disturbance between founder and members as disruptive to the works he intended it to do. Two weeks after the formal clothing of the women as novices in the Little Company of Mary, he deposed Potter as superior, placing Elizabeth Bryan in that office. Potter recalled the event:

> A series of statements by the sisters (I think principally influenced by one or two) had the effect; and one day Canon Douglass arrived and the Sisters were summoned. One, M. Agnes, told me after that she thought it was a Chapter of Faults and was preparing. But, however, the poor Canon gave a Conference of sins of the tongue, sins against charity and then said the Bishop had put me out of office and Sr. Elizabeth was to take my place. I was certainly surprised that the Bishop had not said a word to myself, but had sent down so suddenly, but I was still more surprised when the Bishop, the next time I saw him, with a kind of apology said "I stood by you as long as I could"…I suppose not being much used to women's natures was the reason I had not noticed any disaffection. To all appearances, the Sisters were very contented – religious, obedient and polite in their manner … I was edified by them.[202]

Competent and efficient, Sister Elizabeth Bryan now coolly assumed leadership, neither protesting the appointment nor seeking to avert the next blow to be delivered to her friend and the founder of the institute. Not content with deposing her from office, Bagshawe, in what appears as an extraordinarily petty move, sent a message to Potter advising her that she was forbidden to speak with any of the sisters. She was to spend her time writing and saying her prayers.[203] This was a crushing blow and one that outraged and angered the two youngest members the community, Sister Cecilia (Mary Eleanor Smith) and Sister Philip (Edith Coleridge). Smith reported being so discouraged by the situation that she wanted to return home, whilst Sister Philip, a woman of passionate intensity and equal instability, found it so unjust and cruel, that she stormed the two miles into the cathedral and confronted the bishop with his actions. Bagshawe's only response to Sister Philip's anger about "dear Mother's" treatment was to inform her that he would "crush her" as well as Sister Mary (Potter) – a threat the woman threw off with defiance and derision.[204]

It is not to be supposed that the action taken by Bagshawe was entirely personal, or directed solely at Potter. According to members of the diocese, the bishop was "a law unto himself," a man of "strange eccentricities." [205] His hasty and haughty manner led him to act without counsel or consideration of others,[206] and his "peculiar trait" was "to follow his own view at all times."[207] Once set on a path, he could not be dissuaded from it, and in spite of continued representations by members of the community, Potter's leadership was not restored, and Bagshawe continued to run the institute according to his own lights.

For her part, Potter tolerated no criticism of either the bishop or Sister Elizabeth, exhorting the deeply pained Sister Cecilia to use the event to practice obedience.[208] The bishop was the superior of the institute and whilst she may have wished it otherwise, Potter abided by his decision though she found it painful:

> I used to wonder why God permitted this…When I found that the Bishop's views did not agree with strict monastic discipline, though I had never thought that he was to be the founder, still I was very pained. It seemed as though there was no one to lean upon, for I did not think God's grace would come except through the appointed channels – the confessor appointed by the Bishop … even though I doubted his wisdom as Superior of a convent.[209]

Potter's pain and confusion did not prevent her from pressing upon the bishop the need for some form of spiritual development for the Sisters, or for her right to communicate to them her understanding of the orientation of the institute. Finally, after repeated requests, he gave Potter the title of "Novice Mistress," and consented to her holding a regular "formal interview" with her charges. During this time of interview she could teach methods of prayer, introduce her charges to the spirituality of De Montfort and the idea of the institute, but not hold any converse with them regarding the development of their inner life or their religious behaviour. These tasks first belonged to Father Burns, whom the bishop had delegated to act as superior and spiritual director in his place, and secondly to Sister Elizabeth, as superior of the house.[210] Again, Potter sought to make the bishop aware that a novice mistress had certain rights and responsibilities towards her charges and that without adequate guidance, difficulties could occur.[211] It was pointless. He refused to acknowledge Potter's right or insight to guide the congregation along the lines of its unique spirit. Yet, she – and she alone among the community – had experienced religious life, and she alone held the insight into what the institute was about, and what it proposed. She alone of the companions had experienced both the joys and the pitfalls of the spirituality she had assumed. Reason could have suggested that the formation of the members in the specific spirit and spirituality of an institute was better left to one who had travelled the road. No such grace enlightened the bishop, and Potter's continued request to lead the sisters into what she believed was the spiritual heritage of the institute was, in his opinion, a horrifying display of female arrogance. That he thought Potter lacked a truly spiritual and subservient humility, he made clear in his letter of March 23, 1878. "My dear Child" the letter began, and continued:

> I think you told me before that you thought it better that you should be allowed to advise and direct the Sisters in their individual difficulties, trials, failings, etc, and I replied that I did not wish this work to be done by you. You again press it upon me, and I again reply that I do not wish you to do it, adding that I do not think you in anyway fit or competent for the office. Any advice or direction not given by the confessor or me will be given by the Reverend Mother. The "Formal Interview" was not one for spiritual direction, but only that the Sisters might be taught methods of prayer and the

nature of "De Montfort's True Devotion". Lectures in ascetical teaching, like those in any other department of theology are generally given in formal interviews. Teaching a science in one thing, and applying it to individual cases is a very different one. The first I wish to be done by you, the second by the Rev. Mother. The necessity of "denying ourselves" can be perfectly taught (as it was by our Lord, as it is in the pulpit) without any enquiry into the way in which individuals practise it. Since you feel that you cannot do the one without doing the other it will be better to do neither, and leave them to be done otherwise. Perhaps you will teach most usefully by showing us all how perfectly you can mortify your own views, feelings, and wishes in this as well as in other matters. Really when you tell me that you "wonder at me" for taking the Spiritual direction from you, and that it "was not right to do so" I cannot but feel very much shocked at the difference between your principles and your practice. The Saints have felt their unfitness to guide others, and have refused offices of the kind till they were forced on them. I wish Grignon de Montfort's devotion to be understood and practised. It does not seem to me to be so very hard to understand. I shall take care to have his life and works read and studied by the Sisters. As for practice, especially the foundation practice of self-denial, we all of us fall short in that – but I think you are mistaken if you think your sisters do not try to practise as well as you. They have their faults, as yet very much subdued, but I know none among them, who has so much that still needs subduing and mortifying as yourself. To take the last and lowest place in all things till you are bid to "go up higher." Our Blessed Lord's teaching and the practice of the Saints. I cannot see that it is yours, and when I see you teaching the world spirituality, and at the same time manifesting in your conduct so great a lack of humility, I sometimes tremble, and wonder whether I am wise in letting your books come out as I do. I hope you will take what I say to heart.[212]

Aiding the bishop's interference were the tales carried to him by women penitents he had placed as postulants in the community. The effect of his encouragement to the sisters to "speak freely" about the daily round of convent life and other members of the community was to create disharmony.[213] The situation rapidly deteriorated when, early in May 1878, the bishop sent more of his own penitents as postulants to the order.[214] One in particular was to contribute much to the tension between the bishop and the founder. As Sister Cecilia remembered her, the bishop's candidate, Mrs. White:

> [was] a widow, who came to us early in 1878 – The Bishop clothed her after a week or so and made her at once the Bursar…she was an extremely aggravating person, about 50. Most repulsive in every way, she had eyes like a ferret, added to these a little celestial nose, high cheek bones and a very high colour, I can never forget her meanness and severity. She was in so many ways thoroughly unlovable and unmotherly for some couple of years we had to bear with her.[215]

It is hardly a flattering portrait, but it reflected much of the reaction to Mrs. White, who following her hasty entrance into the novitiate was given the name Sister Francis. Grist to the mill of those who sought to prove Bagshawe's incompetence, Potter's madness, and unsuitability as a founder, Mrs. White was the stuff from which scandal bred. According to documents sent to Rome complaining of the bishop's government, White had followed

Bagshawe from London, where it was alleged "she was the concubine of a man who at his death left her a considerable sum of money," some of which she had offered to the bishop.[216] According to the complainants, the woman was troublesome, the cause of much disedification in Nottingham, due to her drinking habits.[217] She was encouraged by Bagshawe to go and live at Mansfield, a town some seventeen miles from Nottingham and the cathedral. Further problems occurred which gave even greater scandal. There, White brought a house in which the bishop opened a chapel for public use.[218] He first placed a resident Irish priest in the district to act as its mission rector, but "his drunken habits made it necessary to send him back to Ireland."[219] Bagshawe then arranged for a priest from the cathedral to go to White's house in Mansfield each Sunday, so that the local community could have their Mass. It was a disaster and things came to a head when she refused to allow the priest admission. According to the reports of the incident:

> all this time, however, the woman White was giving dreadful scandal in Mansfield by her notorious drunkenness. She would frequent common taverns and dance and drink there till a very late hour of the night. Indeed, she was on one Sunday morning still so drunk that when the priest arrived from Nottingham to say Mass, she refused him permission to do so. [220]

The bishop then arranged for Mrs. White to go to the Praemonstratensian Nuns at Spalding, (which was, according to the priest authors of the document, "a very Protestant town"), in order to make a retreat "in hope of her reformation."[221] White "repaid their kindness by going out into the town and returning to the convent mad with drink."[222] In response to the attempts of the Sisters to quieten her, White:

> threw open the window over the street, and collecting a great crowd by her cries, shouted out to the people that she was being kept a prisoner in the convent by force and against her will…then the sisters had no option but to open the convent door, and allow her to leave. [223]

This behaviour and other of White's actions, bear remarkable similarity to the urban myths regarding convents and nuns which devolved from the anti-Catholic crusades that ebbed and flowed throughout the whole of the nineteenth century.[224] Whatever the truth of the information supplied to the Holy See, however, the fact was that Mrs. White *was* a problem – to herself, the bishop, and the community. She was not alone. Other women who entered the community created division and dissension. Some like Mrs. White, brought scandal: a Miss Pritchard, noted as being "very clever and boasted of having been in fourteen convents," also had a problem with alcohol. She left the house without permission one evening and was returned to the community the following morning, lying on a plank and accompanied by a roistering crowd from the local tavern.[225] Others sent by the bishop to far distant mission chapels or to nursing cases found their lives shaped differently because of their encounters and simply left. Still others found the discipline and the work too hard. They also left. Mary Fulker, Potter's friend and supporter, entered the community late in 1878, and did not stay. Her volatile temperament was totally unsuited to life in community. Sister Philip Coleridge, quite literally broke down under the weight of her own ungovernable rages, during which she physically assaulted Potter[226] but struggled on with the life, never really sure that she wanted to be there.[227]

The blunt reality was that conventual life was a microcosm of the wider world of Victorian women of the middle and lower classes. Convents attracted the "waifs and the strays" among Victorian women, even as they attracted women who had an ambition to be united more closely with God within religious life.[228] The problems, hopes, dreams, agonies and ecstasies of the women who inhabited the broken down building in Lenton Street, Hyson Green, were real. And just as real was the loneliness, isolation, and lack of opportunity that drew women to search for a lifestyle that could give importance, worth and meaning to their womanhood. Like their sisters in the world, they suffered the same tensions and weaknesses. Their addictions, whether to alcohol or opiates, mirrored those of the wider community,[229] but they were the women who, in all their frailty and with all their eccentricity, Potter hoped to meld into a community. These were those who, she believed, would make a difference in the world as they grew into their own wholeness and holiness.

To achieve this, they needed a stable way of life, opportunity to learn, reflect, and practise the art of prayer and asceticism. With the bishop's restrictions in place, however, Potter had no real answer as to how this could be accomplished, and no support was forthcoming from Mother Elizabeth who, using her role as superior, continued to block Potter's attempts to form the community in the spirituality she believed appropriate for it. In pain and confusion at what was happening to the institute and the people within it, Potter wrote to Bryan:

Mother dear, I do appeal to you. Do you love [True] Devotion? What do you think about the work you are directing? Will you help me, or rather will you let me help you? You know well how I wanted when you were first made our Mother, to do all I can to assist you. I was repelled in that, whether by you or the Bishop I know not. I had hoped you would have been anxious to have carried out certain things, I do not say my views, but what I believe are God's views regarding this work …I do not say it is your natural disposition to like commanding, but it may be that with the possession of power comes a dislike to interference in the exercise of that power, and say, dear Mother that this rule, I do not say despotic – that it is not – but this taking a stand apart, acting alone without consulting the sisters' feelings, my own included I think in acting thus, you have not acted well or wisely…I have glossed over openly before the sisters what I could not gloss over to myself, certain things you know we disagree upon, such as the rule, strict obedience etc. which it is certainly not my place to speak to you about, but as regards the form of government I certainly think that if you would consider we are a Community, you the directing member of that Community, you would see that they might naturally expect to be taken a little more into counsel, to be told anything concerning the good of the Community; council to be held; opinions given; decisions

referred to the Bishop; a government similar to the church itself…From the commencement you know, I began that plan of meeting and taking counsel together.

I shall keep to the Bishop's wishes, but it is with a very grieved heart and with as
strong a conviction there is something wrongs, as I am convinced I am right in obey-
ing. Will you speak openly to me? Will you tell me a little more of your thoughts about
our work? You can never love the Sisters as I have and do. No one knows how I have
suffered for them though I do not wish to speak of that. I have prayed, suffered,
laboured for them, before there was any chance of a home for them. Now we have that
home they are in one sense more estranged from me than strangers who can speak and
confide. [230]

Pained, puzzled, yet determined to make the best of it, Potter used her isolation from
the group to prepare the formal interviews, and these resulted in a series of lectures on the
spirit of the institute.[231] These were not appreciated by some of the aspirants. Reacting
against the discipline Potter sought to inculcate in the community by words and example,
they were "continually going down to the bishop with tales against [Potter], calling her
silly and a fool etc." [232] The bishop's attitude to Potter hardened. It was an uncomfortable
and difficult time, made more difficult by Sister Francis (White) who had been given the
job of bursar for the community. Her pettiness knew no bounds, and she appeared to
delight in refusing supplies to the sisters, or removing from them what they had. Towards
Mary Potter, she seemed to bear a particular grudge; turning the gas off and removing tow-
els and other things from her room so that she could neither work at night, nor apply bel-
ladonna plasters to a painful breast tumour. [233] Her presence brought more dissension to
the community, as she also made it her business to act as informant to the bishop and was
not above "embroidering the lily" in her tales of community happenings.

By July 1878, the works of community were manifold. The day school was successful,
and the tasks of nursing the sick, visiting the poor and providing help to families in need
were taking up much time. In spite of the pressure of works already undertaken, the
bishop now decided that, though they had only one trained nurse and no practical midwives within the community, the sisters could also involve themselves in maternity work.
Sister Philip's expertise was called on so that members of the institute could continue to
learn practical nursing skills and a Doctor Hatherley was engaged to provide a rudimen-
tary knowledge of medical matters.[234] Without resources, the community struggled along,
and when the financial support of the sisters became a difficulty, various members of the
community were instructed by the bishop to go begging in the surrounding towns and villages. It was often a fruitless, demeaning undertaking, but if the community was to survive or expand, it had to be self-supporting, and Potter's congregation lacked patrons.[235]

As the year progressed, so did the crises within the little community. Funds were des-
perately needed and the conflict with the bishop showed no signs of diminishment. Potter
and Sister Cecilia, in spite of being ill, were sent on an expedition to London to raise funds
and garner any support that might be available. The two sisters were absent from the community for almost four weeks, and from reports of the journey, the returns were small.

Father Selley, once made aware of the problems, volunteered to assist by taking up a subscription among his penitents: "say[ing] they do nothing for him so they can do it for us instead of him."[236] Relatives and friends sometimes gave what they could afford but, as the report for three days' begging in August suggests, the gains were minimal: "Saturday, called three places, 8/–…Monday my cousins and two others, 18/6, Tuesday, Greenwich, Mr. Knill out, another lady 1/6, Mrs. O'Neill 5/–." The grand total for the weeks away from the house added to £17/6/9, from which "we shall have to deduct expenses, then again … our board at the convent."[237]

Begging was part of the lives of many of the religious communities, and there were rules and regulations which governed how, and who one could approach. Potter spent much time on the journey, writing to various bishops seeking their permission to beg within the diocese. Some were welcoming, others were not, and still others could not afford to let another congregation "poach" the ground already needed by one of their own. The bishop of the diocese of Plymouth, the Rev. William Vaughan, failed to reply to a request to solicit funds, while Bishop Francis Kerril Amherst, of the diocese of Northampton, responded with kindness but refused permission on the grounds that: "he was obliged to reserve his diocese [as] a hunting ground for the Sisters of … [name indecipherable]."[238]

Not all congregations of women religious were forced to beg for sustenance and support for their charitable works. Where communities provided services to the local Catholic community, which could bring in an income, the need was much minimised. Institutes, which could provide quality education to middle-class students, could charge for the privilege, but for other groups, working among the poor, subscriptions or pledges were vitally important if the work was to survive. The convent of Our Lady of Pity, a work of the Poor Servants of the Mother of God, sought "money, food, wine, old sheets, blankets and clothing" for their ministry to the destitute.[239] For the Sisters of Charity of St. Vincent de Paul, the situation in 1878 was difficult, and they were "compelled to entreat the continuance and increase of the charitable assistance" so necessary to the carrying out of works of mercy. As their advertisement stated, "A heavy debt still weighs upon the house: the support of the sisters, and of many of the poor children under their care, depends on casual subscriptions and donations."[240] Still other groups required funding by alms collected by the sisters themselves. This was the situation of the Little Sisters of the Poor.[241] Their attempts to beg for funds in Bristol in 1863 brought accusations of "papal aggression" from the Protestant crusade, and the hope that few Englishwomen undertook such work.[242] Responses to such endeavours were never great, though within the larger cities such as London, there were networks of wealth and patronage, which offered some support to varieties of charitable works and groups of sisterhoods.[243]

Potter desired to fund her Little Company through works performed by the sisters. This, she believed, was essential to its practice of poverty. It was, however, an ideal constantly thwarted by the demands of the mission and by Bagshawe's refusal to enable the contemplative members to be established. The need to be self-funding eventually led to a further distortion of the original vision, as the community sought and failed to balance paid care with assistance to the poor. In 1878, however, the hope was still alive:

> Regarding our present means of subsistence, we have unsuccessfully tried to earn our own living, our numerous works for the poor keeping us employed day and night, but we hope in time to be self-supporting, aided by charitable people who give to us regardless of religious principles, annual subscriptions and donations as to any other charitable institution. We at present avoid incurring debt, personally solicit alms, both for ourselves and our poor, but we would prefer earning our own living by any means the place we might be located in afforded. [244]

Bagshawe was not overwhelmingly happy with the results of the begging tour undertaken by Potter and Sister Cecilia Smith. Nor was he happy with the fact that the poverty and the trials of the community were being noised abroad. He wrote to Potter blaming her for a letter he had received from Sister Clare of Kenmare, in which she alluded to the financial problems of the community, and suggested that some of the sisters be sent to Dublin hospital where they could "learn about confinements."[245] Bagshawe was outraged at the interference and chastised Potter again for what he perceived as her interference: "The use God made of you in founding the institute may give you as much interest in it as you please," he wrote:

> but it does not give you any right to mould it as you like unless in perfect submission to your Superiors. Tell me your views, but accept and be content with my decisions. I do not in the least wish to throw you off or get rid of you, but I am frightened at your reliance on your own judgement and [the]canonising of your own opinions as inspiration. [246]

Potter denied the charge of encouraging Sister Clare, but tensions in the community were growing steadily worse. Bagshawe persisted in his attempts to drive a wedge between Potter and Mother Elizabeth. "Sister Angela" he informed Elizabeth Bryan, was "a trouble," "meddlesome" and a woman who "had a trick of seeking to have things her own way by petitions, suggestions, arguments etc, in a manner which is often troublesome."[247] Bryan does not appear to have refuted such claims. As a woman who enjoyed the position of authority, she was undoubtedly shrewd enough to realise that to cross the bishop was to risk her own position. There were other problems facing Elizabeth Bryan as superior of the house, which exacerbated the tension. Quite simply, she was out of her depth in terms of managing a religious house.

Bryan had been placed in a position of authority over a group of women who were, by public proclamation of the bishop, "a new religious order." Lacking any knowledge of religious life, its meaning or ultimate purpose, and unwilling to appeal to Potter for help, she turned for counsel to the superior of the Nottingham convent of the Sisters of Nazareth.[248]

Mother, Mothers Cecilia, Gertrude and John, Xavier, Srs de Montfort, Edith (white novice) in the garden of via Sforza, Rome, circa 1989.

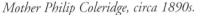

Mother Philip Coleridge, circa 1890s.

The Sisters of Nazareth had come to Nottingham in 1876 at the invitation of Bishop Bagshawe. In 1877, under the superiorship of a Sister Alphonsus, the community "had been harbouring thoughts of discontent against their superiors thinking they were being treated with insufficient consideration."[249] They took their complaint to the bishop and he, "with more impetuosity than prudence," believed the tales the women told him, and carried the complaint to Cardinal Manning. The issue escalated into a full-scale enquiry. The behaviour of the founder of the institute, Victoire de Larmenière (1827–1877) and her governance of the sisters were scrutinised, and found to be exemplary. Exonerating the superior and her council, Cardinal Manning determined the action was one of mischief. He did not impose a penalty on Mother Alphonsus and the malcontents, "leaving it entirely to [their superiors] to act as they thought fit towards those members who had so grievously offended [them]."[250] Neither Lamenier nor her council acted against Mother Alphonsus. She returned to Nottingham, and it was to her that Elizabeth Bryan turned for advice regarding how to lead the community.[251]

The advice given by Mother Alphonsus and the corresponding alterations Elizabeth Bryan began to make to Potter's community structure were far removed from the vision of the community which had inspired and encouraged women like Cecilia Smith, Agnes Bray, or even that tormented soul Sister Philip Coleridge. These members of the community, angered by what they perceived as a betrayal on the part of Mother Elizabeth, vented their displeasure.[252] The result was that Bryan became more aloof and controlling, and the sisters less and less involved with community decision-making. An opportunity for Potter to address the issue came when Elizabeth Bryan taxed Potter on her criticism of her government and her lack of obedience and docility to her as her superior. Potter responded in frustration:

> I feel it very much that I hurt you, but what can I do? I may not speak to you myself, and the sisters say they may not. That is one complaint I know they have, that they are told to be simple, but they may not speak simply to you and you do not to them. Now I know much more is said than I hear – they will not speak before me, because they know I would not listen, except when I thought I could explain. There is a thought among them that whenever you go to Nazareth House you come back different. It has put however into my mind that perhaps Rev. Mother has been advising you as she did me, which advice I do not think suited to our Community. One spirit differs so much from another that Rev. Mother could do harm instead of good, advising you according to the spirit of their Institute…
>
> …I would ask you if you feel aggrieved with me about anything, put yourself in my place. If this work had been a plan of my own, I should probably have said I could not give the whole direction to another. As I do not believe it is a plan of my own but a work of Almighty God's and one especially dear to Him and therefore specially crossed, I leave it to God, telling him He must look to it. At the same time, I feel grieved when I see things going differently to what I hoped, but my confidence in God is not shaken. If this Foundation were to fail, another would prosper, If it failed in this country, it would succeed in another. If it were suppressed in this century, it would arise again in another. Please God I will ever hope in Him, knowing that though He does not [cause] everything that happens, he permits it and can and does draw good out of evil.[253]

The plea that Mother Elizabeth look more carefully to her own beliefs about the institute she had joined had little effect. The distance between the two women remained, but in September 1878, a new situation arose which would lead to a critical moment in the institution's history – Sister Francis White became Assistant Superior of the house. By virtue of her office, she had:

> the duty of assigning from day to day, or from time to time, the various works in the house, as cooking, scouring washing, cleaning up etc., etc., among the sisters who may be at home at the time, distributing to each one her share of labour. [254]

Whether through a genuine insensitivity or plain spite, Mother Francis now began a campaign, which affected the whole community. It was customary for those who were ill or needed rest to gain the necessary permission from the assistant or the superior, if she was in the house. It was also customary to receive such permission. Mother Francis, however, refused to accept that sisters were ill, placed heavy duties upon them, and failed to give them permission to be exempt from offices when other pressing matters came to hand. An enormous sense of injustice grew within the community exacerbated by the fact that the bishop had exempted White from any other duties within the house or in the mission.[255] The community was in an uproar, and when Mother Elizabeth fell ill in the

October of 1878, things only got worse, for Mother Francis took over her authority. Community meetings were not held; Chapters – at which either the bishop or his delegate was to preside – were cancelled without notice; and community routine and prayers were not followed. White now began to report Bryan to the bishop, accusing her of "disobedience," because of her inability to attend to community duties. The variety of tales being carried by White confused even Bagshawe. On November 27, he wrote to Mother Elizabeth clarifying whom he wanted in charge of the community, and how it was to operate in light of Bryan's own illness:

> I fear that there is still some want of clear understanding of what I wish as to the government of the house, and I cannot quite gather whether you or Mother M. Francis are governing it at present. She tells me of Fr Herbert having reinstated you on the same evening when I had been there; yet you do not seem to be attending to all the duties of the Office nor as yet well enough to do so. I think it would be better in every way that you should remain on the sick list until you are quite able to get about again, appoint and supervise the work, hold chapters and fulfil all the duties of the office. I am told there was not a Chapter last Wednesday and yet do not know whom to hold responsible for the confusion, yourself or Mother M. Francis. When you are strong enough to resume all your duties, then announce the same to the community … I wish the Acting Superior for the time being to have the whole responsibility, so she must have an undivided authority and therefore I have struck out some words of the Rule, lest they should lead to misunderstanding.
>
>   I have directed her whenever she is in office, and for the present until you resume office, to lean to the side of believing too much rather than too little in the Sisters ailments. For yourself while ill, you will not be liable to be called on for any work whatever. [256]

The bishop's flexibility in terms of changing the rule of the institute to meet particular circumstances did little to create a stable environment. The "full authority" which White now possessed gave her an unprecedented power over other community members and it could not have come at a more inopportune time for Potter herself.

Early in 1878 Potter had begun to experience great pain in one of her breasts. She had done nothing about the discomfort, which worsened over the year. By the end November, it had become obvious to all that something was gravely wrong, yet Mother Francis refused to accept that Potter was ill, and when she sought exemption from community offices or work, White complained to the bishop that "Sister Angela" was seeking to avoid her duty.[257] Mother Philip, as infirmarian, finally rebelled against White's injustice, and took the matter into her own hands and called in the community's doctor, Dr. Hatherley. His diagnosis was that Potter had cancer and that the breast should be removed immediately. The operation was set down for December 8. Permission for the surgery was needed, and so Potter approached the bishop. With wry humour, she asked permission to "give away community property" and Bagshawe, only a little discomforted, gave his consent to the operation.[258] How little he understood of the severity of the procedure, and how defensive he was of his protegée Mother Francis, may be seen in his letter to Mother

Elizabeth, who, finally stirred from her lethargy and united with Sisters Cecilia and Philip, complained to him about Mother Francis' rule and treatment of Mother Potter:

> If any dispensation is required by M. Angela and refused unreasonably, let M. Mary Angela write or come to me about it, or if she cannot let her get someone to write in her name. If you mean that she tells me through you that she is now being forced to attend community duties for which she is unequal, I dispense her from doing so until I can speak with Mother Mary Francis on the subject…I am sure you three would be far from consciously opposing or thwarting Mother Mary Francis, … your disapproval of her being in office as she is might easily lead to some unconscious want of confidence and cordiality, which she might be able to perceive more easily than you would do…. As for Mother Angela, my impression is that she has a trick of seeking to have things her own way by petitions, suggestions arguments etc., in a manner which is often troublesome. Let her genuinely seek to find out in silence the real wishes and meaning of the Acting Superior, and conform to them without so many words.[259]

The operation – a primitive procedure – took place on a table in the community house. Potter could not be anaesthetised due to her heart condition and remained conscious throughout. Suffering intense pain she sought to cheer up the witnesses to the surgery and prayed throughout, and whilst edified by the endurance, the horror of the surgery remained with those who witnessed it.[260] It was a horror to be revisited six months later when Potter's other breast was removed under the same conditions.

The slow and difficult recovery Mary Potter faced over the December of 1878 and January of 1879 had at least one positive effect. The founding members of the community, perhaps frightened by the founder's close brush with death, were drawn into a unity of spirit and purpose. For the first time since the initiation of the community in 1877, they spoke with one voice. Even Mother Elizabeth, worn out as much by the bishop as by the antics of Mother Francis, found support in the strength and aggression of Mother Philip, and the loyalty of both Sisters Cecilia and Agnes. Potter, encouraged by the unanimity, requested that the bishop hold elections whereby the community could decide who it wanted as superior of the house. This he agreed to do, confident that his choice for the post – namely Mother Francis White – would be elected. To his chagrin, the vote of the small community was firmly behind Potter, and on February 12, 1879, Mary Potter was re-established as the community leader.

Bagshawe's dismay was made obvious when, on February 14, he wrote to Potter withdrawing financial support, and placing the community on notice that they were now to finance themselves:

> The Community has now decided for itself as to those who are to have the management of its affairs, and it is now necessary for me to define the extent of my responsibilities towards it. I will pay the outstanding debts to the extent of £60, some time in the course of this year, according as they press. You must let me have an exact list of them without delay. You need not pay any of them yourselves i.e. so far as the £60 go.

For the future, I enclose a check for £10 as a donation to help you make a start, and give you time for arranging affairs. It is for the purpose of enabling you to begin paying ready money for everything without exception which is had or ordered for the future – and if anyone of you orders anything on credit it must be ordered in her own name and on her own personal responsibility exclusively – No one must order anything in my name, nor will I be responsible for anything… I desire that an exact statement of the financial state of the house, with a complete list of its debts, together with this letter, be at once laid before all the Sisters, and placed so that anyone may refer to them at pleasure, and I also desire that every week, at the Chapter of Faults a balance-sheet of assets and liabilities, that is, of money in hand or coming in, and also of debts owing, be presented to the Community and left for reference… You will also have to consider what has to be done as to Minnie Croker and the new Postulant. It will be the Superioress and not I, who will have the responsibility of incurring debt for them, if ready money be not forthcoming. [261]

There was certain petulance in the bishop's decision to withdraw financial support. The little community had struggled to provide for its needs, and if debts had been accrued, they were debts incurred in his name as superior of the house, and with his knowledge and consent. His protegée, Mother Francis was, after all, the bursar, and had kept tight control over the monetary affairs of the community. The bishop was angered further, when his request for details of the community finances failed to be forthcoming. Mother Francis, whose charge it was to prepare and present the documents, had simply failed to do so, and when asked for them by the bishop denied knowledge of the task. Once again, the bishop believed her and wrote again to Mother Potter:

Sister Mary Francis, having called to see me, I asked her when I was to receive the list of bills, (and the bills themselves) owing by the community up to the receipt of my letter. She said she did not know she had to prepare it. There must be some mistake. Please therefore let me have at once the complete statement of everything owing by the Community up to that date, as well as the actual bills – the assets of the community up to the same date, whether in money owing to it, or in stocks of books etc., still remaining for sale… they must of course be deducted from the amount owing – that is to say, to clear you up to the date of my letter, I must take to myself both your debts and your assets. This I am willing to do, and discharge the balance of your liabilities, provided it do not exceed £69.[262]

The task was completed and Potter sought to bring to the community a sense of order and commitment to the vision. It was to prove a far more difficult task than she had anticipated. The works of the community were demanding enough, but her concern was for the sisters in her care. "No one could know the suffering being Mother has brought upon me," she wrote to Father Walker. "If a sister is in a wrong state I feel it in my soul without her telling me, as likewise I feel relieved and joyous…when the temptation is gone or the sister is sorry."[263] The burden of leadership was made heavier by the breakdown of Mother Philip Coleridge. On October 15, 1879, Potter wrote a letter to Father Walker, seeking his assistance determining if there were any signs by which "possession" could be known "for I feel almost inclined to think I know someone possessed."[264] The following week, in response to a letter from Walker in which he evidently encouraged her to tell him more of the problem, she wrote again, this time telling him of the trials she was undergoing with a particular sister. "There is a sister here," she wrote:

> One whom I have constantly with me, whom it would be a relief to my mind to think possessed. It would have saved me many bitter tears if I had known such was the case. The sisters do not know what I tell you; they know she is passionate and grieves me a great deal, but they have never seen what I do, almost every day. I have known her to take off her crucifix and throw it on the ground, then her rosaries and her religious clothes. Then in her fits of passion she will swear and say terrible things and at these times seems possessed with an intense hatred for myself. I do not like to tell you and yet feel urged to, she seems as though she would kill me. Her face looks simply diabolical, and she will gnash her teeth, seize me, shake me violently, strike me, knock my head against the wall, spit upon me. Being my infirmarian I had to be obedient to her and in her tempers she would, after getting me ready for Mass, hinder me going …Benediction the same…. [She has called me] into a sister's room, she has got angry while talking, taken me round the throat with her two hands, lifted me up, shaken me…. She will make a dart across the room to me, squeeze me around the throat as if to strangle me, knock me about and, if I am up, pull me about, spurn my veil, spit on my blessed ring. She really does not seem to be able to contain herself at these times. I do not think she recollects…[afterwards]…all she does, but still she tells me she fears some day she will do something dreadful and be lost. What makes it still more painful is the love I have for her.[265]

It was an extraordinary situation, and speculation might ask if Potter was exaggerating the violence of the relationship. From the evidence provided by scraps of notes from Mother Philip however, the rage and the violence were real. In these, she expresses a constant remorse for her ungovernable rage and brutal behaviour.[266] The pathology behind the actions remains undiagnosable, but Coleridge was a woman undergoing intense psychological disturbance. Later letters to her confessor, Monsignor Kirby of the English College in Rome, reveal a woman suffering from painful self-doubt, a lack of conviction about her own conversion to Catholicism, and a deep doubt about her own vocation.[267] Potter did not reject the woman. After a further period of violent behaviour, Coleridge "threw herself" on Potter's protection, and begged for her spiritual support. It was forthcoming, and Potter was able to report to Walker that:

> even now she is not like she was, that is to say, though she does such fearful things, she does not remain a day in her passion and she is so sorry. She has such desires to be better.[268]

If these internal trials were not enough, further tensions mounted as the bishop, unable or unwilling to leave the community to govern itself, placed more pressure upon it by planning further expansion within the diocese, and ordering Potter's small band to undertake new works. It was an onerous task, for the community numbered little more than ten members.[269]

Expansion

In June 1880, pressured by the needs of the diocese, a further deficit of priests, and the continual desire to expand the influence of the Catholic church, Bishop Bagshawe made a decision that he would profess the first members of the institute. Workers were needed if expansion was to take place, and, in spite of the difficulties between himself and members of the community (in particular the founder), the congregation had proved an asset in the diocese. Branch Houses, staffed by the sisters would provide a means of opening chapels, churches, and schools. As superior of the institute, he could determine the works of the community, and indeed force their compliance. But the decision so arbitrarily taken by the bishop posed particular problems for Mother Potter. While glad for profession of vows, there were certain irregularities that needed to be addressed. None of the sisters the bishop was proposing for profession had followed a novitiate; Rome had not been advised of the inauguration of the institute and the rule was yet unfinished. Such foundations as the bishop was now proposing would again mean that no formation could be given to new members, and any hope of living the essential charism of the congregation would be further negated as works proliferated and rules failed to appear.[270]

This direct interference and stalling of the founder's desires was no new situation for women religious. As the historian Margaret Susan Thompson has pointed out, a bishop's primary concern was directed towards fostering the growth of his diocese, and no mother superior or sisterhood could be allowed subvert that goal.[271] Where congregations did manage to evade the interference of the local ordinary, one solution – as Mary Oates has illustrated – was for bishops to create diocesan congregations. These offered the advantage of placing power of the institute into the hands of the bishop, whilst at the same time providing a source of labour for the diocese.[272] In the case of Potter's institute, the reckless abandon with which Bagshawe altered rules of the congregation indicates the manner in which he sought to control its structure to suit his own ends. While this had the advantage of advancing the growth of the diocese, it also had the effect of negating the founding vision and charism of the congregation.

In the face of Bagshawe's persistent interference Potter's desire to have the institute regularised and recognised by Rome increased. She requested permission from the bishop to put her case for approbation before the Holy See. Bagshawe denied the request. Approbation of the institute by Rome would remove the bishop's control of the institute, as it would become an institute directly under the authority of Rome. It also meant that Potter, as Superior General, would have the power to determine the nature and scope of the institute. She could accept or commence branches of the institute outside the local diocesan borders and govern the inner life of the community according to its duly approved constitutions. Gaining such approbation however also required a letter of approval from the bishop himself. This he refused to consider.

Bagshawe refused to permit application to Rome, so Potter gave an obedient if reluctant acquiescence to the founding of the Quordon mission. Writing to Father Henry Walker, parish priest of St. Austin's Kenilworth,[273] Potter gave the news:

> Just a few lines to say that I am going to help make a new home for Our dear Lord and want your prayers for its success. Next Sunday morning we have clothing of two postulants then we are to be professed publicly; the Bishop will offer Holy Mass about 10. In the afternoon, five of us are to start for Quordon, a little village about one mile from Mount Sorrel. I am trusting providence greatly, going where apparently we shall have no Priest.[274]

It was not that the mission work undertaken by the small community did not appeal to Potter. It did. In her eyes, it was "one of the works of the Little Company of Mary," and was a source of delight and a work Potter viewed as particularly suitable for women vowed to service.[275] Seeing members of the community as co-workers with clergy, Potter's view of women's work in what she termed "mission" foundations was that the sisters were, like their male counterparts, itinerant missionaries. This was an impelling vision, one that would later motivate the quick dispersal of the community throughout the world.[276] Unlike the "pious ladies engaged [by priests] to help them," who were "changeable, capricious and easily given to take offence," women religious worked only for "the glory of God" and their disinterested involvement was a source of strength for the church.[277] Besides, mission work provided an opportunity to evangelise, to preach the good news, and to make a difference in the world:

> It is very evident that God wishes us to be occupied with His vast family, since He has so blessed this work wherever the Little Company of Mary have engaged themselves helping the priest with his mission work – what blessings have been attached, what souls saved. Conversions, instructions, united with out interior life, help to our own sanctification as well as to the extension of God's kingdom. The presence of the Sisters gave a certain spirit to the people, if we may express it so. The seeing in practice what the priest preached was more effectual than the sermons themselves.
>
> Religion was not then theoretical. They saw it practically carried out – the sick administered to, the suffering consoled and comforted, the poor fed, and children instructed and the ignorant learned to love our Lord and His Spirit entered into them…The poor are His favourites, and we love them because he loves them.[278]

There is little doubt that the work of the community made a difference in the local church. Case records from Hyson Green illustrate a terrible constancy in the calls to nurse cases of consumption, "malignant scarlet fever," typhoid, cholera, dropsy, heart disease, bronchitis and other illnesses.[279] The death rate was high in the overcrowded corporation housing of the working-class, and children were often the victims of epidemics which raged through buildings. [280] Deathbeds became the place of many conversions, and the mission sisters fought valiantly with "protestant" ministers for possession of the souls of the dying, rejoicing with each soul "won for God" by conversion to the "true faith."[281] Mission work also involved the regularisation of marriages for there were many in the community who had "married outside their faith." De facto relationships also fell under their brief, as did the reform of drunkards, and the promotion of temperance leagues.[282] "All manner of spiritual and corporal works of mercy" were carried out by the mission sisters [and these works] the Bishop "deem[ed] worthy of his paternal and cordial patronage," the very success of the women prompting his desire to expand the influence of the community to outlying areas.[283]

On July 4, 1880 Mothers Mary Potter, Elizabeth Bryan, Agnes Bray, Cecilia (Mary) Smith, Philip (Edith) Coleridge, and Francis White professed their vows.[284] Following the ceremony, Potter accompanied four "mission" sisters to Quorndon, "a pretty, little village, … with no resident Catholics" one mile from Mount Sorrel, and linked to Nottingham by rail at Barrow-on-Soar.[285] "A very nice priest from Ireland" was promised to be in residence soon after the sisters' arrival, and the mission was begun in a small cottage alongside "a pre-Reformation Church and churchyard, and house for the priest."[286] In spite of having no congregation, the small community was hopeful "of being the means of making a Mission."[287] By August 3, with a priest appointed and in residence, the mission began to take shape:

> We had daily Mass and Benediction two or three times a week. There was plenty of mission work to be done and a school to be opened. A postulant who was a certified teacher saw to that, but on Sundays we taught catechism and gave instructions, as time went on, several converts were made.[288]

Members of the neighbouring mission at Barrow also gave support. Without a priest themselves, the Catholic community:

> would come over and help us and we in turn would do anything for them, and strove to encourage them in their Altar and choir duties by letting them play and sing for us when they came for Benediction and so on, which they did constantly…and the hearty way they sang was always very refreshing.[289]

As Quorndon began to flourish, the bishop decided to open yet another mission and again requested sisters from the convent at Hyson Green. In September, a mission was established at Eastwell, but this was neither as successful nor as happy as Quorndon. Eastwell was a "sadly neglected place, [with a] fine old-fashioned house, pretty little church and cemetery attached."[290] The parish priest however "is in great difficulties, is even summoned to court." Potter found the situation with both priest and people difficult, as the bishop had given her instructions to take over the administration of the parish:[291]

> We are to provide for [the priest] there, and even to take the offertories. Poor old man, he seems very unfit for his post both temporally and spiritually, and we have orders

from the Bishop to look to everything. I was shocked to find apostasies and wicked things going on in such a beautiful little village.[292]

By November 1880, following an outbreak of scarlet fever which again placed Potter's life at risk, the community was swamped by the works of the various houses and the stresses of the tasks they were undertaking. The bishop, unwilling or unable to see the tensions and the difficulties the works created, persisted with his expansionist policies. The small community, whose membership had risen to fifteen by the end of 1880, and twenty-two by the end of 1881, was asked to take on the care of the church in Colston Bassetts. They now had care for the missions in Quordon, Eastwell, Hucknall, Bulwell, and Colston Bassetts. It was becoming an impossible load for the community to sustain, particularly as it coincided with problems Bagshawe was experiencing with his imported priests. In January 1881, Potter wrote to her friend Father Walker of the burdens that she now carried as a result of clerical failure:

> You must please pray that I may be able to do what the Bishop has this week put on me. There are difficulties in the Mission for want of money, and the Priest raised money upon the Remonstrance and sent away the assistant Governess, just as the Examinations are coming etc. So the Bishop has made the Priest his curate, taken the responsibility himself, and asked me to look to the temporalities and school of the mission. I am now more overwhelmed with work than ever, committee-men, workpeople, collectors, school business, the two Branch Houses, school difficulties at Quordon and Barrow.[293]

For all the difficulties, postulants to the order were coming in their ones and twos, and the growth augured well for the congregation's future. Potter, while pleased with the growth, still anguished over the lack of an adequate formation, and fulminated at some of the candidates the bishop persisted in sending. In July 1881, there were problems with a new member "behaving in…a terrible way, and threatening to go to law for defamation of character."[294] By September, the situation had worsened considerably and they seemed to be living "in the midst of sad scandals."[295] There appeared to be no respite from the problems. The community, she told Father Walker, was "in a sea of trouble; one sister wanting a dispensation from vows," and "the law business…still hanging over our heads [which] unless God interferes may be a cause of great scandal."[296] In April 1882, despite recurrent difficulties, the bishop demanded the opening of two new missions in Melton Mowbray and in Osgodby. Further postulants arrived, "very good children, with one or two exceptions for our trial."[297] By August 1882, however, Potter was writing in unguarded terms of the problems being foisted upon the community by the bishop's "forc[ing] another postulant upon us which has rather raised up old sores."[298]

The cause of the latest problem lay with a Miss Paradon who, in spite of ill health, was admitted to the community by the bishop. On taking a nursing case, she had complained to the bishop that she had "hurt herself considerably in lifting a woman who had fallen into a coma in a case taken just before her last illness."[299] Regardless of her being ill equipped for the demands of the work the bishop himself was laying upon the community, he desired that she remain with the community because he believed that:

> 1. Her ailments will mend in time and she will be able to be generally useful then,
> 2. Because in any case I think she will be of great use to the community in various ways even if she does not go nursing. She wishes to be a religious, and thinks she could well manage the routine of the convent, with perhaps a little exception at present. I should like her for some months to come to be kept in the convent observing the Rule and doing needlework or any other light work writing or otherwise, which might be found for her. I am sure she will get better and stronger with a little patience. I wish her to be excused all laborious work, and if she needs it, to have some indulgence as to not rising so early; otherwise to keep the rule as I have said… Let her continue as I have said till the time comes when she might be able to put on the habit.[300]

Dissent about the quality of the candidates and their function within the community continued to create difficulties, and served to highlight the on-going problem with Mother Francis, whom the bishop had also withdrawn from cases. Mother Philip Coleridge, full of anger at "idle" sisters like Mother Francis and Miss Paradon, confronted Bagshawe, who wrote to Potter of the encounter:

> In reply to your letter I would say that I think it is better not to disturb the arrangement last made with Mother Mary Francis, that she was not to be asked to take outdoor nursing. If you want Mother M. Cecilia, her time is up, and if you have another available sister to send in her place, she can be recalled, after reasonable notice given to the patient. Mother Mary Philip urged very strongly that Mother M. Frances ought to be sent to cases, and when I told her that I had arranged otherwise, spoke of the injustice of placing on the community the burden of an idle sister, blamed me for acting without the Council, said that she had been advised on a previous occasion to appeal to the Cardinal against me, and alluded to the probability of herself leaving the Community. I am quite sure that Mother Mary Francis, through her disobedient humours is a burden to the community. I thought it was one which the leading members of the Community were willing to bear at my particular request. If I am sufficiently informed that the case is otherwise, I will consider what other provisions I may be able to make for her. – But, while she remains I should be glad if the Question of the work to be assigned her were now considered as settled, as if it is continually raised, no one can have peace. I regret much to find Mother Philip still in heart opposed to the entire dependence of the Community on the Bishop's will, and evidently desirous of a fundamental change in this respect. As it is now the second time that she has seriously and formally made objection to the fundamental principle of the Community (besides previous difficulties) I fear she is likely to cling to it, and if so, she will not persevere.[301]

Mary Potter shared Mother Philip's discontent. The bishop's continued control of the institute was crippling the community, and destroying its fundamental spirit. Unless the situation changed, the community was in the very real danger of fragmentation, and probable death. The situation could no longer be tolerated, particularly as the ever-expanding mission work placed its demands upon young and untried religious. Potter made her decision. She would go to Rome and seek papal approbation. Applying for a change of status from a diocesan congregation to one of pontifical right would at least remove direct control from the bishop, and give a degree of autonomy to Potter and her rule of the congregation. An approved rule could be appealed to in cases of dispute, and if it could be designed with clear-cut parameters, Bagshawe would no longer be able to dictate the works or the structure of the community.[302] Potter wrote of her reasons for desiring change in a submission to the Holy See:

> The bishop in receiving me and my Little Company, approved entirely the object the work and the spirit of the said Society, but added to the already devised rules an organisation, and gave to it a constitution. In force of that Constitution, in the Chapter "The Authority of the Bishop" [he] has been made responsible for the observance of the Rules and has reserved to himself the right of Superior General of the Society and governs the society all other superiors and council being only his representatives and advisers. We have always experienced the Bishop exceedingly kind and good, but we feel bound and have been advised to represent to the Congregation that under such arrangement, the order discipline and spirit of the society have suffered very much, because the Superioress and the council having no real authority, the Bishop can interfere with the smallest matters even of the internal life of the Convent and nothing can be enforced without his sanction. More particularly in matters of religious vocation, the Bishop solely decided upon the admission and retention of subjects. Postulants have been admitted and Novices retained to whom the Superioress and Council objected…not having a religious spirit and having full freedom to refer to the Bishop as their superior at any time [these] cause considerable annoyance to other sisters.… Also, the fact of the council not having the power to protest the Bishop's arrangements many and many have been the evils and scandals that have arisen from the fact of the Bishop placing the sisters to work in parishes with bad Priests. Likewise, new foundations must be opened whether the sisters think the said foundations can be prudently entered upon or not… The duty of the Superioress in the present rule is to enforce the Bishop's wishes and directions, she cannot therefore represent (together with the Council), the Community, and look to its interests conscientiously, obedience to the Bishop hindering many measures being taken for the general well-being of the community. Therefore, I and the Council of the Society, anxious to avoid any seed of corruption or element of disorder in the Constitutions and Rules of the Society, supplicate the Holy Congregation of Propaganda to change the chapters upon the authority of the Bishop, the Council and Superioress … giving to the Mother Superioress and the council, their proper authority and restraining the Bishop to his own right of Ordinary of the place. [303]

Other complaints were contained in the supplication to Propaganda. The bishop, Potter stated, had neglected to enforce parts of the original plan: "the all important point of Novitiate" had been put aside. The role of the Novice Mistress was not made "sufficiently important"; the practice of poverty was not emphasised. In addition, the contemplative members of the community were not being developed or encouraged.[304] At the root of the submission lay a power struggle for control of the institute. If the integrity of the founding vision was to be maintained, the bishop's control over the congregation had to be lessened. There was little option. If an end was to be made to these "sad circumstances," the journey to Rome was essential. As Mother Cecilia Smith noted:

> Mother felt it was absolutely necessary to go to Rome, not only to obtain a Blessing and approval on her rule, but in order also that an end should be put to these sad circumstances. At first the Bishop gave a decided refusal to her going, saying that he was going himself and would see to anything she wished. She waited for a time, but one morning, she sent Mother Philip down to the Bishop for permission to go to Rome. While Mother Philip was gone, Mother spent the time in the little Chapel. Happening to make a visit to the chapel myself, I saw her tapping at the Tabernacle door, and then, sometime afterwards, I met her coming down from the chapel, she appeared radiantly happy and said, "My child, I am going to Rome." "But Mother," I said, "the Bishop won't let you," and she answered "Yes he will." And she was right, for when Mother Philip returned, she brought the permission for Mother to go, on condition that the Doctor gave permission and that M. Philip travelled with her. Then Mother said I should also go with them.[305]

On September 24, 1882 the party of three women left Nottingham for Rome. Potter's family provided funds for the journey, and the task ahead was clear. They were to seek approbation from the Holy See, and through such means regularise the congregation, removing it from the control and interference of the bishop. It was not a decision Potter took lightly, and was to bring its own problems.

SECTION 4

Expansion and Consolidation
(1883–1913)

Expansion and Consolidation (1883–1913)

Mary Potter's decision to go to Rome to seek papal approval for her institute was to prove a critical moment in its history. Tired of the interference of her bishop, distressed at the loss of what she perceived as central elements of the life she had been called to bring into being, there were no other options available to her. As this section demonstrates, while pontifical approval did secure a modicum of protection from interference by local authorities, such protection came at a price.

Faced with the pressures of political upheaval in Europe, the loss of temporal power, and a need to consolidate its spiritual leadership,[1] a new ultramontanism emerged within the Roman Catholic church, as the papacy sought to create a new spiritual hegemony to replace the loss of temporal power.[2] This new ultramontanism brought with it the determination to create a parallel world of solid, stable Catholic life where adaptation of religion to culture was turned upside down and culture converted to religion, then "Romanised."[3] The result was "a uniformity of discipline, liturgy and piety," a religious life-style comparable to that of Italy, and the development of an infrastructure through a massive and comprehensive building boom.[4] Hospitals, schools, orphanages, convents, and monasteries were built on a large scale and represented not only the "success" of Catholicity, but the power it held.[5] As Mary Magray has pointed out, this was an infrastructure built upon the religious virtuosity of the women whose care, solicitude, and determination founded, staffed and continued to support such works of charity – the nuns.[6]

Margaret Thompson has suggested that "instrumentalism" was an important factor in the emergence of many of the religious orders of women in the nineteenth century and was in part generated by the increasing need of the church to provide a total "Catholic" social identity.[7] Yet, even as the institutional church commended and utilised the invaluable labour of women, churchmen reacted with disquiet.[8] Mary Potter would find out that clerical and hierarchical response to any activism they regarded as threatening to their own authority or as serving to advance to the cause of women or their autonomous role in the church created tension and at times outright conflict.

The need to harness the social activism of nuns and the power of their religious virtuosity combined with the relentless pressure on the papacy to create a human face – a self-contained structurally complete secure Catholic culture, which could serve and defend the

faith of Catholics from cradle to grave. Religious women were to be for the church a
Catholic variation of "the angel of the house," the:

> menders and fixers, tireless workers who seldom complain, doing all for 'love' and ask-
> ing no recognition in terms of increased authority or say in certain matters directly con-
> cerned with their work.[9]

To assist in that process, and to stabilise relations between religious women of the new
active orders and local clergy, the church had to come to some definition of just what it
was that these groups of women were.

They were unrecognised in canon law as distinct entities in their own right, given recognition on the basis of utility and service. The processes of the church began to seek ways
of naming, claiming and aiming the work of different bodies of women that had emerged
over the nineteenth century. Prophetic in their assumption of new roles and public pro-
files, the women who initiated religious communities lived in a tension with the hierarchical church. Not considered real religious because they were active, unenclosed and
without solemn vows, the ambiguity of their existence reflected back on the hierarchical
church. But appeals for recognition and papal approval increased over the century.

By the middle of the era the church had entered a process of stabilisation regarding its
active institutes of religious life. Increasing demands for pontifical recognition led to
norms for approval being laid down. There was still resistance to acknowledging active
apostolic institutes as "true" religious so constitutions or rules were not to reflect any of
the privileges of the old monastic orders. No references to scripture, to theology, to writings of the church fathers, to spirituality or to "religious profession" or "religious life" were
permitted.[10] These restrictions were critical for Mary Potter, who believed that she had not
been called to create a new religious institute, but a new religious order, with a primary
purpose unrelated to the activism of so many of the other new congregations.

Potter's conviction regarding the charismatic nature of her order, and its total ecclesial
significance, held little value for those charged with approving or rejecting the congregation. It was to remain unimportant until the promulgation of Paul VI's *moto proprio*,
Ecclesia Sanctae, of 1966. There, for the first time, the terms "charism," and the "charism
of the founder" were used as definitive and necessary elements of religious life – which was
now seen as a gift of the Spirit to the church and world.[11] Potter would well have understood the statement contained within that document, that:

> the charism of the founder …[appears as]… an experience of the Spirit, transmitted to
> their followers to be lived by them, to be preserved, deepened and constantly developed
> in harmony with the Body of Christ, continually in a process of growth.[12]

It was a precise statement of her belief. From 1875, she had claimed that she had been
given just such a gift of the spirit, and that her responsibility was to enable it to be brought
to birth in her congregation.

The nineteenth-century church lacked a theology of charisms. It did, however, possess a long-standing reluctance to admit to the action of the Spirit (a result of the Montanist crisis of the second century[13]), and an equally long-standing and even greater reluctance to believe in women's ability to have direct interaction with the divine. The church was interested in creating a "catalogue" of rules and regulations by which religious orders could be defined according to structure and purpose, and approved on the basis of those factors alone.

By the time Potter reached Rome in 1882, the norms of the church regarding women's institutes of religious life were already in process of formulation, and Potter would find her charismatic ideal pushed to one side under the legal requirements of approbation.[14] A growing body of canonical definition surrounded, manipulated, and determined not only what women did, but also how they did what they had to do. As the process of approbation continued, this lack of emphasis on the charismatic reality of the congregation (and therefore of its mission in the church) suffered a stinging blow. The particular unity between the active and contemplative strands of the life and its ministerial diversity was channelled into a single-stranded ministry, that of nursing. Her "spiritual mission" – to draw the church to a realisation of its call to live the mystical life – was lost to the activism imposed on the institute by the church and, it must be said, by the institute's own need for economic survival.

As Thompson has pointed out, compromise was often the cost of papal approbation.[15] Validation of an institute by pontifical approbation secured at least some protection from the manipulations and predations of local bishops, intent on securing support structures for their dioceses. The cost of the compromise was high. Acceptance of the institute as a part of the church meant that Potter's essential belief in her spiritual and theological insight was forced to bend before magisterial determinism. In many ways, compromise was forced upon her as a loyal daughter of the church. Mystic and prophetic though she might be, if she were to remain united with the traditions of the church and of religious life, then that compromise was inevitable. It had unfortunate consequences on the development of the congregation. Nursing, an offshoot of the principal "work" of the congregation became the determinant of its identity, thus placing it within the "structure" of an institute of active apostolic life. With that decision, the open-ended, evangelical, charismatic vision of the Little Company of Mary became conformed to the "Institute of Nursing Sisters called the Little Company of Mary."[16]

Yet, even as the congregation grew, the charismatic and apostolic flexibility envisioned by the founder vanished as the increasing tendency of the Roman and Romanised church to carve its apologetic in stone and mortar impacted on almost every foundation the congregation made over the period of expansion.

Apostolic flexibility was not the only element to suffer with the restructuring of the nineteenth-century church. Potter's distinctive form of religious life rested upon a premise that its primary function was to speak a prophetic word to both church and world about living the Christian life. This prophetic word could only be spoken if the specific spirituality of the institute could take root in the heart of the members. The increasing tendency of the church, however, was to define and prescribe the prayers and pieties of the sisters. Canonical hours were laid down, as were detailed prescriptions for the manner and content of prayer.[17] Potter's original concept of a mixed contemplative and active community would again suffer under the prescriptive definition of the church, and its essential blending of a contemplative and active life became lost.

The forceful restructuring and re-integration of women's religious institutes also destroyed a fundamental part of the belief system of the institute Potter had founded. Unafraid of the modernising world of which she was a part, Potter's world view was towards integration not isolation. Her place, and the place of her sisters, she believed, was in the battlefield of life, where souls suffered their most grievous isolation and loneliness. But, as the church reacted to the process of modernisation, it reacted also against the movement of women towards autonomy. The new centralism of the church re-established an ideology of women's infantility. The good nun was like the good wife, submissive, subservient and compliant to the demands of the male hierarchy. Needing protection, she was to be removed from a world in which her own weakness might draw her to sin. Enclosure became a means of again removing women from the world's contamination, preserving their virginal purity, while, at the same time, restricting their sphere of influence.

Potter would now be faced with learning how to live with the politics of compromise. Loyal woman of the church, she accepted the rulings given to her, preferring compromise to non-acceptance. As a good Catholic, she believed that within the church lay her salvation, and that the institute she had been called to create was *for* the church. In spite of the comprises necessary, however, she maintained her belief that the Little Company of Mary was a body of women who were to be mothers to a world in need. Their place was *in* the world, and they were to be mothers *to* the world, acting as spiritual midwives, aiding the birth of God in the souls of others.

Against the growing tendency of the church to reduce the power and the autonomy of women as disciples and actors in the drama of salvation, Potter sought to maintain the evangelical and outward thrust of the institute. Letters and conferences poured from her pen. Each addressed aspects of the life she believed she had been called to initiate within the church. Each sought to exhort the members of the institute to take greater care of the "charism" they shared. Against the increasing trend of ecclesiastical law to control and trivialise what she regarded as the unique and unrepeatable "spirit" and spirituality of religious institutes, Potter sought to maintain the focus of her community. However, as this section reveals, the hard reality was that the brave sweep of her vision for the congregation ultimately bowed under the weight of ecclesial restructuring, to be called to renewal some fifty years after her death.

The Journey to Rome

Potter's journey to Rome began with subterfuge. When Bishop Bagshawe gave permission for her to leave Hyson Green and journey to Rome, he did so because he thought her illness and growing physical infirmity were life-threatening. The operations to remove her breasts had left her debilitated, she was recovering from an attack of scarlet fever, and her recovery was not hastened by the ever present reality of her weakened heart, or the malignant tumour that had invaded her shoulder and arm. Believing that she did not have long to live, and perhaps regretful at his own part in the woman's decline in health, he gave her permission to leave Nottingham to visit the Eternal City. Concerned about the effect of the journey, he instructed Mother Philip – the only accredited nurse in the congregation and community infirmarian – and Mother Cecilia to accompany her, in case her health deteriorated further. Providing the three women with letters of introduction to various prelates and priests, he watched their tearful farewell from the community, without realising that the journey Potter was making was to seek approbation of the congregation as an institute of pontifical right.[18] He was not to see Mary Potter again for four years.

On September 24, 1882 when the three women left Nottingham, Potter alone was the life of the party. Armed with Bagshawe's letters of introduction, a half-written rule, and three one-way tickets to Rome, she was convinced that something would happen to bring the institute to its fulfilment.

Her two companions were less than happy. Cecilia Smith, whose experience of travel had been from Portsmouth to London (return) and London to Nottingham, was over-awed at the prospect of foreign travel. Mother Philip Coleridge, in whom a great dread of the sea combined with a rooted distrust of all foreigners, viewed the prospect ahead with foreboding.[19] As it turned out, her pessimism was justified.

Ill-health meant the journey was to be staged. A short stopover was made in London, where Potter met up with her brothers, and then it was on to Calais. The crossing was difficult, cold and unnerving. Mary became ill, Philip was seasick and poor Cecilia Smith developed a large and painful abscess on her face. Succour was sought and given by the Sisters of Le Sainte Union in Calais, and though Cecilia Smith was "feeling very lonely and miserable in a strange land," and Philip Coleridge ready to return home, Potter urged her companions on. [20] Paris was reached without incident, but Mother Philip's xenophobia refused to rejoice in the delights of the city: "We were all nearly knocked down and run over," she wrote to the community, "such bustle and confusion. We got into an open carriage; the driver was either mad or drunk, he dashed along, more like a fire engine than anything else."[21] However, the network of convent contacts and the hospitality at the convent of the Sisters of Marie Auxilatrice on Rue de Bac somewhat soothed the travellers' misery and, on October 5, the party set out by train to Turin. In a dreadful moment for her two companions, Potter, who was still ill from the trials of the crossing, suffered a heart attack. Her companions, convinced she was dying, broke the journey at Mâcon, where refuge was sought at a convent of the Good Shepherd Sisters. These sisters, unable to read the documentation provided by Bagshawe, at first refused to receive the three women, believing them to be impostors. Finally, hospitality was offered and Potter put to bed.[22] Mother Cecilia was greatly unimpressed by both the hostility and the surroundings:

"The building looked like a prison and reformatory attached...the windows were all barred and through the bars, a lot of wild-looking girls were gazing at us."[23] Nor was her spleen improved when, seeking a consoling cup of tea, she surrendered the trio's precious "bag of tea" to a sister deputed to care for them. The entire bag was returned as "a huge jug of boiled tea leaves, no sugar or milk...they [had] emptied the whole bag, and brought the leaves for us to eat."[24] Further indignation was experienced on the morning of their departure, when she was woken by "the iron knuckles of [a] sister, [who] with all her strength ... rapped them on my forehead saying: *'Benedicamus Domino ma bon [sic] soeur'.*" [25] Mother Philip, witness to the awakening, and fearful of similar treatment, sought refuge under the bedclothes, calling on Potter to protect her from the onslaught.[26] Despite the difficulties she was experiencing, and unwilling to let physical weakness delay the journey, Potter made the decision to press on, convinced that it was imperative to get to Rome.

The disasters continued. Leaving Mâcon, Mary Potter suffered another major heart attack.[27] "It was dreadful...we feared she would die," wrote Mother Cecilia, but, taken to a hotel in Aix-les-Bains, Potter again recovered enough to declare her intent to continue the journey. They arrived in Turin and the Sisters of La Rétraite gave them hospitality. There, Potter rested for two days. Finally, on October 10, 1882, the trio entered the city of Rome, with little money, no place of accommodation prepared: the first task was to find bed and board.

Again, letters of introduction proved helpful, and these directed them to the Trappist Monastery in St. John Lateran, where a friend of Bagshawe was to help provide accommodation. He, however, was away, but temporary accommodation was found with another community of Good Shepherd Sisters, whose convent was near the monastery.[28] There, plans were laid for the next stage of the venture.

Amongst the letters of introduction Potter held, there was one addressed to the *Maestro di Camera* at the Vatican, Monsignor Luigi Macchi. The day after her arrival, Potter went to the Vatican to call upon the prelate. He received her cordially, and invited the three to join a French pilgrim group, which was to be received in a public audience by Pope Leo XIII the following day.[29] It was a fortunate meeting, for Monsignor Macchi became an invaluable friend to Potter and her institute, becoming its Cardinal Protector in 1893. On October 21, 1882 – again at the instigation of Monsignor Macchi – the three sisters attended a papal Mass, and in a private audience following that event, Potter was astounded to hear herself invited to remain in Rome:

> On the following Sunday, Feast of our Lady's Purity, we heard the Holy Father's Mass and received Holy Communion from him in His own private chapel...there was a Mass of thanksgiving after which we were presented by Monsignor Macchi, the Maestro di Camera. We had taken the Banner with us, and now Mother whispered to me to take it to the Holy Father, upon which His Holiness looked up at Monsignor, saying "E' questa la Fondatrice?" (sic). But at that moment Mother was kneeling at His feet.... She

asked him to bless us and our Rule and then she would be content to return to England again. "But" said His Holiness, "Perche? Why not remain in Rome? The gates are wide open to you." With this, he blessed each one of us. Then Monsignor Macchi told Him we were going to breakfast with himself, at which the Holy Father smiled and said "Mange bene." After the above invitation of course, dear Mother made up her mind to stay in Rome.[30]

When Potter left England, it was with the hope that "Jesus [would] be in the heart of the Holy Father and speak visibly" so that she would know what it was God wanted of her.[31] With Pope Leo's apparent invitation to remain in Rome, that hope seemed to be answered. After the meeting, Monsignor Macchi informed Potter that the Pope had not simply made an invitation. She was to consider it a request, and the sisters were to commence their nursing as soon possible, with the view of opening a hospital in Rome. It seemed all too good to be true – an omen of the church's recognition of the institute.[32] While Potter had not yet decided to remain in Rome, the invitation extended by the pontiff was a matter of great heart for her.[33]

There was a certain incongruity in Leo's request to the three sisters who had been presented to him. Potter was without funds, patronage or accommodation, and had small hope of establishing a home, much less a hospital. She had come with a specific intention, and with no thought other than she should find the mind of the church regarding her institute. It was, however, a suggestion in keeping with Leo's avowed intent to create a Catholic culture, and perhaps reflected the tensions under which the papacy, the religious orders, and the national Italian church were labouring.

Political upheaval and the ongoing struggle between church and state following the suppression of the Papal States in 1870 had left the papacy vulnerable. Religious orders had been suppressed, and the goods of the church appropriated by the government. Restrictions were applied to church ownership of property, and the Italian government insisted on applying to the property of the Congregation of Propaganda, the law regarding ecclesiastical goods, which had to be converted into Italian securities.[34] In an economy already vulnerable, this meant a serious loss of church funds, and a commensurate limitation of the services offered by Italian religious.[35] Crippled by the anti-clerical laws, convents – and the work force they provided for the church – were in a crisis.[36] Foreign nationals, however, could hold property, and foreign religious were not subject to the same restrictions as their Italian counterparts. [37] Pope Leo XIII, that most political of popes, knew full well that the creation of internationally owned and privately funded institutions, could do much to portray international support for the "prisoner of the Vatican," and prove the power of the spiritual – if not the political – hegemony of the church.[38]

It was, however, a prospect for which Potter could not hold out much hope. But if the notion of building a hospital was out of the question, the suggestion to commence nursing made good sense. English nurses were valued in a country filled with expatriate English-speaking nationals, and invaded by hordes of pilgrims and visitors in the winter season. In a country in which typhus and cholera were frequent visitors many fell ill. Disease and illness respected no class or church divisions and aristocrats and artists, seminarians and secretaries succumbed to the many "fevers" Italy produced among its visitors.[39] As Italian health services were at a primitive level and illness common, qualified care could provide something of an income for Potter and her small community and gain potential supporters for the congregation. Few foreigners sought the care of Italian hospitals, which, according to observers:

> were in a pitiable state; the nuns in charge only saw to the administrative part, or at the most gave out food and medicines. The actual nursing, if any, was done by women of the lowest and commonest type, rough, and incompetent, since nursing was considered an occupation totally unfit for a refined or educated woman.[40]

Religious who were trained and prepared to nurse within the homes of the sick would be a positive benefit.[41] More pragmatically still, if there was demand enough to provide a living for the community, it could assist the process of approbation, proving the ability of the institute to be self-supporting.

With the help of Monsignor Macchi, and a Polish countess the trio met in a shop in Rome, word of the "English Sisters" and their ability to nurse in the homes of the sick spread through the community. Fortunately for Mary Potter, demand soon outstripped supply, as Mothers Philip and Cecilia gained a reputation for quality care. Cases multiplied. An American doctor in Florence, hearing of the "English nurses" in Rome, wired for their assistance[42] and less than three months after their arrival in Rome, Potter was pleased to report to Father Walker that:

> We have not been three months nursing and have received £30…they pay so well here and so glad to get English. Another season we should, I am sure, be able to put by plenty for the summer months…I do think it very possible the sisters may get cases [in] various parts of Italy. One has been to Florence, another to Milan, so they will be known about.[43]

Yet, even with the popularity of their nursing, the community was in straitened financial circumstances. The depressed state of the Italian economy made living difficult, prices for food and other essentials were high.[44] As their impoverishment became known, support came from all sectors of the Roman society. A Miss Bell, ex-governess to the Princess Borghese, befriended the sisters and gained her employer's patronage for them. The Misses Barry, English visitors to Rome provided food and other essentials, as did the Glesley family from Meridian Spa in Leamington.[45] These "were not Catholics" Mother Cecilia noted, "but that made no difference in their kindness to us."[46] In ecclesiastical circles, a growing number of contacts were made with English, Irish and Italian clerics positioned with the Vatican hierarchy. This was a process aided by an outbreak of typhus in the seminaries of the Scots and English Colleges. The Cardinal Vicar of Rome was petitioned to give permission for a sister to nurse the students, and the *Annals* recorded with some pride, that one of the sisters was the first woman to enter the male dominion of the Roman Colleges.[47] So successful was this venture that nursing clerics became a regular occurrence.

Not all clergy were as welcoming of the sisters' ministrations. The belief of some Italian clerics, stemming from previous experience with Italian religious, was that the sheer weight of numbers of sisters necessary to attend one patient was overwhelming. As one old Curé remarked, when asked if he would like to have the English sisters nurse for him in his parish: "No! I would not! We had Monsignor Amadore ill, and he had to have three sisters, two to mind the patient and the third to mind the other two."[48]

In spite of such views, clerical support for both Potter and her institute strengthened. Cardinal Howard, the Jesuit Father Cardella, Cardinal Simeoni of Propaganda and Monsignor Guardi, an under-secretary with Propaganda Fide all became friends of the community, and allies in the cause of the constitutions, along with Monsignor Macchi and Monsignor James Campbell, Rector of the Scots College. But this encouragement, whilst important to Potter, did not provide accommodation or financial aid. As the months progressed, a need to find suitable and permanent accommodation became a pressing problem. No longer able to stay with the Sisters of the Good Shepherd, the trio moved to lodgings provided for them by the Sisters of La Rétraite in the Piazza degli Apostoli. An injection of funds from Hyson Green enabled a further move into what was alleged to be "a very respectable lodging, in the Via St. Chiara."[49] This proved to be a squalid house inhabited by things other than human. Cecilia Smith yet again was discomforted by the experience and conveyed her impressions: "Oh! The dirt and the animals, worse things by far than mosquitoes. We were nearly eaten to death. It was a most undesirable place."[50] However, fortune appeared to smile on the group with the appearance of "a smart little enterprising American":

> A Mrs. St. John Harper called upon us, hearing we were strangers in Rome. She was a smart little enterprising American, and offered to help us in any way she could. So one morning Mother sent me out with her to visit some churches and do a little shopping. Eh! Now I well remember this first shopping. She took me to a pizzicheria near S. Agontino; there was ham, butter and cheese to buy. She had a good taste of each and then told me to do the same. We seemed to be having a small meal in that shop and how ashamed I was…Since we had to move again she said she had a nice little apartment near S. Peter's in the Brogo Nouveau and she could let us have a couple of rooms. It sounded nice and inviting, especially to be near S. Peter's. So we went. Alas, there were more than a hundred steps to get to the top. Poor Mother! Every morning I went out with the good lady to the Carmelite Church for Mass and Communion about 5.30 am, after which we brought bread and butter for our breakfast which on going back I prepared.[51]

Mrs. Harper proved a friend to the trio, teaching them Italian and accompanying Mother Cecilia on errands. However, her hospitality drew the attention of other English

and American women in Rome. Unbeknown to them, the "enterprising little American"
was Lizzie St. John Eckel (Mrs. L. St. John Harper), daughter of the infamous author of
The Awful Disclosures of Maria Monk. In what appears to be a case of the sins of the mother
transferred to the daughter, Mrs. St. John Harper, though a practising Catholic, was an
unwelcome member of the English-speaking Catholic community.[52] Potter and her two
companions were soon visited, and informed that they were creating a scandal by their
association with Maria Monk's daughter:

> The Honourable Mrs. Montgomery called upon us…[she] was shocked to think we
> were with this person. She suggested we should come away at once. She herself was a
> tertiary of St.Francis and said she knew some American Franciscan nuns who would be
> glad to have us, these lived in the Via Alfieri near St. John Lateran and the Scala Sancta,
> so we accepted the kind hospitality of these nuns. That part of Rome…was all country,
> there was a lovely field in front of the convent in which white sheep [grazed].[53]

Potter, glad to think of accommodation in more convenient surroundings expressed
interest in the offer, and upon visiting the proposed house found it offered a self-contained
section big enough to accommodate sisters and some nursing patients. A large, rambling
house, with a separate entrance, it offered real independence.[54] The superior of the community, in what appeared to be genuine interest, assured Potter that she could have as
many rooms as required in order to expand the work of nursing, and encouraged her to
consider bringing more sisters to Rome.[55] Delighted with the encouragement, Potter sent
a request to Hyson Green for three more sisters, and then found herself in an awkward
predicament, as pressure began to be applied by the Franciscan community to amalgamate
with them. It was a request emerging from the changing demands of the church regarding approval of new institutes of religious life.

By the last quarter of the nineteenth century, the overarching tendency of the church
was to restrict the development of new institutes of apostolic life. As Father Gomer Peeters
told Alice Ingham (founder of the Franciscan Missionary Sisters of St. Joseph) in 1878,
there were great difficulties gaining approval for new orders. They now had to demonstrate
"a peculiar characteristic of work and spirit, by which Divine Providence shall point out
that a new order or congregation should be formed, different as it were, from the various
religious congregations already existing."[56] Evidently finding some difficulty in gaining
approbation, Montgomery's group, sought to align Potter's work of nursing of the sick and
the dying to their own Franciscan rule. "Great discussions" went on, and pressure was
brought to bear on Potter by other supporters of the Franciscan community, who added
their own methods of persuasion to take the habit and rule of the Franciscans, and continue the special work of nursing.[57] "I do not think that I am judging that it was a little
plot that we might join the Franciscans," wrote Potter:

> She, Mrs. Montgomery did not herself openly propose it, but it was connived at by oth-
> ers. In fact, one lady, Marchese S…(sic), came, as she said with a message from Cardinal

Simeoni that we should become Franciscans…I told Cardinal Howard of the advice of the various ladies and of the particular message the one mentioned above averred to have received from Cardinal Simeoni. The Cardinal said: "Oh, these ladies…."[58]

Potter refused to consider the offer, convinced that the spirit and idea of the institute which had brought her to Rome could not be amalgamated to another congregation.[59] Just as she could not accede to the demands of Bishop Bagshawe, she could not submit what she perceived as the originality of the vision, and its divine inspiration to an already existing form of religious life. Her institute, its spirituality, framework, and inner orientation demanded its own imperative, and from the outset she had sought to create a form of religious life which reflected what she believed was its essential difference.[60] The conscious choice to reject amalgamation with a Franciscan rule, was based upon the fact that to accept:

would have meant giving up all that the spirit of the Little Company of Mary implied, – the great devotions – Calvary, the Precious Blood, the Maternal Heart, the constant intercession for the dying, – all that had been shown …as forming the interior spirit of [the] Institute, and keeping only what was more or less secondary, the exterior work of nursing.[61]

There were, according to Potter, "many flowers in the garden of God's church," and it was essential that they bloom where they were planted.[62] It was a naïve expression of the theological insight offered in a much later time by J.M.R. Tillard. If the spirit of the institute – its charism – was to be preserved it needed a structure, but one that was creatively fashioned to support it:

A charism needs structures if it is to be incarnate and its survival does depend on the where and the how. It requires – and it is often a matter of life or death for it – this practice and not that other, this institutional expression and not that other, this attitude of prayer and not that other, this style of personal relations and not that other. One does not plant corn in a field of rye.[63]

The firmness of her refusal of amalgamation brought unfortunate results. Whether through pique or pressure, there was a sudden reclamation of the accommodation previously so generously given, and again, the search was on for suitable housing – a task made more urgent by the arrival of Sisters Catherine, Michael, and Rose from the Hyson Green community. With the help of a Franciscan friar, Father Luke Carey, an apartment was found on the Via Purificazione, and in the spring of 1883, the community was established in its new home.[64] By the end of April, the expanded community was employed nursing, in their homes, the rich and poor of Roman society.[65] It was a work that would continue, and was a source of status for many.[66] Evelyn Underhill (1875–1941), visiting Rome with her mother in 1910, experienced the ministrations of the sisters:

Mother fell ill when we had been in Rome quite a few days and is only this week beginning to go about again, so travelling has been an impossibility…Fortunately her illness was at no time dangerous, though trying: and we had a most delightful Blue Sister of the English "Little Company of Mary" to nurse her.[67]

Shortly after this, Underhill herself became ill and as she told it:

> The Sister after a day [of illness] coaxed me to see a lady doctor she knew, as I cordially disliked the doctor the Missis [her mother] had. Unfortunately I consented and the tiresome creature, though a very agreeable woman has turned out to be one of those terribly scientific hospital products who treat everything as an illness and by rule! Having found my bronchial tubes rather stuffy she at once pronounced it bronchitis and I have now been kept 5 days in bed and simply starved – nothing to eat but milk and a little soup – all for a common cold…even the Missis thinks it absurd, but these two women take not the slightest bit of notice of either of us! The poor Missis is bearing up well, though of course she is having a very dull time of it, no one to go about with but Sister, and she may never drive in an open cab![68]

So it was that care of the sick became the most significant identifier of the institute of the Little Company of Mary. Originally perceived as an outcome of caring for the dying, and one of the activities of the institute, it was now seen by those outside the community as the predominant and single work of the order. Certainly, it had enabled an income and given new status to the institute. As will be seen, however, the identification of the Little Company of Mary with its nursing apostolate was to create further problems for Potter as the shape of the congregation, its multi-faceted flexibility and its contemplative dimension, were once again submerged, this time by an increasing body of legal requirements.

Shaping the Constitutions

Potter's journey to Rome, and her subsequent working towards gaining pontifical approbation, had been undertaken with the specific intent of protecting and preserving the essential spirit (charism) and structures of her institute. Her first conviction was that the Little Company of Mary was to be a religious order, "whose spirit and model was Calvary."[69] This inner spirit was to be formed through the practice of the spirituality of abandonment she had found expressed in De Montfort's *True Devotion*. Through the practice of that spiritual path, the members of the community would be transformed into images of Mary, who was herself the perfect disciple and the mother of humanity, missioned by Jesus to preserve, protect and defend those for whom he died. The first article of the Rule for the Hyson Green community had elaborated the elements of the congregation and named its essential spirituality and guiding principles:

> The Little Company of Mary is founded with the object of honouring God, in special union with Mary. To arrive at this, the Sisters give themselves, body and soul with all that belongs to them into the hands of Mary as the Venerable Grignon de Montfort teaches in his work "True Devotion towards the Blessed Virgin." They act thus after the example of the Son of God incarnate. The sisters seek to be moulded by Mary so as to become the perfect likeness of her Maternal Heart, wishing for what it wishes and con-

forming themselves to her spirit. They have, with Mary, a special devotion to Jesus dying on the Cross and for the salvation of souls for whom he died, particularly the agonising, for whom they have a special zeal and devotion. [70]

The distinctive element of the rule the community had adopted was its primary concern to give glory to God by the practice of a contemplative spirituality which would then flow out into their special ministerial concerns – the salvation of souls and prayer for and care of the dying. The preliminary focus was to become the images of Jesus their rule called them to be and the essence of the vocation lay in the ability of the sisters to be transformed by their spiritual practice into living images of Jesus and Mary, "who went about everywhere doing good."[71]

Through the practice of the spiritual path elaborated by De Montfort, adapted by Potter, the members of the institute would learn to subdue self, to become empty of all things "to make room for Jesus." The end of the spiritual pathway was to permit Jesus to live in the soul: "Jesus dwells in the soul that is emptied of self. He is to the persons who thus possess Him as their very heart."[72] When this union occurred a new relationship, a new way of living commenced in which "all we think and do is virtually, if not always actually, in union with Him." United "heart to heart" with Jesus in themselves, they were also united with the heart of God reflected in creation and the world in which they lived. There, according to Potter's belief:

> You will love from your heart, where Jesus lives in love, you will pour this love upon those outside; you will see God everywhere, you will see him in his creatures, you will love him in them; you could not possess a hard thought of a creature God loved. You could not, possessing within you the Holy Spirit of love…Thus our love will unconsciously show itself, it could not be kept in.[73]

The members of the institute were to live a life of personal oblation: "to unite their every breath…every beating of their heart…to…that strong loving Heart that beat with so great love of the human race."[74] With the Virgin, who "watched at the foot of the Cross…[and] joined her [heart] to the Agonising Heart of our Lord," they were to "plead by the Precious Blood – plead first for the Church, its head and the members … [and those]…who have the greatest need the dying."[75]

The mission of the institute was to reveal to the world that: "the Incarnation was not a mere occurrence…not a transitory act. The union of the Eternal Word with human nature lives forever." Through their own transformed consciousness of the meaning of life, they were to "make a world of beauty in souls for [the] Creator… [and] extend God's kingdom… to restore God's loved world to its God." [76] They were commissioned with the Mother of Jesus to "go like the Good Shepherd, and seek the lost sheep."[77] They were to be:

> Mothers after [Mary's] heart – full of zeal, full of fervour, walking this earth picking up the bruised and crushed ones and placing them on their bosom and bringing them to

Thee. Yes, on their bosom, because in their hearts they ever plead and pray. Plead for the most needy, plead for the most miserable, the most wretched of this earth, those who are most wounded, who have the greatest need. Yes, thus may they be true children… true Spouses of Jesus, like to their Lord. Yes like to Him! Full of love, love by night and day, love for beautiful souls make like to Thee, O God! Yes, it is at Thy throne we learn the value of a soul, precious since Precious blood was shed for it; priceless, for the price was the Son of God's immortal, since it was made by an immortal God, made for himself.[78]

"[A]s sentinels, as witnesses at the portals of Christ's Church that no soul may go forth for whom we have not prayed,"[79] the women of the institute were to be virgin mothers, intercessors for humanity, and through their lives be models and instruments of a perfected humanity.[80] Underlying the spiritual rhetoric there lay a claim to the independent and self-acting power of women, transformed by their prayer into radical disciples.

Taking up and controlling the image of the Virgin as *Mater Hominum*, the works of the institute were in response to the needs of society. Saving the special concern for the dying and the interior practice of constant intercessory prayer, practical expressions of the internal attitudes were as varied as the needs that arose in the heart of humanity. As work on the constitutions continued, however, Potter was made well aware by her canonical experts, that the rapidly institutionalising hierarchical church demanded an identifying work that was particular to the institute, and defined it in terms of function.

The home nursing done by the sisters was already valued within the community. In addition, nursing was seen as an appropriate service for women. As Welter points out, it was allegedly valued within the nineteenth century because it drew forth the patience, mercy and gentleness of women.[81] Religious nurses, by virtue of their angelic likeness of purity and selflessness could echo the virtues of the domesticated woman of the sickroom. Potter's community had already proved that nursing was practical in terms of income generation. It could be linked with the ministry of prayer for the dying and the expressed concern to assist at their deathbeds, and it met the criteria for papal approval. It provided an identifying and non-negotiable function for the community. If Potter hoped for a more diffuse and open-ended attitude towards apostolic labour, her hopes would be denied. The framing of the institute, according to the wish of the hierarchy of the church continued. Nursing would loom large in the problems Potter faced in the later years of consolidation, and in part those problems directly related to deeper theological issues – the relationship between the charism, the mission, and the ministry of the congregation.[82]

Potter's contention was that she had been "inspired" to create within the church a religious order whose first function was to model a way of living the Christian life in its integrity and to actively engage in the mission of Jesus by "going about everywhere doing good." Echoing the "new" motherhood given to the Virgin on Calvary, the members of the institute were commissioned with her as "mothers of the church." And they were to work at bringing the mystical body of Jesus to birth in his disciples. Centred in the world like Jesus and Mary, the members of the institute were to:

look upon this world as a battlefield, full of wounded and suffering ones, souls sick unto death, injured, disfigured, in which the image of God is defaced or blotted out entirely. It is all too true, and too sad – and sadder still is it to think that those who should help them neglect to do so, through indolence, selfishness, and self indulgence. Our Lady has sent her Little Company, the children of her Maternal Heart into the world to help gain souls to her Divine Son, and how can we be faithful to our vocation if we neglect any means which would lead to that grand end.[83]

The incipient messianism of the vocation – and its potential for excessive activism – was to be tempered by the radical self-knowledge gained through the contemplative life. Only if the members were grounded in the radical distance between themselves and God, and the paradox of the equally radical closeness to God, could a commitment to the life be made. Hence Mary Potter's determination to establish a separate and highly disciplined "monastic" house of formation in which a life of prayer and union with God, could be developed in the aspirant, prior to her being sent on mission.[84] In terms of the mission of the congregation, Potter believed that they could not be confined to one form of action. As problems arose from the concentration on nursing, she continually re-iterated the focus of the institute, illustrating how concern for the dying fitted into her overall perspective:

> You know, dear children, the first object of our foundation is not to nurse, as so many suppose, and it is not right; too many of our sisters allow them to suppose[sic]. Our first object is to model Calvary and form a united body representing to heaven mirroring that grand work of the Holy Ghost: that mystery of grace – Calvary. So on Calvary, we see the figures of our institute. We see Jesus Crucified, shedding his Precious Blood. Our Lady's Maternal Heart pleading by that blood to save souls. We see those three deaths. We watch the happy Dismas and long to co-operate with our Mother in thus saving souls at the last hour. To do this, we go out to attend the deathbeds of Christ's large family. He died for all, we pray for all and visit in spirit the death which we cannot attend in person.[85]

In a world of turmoil and change, the Little Company of Mary was to be a prophetic experience of radical discipleship.[86] By "joining with Jesus in the offering he [made] of his Precious Blood," offering themselves "as living sacrifices …[as] victims in union with the great Victim for us all,"[87] they were to be catalysts for change. Problematically, acceptance of functionalism, meant that the charism of the institute – its motivating power, its gospel orientation and its primary purpose of "building up of the body of the church" – was reduced or even denied by many of its members. Its spirituality for mission was reduced to personal piety as the magisterium began to recommend the practices of devotion appropriate to religious women, and the moral imperative of the community was reduced to the perfection of the individual member.

Functionalism also attacked one of the interior aspects of the proposed congregation: its life of oblation and prayer for the dying of the world. The crucial point of the life of the community was that it was called to evangelise. Again underscoring the missionary thrust of the institute Potter maintained her vision of a group of active and contemplative apostolic women. "We were not founded in God's kingdom simply to nurse," wrote Potter, "we were founded to extend the kingdom of God by making Mary reign in the hearts of men."[88] Whatever the works undertaken, this was the one thing necessary, to provide opportunity for those without knowledge of God to come to that realisation. As she herself expressed it:

> Go then my children fulfil your mission. Go visit the widow, the fatherless, the afflicted, and keep your soul unspotted from this world. But who is the widow, and who are the fatherless you are to visit…? The widow is the soul bereft of its Lord. There are many who deny their Father, though we may not call them Fatherless, but oh, how far they have wandered from that good Father from whom all paternity has its name! Let us bring them back. Let us inspire hope in hearts apparently hopeless. They have seen no power on earth capable of making right what is wrong as they know their own poor hearts to be, and they doubt they can ever be righted again, disfigured, disjointed, broken to pieces as they know their own poor souls to be. They doubt, they trust not his providence, they believe not his power to restore, regenerate, to give them back the light and liberty of the children of God. They doubt that their souls can ever bear the image of God again. Ah Sisters! Let us go forth upon our works…[89]

This diffuse and evangelical position was to be undercut by the revisioning already underway within canon law. That revision would affect her constitution, and be explicitly stated in *Conditae a Christo*:

> Except perhaps in mission countries, no new congregations should be approved which without any specified and proper purpose would embrace the practice of all kinds of works of piety or charity, however different they might be in themselves.[90]

Potter's institute, if it were to be accepted, would have to be defined according to the norms governing religious life – and not by what she believed was the charismatic imperative.

As Potter struggled with the formulation of a constitution and rule which would express the charism as fully as possible within the limitations of the law, Bishop Bagshawe was becoming increasingly irritated. Informed of her decision to seek approbation, and realising that the rule she had taken to Rome reflected his own arbitrary decision-making (and his general tardiness in advising Rome of the establishment of a community within his diocese), Bagshawe now sought to indemnify himself against possible complaint. He prepared and sent to Rome a copy of a rule *he* proposed for approbation, and at the same time expressed his dislike for and displeasure at the proposal to make the congregation one of "pontifical right," with a central government and responsible directly to the Holy See.[91] Potter was undeterred by his displeasure. Convinced that the institute could only survive if the power of the bishop was diminished, a formal novitiate implemented, and the spiritual integrity of the congregation protected, she pushed ahead with her proposals to Propaganda.

Aided by Father Cardella and Monsignor Macchi, she continued to work on the constitutions. A *Lauda*, or brief of praise, was offered but refused, on the grounds that it was often a means used by Propaganda to delay proceedings.[92] Also refused was a suggestion made by members of the curia that Potter should return home to England, as approbation could take a long, long time.[93] This was simply not acceptable to her, and she informed the curial official of that fact. As the *Annals* record:

> With that mixture of gentleness and firmness so characteristic of her, Mother replied that in spite of her poverty and ill-health, she had come to Rome for the purpose of obtaining the approval of the Holy See upon her work and therefore she could not leave until she had some decisions. Her words and still more her appearance and manner greatly impressed the official, Don Enrico Gualdi. He listened to her explanations saying: "This is quite a different matter, and I will do all I can to help you." He kept his word.[94]

Gualdi did support the community, and began to give invaluable help in preparing and presenting the report of the institute and the draft of the constitutions.

While work on the constitutions continued, nursing continued to bring positive benefits, including the offer of rent-free accommodation in a big house on the Via Sforza di Monti. Potter, anxious to find accommodation that would provide stability for her sisters, accepted the offer.[95] By the beginning of 1884 the community was settled, had been accepted by the Roman authorities, and given certain privileges of a religious house, which included their own chapel, and appointed confessors.[96] "A great deal of night nursing" was now carried out amongst the Italian poor, and as their reputation spread, so did requests for assistance.[97] At times, however, there was a mixed reception to the presence of these women, with their sky blue veils and sombre black habits. According to the *Annals*, Mother Catherine was called to nurse a patient at the Quirinal Palace:

> [The patient] was Equerry to King Humbert I and like so many Italian men of that time, had not practised his religion for years. His wife on the other hand was a very pious and fervent Catholic; she was Lady-in-Waiting to the Queen. She deeply appreciated Mother Catherine, both as a religious and as a nurse, and so did the King and Queen who daily visited the patient. It would seem that the underlings in the Palace did not share the same opinion. For when Mother Catherine went to have her meals, she was served on the table in the ironing room with a newspaper instead of a cloth, on the principle apparently anything was good enough for a nun. M.M.Catherine made no remark or complaint about this, and it was only found out by the patient's wife…When she found out how she had been treated there was a great storm "below stairs," for the Marchese was most indignant at the way Mother Catherine had been treated.[98]

Such encounters served only to increase the popularity of the community, and as Clear points out, a certain status came to be conferred on patient and sister alike as success blossomed.[99] More and more, the demands of middle-class nursing pulled the community away from the care of the poor and this was to become a more pressing problem as the century progressed.

On May 31, 1886 Potter received word that the Institute of the Little Company of Mary had been approved as an institute of pontifical right, and given permission to operate for a period of five years *per modum experimenti*. Cardella, Gualdi and Macchi had done their best to preserve the flexibility of the institute, and give it a grounding in the spirituality it held. Consistent with the ambivalent attitude held by church towards these new congregations of women however, there was no reference to the Little Company as a religious institute, or to its religious status. Quite simply, as M. Dortel-Claudot states:

> the name and legal rights of religious had not yet been conceded to the members of Institutes of simple vows…. The jurisprudence of the Roman Curia and also the teaching of canonists denied that Congregations should be called Religious Institutes or their members Religious except in a broad and non-proper sense.[100]

The opening paragraph determined the nature and function of the institute. Potter was now the Mother General of "The Institute of Nursing Sisters, called the Little Company of Mary," and home nursing, which had been a recognised part of the ministry to the dying, was now the "external and principal" manifestation of its interior spirit.[101] It was a work undertaken "by day and night" in which the members of the institute sought to serve the dying and their families: "with an entire devotedness …fulfilling … every charitable office which it is possible to render, and as much as their strength will allow."[102] The vocation of nursing was now elevated to a sacred task, and one of selfless devotion. A variant of the angelic ideal of domesticated woman, it would stand in tension with other elements of the life of the institute. But it provided the Sisters with movement in society. They would:

> nurse the sick of all classes of society, rich and poor, Catholics and Protestants. The only exceptional cases being that in which the reputation of the sister in care of them being compromised. If the sick are in a position in which they can pay, the Sisters will receive remuneration. They will always nurse the poor gratis.[103]

Egalitarian and ecumenical, the "angelic ideal" of the Little Company of Mary nursing sister was further strengthened by the inclusion of clauses relating to the associate members of the institute, and illustrated the separation that was being effected by the church amongst women themselves. The nun was now contrasted with her lay sister, less reflective of the view of women themselves than the problem the church still had with notions of women and sexuality.[104] Potter believed that holiness of life was for all and, in her vision of the congregation, saw it as inclusive of lay or secular membership. Women drawn to live a more spiritual life and to the spirit of the institute, but not to religious life *per se*, could be joined to the Little Company as associate members. These could live within or without the community, share in the mission and ministry, and participate in elements of the community's life.[105] While their presence remained within the constitutions, a clearly defined function was assigned to them. They were to provide a practical means of circumventing the prohibition placed upon religious women in the nursing profession, particularly in relation to the care of confinement cases and other sexually-related illness or disease. The constitutions read:

> The Sisters have attached to their community and under its direction, a maternal society of pious women, who fulfil the duties of midwives and monthly nurses, therefore the sisters will not attend confinement cases, nor bad diseases nor any other surgical operations capable of wounding the imagination, or injuring modesty, except in an extreme and indispensable necessity, and then only after having taken the precautions which the most severe (strict) prudence exacts.
>
> Excepting these cases, the Sisters take care of all sorts of diseases, infectious or not, and all classes of invalids.[106]

The thoughts expressed in the constitutions would find expression in the formalised document of *Conditae*, and later in the *Normae* of 1901. However, the sharp differentiation between the angelic purity and chastity of the "sister" and that of "ordinary" women is worthy of note. By male ecclesiastical decision, women who had forsworn the "sacred shame" of motherhood (and therefore sexuality), were not to be exposed to the temptations of their own biological reality. Potter, whose sisters had already embarked upon the care of confinement cases in Hyson Green, had no such qualms.[107] Birthing children was the role of women, whether spiritually or physically, and it reflected the maternity of Jesus. The careful inclusion in the constitutions of exclusion clauses "except in an extreme and indispensable necessity, and then only after having taken the precautions which the most severe prudence exacts," enabled pre- and post-natal care to be carried out, and the work of midwifery to be undertaken in certain situations.[108] It was a decision Potter would appeal in 1905, when by a special decree of the Sacred Congregation of Propaganda, permission would be given to undertake maternity nursing provided they chose "only the more mature sisters."[109]

Hard work on Potter's part, and the help given by Cardella and Gualdi, had resulted in the inclusion of other elements of the vocation Potter believed was to be lived by the sisters. The constitutions acknowledged that the Little Company was specifically oriented to the "conversion of sinners," and the "promotion of new missions." Careful work on the constitutions preserved the integral, evangelical thrust of Potter's vision, even as it was made subordinate to the primary work:

> The Little Company of Mary is to work for the conversion of sinners and for the reception of heretics and infidels into the bosom of the Church, by visiting, exhorting and helping those who may require help, but always in co-operation and under the direction of the Priest of the Parish in which they live. …[The Sisters] are to assist in the formation of new missions, in instructing gratuitously, or with the help of a small remuneration, in schools where the appointment of a master or mistress could not be paid by the Mission…[they] will also undertake other spiritual and temporal works of mercy when there is any occasion for doing to…[110]

The flexibility of ministry thus offered by the constitutions – whilst preserving the integrity of the special concern for the immediacy of the needs of the dying – expressed for Potter the basics of the mission and ministry of the institute. What it lacked was the definition of the institute as a religious order, express mention of the particular De Montfortian spirituality so central to the institute, and all scriptural references. These, according to the mind of the church, were things reserved for the real Religious Orders, the contemplatives, and their exclusion gives indication of the unresolved status of the new, active religious institutes the church was attempting to define.[111] What had been omitted by the formalised constitutions, Potter would seek to consolidate through her own conferences and instructions upon the meaning and intent of the rule.

While the work of nursing would bring its own problems and cause much heartache for the founder, the approbation of the institute as one of pontifical right gave great joy. It was now recognised, supported by law, and could expand. The principal cost, in terms of Potter's initial vision, lay in the refusal of the church to sanction the dual contemplative/active nature of the institute and its inability to see the specificity of the charism. Unless these two elements could be resolved, and an integral unity between the charism and ministry be maintained, the congregation would not be formed according to its founding vision. As will be seen, however, further changes in church attitudes to religious institutes would not be helpful to the process.

With the preliminary decree of approbation came – a *sanatio* – or validation of the "irregular" (non-existent) novitiates of Potter's first companions. Potter herself did not need a sanatio, the curia decreeing that she had made a canonically approved novitiate in the Sisters of Mercy. This document opened the way for the original members of the institute to make public profession of their final vows. The approbation came none too soon for there were already invitations to found new houses of the Little Company of Mary.

Further Expansion: 1885–1903

Between 1882 and the approbation of the first Rule of the Little Company of Mary in 1886, care of the sick had occupied much of the time of the small group of sisters stationed in Rome, and it had brought them to the attention of influential laity and cleric alike. In 1884, Bishop Patrick Moran, bishop of Ossory in Ireland, came to Rome to receive his appointment as Archbishop of the Australian church. Visiting an Australian in Rome, who had fallen foul of the Roman "fevers," he learnt of the existence of the "English sisters,"[112] and on making further enquiry from his friends in the Irish College, received glowing reports. Impressed by what he had heard of the community, and anxious to build up services within the Australian Catholic church, Moran voiced the opinion that he believed it was probably "God's will that the Little Company be established in Australia."[113]

Moran made a formal approach to Potter in 1884. Caught unprepared by such an invitation, she vacillated between acceptance and rejection. The invitation was flattering, but she was ambivalent about it: the congregation was not yet approved, its rules were still being formulated, and there was, "only a simple blessing on our works and an encouragement to proceed."[114] Besides, the institute was still technically a diocesan congregation, under the rule and authority of Bishop Bagshawe in Nottingham. He would have to be asked for his opinion on the matter. Potter notified Bagshawe of the invitation, and on May 14, 1884 received an encouraging letter in reply. Bagshawe had no problems with such a foundation: "I think you should accept the Archbishop of Sydney's offer," he wrote:

> but I should like you to get some instructions as to how the distant community would be related to the Mother House in practice. Clear up these points. You would then more or less have to get volunteers, i.e. send those sisters who would not mind going away from home practically for life. For communications except by letter would be, I fear almost out of the question.[115]

In spite of Bagshawe's qualified support for the idea, Potter could not bring herself to accept the offer made by Moran, who received the news with some genuine regret. The following year, however, when called to Rome to receive the "red hat" of Cardinal,[116] he again made formal application for a foundation to be made in Australia. This time he enlisted the aid of Monsignor Kirby, Rector of the Irish College and a friend of the Little Company and its founder. Though the constitutions had not yet been approved, or the institute given its status as a pontifical institute, Potter felt she could not refuse. Discussions of the works the sisters would undertake were exciting to Potter, particularly the cardinal's proposal to have the sisters staff a deaf, dumb and blind asylum. Seeking to protect the foundation from any alienation from its spirit or purpose, she sought to gain the new cardinal's co-operation and support in maintaining fidelity to and unity with the parent stem. She requested that he write a formal letter to the College of Propaganda:

> promising that no attempt should ever be made to separate from its present stem in Europe, the Little Company of Mary, whom he had offered to plant in that part of the Church.[117]

It was an astute, if manipulative move, taken as an insurance against interference with the spirit or the identity of the congregation. The cardinal, somewhat taken back by the initiative, needed some persuasion to commit to paper on this point, but "promised when I persisted, that though I did not doubt his word, it was necessary to have a formal letter to that effect."[118]

Hoping to avoid the "splits, rents and dissension so disgraceful in the history of the Church,"[119] Potter's initiative illustrated her growing recognition that active defence of rights was important against the power of overzealous and at times abusive episcopal authority. Leslie Liedel points out that, as episcopal power became more concentrated, this was an increasingly important learning process for many other leaders of women's communities.[120]

With Moran's formal acceptance of the terms laid down by Potter, the foundation was agreed upon. Five sisters appointed to the mission would accompany the new cardinal on his triumphant journey home on the *SS Liguria*, due to depart Plymouth on September 16, 1885. There was a limited pool of sisters from which to select a mission community and, as Moran had asked that no novice be sent, selection was even more limited.[121] The leadership of the mission community also posed a problem. Wanting to assure herself of the spiritual competence of the superior of the mission, she anguished over the decision, finally appointing Mother Raphael Byrne Farrar, aged 25. Four other sisters were selected: Pius Kelly, 36, Josephine Wroughton, 29, Pierre Dillon, 28, and Brigid Rosser 20. Mother Rose Mowles from the Roman community was to be assistant to Mother Raphael, and in this combination, Potter believed she had a well-matched leadership team where "Mother Raphael's spirituality and Mother Rose's order and discipline [would] set a stamp on the Little Company of Mary in Australia."[122] In a letter dated August 6, 1885 Potter advised Moran of her choice of community – and of her enthusiasm for teaching the deaf the new art of lip-reading:

Your Eminence and Rev. Father in Jesus and Mary…

I enclose the names of my children whom we think it well to commence the new foundation under you. Would you wish to reserve two to be trained to undertake the deaf and dumb and blind asylums you spoke of, or would you prefer another two to be trained and sent in a year or two. I have ascertained where the Sisters can be trained for the deaf and dumb asylum according to the ordinary system, but have yet to learn where the newer systems of lip motion could be taught the Sisters. This is so wonderful that I have heard you may speak with the deaf, and now know that they are so, from the wonderful way in which they have been taught to watch the motion of the mouth.

You will not mind my asking for a written agreement that no attempt will ever be made to separate the Sisters from the Mother House in Europe. Your word would be sufficient but for the sake of those who will succeed you, it seems wiser to have such an agreement that it may be well understood such a thing could never be done.

Last year, Dr. O'Hara said that in case of necessity one or more Sister might be sent back (& their expenses paid) to Europe. This seems asking a great deal, and I would only ask it for one Sister. Circumstances might make this necessary…[123]

Circumstances would make it necessary for one of the band to return from Australia, but the group of women chosen for the task now set about preparing for the journey. Not all were over excited. Mother Raphael was terrified of the appointment. Potter wrote to her in encouragement:

My darling childie, my little angel Raphael, God Bless you. I am writing this, not knowing whether I shall see you to say God speed or not. God direct, and may His Sweet Providence rule over – rule all for our good. When our hearts are full, as you wrote – poor little soul – one knows not what to write. We cannot say what we feel. Well, you will draw now within yourself, my little one, and speak to Jesus in your own heart and He will tell you what I would say to you, our own Jesus, our Brother, Father, Lord and Love.

Love him my childie, more and more. Let your life be pure love. Show your love for dear Jesus by your love for those of His that He has given you to take care of for Him. All the love you show them He will take as done to Himself. You will do your work for Him well, my childie, will you not? You will give him the very best. What a happy home He will have with my little children. What pleasure for me to come some day to see it, if God wills.

Ever one in Jesus and our Mother's heart, little Raphael and her loving mother, Mary.[124]

To the mission sisters she wrote a general letter of encouragement and advised them of the travel plans laid down for them by Cardinal Moran:

Little ones and older, God bless all. Let us cluster round our Mother's Heart and think of this new honour that we are to give her by spreading her work in this far-off land. Happy those who are called to cross the wide Ocean on this mission. Their Mother will be with them in a very special manner, if they are faithful to grace and are generous, not shrinking from the suffering, from privations, from much that it is not possible to say beforehand, but which may be trying to your nature, unless you are resolved to suffer all for love of Jesus, to keep happy through sick and suffering, to hide from others any pain of mind or body you may feel, to have a smile and a kind word for all, to do all the acts of charity possible and keep to the spirit and even exercises of your Rule. [125]

The Cardinal laid great stress upon the little Chapel he will have on board ship, where the nuns can chant their office and have their spiritual reading etc. etc. as the nuns did last year who went out to Australia. This Cardinal is a most holy strict man. The Holy Father has spoken of him as one of the holiest, one of the ablest etc. etc. whom he had chosen to do a great work in this new world, and so on. But to prove to you his great idea of religious life, he said he thought it better not to send a novice. The voyage would be too distracting for a novice, she might not preserve her recollection. So dear children, I hope you will not allow the distractions to disturb you.[126]

There would be little time for distractions. The six Little Company of Mary sisters and eight other religious joined the *SS Liguria* in Plymouth, all bound for Australia, and the daily timetable the cardinal drew up for the voyage kept them busy from morning prayer at 6 am until night prayers at 8 PM.[127]

The Australian foundation continued to hold an affectionate place in Potter's heart, but it was destined to create significant problems, and for all the cardinal's agreement, the time would come when his own national interests challenged the authority of the Mother General. In the meantime, however, other invitations for foundations were arriving.

In 1885, Count Arthur Moore of Moresfort, Tipperary, whose wife had contracted enteric fever on a visit to Rome, made a vow that should his wife recover, he would estab- lish a branch of the Little Company of Mary in Ireland.[128] His wife, entranced by the nursing care she had received also "got the good thought that she would like to provide her poor people on the estate in Ireland with the same comfort in sickness that she had."[129] In 1886, the Moores began to pressure Potter to establish a community, and had already approached Bishop O'Dwyer of Limerick for his support.[130] In that same year, demand came from Florence, where the combined resources of the bishop, an American doctor and three Scottish Presbyterian women were placed at the disposal of Potter's community, if only she would establish a foundation in that city. Potter was faced with a problem. She had fewer than fifty sisters, only thirty of whom had made vows.[131] If foundations in Italy or Ireland were to be made, they would have to come from the already pressured Hyson Green house. When Rome continued to make its demands, Potter had to make yet another request for more sisters from the home community. In December 1885, she wrote to Mother Elizabeth Bryan:

> We are indeed sorry to take more Sisters, but you know Rome must be kept up for the good of the whole community. Rome is like an English colony. Already complaints have been made about our not visiting enough, and they expect to be looked to with English sisters in Rome etc. Evidently, we have not been able to supply the want.[132]

With a certain degree of relief, she informed Mother Elizabeth that another English community, that of the Magdalen Taylor's Poor Servants of the Mother of God, was to take up residence in Rome.[133] This, she hoped would bring some ease to the demands being placed upon her little band. Taylor had come to Rome to seek approbation of their rule, and had received an invitation from Leo XIII to "settle in the English quarter [and] look to the English."[134] They too elected to stay, and set up house at 16 Via S. Sebastiano where they established a laundry: "in order that the sisters might support themselves, and at the same time offer a means of livelihood to a few poor women and girls."[135] To help the community settle in, Potter and her community "took little useful items for the sisters," and wrote to Elizabeth Bryan of the support the community could offer:

> It is a good thing as really there is more to be done that we can do. I think we have done some good by letting it be known what need there is of active work in Rome. I do not think it was realised before the amount of proselytism etc. going on…I have taken the opportunity of the sisters coming from the Poor Servants to bring ours out with them…[136]

Financial burdens were simply part of the struggles for congregations seeking to gain approval from Rome. While Taylor held the patronage of Lady Georgiana Fullerton, money was scarce, and unless supported by the philanthropy of wealthy patrons, there was a struggle to survive, particularly when other foundations or houses also needed support. For Potter and her small band, there was a constant pressure. Hyson Green and its expanding community needed finances and while work was multiplying in Italy, and a good number of their patients were wealthy, not all contributed to the care they received. Delay in payment meant delay in the ability of the community to pay its own bills, or fund new enterprises, as Potter noted to Elizabeth Bryan:

The cases are sometimes slow in paying. Count Moore has never paid yet…We have three sisters in Florence. The cases pay well there. The Dr., I think, presses for it. We got into disgrace before, taking sisters for Rome, but what is to be done? We must have money. They do press for a foundation in Florence, but who have I for Mother, that is the difficulty, or else there is, in every way, a grand field in Florence…. [137]

In the beginning of 1886 Potter was contacted by the Misses Murray, Scottish Presbyterian women who were residents of Florence. If a community were to be established in that city, they told Potter, they would make available the sum of £2000stg. to assist in the establishment of the mission.[138] The generosity of the gift overwhelmed Potter, and she decided to accept the offer, and requested Mother Cecilia to commence the foundation:

Mother wrote to me giving me the blessing of obedience and told me to first of all see the Archbishop of Florence…and to take with me a certain holy lady (English) but who lived in Florence and she would interpret for me, for I knew no Italian… His Grace received us with much affection and having heard all about our work and the spirit of the Little Company gave his permission to begin at once in the Diocese of Florence, he blessed it and hoped God's blessing would rest upon it. This lady (Miss Ram) was most kind in going round to the different offices for the various permissions etc…

Then I let the good Misses Murray know, and they who were anything but demonstrative folk clapped their hands and offered at once to find a place for us and help in every possible way they could.[139]

The "good Misses Murray" found an apartment on the top of a house in Via del Campuccio, Florence. Filthy-dirty and in need of some hard cleaning, the "one redeeming feature" was the view from the windows of the Torrigianni Villa.[140] With the aid of the youngest of the Murray sisters who was called "Mother Abbess" by the others,[141] the apartment was cleaned and furnished with the assistance of rich and poor alike:

…things [arrived] from friends in the shape of various items of furniture; small carts with boys appeared down in the street, and our neighbours heads [sic]were out of windows on every side … one small girl brought us a little Persian kitten, with 'tante complimenti' from her mother and offered to do anything we wanted…one lady gave us a nice clock, another a bowl of gold-fishes and a rather handsome tablecloth.[142]

So Florence was established. A small community of sisters established themselves and began their nursing practices. In the December of the same year, an "English mission" was commenced as part of the foundation. The mission, which provided use of the convent chapel, lectures, spiritual instruction and the services of a priest to the local residents, proved so successful that the ecclesial authorities offered Potter a small church off the Via San Guiseppe, for the "English Church" in Florence. Whilst willing to take responsibility for the organisation of the mission, Potter was unwilling to take responsibility for the church, preferring instead to find an English priest to claim it as his "parish" in the winter months which brought so many visitors. As she recorded in her notes:

> I went to Florence, took the house in via Ferruccio and commenced the English sermons, which I had long contemplated. The Jesuits at Fiesole had promised to preach, but for some reason or other seemed not able to comply. I wrote without any particular reason to Monsignor Harrington Moore, whom I met a few times…he had tried the same thing on the Riviera, but through some jealousy had not been able to succeed. For some two of three winters, he remained with us, and his preaching gained some notable converts. The present Church of San Guiseppe was offered to us and we, thinking more good might be done if a proper English mission were established, offered it to Monsignor Moore, who after some consideration accepted the offer.[143]

It was an outreach vital to Potter's understanding of the evangelical thrust of the institute. Teaching, instructing and providing opportunity for an education in the faith she held so dear was also reflected in the constitutions of the community. There it was stated that the entire institute was dedicated to:

> work for the conversion of sinners, and for the reception of heretics and infidels into the bosom of the church by visiting, exhorting and helping those who require help, but always in co-operation and under the direction of the Priest of the Parish in which they live.[144]

It was an evangelical fervour that would prove hard to maintain as expansion continued, hierarchical control increased, and internal problems continued to beset the order.

As 1885 moved into 1886, the tensions in Hyson Green were again mounting. The bishop, angered by changes to the rule which undercut his authority as superior, established the principles for a separate novitiate, and gave a relative autonomy to the founder, began a new muttering of complaint. Friction between himself and Mother Elizabeth Bryan was a constant irritation, the sister replacing Mother Raphael as Novice Mistress he considered a source of great dissent, and there were outstanding financial difficulties associated with Hyson Green and the surrounding missions.[145] To cap the situation, Francis White was still creating problems within and without the community and the bishop seemed powerless to do anything about his protegée.[146] Potter, he believed, should come home and set things to right.

In the event, she did return to Hyson Green but only for a short time. The authorisation of the constitutions in May of 1886 meant that the way was now clear for Potter and her first companions to make their final profession in a formally established religious congregation. In the light of the problems existing in Hyson Green, Potter made the decision to return to England, where she and Mothers Philip Coleridge, Cecilia Smith and Agnes Bray could make their final vows with their old companion, Mother Elizabeth. The new Mother General and her companions gathered in the chapel at Hyson Green on the September 17 and Bishop Bagshawe, his peevishness forgotten in the power of the liturgical moment, received the final profession of the five women he had first welcomed into his diocese nine years previously.[147]

Following her profession, Potter now acted with the authority of her new status as Mother General. To the chagrin of the bishop, she withdrew sisters from the branch houses, dismissed from the congregation several unsatisfactory subjects, including Mother Francis White, and consolidated the novitiate.[148] That task achieved, she turned to the recurrent request to establish a house in Ireland.

Count Arthur Moore, anxious to fulfil the vow he made on his wife's illness, came to visit Potter in Hyson Green. His consultation with clergy in Ireland had found that Bishop O'Dwyer of Limerick was willing to receive the sisters. There was possibility of a hospital – albeit abandoned and in need of renovation – for the sisters to staff and run. Here they would provide the "all but voluntary labour" to staff an institution paid for out of tax-payers' money. They would have no control over finances, nor over management. It was a good option for O'Dwyer, for, as Clear points out, nuns cost less than lay nurses "and they never complained about pay."[149]

Negotiations commenced and, following Potter's return to Rome in 1886, dragged on through 1887. Agreement was finally reached that the foundation would take place in 1888. Six sisters were to be provided to staff the hospital and the bishop and the hospital board were to provide an annual sum of £100 for their services.[150] In the summer of 1888, Potter again returned to England and, when further delays and an altercation occurred in Limerick between the new superior, Mother Veronica, and Bishop O'Dwyer,[151] Potter made the decision to go to Ireland and attempt to sort out the difficulty. There she experienced at first hand not only the excitability of the Irish, but also the depth of their passion and politics regarding successive injustices in the Land Acts. In the long-running war between government-backed landlords and rebellious Land League tenants, Irish sensibilities had been affronted by an intervention of Leo XIII regarding the use of lawful and unlawful means to settle political disputes. As an English woman, Potter was fair prey for the Irish nationals, particularly when she dared to defend the papal intervention, or implicitly to condemn Irish policy:

> A holy and learned young priest took up some remark I made about the land league. I saw his face cloud, and he said: "I have never approved of the land league myself, but I should not like, for that reason, to disapprove it in others." I said "Father, you must dis-approve what the Holy Father disapproves." "It is not the Holy Father," he said, and like many other said, "He should not interfere in politics." "You have not read his let-ter… he says you are quite right to strive for your lawful right, but you must do it by lawful means…We were talking in the meadows, and a man working at a lime-kiln stopped to listen. I did not mind his hearing but it was not wise in those days, as the event proved…A night or two after, we were at Recreation in the evening. I was on my couch and the Sisters were practising at the other end of the room. I could not get them to understand what I was saying, and did what I rarely do, rose up from my couch…a report sounded, and a large piece of metal was shot onto the couch where I had been

lying. The report and the light was worse, evidently through having in some way caught the gas and a large piece of piping was also shot on to the couch. We all looked at one another and they left off playing as may be imagined and cowered round the turf fire. Whether a ladder had been made use of, which was outside the window, whilst the men were scraping the walls, we never knew and we never went out to see. It was a matter we tacitly seemed to understand we would never speak of. [152]

In spite of political terrorism and priestly prevarication, St. John's was finally opened on October 10, 1888. Soon after the opening, Potter was ordered home to Rome, ill once more. However, her problems with Ireland, the Irish and Bishop O'Dwyer were not yet done.

As Catriona Clear notes, Bishop O'Dwyer's despotism provided much heartache for the first superior, Mother Veronica, and the *Annals* of the community are testimony to his terse accusations of disobedience, disruption and negligence.[153] In 1892–3, he earned the ire of Mary Potter, when, on being approached to give the mandatory letter or recommendation for final approval of the institute, he refused to do so, on the basis that "he would like [it] to be more under Episcopal control."[154] Potter, was not about to surrender the Irish foundation to the hands of a bishop who, she believed, neither valued what a religious was, nor supported their endeavours. Tired of the dispute and the lack of co-operation exhibited by O'Dwyer, she instructed her deputy, Mother Catherine Croker, on how to approach the man:

> I think you had better call on Bp. O'Dwyer and ask formally for the letter of recommendation for the final approval. If he refuses, then put it to him plainly, that "a house divided cannot stand." If we are not in harmony with our Bishop we would rather not remain, but would pray first, then part in peace, leaving it to his sense of justice what indemnity should be given for what we brought to the Diocese…One thing I must tell you. Keep to our principles and idea of perfection. I do not think I mistake the Bishop when I say that I do not think he has an idea of a noble nun. I have reason for what I say. He would attribute motives that you children would never think of. Therefore, I want you to be firm with him and show him that it is no import to us to have a large Hospital or building, but we want to be where we can do good and carry out most perfectly our Rules. That we have not ambition in our works. I cannot understand what kind of nuns he has been intimate with, but it seems to me he must have known some little-minded ones. I can say that after the various tussles we had had together, he came to say goodbye the night before we left and seems much affected, apologized for anything, and then, shaking hands, said, "You were right Rev. Mother, and I was wrong"…Simply ask for his letter, the others have already sent theirs in.[155]

O'Dwyer would give his consent, but, as Liedel points out, such personality clashes could be expected between bishops and strong-minded women religious, and Potter, for all her physical infirmity, was far from mental vapidity.[156] Her fundamental concern lay with the maintenance of the spirit and the charism of the institute, and the clash of wills between herself and O'Dwyer was representative of the problems she would continue to find as congregational expansion continued.

On the April 24, 1893 the decree of final approbation was signed, and the constitutions given for perpetuity. There were few changes. No recognition was given to the Little Company of Mary as a religious institute, the one concession being that the sisters now made public "profession" of vows. Perhaps the most significant change was that those who desired to leave the congregation after either temporary or perpetual profession now had to seek permission from the Holy See.[157]

In the same year, a foundation was made in the United States in Chicago. In 1894 sisters were sent to Malta. By the end of 1896 three new houses had opened in the diocese of Westminster, and Australia had opened another new venture.[158] A foundation in Fiesole was established in 1899, as was a further house in Adelaide, Australia, and a South African foundation was begun in 1902. In 1905, a second Irish house was opened in the parish of Fermoy, in the diocese of Cloyne. In Rome the pressure for a hospital continued so that by 1907 Potter and her community had built a hospital and Mother House in San Stefano Rotondo. In twenty-eight years, the community had expanded beyond anything Potter had imagined.

One foundation in particular delighted her, that of Commercial Road, in the East End of London. At the invitation of Cardinal Vaughan, a mission house was established in the parish of St. Mary and St. Michael in 1896. Based among the poor, the little community sought to minister to those whose lives William Booth had typified as "a population sodden with drink, steeped in vice, eaten up by every social and physical malady, these are the denizens of Darkest England."[159] There the sisters carried out a variety of works, and the house was open to those who needed to come for food, help or support. In Potter's eyes, it was an expression of what one of "Our Lady's homes" was to be – a place of refuge for the wayfarers of the world. They were to be fed, housed and cared for as honoured guests.[160] The sisters "visited the sick, collected alms for the poor, fed the hungry nursed the dying, did moral rescue work among women and children."[161] It was a foundation begun with some excitement, as anti-Catholic sentiment and the conviction that convents were snares for innocent and reluctant womanhood was a persistent sentiment in Protestant England, even as late as 1896.[162]

The night before the opening on January 20, 1896 Mother Catherine Crocker and her companion Sister de Sales were preparing for the opening Mass when they discovered that the windows of the room they were preparing for a chapel opened directly onto the street. Mother Catherine, feeling that such high visibility was "not quite desirable in the rough and rather curious neighbourhood,"[163] undertook to remedy the situation. Having no time to purchase opaque glass, or to put curtains across the windows, the two founding sisters set to work at a makeshift solution. As the *Annals* record it:

> Mother Catherine thought of "frosting" the glass with whiting dabbed on with a cloth. They set to work, and when it grew dark, lit the gas. The door bell rang vigorously and to their surprise there was a stalwart policeman on the doorstep, who told them they better put out the gas, as the people in the street said there were two nuns…trying to

escape and were signalling for help; to the Sisters' horror there was a crowd of excited people outside the gate, who apparently had insisted on the policeman coming to rescue them.[164]

Life in Commercial Road would continue to provide its own excitement, none more so when enthusiasm to save the souls of the urban poor involved the community in unusual ways. House-to-house help, feeding the hungry, nursing the sick and clothing those in need brought their own rewards to the community, but excitement was added when the curate of the local parish, Father Amigo (later to become bishop of Southwark diocese) or the Jesuit Father Bernard Vaughan came of an evening. These were exponents of the art of "street-preaching", and their energies were directed to those living within the warrens of courts and alleys of London.[165] The two men would arrive at the convent:

> borrow the community bell, a long suffering harmonium on wheels, the organist to play, and the rest of the community to sing hymns, and all would go off to some court or alley of the worst reputation leaving one of the community at home to mind the house and have some hot cocoa ready for the missioners when they returned. The Father would go ahead ringing the bell, and when a sufficient crowd was collected, the harmonium was put up against a wall, a hymn was sung, and the priest standing on a box would deliver a stirring sermon.[166]

If no conversions are recorded as a result of such theatre, there can be little doubt the sight of bell-ringing black-clad clergy and a gaggle of blue-veiled nuns brought laughter if not devotion to the darkness of "outcast" London. Commercial Road was the place where Potter's love for the poor found its satisfaction and, next to Hyson Green, was perhaps the truest expression of the mission work of the Little Company of Mary. Following her last visit to Commercial Road (and England) in 1899 she wrote of its effect on her:

> There is something in mixing with the poor which brings us close to God, and after my return from Rome, with all its grandeurs and graces, with the constantly seeing the Holy Father, with the holy priests who are true friends, the visiting the shrines, the bodies of Saints, the magnificent functions of the Church – with all this – when I went again among the poor, I said, "Life is worth loving" as I carried one little thing or another to relieve the sick and brought the love of God into their souls.[167]

Expansion did not come without its own cost. As the community spread across the world, Potter was faced with the enormous challenge of maintaining a spirit of unity within the cultural differences, and of ensuring that continuity with the founding vision, or essential spirit, of the congregation was maintained. Her considerations of potential expansion and the need to retain control of the institute, had led her to chose a highly centralised form of governance based upon that of the Society of Jesus. As Mother General of her congregation, Potter was charged with "the care of the Observance of the Rule and fervour in the whole Congregation that she governs."[168] Supported by a council of five, her authority over the congregation was absolute. "Her authority is full and entire over all the houses, the superiors and the members of the Institute."[169] To her and her council was reserved "all negotiations concerning new Houses and the extension and commencement of the Congregation." She was the one to "treat with the Ecclesiastical Authorities… examin[ing] deliberately … the propositions made to her, [assuring] herself before all that the Sisters will be able to observe their Rule and will not want necessaries."[170] To maintain unity and preserve the traditions of the community, she was to "keep herself informed of all that passes of importance in the different houses of the Institute." She was to do this by "a correspondence carried on with all the Provincial and Local Superiors," and through this means, "help the Superiors by her Counsels, reprehend them for their failings correct their faults and console from time to time."[171] It was a formidable undertaking, and with the dispersion of the community across continents, one that became increasingly frustrating, as the mission foundations themselves expanded. It was an undertaking necessary if the unity of the spirit and the charism of the institute were to be kept intact.

The separation between local communities and their Mother House gave a distinct advantage to local bishops. Distance provided a barrier between the control and influence of powerful leadership, and many a local bishop, having invited a religious community into his diocese, then sought to force it to operate in the way he considered best.[172] Thus, Cardinal Moran, for all his commitment to the document he signed to preserve the integrity of the first Australian foundation, pressured the community in numerous ways. In March 1886, less than one year after their arrival, the community was approached by Moran and told that "he was presenting a hundred acres of land at Pennant Hills for [a] hospital, and that he was very anxious for us to begin building soon."[173] The sisters refused the offer, on the grounds of its being "too far away for patients to come."[174] Another offer was made of land closer to the city of Sydney. "Fearful that they might fall under the Cardinal's greater displeasure the community accepted this offer."[175] The foundation stone was laid in October 1886, and by 1889 the first wing of the hospital was opened and blessed.[176] The following year saw the opening of an "Institute for the Female Insane." Soup kitchens and a women's refuge were opened in 1894, and in 1899 an institute for the blind. All of these works were undertaken at the instigation of Moran, who, according to Sister Brigid Rosser "urged us so earnestly to do it, we just had to do it."[177] And it was done, with the support of wealthy Catholic patrons, but without the permission or the knowledge of the Mother General.

For women like Brigid Rosser, a daughter of Dublin, it was all terribly exciting and stimulating. "Grand Social Reunions" (fundraising) took place, where "The Prince of the church, the King's Representatives, the Elite, the homely, ever generous subscribers…enjoy the sunshine of each others presence."[178] It was, however, a long way from Lenton Street, Hyson Green, or the shambles of Nottingham, where Sister Brigid had begged for food for the poor. It was a long way from Potter's own understanding of what the Australian mission was established to do, and how it was to operate, as she informed the mission leader, Mother Raphael Byrne Farrar:

> [N]ow comes news of a Night-refuge to be opened and no word spoken in Council. A sister to be removed – no Council taken. Now I cannot have this! If you do not know your Rules you have had sufficient letters written blaming you for acting and undertaking works without the blessing of Obedience, asking permission as your Rule prescribes. You acknowledged you were wrong, making excuses for the distance and time to get an answer... You are told to take Council together on the spot, and if thought well to decide at once, leave [is] given. You act independently and evidently have not faith in Council as you should have....[179]

Moran, as Potter well recognised, was a man driven by the needs of his own diocese, and very conscious of his own episcopal powers. "A Bishop who is wedded to his diocese," she wrote to Mother Raphael:

> is bound in duty to look to that before all things else, as likewise a superior of a community has to look to her community and its good before the good of the diocese... the two duties must certainly come into collision unless a Bishop has diocesan Sisters, that is, Sisters who are founded for the good the diocese, which some bishops have... The two opposite duties, of a Bishop looking to his diocese and a Superioress to her community must come into collision unless the duties are well defined before they are located within a diocese.[180]

Moran and his brother bishops expected blind obedience from "the good sisters" and when it was not forthcoming, were not above applying pressure. In 1895, Moran threatened to close all houses operated by the Little Company of Mary if the founder persisted in her demand that delegates be sent to the General Chapter in 1896.[181] That threat brought censure from Propaganda. In 1899 he again sought to control the institute by informing the local communities that no sister could be admitted to the congregation, receive the habit of religion or move to another diocese without his prior consent.[182] Again, Propaganda was called to defend the integrity of the congregation. They chastised Moran for his interference, and reminded him of his previously given promise:

> It is true, concerning this meritorious society, that you have tried to form a Community separate from the Mother House. Your Eminence will remember that in one of your letters written in Rome on 10 August, 1885, to the Superior General, you expressed in these terms, translated from the English – "If your Sisters come to establish a house of your Religious Community in Sydney, I believe it is just, according to your request, to put in writing that I have given a guarantee in words, that nobody shall make me separate from the Mother House, the community which is to be established in Sydney, or in other districts of New South Wales, under my jurisdiction.[183]

Threat and counter-threat, as Liedel notes, was part of a process of role definition, and episcopal hierarchy often found itself at loggerheads with the power of a mother general.[184] Religious women were valued not for the spiritual realities their lives might represent, nor for the charismatic integrity of their vision of the Christian life. They were resources necessary to local churches to provide a visible, institutional and cohesive Catholicity. In their desire to build up the resources of their own diocese, it was not uncommon for bishops or their clergy to suggest, threaten, or cajole members of a community to separate from its parent stem and place themselves under local authority.[185] The Australian foundation of the Little Company of Mary was to provide Potter with just such heartache in 1895, as five members of the community, supported by local clergy, considered separating from the parent stem.[186] Propaganda was again called in and the tensions eased, but the fact that it occurred at all was an indication of the lengths to which local ecclesiastics would go to ensure their control over the much-needed works of women religious.

As founder, Mary Potter had sought to avoid some of the difficulties of the mission communities, by building a principle of subsidiarity into the constitutions. Believing that a united community had its own spiritual resources, she had established the principle whereby local councils (communities) could discern together when immediate decisions were to be made. Without abrogating the right of the superior general, local "Provincial Vicaresses" together with their "consulters" could "take Council [sic] together on the spot, and if thought well to decide at once, leave given."[187] When that principle was not followed, and independent decisions taken by a local superior or "vicaress," Potter considered it a betrayal of the right of the community to discern and decide appropriate courses of action. Perhaps motivated by her own experience of the dissension caused within the Hyson Green community when Mother Elizabeth acted independently of the rest of the community, Potter refused to permit similar independent courses of action on the part of others. As Mother Raphael Byrne Farrar had discovered to her discomfort, failure to live out the unity of purpose by common discernment and decision-making earned a sharp rebuke.

Historians of religious life, Ewens, Clear, Magray and Thompson among them, have all alluded to the difficulties experienced by women religious transposed from their own cultures and inserted into the mission of local churches.[188] Distanced from the Mother House, subject to political, social and religious pressures and expectations different from those in their country of origin, religious women were sent out to mission foundations, and often found themselves in conflicted situations. Yet, those who established the foundations also suffered tension. How could the spirit be maintained in the distant foundations? How were new recruits – born of different time, circumstance and place – to be "enculturated" to a community whose origins were significantly different? Centralised government undoubtedly presented major problems for local churches and mission communities, but it was also a problem for mothers general. However, it was Potter's conviction that only a highly centralised model of governance could protect the spirit of the institute, ensure a degree of freedom from the depredation and manipulation of local clergy, and maintain what Thompson identifies as "the right to follow their particular rule and to live out their distinctive charism."[189]

Consolidation and Commitment

As tensions with local episcopal governance and clerical interference increased, the need for unity permeated many of Potter's interventions. Sisters who were discontented began to grumble and complain, and won supporters in their criticism of the demands made upon them. In 1891–2, scandal and dissension from within the community caused great pain to those close to Potter. A Doctor Thompson of Nottingham took a strong dislike to the order and let it be known that he had set up a fund for any sister who wanted to leave.[190] Two of the sisters, unhappy with their superiors, had found in him a ready ear for complaint and, with his encouragement, one left. Accusations regarding Potter, her illness and her treatment of the sisters made their way to Rome and a "bank" was established for any in the Roman houses who wanted to be quit of such an onerous life.[191] Such accusations and defections brought Mother Philip Coleridge close to despair. When another sister left, "and incurred in the house a debt of £300 to £400 stg., and in another house a debt of £100 stg.," Coleridge wrote in anguish to her confessor:

> we have no money to pay it or meet bills – Father, if it is a sign of love this cross, our Lord must indeed love us… [I] do feel tempted sorely…one cross comes with another, each harder and more painful to bear…Poor Rev. Mother, God tries her and she is so patient – but I rebel.[192]

Mother Cecilia, another of the first companions, also suffered. As the tensions became obvious she too wrote to Monsignor Kirby:

> Miss Brady has now put aside our Habit, and is attired as a secular. The Card. Vicar commanded this under pain of further excommunication, and I believe she had to present herself to the "Cardinal Penitentiary" poor unfortunate child and yet she can say she is perfectly happy – but she has nearly broken our Mother's heart – her statements have been so untrue, and she certainly has tried to injure our Little Company…She is still here in Rome, I fear she means to stay on which will make it most unpleasant for us – we hear daily such sad things and we find all this evil commenced through herself and another sister acting deceitfully – going about telling seculars they were unhappy and asking their advice, at the same time speaking of supposed abuses in the convent which never existed at all. They also said the Rule was not being kept…Poor Rev. Mother is so crushed with all of this, at the same time so patient, loving and forgiving towards this poor child.[193]

When Miss Brady (Sister Guiseppe) was finally released from her vows, the founder expressed her sorrow to Mother Cecilia:

> God bless my children all…I felt your sympathy. I cannot trust myself to write much or Mother Philip Catherine and Michael, who are out for an airing, would return and find what I cannot bear my children to see – tears…She is gone, she is to me as one I loved dead, whom we remember to think of, to speak of only of what is good, but she has shown me how Jesus loves all. This sad sorrow had made me understand better the

love of dear Jesus for sinner, for despite what has passed, I love better, or know better how I loved my poor lost child.[194]

The truth of it was that many women who entered the Little Company found it difficult and demanding. Immense fortitude was necessary to enter the homes of the sick, the dying, and the poor. Risk of personal contagion was high, and the sheer drudgery of caring for others, sometimes on a twenty-four hour basis, for days on end, drained the spirit. Potter, for whom illness and suffering was a window of opportunity, a moment for pastoral care of the soul, knew that without a strong personal life of prayer, a genuine vocation to the life, the carer herself suffered.

The Contemplative Spirit of the Institute

From the outset, Potter had sought to create a process of formation in which a meaningful relationship with God could develop. Prepared by seclusion from the world in a semi-monastic environment marked by strong discipline and a life of intense prayer, the women of the institute who were called to mission work would be grounded in God.[195] Selfless dedication to the cause of saving souls could not be achieved without the necessary correlative of recognition of a self-hood. And the reality of self-hood, for Potter, came from discovering the self as in God. The congregational spirituality – the "Path of Mary" – was the means of such grounding and thus provided the basis for true self-realisation. Potter's conviction was that, having the mantle of a strong-minded spirituality, the moral authority of one's own experience of God, and a strong linkage with the spirit and charism of the institute the women would be protected from the destructive forces of inadequacy, doubt, and fear. It was a belief that links to the theological view held by Karl Rahner who states that "without any experience of God, however non-thematic and non-reflective in character, experience of the self is absolutely impossible."[196]

Where such self-definition was not present, problems of adjustment occurred. Where there was a lack of charity, a spirit of dissent, nervous illness, or physical addiction – to alcohol, morphine and other drugs and stimulants – there was a question of spiritual and psychological aptitude to live the life. Quite simply it was hard, and not all were called to it. Holiness was not the prerogative of the cloister. "We could consecrate ourselves to God's service without becoming religious," she told her sisters, but as religious, they were called to be "the immensity of God bound in a body."[197] Not all could bear the burden of such reality. Not all wanted it. But for Potter it was the reality of religious life in general and the life of the Little Company of Mary in particular, for it described the fundamental option of the spirituality of De Montfort that Potter had adopted for the institute. Only if the sisters could realise themselves as "nutshells encasing God"[198] could they bear the burden of the ministries asked of them among the sick, the poor, and the dying.

Within what Potter called the mission houses, or branch houses, where local needs and the demands of the mission required the members to be out among the people, the ordinary rule could not be kept in its entirety.[199] Exempt from the full round of silence, personal prayer, and community devotions, the life of a mission sister was intense and unless the sisters' lives could reflect the integration and essential unity between contemplation and action, the works would continue to pressurise and bring conflict.

Potter's own religious experiences determined her position. She had learned through her own journey that the dialectic of the mystical life was not a withdrawal from the world, but an integration within it. Reflective of the belief of philosophers such as Wapnick and Hocking,[200] the concept of the mystical life she espoused for the institute was a renunciation:

> not of the world, but merely [the] attachments and needs relating to it…once…able to abandon these dependent social needs and …freed of the pull of the social world, he experiences the freedom to live within society in conjunction with his inner strivings, other than experiencing society's customs and institutions as obstacles to …self-fulfilment.[201]

Potter's perception of the necessary dialectic between contemplation and action was expressed in the term "liberty of spirit." Liberty of spirit was achieved by entering the mystical "path of Mary," by ridding oneself of "the spirit of the world," but not the world itself, and living within the intimacy of relationship with God who was present within his own creation.[202] Her instructions on living the spiritual life were many and reflected her own belief that freedom from worldliness gave the essential freedom to love the world:

> if we strive to guard our heart that no earthly love usurps the place of our Heavenly Lover, our God; if we keep a worldly spirit away from our souls that God's Spirit may live there. It is easy to give admittance to a foreign spirit, to set up some idol in our hearts – not Jesus who alone should be the God of our hearts, and when we do this we cannot echo God as we should… If we put some substance between a magnet and a needle, the needle cannot fly to the magnet… Let us beware, let us be on our guard…[so] there will be no barrier between us and God.[203]

In their lives of intimate relationship with God, she advised her sisters, they were to imitate Moses on the Mountain of Sinai.[204] Like him, they were to plead for the people of Israel (the suffering of the world), and have the audacity to ask to see the face of God.[205]

The promise to the members of the institute was that they too would see God's glory and, filled with that vision, go back down the mountain, "magnificent with the power of God within them."[206] Living lives of "holy familiarity," they, like Moses, would brook no refusal of mercy from God, their love for the glory of God reflected in each particle of creation would become "the moving power of this world." [207]

Such a life demanded time to develop, and Potter had fought hard and long to gain the right to have a formation adequate to the task. While the community was "not [to be] afraid of admitting postulants," it was also not to be afraid "of keeping them too long in their state of probation when you have the slightest doubt whether they are suited to follow Mary to Calvary."[208] All members of the institute were to enter the path of Mary and were to renew themselves in the spirit of the devotion on an annual basis.[209] Formation was flexible in that it would:

> vary according to the individual character, but it may not be less than three years and it may extend in many or most cases to five or six years, it being most essential that Sisters … should have a very deep foundation of religious virtue, or they might dwindle into mere nurses and the beauty of the true religious pass from them. This may easier happen with Sisters whose vocation calls them away from the restrictions of convent life than with those who do not quit their convent, therefore the need of a more than ordinary long Novitiate with us.[210]

Though the aim was laudable, there was a persistent refusal on the part of the church to hear arguments regarding the specificity of this particular expression of religious life. As the church began its process of providing a canonical framework that would be applied to all women's institutes of religious life, the specificity of particular forms of the life was ignored. There was gendered bias. Women religious could not extend the time of temporary profession in cases of doubtful candidature, or in those instances where a longer period of formation was needed or considered beneficial. This was not the same for some male orders. Moreover decisions made by the community regarding the suitability of candidates to make vows, could be overturned by male clerics. It was an issue that pained Potter. The problems that resulted were not only detrimental to the women themselves but difficult and painful for the community to bear. There *were* particular tensions in the life of this blended institute, and they needed particular care and controls:

> As so many sisters in our life might get nervous or other complaints which would make it unwise making perpetual vows (it is not kind to themselves also), the brain may become confused, the will enfeebled through physical complaints so common in the present day, and if it is through work or during work in the convent, it is not fit to send the sisters into the world, but bear with them, as we do our own family…if we had the same power as the Jesuits of reserving perpetual vows we might not have allowed them to make perpetual. Bridget too we seemed forced to let make perpetual vows, though we did not want to, with that sad habit, and she has again relapsed, either drugs or drink.[211]

A fierce tenderness drove Mary Potter to cherish, chastise, and rule her sisters. They had been called to "offer their lives in union with the great Victim of us all,"[212] and the fundamental orientation of the order was not to be manipulated. The community had been established to "stand at the portals of the world," and no bishop, no cardinal, no work was to take away from the centrality of the mission to save souls.

"Our Lady's spirit," she wrote to Mother Cecilia, was not to "[dwindle] away to please the Bishop."[213] And the complexities of that spirit reflect much of the paradox of Potter's own life and understanding of the place of women within the church. She was caught between the politics and the paradox of submission and self-determination; between respectable surface and inner rebellion. Using the power and authority given her by highly personal and idiosyncratic religious experience, she had formed a body of women around a notion of maternal care – but a maternal care surrounded by military metaphor. Controlling and manipulating the social image of maternity and motherhood, the women, dedicated to emulating the maternal love of Jesus, and imitating the maternal love of Mary, were warrior-mothers. The world was a battlefield across which these women walked – disciplined, "immaculate," and powerful in the cause of the kingdom:

> We may have become somewhat nerveless, passively submitting and going our way quietly, but needing a spur to remind us that "the kingdom of heaven suffereth violence" and "the violent alone shall bear it away." Yes, we must do violence for the sake of the those who are threatened with losing their immortal souls. We must go out onto the battlefield, we must pick up the wounded and anoint them. We must bring to them the treasures of the Precious Blood. The merits of the Sacred Humanity of Jesus are at our disposal. We must bring them to all around and we must plead with the Eternal Father, by the Passion of Jesus, by his passion and death, to show mercy to the world.[214]

Doing "violence for the sake of the kingdom" meant, where necessary, standing against the manipulations of clerical authority. Mary Potter well understood the gendered dynamics that occurred between religious women and the economically, socially and politically powerful bishops who ran the dioceses. Her experience with Bagshawe, O'Dwyer and Moran demonstrated a growing awareness of their capacity to denude and denigrate women's capacity to serve, guide, and rule in their own right. There is no doubt that she used both her position as a religious and her religious beliefs to extend her control and influence over the men who sought to manipulate her.[215]

Alienated from authority within the church by virtue of her sex, she used the power of ecclesial authority to defend her rights and the rights of those under her. The Rule, and the church authorities that approved it, became the means of countering the tendency of local bishops to control the women of the institute. "Are we then to suppose that the church approves a Rule which she does not expect to be obeyed?" she wrote to Cardinal Moran,[216] and echoed the same sentiment to Propaganda. The intent is clear, Moran is to be as obedient to the prescripts of the church as the women themselves:

> Why should the Church approve a Rule which cannot be kept? Why should his Eminence Cardinal Moran say – this Sister or that shall have this or that office – when the Rule expressly order the officials to be elected within … the Company itself?[217]

Working between the polarities of submission and autonomy, Potter manipulated systems and people in the cause of what she presented as a "divine imperative." Without desiring to impute motives beyond those that she herself honestly perceived, her sense of her own at-one-ness with her God empowered her action. "I cannot but feel I have had a call from God," she had written to Monsignor Virtue in 1874, and that call, with its inner compulsion, was to bring to birth within the church an institute of religious life. Her fundamental and driving vision was that of the maternal love of Jesus for humanity. Theologically, it was this understanding of a particular window on the gospel that constituted the charism.[218] The maternal love of Jesus was to be incarnated in the lives of the members of the community, who in turn would take it to the world, and bring it to birth in others. This was the mission: this was the charism and the passionate self-sacrificing love and commitment that she expected from those women who were drawn to follow her. As Magray has pointed out, however, not all who entered a religious institute, possessed the same degree of passion or commitment as their strong-minded founders.[219] Nonetheless, Potter's determination was that a strong, disciplined body of women was necessary if the work of "ordering this world for God" was to be done.[220] Intelligence, education, and commitment were needed, and the constitutions framed the necessity, ensuring that all had requisite educational skills to undertake the works of the institute.[221]

This intellectual formation of the institute was to prove difficult, as a continuous flow of semi-literate and illiterate postulants had entered the community from its foundation.[222] Victims of a society in which a basic education for girls of the lower classes was a four year program of domestic skills, some reading, and religious education, they were, as Grainne O'Flynn points out, representatives of an insouciance regarding the education of women.[223] Potter, though convinced that "great good is done by showing but one soul the way of Mary," and unafraid of admitting postulants,[224] took it as an insult that "some priests have the unreasonable thought in sending us subjects that they need not be educated."[225] The egalitarian outlook of the congregation and the absence of demand for a dowry were possible inducements for some to enter religious life but there is room for suspicion that those who appeared docile and compliant contributed to clergy selection of candidates for they met a commonly held image of "good useful subjects", particularly when both nuns and nurses were seen as servants. Education for the "domestic" tasks of religious women and lay nurses was not deemed necessary, for as Margaret McCurtain points out, one of the perceptions that had to be combatted by Catholic women through the nineteenth century "was that the quality of recruitment of the general nurse was quite low."[226] Yet for Potter, education was necessary if the works of the order were to be performed intelligently and skilfully:

> Instruction, especially about all that is necessary for the purpose of the vocation to the Little Company of Mary, will not only make the sisters more useful to their neighbour, but will also help them much in the service of God and for their own perfection, if it be not separated from true humility.[227]

To encourage a love for learning as well as a desire for God, each house was encouraged to:

> put by a little time for sisters who are capable of study to read so as to be able to do good, and to know how to give an answer to 'the hope that is in us,' as we are told by the Holy Spirit.[228]

Letter after letter flowed from Potter's pen, encouraging, admonishing, and guiding individuals and communities. To one she commended the use of wine for her health;[229] to another the need to live in harmony with her rule: "for God will not ask you about hospitals and night refuges… but he will ask you if, in thought word and deed you strove to live your rule."[230] To puncture the arrogance and pharisaism of those who hid behind a judgmental piety, she reminded them of the frailty of human nature – and their own vulnerability to sin:

> You turn away with a shudder from a degraded woman, a tipsy man, a murderer. They are, however of the same flesh and blood as you. One touch of nature makes the whole world kin. You may be like them. You may be surprised into greater sins if you fight not with the lesser ones – but fight![231]

To those ashamed of being born poor, and revelling in their newfound status of religious life, she dealt a swift word of disgust at their lack of humility. There was no shame in being poor, she told the novices in Rome, but there was a certain shame in the want of the "truth" that was humility, in failing to recognise the fact.[232] To all she wrote of the need to "plunge into the abyss of loveliness, of joy, of power" that was God:[233] God who was "Father, Mother, Brother, Sister, Friend – All."[234]

Informed by her own insights into the relationship between God and humanity, Potter sought to bridge the gap she saw between living the integrity of the Christian life and the suffering world. Suffering, as she perceived it in Jesus, was the "touchstone of love." If the community were to be formed into a cohesive band of women dedicated to renewing their world, then they were to live according to the spirit of the institute. "A true spouse of Jesus must follow the Lamb of God on earth as much as she hopes to follow him in heaven," she wrote in *Brides of Christ*, and continued:

> Following means literally walking in another's footsteps, imitating their actions or being guided by their example. Following the Man of Sorrows therefore necessarily means a life of poverty, subjection and contradiction.[235]

The poverty, subjection and contradiction of this Man of Sorrows, was expressed for Potter in the three vows of religious life: poverty, chastity and obedience.[236] Traditionally accepted as the vows that defined religious life *per se*, they also represented the life of the disciple and were based on the scriptural invitations of Jesus to take up his cross, and follow him.[237] Not an end in themselves, but a framework for a way of life, the vows were subject to canonical definition, but also to shades of meaning and emphasis.[238] Potter emphasised two: the vows of poverty and obedience. These she situated in Jesus and the Cross, where she found both abject poverty and absolute obedience to the will of God:

> An order whose spirit and model is to be the spirit of Calvary, and has Calvary as its model, must practise poverty in its integrity and therefore its members, like poor people, must earn their living.[239]

Sharing a concept of poverty more in keeping with traditional mendicant orders, she sought to refuse ownership of property:

> I am now writing to you to tell you some one must have written you misleading you regarding my view of property holding in the Little Company of Mary. I am not anxious for the Community to possess property… We do not require to be owners of houses or lands. We offer to God the daily pains we encounter, and trust to him.[240]

Without the ties of property, the community was freed to go about the world "[doing] all that was required of them."[241] Obedience was a "sign of the Cross," and was a mechanism through which the mission of the institute could be carried out. "Dear Sisters," she wrote, "we can have no surer sign that we are living by the sweet spirit of Jesus and Mary, and being a delight to the Eternal Father than that we are zealous and obedient."[242] Obedience was to be practised ruthlessly, providing an opportunity to growth in the virtues necessary "to be fruitful."[243]

> What should we think of one who having been given money for the poor, spent it on herself? This is exactly what they do, who living in a community founded to save souls are not unselfish and zealous in their work, but use their graces only for their own good. Sisters of such type may save their own souls, but they will not help others to do so. They grow into selfish beings, and are no more like a generous devoted spouse of Jesus than a Pharisee was like an apostle. Exteriorly they may not be disedifying; they may love to be punctual, they may do their duties carefully, just as many worldly people acquit themselves of their social duties; but the burning zeal of souls, the heroic self-forgetfulness, the extreme generosity and the Christlike self oblation are wanting them.
> My sisters! I beg you not to relax! Spur yourselves on. Be not deceived by an specious reasoning such as "I must take care of my health for the community's sake; must be prudent for religion's sake"…Happy for us if we injure our health under obedience, or even shorten our lives through zeal for God. Indeed, we might lawfully pray to God to grant us the great gift of self-oblation.[244]

Self-oblation, expiation, the voluntary "self-offering" of the lives of the community, all speak of a theory of substitution – a belief in the positive power of offering one's life that others might have life.

Woman of the church

As a woman of the church, Potter's loyalties stood within traditional Catholicism. Aware of the trials of a church struggling to maintain its balance in a modernising world, she interpreted the political imperatives ranged against the papacy as a time when "the kings of the earth [have] stood up and leagued themselves against the anointed of the Lord, his vicar."[245] While sharing the devotional and defensive ultramontanism of her own period,[246] she also believed that "the church, the spouse of Christ, replicates within herself His life."[247] If the church was to enter more fully into this "share" of the passion, learn from it and grow through it, the virtues of the Cross were to be more fully realised in all its members.[248] Her Little Company, as a religious order – and thus part of the church – was to demonstrate the radical fidelity necessary, even in the hour of the Passion. In imitation of Mary, the Mother of Jesus, who "by God's appointment, stands out to us as Mother of God's children,"[249] it was to stand supportive of both Christ and the "apostles" (the church in all its members). In a clear statement of militant Catholicism Potter wrote that the Little Company of Mary was:

> [S]pecially bound to represent the Church, to stand up for it in its day of trouble, the time of its passion; the sad time which has now commenced, the worst of which indeed is yet to come. We are banded, vowed together for one special object. We know no distinction of nationality. We have left home and friends, we have put away even our individual selves, I mean all personal feelings and interests. We are resolved to fight for God and his interests in the day when the princes of this earth stand up to fight against him, to oppress, to crush, to kill, if possible, his church… We will prevent her children being lost to her, we will place ourselves at her portals, the death beds of her members. We will allow none to go forth for whom we have not prayed, for we will pray for all. We will plead before the throne of God.[250]

Just as the Mother of Jesus was "brought out of retirement" by the Passion of her son, the women of the Little Company of Mary were drawn from their "retirement" of prayer and contemplation to be "apostles to the apostles." Women in the church, they were to "[take it] upon themselves to help row Peter's Barque."[251] In a communion of labour they were to contribute to the mission of the church, evangelising, healing, ministering to those in need; they were "the lifeboat" of the church and had various missions to carry out. Bearers of the good news of Jesus' saving love to all – "from the Pope to the peasant"[252] – they were to emulate the women who remained faithful in the moment of Jesus' passion:

> In the time of our Lord's passion, the women seemed to gather strength and courage to face the world for his dear sake. We know the women of those times lived more retired than the women of the present day, and yet those women came boldly forth to follow Jesus whom they loved at the time when others forsook him. We likewise know that the holy women mentioned by the apostles laboured publicly with them, following them from place to place…Yes, my children, you must go forth into the world.[253]

Implicit in this statement is the belief in the moral superiority of women at a time of crisis. Their fidelity to Jesus, their courage at the cross and their compassion at the tomb made them bearers of good news to those who scurried fearful away. Again Potter moves close to that apocalyptic feminism described by Helsinger, Sheets and Verder, an image of woman as "saviour" ushering in a new era of community and love.[254]

"Going forth into the world," however, was to prove a problem. Even as Potter's enthusiasm for the task she believed allotted to her Little Company overflowed in her writings to her communities, changes both within and without the congregation were challenging the dynamic, apostolic call to evangelise. There was a growing tension within the order as nursing began to shape the image the sisters themselves held of the institute.

By 1906, with a membership of finally professed sisters numbering somewhere close to two hundred,[255] hospitals claimed the attention of sisters in Ireland,[256] Australia,[257] and Malta.[258] In the same year, the new Mother House of the Little Company of Mary opened in San Stefano Rotondo. A cruciform building, it housed the Roman novitiate and community, and a hospital wing, which finally fulfilled the hope for a "British hospital" that Leo XIII had expressed in 1882. It had a difficult birthing, for Potter's choice of a building site cut across the desire of Cardinal Merry del Val,[259] Mother Philip Coleridge and a number of other sisters, to build close to the Vatican. Potter, however, chose a site outside the city walls, amid "the hovels of the poor."[260] Her "grand plan" for the building was that it should be a place for the poor as well as rich, and that it was to be a training school for Italian women to learn nursing skills.[261] Whilst welcoming the thought of having a hospital, Mother Philip Coleridge was not enamoured of either of the other two aspects of Potter's plan. Once again turmoil and dissension broke out, with Mother Philip seeking to gain support of the community to overturn Potter's decision.[262] Potter, though barely able to walk and suffering from a painful malignant tumour of the shoulder, held out against pressures applied from both the Vatican and her community. Though the discord was perhaps even greater than that which had nearly destroyed the small community at Hyson Green, Potter stood against the pressure and the incipient ethnocentrism of the community, and slowly gained their approval to go ahead with her plans. Mother Cecilia Smith recorded her own distaste for the idea of a nursing school and of the:

> first ungovernable girls who presented themselves to train in our Nursing School of St. Gregory, and I may add here that very few of us wanted this School but Mother with her usual prophetic mind, saw far into the future and said, 'How much good would be done by it, and how many souls as well as bodies saved by a good band of religiously trained nurses'. All the same, many of us did not want the work, however, Mother with her usual sweet patience prevailed, and said 'Oh do be patient with these girls…be mothers to them'…The first probationers were very undisciplined and difficult to manage; they gave any amount of trouble at the commencement and tried our patience to the utmost. We would tell Mother that she must send these girls away, we could not put up with them any longer. In her own gentle way, she would say, 'send them to me', and they were sent to Mother's room. Meanwhile Mother would have something nice to give them, receive them as if they were 'angels', talk to them of God and our Lady and even ask them to sing to her. Then they would leave, promising to be very good, and so they were for a while. Mother begged us to be patient, assuring us that later on, we should have time to rejoice.[263]

If the building of the Mother House and the establishment of a nursing school created tension, Potter was far more concerned by a growing attitude among the community members that they should move away from the missionary role Potter had always valued, and become established in institutions. It was an attitude she believed would not only destroy the apostolic and missionary stance of the community, but also take away from the fundamental spiritual purpose of the institute. Yet, the signs were ominous that this was a trend that could not be easily stopped.

In 1902, the Vicar Apostolic of the Eastern Cape Colony (South Africa) had asked Potter for a foundation in Port Elizabeth. In 1904, a mission house was established in Prospect Hill. After four years of living in squalor and working among the poor of the district, the community moved to Walmer and quickly established a convent and small hospital capable of receiving twenty patients. England and America were far slower to move to institutional care,[264] but the shift was inexorable, and brought with it a lessening of the broad-based apostolic commitment Potter believed was essential to the charism.

As an adjunct to Potter's desire to pray for and, where possible, care for the dying, nursing had been an important aspect of the work of the community. As Potter saw her community expand across the world, and the trend towards institutional nursing care take root within the various communities, she once again wrote in defence of the spirit of the institute:

> God be praised, how wonderful are his ways; He gives us grace to have the joy of working for Him, but He most strictly requires correspondence with grace. We shall have to give an account of our stewardship... In a certain sense it is the same with out spiritual gifts, they are bestowed on us for a purpose. They must be used for the end which they were bestowed upon us, otherwise we make rapine in our holocaust. How is it in our religious life, we are simply bent on what regards our exterior, that we have merely to become perfect in nursing, we are very mistaken.
>
> In the commencement, the Sisters nursed and taught, they instructed and prepared children and others for the Sacraments; they explained to them the 'Path of Mary', they had them consecrated, and were proud at each fresh soul they placed in Our Lady's arms, and they would relate with joy the conquests they had made, and those whom they had gained to God.
>
> It does not make up to me for all this now, when I hear Sisters speaking of the grand cure they have made of some patients, whom the Doctor thought a hopeless case; of some successful operation, where their skillful attendance has been praised, and so on. Ah, no; it used to be a very different tale, though it is quite right, it is a duty in fact, to use all our energies in attending our patients and not disgrace Our Lady's habit. This we should do, and not leave the other undone, the grand work for which we are. We are not founded in God's Church simply to nurse, that is an addition. But we are founded to extend God's Kingdom on earth, by making Mary reign over the hearts and souls of men, and by striving in every way within our reach to help them in their last dread agony.[265]

Constantly she strove to maintain the charismatic and missionary impulse of the community. The work of prayer for the dying was essential and was based upon her own understanding of the experience of death conflated with her concern for those who faced that experience without knowledge of God's love and mercy:

> Devotion to the dying was a distinct inspiration. I had never seen anyone dying, or been mixed up with death in anyway, but I believe God had made me experience since what those 'agonies' are – what the word 'agonies' means. It is certainly not given to those moments when the soul has to severed from the body without meaning. Some years ago, on the Feast of St. Gertrude, these agonies apparently commenced. Those around me thought I was dying, though they knew not what I was going through. How describe? Suppose a member of the body – only out of place: This is agony until replaced. Now, is this can be imagined all over the body. A powerful, strong wave sweeping over the shrinking body and withdrawing the life partly – there is a vacuum – the sufferer is breathless and gasps – the life seeks to return, but another powerful wave sweeps again with resistless force, withdrawing still more of that life. Again and again comes that mighty wave. Ah! Pray! The suffering may be silent, and show nothing – too weak to give any sign of what is going on. The children of Faith know that their God is love – and that they must bow to him at this moment when his instituted penance for sin is being executed. They have a special Sacrament instituted to support this penance. But imagine a soul without faith, feeling this mighty power, knowing that an omnipotent being alone could withdraw from that tenement it has held so long. What might happen? May God avert it… Jesus, pity![266]

This dark vision, which of itself can be related to the Christian tradition as the death of the self, which is associated with mystical union, Potter translated to the dying.[267] Those "without faith" suffered the terror of the moment. These were the truly poor, who faced their ego-death without the hope of future life. Because "the hour of death may be and is… the hour of birth,"[268] the dying needed spiritual midwives, who were prepared to enter the labour of dying so that others might know life. Whilst it is true that in nineteenth-century thought, "angels 'do most especially minister" at a deathbed," as Michael Wheeler so aptly put it,[269] the members of the institute were not merely ministering angels, nurses bringing solace and comfort to the afflicted. They were missionaries, and their principal object in life was "to go about this beautiful world to draw God's creatures to love him. We have filled then the end of our creation."[270] Very close to apocalyptic feminism once again, the women of the institute were empowered to act as intercessors for humanity and were placed "as sentinels, as witnesses at the portals of Christ's church that no soul may go forth for whom we have not prayed."[271]

As Potter sought to maintain the spiritual focus of the institute, changes were taking place in the organisational structure of the church, which would render her task even more difficult. In an attempt to control and codify the explosion of new religious orders, two new documents came into force, which would attack the charismatic intensity of Potter's vision, and confirm the members of the institute into a single-stranded congregation, with an identity tied to ministerial functions.

Charism and Canon Law: The effect of canonical legislation

On December 8, 1900 Pope Leo XII promulgated the first of two documents which would begin the process of removing women from more innovative patterns of service.[272]

Conditae a Christo applied the prohibition that no new congregation should be approved "which, without any specified and proper purpose would embrace the practice of all kinds of works, of piety or charity, however different they may be in themselves."[273] This legislation had already found its way into Potter's constitutions, seven years earlier, with the definition of the group as the "Institute of Nursing Sisters." Furthermore, bishops were not to permit any new foundations "unless it be provided with the necessary means of support," and they were to be cautious "even reluctant" in approving as congregations "religious families of women who would wait on the sick in their homes day and night."[274]

While *Conditae a Christo* was not retrospective, and did not annul the approval given to Potter's congregation to attend the sick and the dying in their own homes by day and by night,[275] it was a portent of what was to come. One year after *Conditae*, the *Normae* of Leo XIII were promulgated, and these too, significantly shaped the evolution of the Little Company of Mary, as did the slow but steady integration into hospital ministry.

Where *Conditae a Christo*, had set out to make clear "the rights of the Bishop in regard to institutions of simple vows, whether diocesan or non-diocesan, and on the other hand, the rights and duties of Superiors towards diocesan authority,"[276] the *Normae* "described with precision" the form *all* constitutions for religious women should take. Not laws in the canonical sense of the word, the three hundred and twenty five articles of the document established a principle that would remain in force until 1965.

According to the *Normae*, the fundamental belief of the church regarding institutes of religious life was that it was "substantially the same for all, and therefore the various constitutions will practically resemble one another."[277] The charisms of religious orders – those refraction of elements of the Christian life that were to be lived more fully by all Christians – were now negated. Religious institutes were to be distinguished by differences of work, and not by charismatic virtuosity: "The difference [between institutes]," the document declared "will chiefly consist in what regards the special work of the order."[278] It was a critical and destructive declaration. In the absence of a distinct theology of religious life, or of the nature of the charisms in the church, the desire of the hierarchical church to control and contain the emergent orders brought with it a homogenous uniformity.

Again, the *Normae* underscored the shift already visible in the Little Company of Mary constitutions of 1893. The "principal end" of each congregation was "the sanctification of its members by the observance of the evangelical counsels and of its constitutions."[279] The "secondary purpose" was to be clearly determined, not to be identical with that of any other congregation, and not to embrace too many distinct works.[280] In addition, the *Normae* forbade the use of terms clearly used by the "real" Religious Orders that took solemn vows. These included the words "Religion," "Rule," "Monastery," or "Nuns."[281] Furthermore, their rules were to make no use of quotations "from Holy Writ, Councils, Holy Fathers, [or] Theologians,"[282] and no religious institute of simple vows could append to itself a "third order" or association of lay persons. This once more was the "exclusive privilege" of the older "monastic orders."[283] A religious congregation of simple vows could, however "aggregate to itself pious persons of the same sex as the congregation, prescribe them a certain mode of living and make them sharers of its merits."[284] In addition, "special guarantees" were now required of congregations of women who "day and night wait on the sick in their homes, or who take care of the household of poor or labouring families."[285] Sisters could no longer wait on the sick outside their respective cities, "unless there be two," especially at night. If nursing in the home, they had to demand a special dining room. They could not "wait alone upon men living in furnished rooms."[286] Maternity nursing was forbidden, and "approbation will generally be refused to congregations of Sisters devoting themselves to works which do not seem suitable to them, such as taking direct care of infants or of maternity hospitals."[287] A document that reflected the basic anthropology the church held regarding its women members, the *Normae* thrust women back into a role that the evolution of new forms of religious life had lifted them from – childlike dependency. It presented women religious as infantile, lacking in prudence, susceptible to temptation, without discernment, and above all, in need of male protection – lest they cause scandal to themselves or to the church.[288]

When placed against Potter's initial vision and the primitive rule the impact of the *Normae* is clear. All direct references to the originating spirituality, carefully spelt out in the interim constitutions as following that of De Montfort vanished. Over time, the flexibility of works, and the ability of women to work outside of the community as individuals was further restricted as the church imposed a modified enclosure on all congregations of religious women. The secular branch of the institute – those women who were associated to the Little Company and shared their mission – was abandoned. Whilst the document stated that it was not retrospective (thus technically ensuring that the Constitutions given to Potter in 1893 would remain in force), the effect of the *Normae* was to alter the shape of the institute. Local pressures to comply with the document created discomfort for many of the communities. Criticisms were levelled at the Little Company of Mary "by some Ecclesiastics at our not keeping Rules to which the 'Normae' oblige so many religious."[289] It was a charge Potter refuted vehemently, citing the fact that the rule of 1893 was approved by Leo XIII *in perpetuum*, that the injunctions of the *Normae* were not retrospective and thus did not apply, and that she was:

> not at all uneasy as to the non-observance of the Rule for which some of you have expressed unease. I could not have higher Authority and Sanction than that of the Holy Father Himself [290]

But the effect of the *Normae* held. As expansion of the Little Company continued, and more houses were established, the fact was that bishops now saw them as members of a nursing institute, whose services were useful for creating that infrastructure so necessary for the church. This brick and mortar apologetic stifled the innovations of sisters, who in the early years of the foundation, had broken through the ambulatory limits imposed on women's mendicancy; undertaken missions and ministries that echoed the apostolic focus of male orders; and generally gained standing through their willingness to risk all in the service of the needy. Their creative powers were now channelled into corporate ministries and used as the base upon which an alternate "Catholic world" of schools and hospitals, orphanages and asylums was built.

Potter, however, was not convinced of the validity of such direction for her institute. Just as she believed the community had not been called into existence to nurse, so she believed that "large hospitals or other works may not increase its beauty."[291] There was a danger her sisters "would lose entirely her spirit if they preferred grand hospitals."[292] The world was the domain of these women, and their enclosure. "Let this be our principal object in life," she wrote to her sisters:

> to go about this beautiful world to draw God's creatures to love him. We have fulfilled then the end of our creation. Dear children. Our whole lives are devoted to saving souls, and our consecration to this – the grandest work that can be done – gives to our acts a great grace. We may seek it here or there to do this or that. What can be greater than serving God and saving souls? By God's helping grace, we seek to bring him souls[293]

Feminine social action in the world was to remain troubling to the magesterium of the church. It was a problem resolved by the 1917 Code of Canon Law, which imposed a modified monastic enclosure upon all women's congregations. Now, the world was "shut out" and a quasi-monastic state evolved, which was also based upon concepts of moral activity rather that on the charismatic dimension.[294] This would continue to surround active orders until the Second Vatican Council in 1962.[295] It was to have disastrous consequences on the charism and spirituality of Potter's Little Company of Mary. The growing tightening of the regulations governing religious institutes, eventuating in the *Normae* (and ultimately in the 1917 Code), undercut not only the missionary activities of women, but also their distinctive spiritual virtuosity and their charism. In 1920, in accordance with the new code of Canon Law of 1917, the constitutions Potter had anguished over with Cardella, Gualdi, Macchi and her own sisters, were revised in the light of the church's demands of the commonality of all religious orders. By this time, hospitals had replaced the home nursing of the sisters. Some continued their thankless rounds among the poor. Few engaged in any form of evangelization. There were no associates. The spirituality of the institute had been codified and modified. Mary Potter's published writings to her spiritual daughters had been edited, and all that did not accord with the new code of canon law, removed. These modified texts became the "foundation documents." De Montfort, now relegated to a half-life, rested on library shelves – an anachronistic self-denying spirituality in a modern world.

Potter could do little to stop the increasing institutionalising of the work of the order, or the gradual erosion of its charismatic focus. Increasing physical debility prevented her from visiting the far-flung houses of the institute, and slowly her control over the congregation became less and less. From 1906 to 1913, she lived within the confines of the

Mother House at San Stefano Rotondo, built in the hope of bringing the twofold nature of the institute to reality. The compromises affected by the search for approbation and the expansion of the congregation brought her suffering – the more so as she witnessed the ever-increasing movement into institutional care and the corresponding weakening of the missionary endeavour of the congregation. She had sought to ensure that the spiritual focus of the institute would remain steady. Equally she had endeavoured to maintain and encourage the missionary outreach of the community, but the inexorable wind of change blew across her congregation, as it did others. Now the protection she had sought from the church vanished as canonical decisions regarding the nature and function of religious institutes of women were codified and drawn into a common focus.

Isolated from the community by an increasing severity of illness, the remaining years of her life were spent in prayer, in writing to her beloved sisters, and in filling notebook after notebook with a journal of her inner life.

The union with God that she had experienced as a young woman "went on increasing,"[296] as did her love for the world in which God spoke to her. "[E]verything [was] of interest and importance for all [was] connected with God's glory."[297] The passionate love for God that had claimed her in her mystical experiences remained. Her notebooks and jottings proclaimed the agony and the ecstasy of her calling: "How can the finite human soul contain God?" she cried:

> "Thou visit me and my soul is filled, I can no more… I must go to Thee, for my whole being is filled with Thee, with desires for Thy coming in this world, Thy glory in the next.[298]

The apostolic longing for God's reign in the world remained. Her prayer of intercession echoed throughout her writings, and for the institute she founded, she continued to pray:

> Give to Thy Mother's Company mothers after her own heart, full of zeal, full of fervour, walking this earth picking up the bruised and crushed ones and placing them on their bosom and bringing them to Thee. Yes, on their bosom, for in their hearts they ever plead and pray. Plead for the most needy, plead for the most miserable, the most wretched of this earth, those who are most wounded, who have the greatest need. Yes thus may they be true children of her who brought them, true spouses of Jesus, like to their Lord. Yes, like to him! Full of love, love by night and day, love for beautiful souls made like to Thee O God! Yes, it is at Thy Throne we learn the value of a soul, precious since Precious Blood was shed for it; priceless, for the price was the Son of God; immortal, since it was made by an immortal God, made for himself.[299]

Filled with a profound awareness of the presence of God in the created world, Potter's spiritual life was one of intense adoration and deepest intimacy. It was, however not world-denying. The world was charged with God's grandeur, it was a "lovely life, [a] beautiful world" full of infinite possibility and "one of the glories of the universe."[300] To see it clearly, however, one needed to step out of blindness and see the world as God saw it:

If you could rise out of it and [stand] in some part of the universe, you would see a radiant orb, reflecting uncreated beauty, brilliantly radiant, with rays of Divine light lighting it up everywhere, the attributes of God reflected from all its parts. {And} what is the object of this world? Why is it created and placed in the universe? What is the position of the human race? Why! To reflect him, to mirror his beauty, to reflect the light, the radiant loveliness of the Divinity. Ah, ponder. Is this what the world is doing? Are you, in your little circumference striving to do this? Has the majority of mankind this attitude? Even with the good, is there not a certain unhealthy tone as regards their indifference to the world and an air of not minding what happens to the world so long as they get to heaven? Is this not ignoble? Does it show love of God and desire to extend his kingdom on earth? If there is beauty in the world, it must be reflecting the Divinity, and we can multiply these reflections, these flashes, reflections of Divine Beauty.[301]

Drawn by an apocalyptic vision of a world, in which the power of women's maternal love could create a unity of mind and heart, Potter's vision echoed much of the times in which she lived. Like other religious women and men, she knew what she knew, and that knowledge begat an extraordinary journey from the damp streets of Southwark to the hills of Rome. There, in the last years of her life, she quietly prepared for her own last journey through the dark. On the ninth day of April 1913, in her sixty-sixth year of life, the thirty-fifth year of her religious profession, and thirty-six years three months on from the day she had stepped from the train in Nottingham, Mary Potter, founder of the Little Company of Mary, did what she had told her spiritual daughter, Mother Philip, she had longed to do, "fly like a little bird to the breast of God."[302]

It was not an uncommon dying. There was no struggle, no agony. According to eye-witnesses, she gave a small cry and "went to Him whom she loved and for whom she suffered."[303] What surprised the community was the effect of her death. An "incessant stream of people of all ranks and conditions [came] to kneel beside her bed, pray and kiss her hand."[304] Tradesmen and Italian nobility rubbed shoulders with priests and prelates. As Mother Cecilia recalled it:

Prelates and priests came uninvited …she was visited by crowds, rich and poor, especially the latter to whom she had always been kind and generous. I can never forget one old man, who sobbed bitterly…the Hall door had to be left open as crowds came from morning to night. [305]

Two days later Potter was buried. The community watched in silence as three of her first companions placed her body in the coffin prepared for her.[306] On the morning of April 11, 1913 priests began arriving at the Mother House to celebrate mass for the repose of her soul. At 10.00 o'clock, a solemn High Mass was begun. The chapel was crowded with "such a mixed congregation, many of whom were non-Catholics."[307] Finally, the ceremonials of the church completed, the body of Mary Potter, founder of the Little Company of Mary, was buried in Rome's Campo Verano. The journey was over.

Those who had been part of that journey remained to guide the congregation into a new phase of growth. The leadership fell to Mother Philip Coleridge. Irascible, temperamental and unsettled, she proved a failure as a leader and was ultimately deposed from office in 1924, following numerous complaints to Propaganda. Potter's own niece, Mother Hilda Potter, then assumed leadership and set about restoring the order to what she considered it called to be. On September 21, 1927, Mother Philip Coleridge died. Bagshawe too was finally forced to resign his office as Bishop of Nottingham. In 1915, he died in the Isleworth hospital run by the sisters he had established in his diocese in 1877.[308]

Conclusion

Mary Potter's life adds a new dimension to the history of Catholic women religious within the nineteenth century. Utilising the rich sources that document her family life, her religious experience, and the foundation of her community, it provides a unique illustration of the struggle faced by women who dared to move beyond the cultural determinants of their gendered lives. Along with other women in the nineteenth century, she claimed her right to an independent and useful life through an appeal to her religious experiences. Removed from historical anonymity her life illustrates the importance of religion in the lives of English women, and the capacity it held to transform, liberate, and give meaning and motivation to social action. An examination of her life reveals the dynamics of the relationship between religious experience and prophetic social action.

Mary Potter lived a complex yet simple life, and it is in the complexity and the simplicity that her value as an historical subject emerges. A woman of her time, her life experiences illuminate issues currently debated by historians, and add to the limited, though growing corpus of material on Catholic women in the nineteenth century. Whether as a woman, a mystic, a founder, an author of theological and devotional material, or a nun, Potter offers a unique perspective on the manner in which a very ordinary nineteenth-century woman responded to her God, her church, and the wider world.

Potter's life as a founder of a religious order within nineteenth-century England, has a particular importance for deepening the understanding of the place and function of religious women within the emergent English Catholic community. Her vision of the essentially charismatic nature of religious life provides an interesting counter-point to the emergence of active congregations of women religious. It was not focused of notions of utility, but on a prophetic and apocalyptic sense of the need for reform in the church and the wider world. This not only illustrates the importance of understanding the particular "spirit" or "charism" of the different congregations, but also illuminates the problems women of religious virtuosity faced, when their world view differed from that of their surrounding culture, and their creativity challenged existing structures. In her struggles to found her congregation, she witnesses to the overt manipulation of women religious by clergy, and to the constant pressures placed upon them to conform to the demands of local bishops, and ultimately to the demands of the papacy.

Significantly it is in the foundation of her institute that further historical relevance emerges. The struggles faced by her community illustrate the complex and contrasting motives women had in responding to the emergence of religious life in Victorian Britain. For some, conventual life offered a place where spiritual imagination and initiative would find its own fulfilment. For others, it was a means of gaining a status not achievable in the wider world. Still others found it a refuge from redundancy and a means of achieving a "professional life." Egalitarian in its outlook, Potter's community drew its membership from the lower-middle- and working-classes. Few had monetary resources, almost half were either Irish-born or of Irish parents. Some were illiterate or semi-literate. Their problems – problems of health, personality, addiction – are made visible in the evolution of the community Potter established. Not all had vocations, and Potter's struggle to maintain the integrity of her congregation, often went against the desire of the membership. Their reactions provide a unique window through which may be seen the hidden lives of lower middle-class and working-class women, and the petty – and not so petty – tyrannies they practised in order to gain a modicum of power or control. At the same time, however, the evolution of Potter's community illustrates the works women performed in their missionary endeavours, for missionaries they were.

But convents were also used by clergy as "asylums" for women who were either necessary to the clergy in terms of their financial support, or problematic members of a local church community. Bishop Bagshawe's persistence in sending unsuitable candidates to Mary Potter's institute reveals his own lack of awareness of the demands implicit in living the religious life. It also reveals his belief in his own authority and right to manipulate and control women's lives. In the complex, often painful relationships with ecclesial authority, Potter's life reveals the difficulty experienced by women of religious virtuosity *and* the manner in which a church in the process of reconstruction could exploit them. Furthermore, it provides dramatic insight into the complex interplay between the founder of a religious congregation and its charism or "spirit," as well as illustrating the conflict that occurred between those unconcerned with the spiritual focus of religious congregations, yet desperate for the practical works they could supply. Potter's quest to gain autonomy from this manipulation of her community by seeking papal approbation is important, for she is a clear example of the way women founders sought to escape the predations of local authorities by direct appeal to Rome.

The emergence of Potter's community also posits questions about the nature of religious life in its nineteenth-century context. The relaxation of penal laws against Catholicism and the restoration of the English hierarchy in 1850 placed immense pressure on the English Catholic church. It was a problem compounded by an increasing church membership and a lack of resources. The importation of religious institutes from Europe facilitated the revival of church, but it also undercut the right of women's communities to work according to their founding charism. Furthermore, the demand for education within the emergent church guaranteed that orders like Potter's, whose ministerial focus was not primarily "practical," nor education based, but dedicated towards spiritual renewal, found some difficulty in gaining hierarchical support or encouragement. That problem was further compounded by the fact that she claimed divine leading, and proposed an alternative meaning to religious life than that traditionally accepted. Furthermore, her insistence upon the primacy of a life of prayer and her belief in the integration of the contemplative life with its active counterpart found no welcome in a church suspicious of the mystical.

Apocalyptic and prophetic in her sense of the need for renewal and reform, and fired by the missionary spirit of the French school of spirituality, Potter's life also sheds light on the growing use women made of a theological paradigm. Building on her original insight into the nature of the charisms of different religious orders, Potter undertook the creation of a community which would reflect back to the church and world a way of living the Christian life. Utilising feminised images of Jesus, Potter called the church to renew in itself "the mother-love of the Good Shepherd" and through her subversion of the domestic ideology of the "angel of the house" she sought to provide – by example and exhortation – a feminine pedagogy of leadership within the clergy. Women, admitted to the ranks of disciples because of their likeness to a God who was mother as much as father, were to provide a faltering faith with a model of fidelity and service through self-giving love. In this, she was at one with other women of her era, whose vision for a better world utilised images of the Virgin Mary and a maternal God to call for the recognition of women's right to participate in the reconstruction of society.

For all this however, her life reflects both the tensions and the transitions of women within Victorian society and the Roman Catholic church in particular. Caught between the politics of submission and her internal drive towards autonomy, Potter's life reflects the struggle of women to assert their right to be agents of social or religious change. For all her invisibility, Mary Potter can be grouped within the pantheon of women reformers of the nineteenth century – Florence Nightingale, Josephine Butler, Frances Power Cobbe, Anna Jameson, Ellise Hopkins among others – for she, like them, had been grasped by a vision of what might be.

Denied a theological voice, she nonetheless used her theological insight to seek change. Empowered by what she saw as profound experiences of God, she believed she had been called to a radical love and service of the poor, the sick, the suffering and the dying. Touched by the contrast between her own experiences of God's love for humanity and the loneliness of the age, she sought to create a place of welcome for "the wayfarers of the world." Limited by cultural definition, historically invisible, she fought, as other women fought, for the right to think, the right to create, and the right to participate in life. An evolutionist of sorts, she looked back to her foundation in God and found God always before and around. Undisturbed by the shifts and changes of an expanding world, she exemplified an attitude best described as possessing a clear eye of simple regard. She knew what she knew. That knowledge was enough, and within it she lived simply and clearly.

Whether seen as woman, as mystic or as prophetic founder, Potter gives new under-standing of women and religion in the context of her nineteenth-century world, and on the role of women religious within it. As a woman among women, she reveals the rich tap-estry of experiences that constitute a human life. Evidence would suggest that these were neither unique, nor exceptional, but she recorded them, and the intimate details of her life provide an insight into how some women responded to the power of their religious expe-rience in the context of their history and historical circumstance. Like other women of her era, Potter lived a precarious life. Convention drove her just as surely as did the flash of brilliance she called God, and in that tension – between the knowledge of "what is" and the glimpse of "what might be," she found creativity. This study of her life and work reveals her commonality with other women of vision. She too dared to dream a dream, speak a truth and create a system through which she sought to change the world. This is the meaning of her life, and its relevance to history.

Notes

Notes for Introduction

[1]   Edward Gilpin Bagshawe (1829–1915), Bishop of Nottingham, 1874–1901. Bagshawe was an Oratorian, who trained under Frederick William Faber. As a social activist and militant Hibernophile, Bagshawe was an irritation to many of the ecclesial body of the period.

[2]   James Danell, (1821–18) consecrated Bishop of Southwark at St. George's Cathedral by Henry Cardinal Manning, March 25, 1871.

[3]   Henry Edward Manning (1808–1892), Archdeacon of Chichester, who converted to Catholicism in 1851, and rose rapidly in the ranks to become archbishop of Westminster in 1865. Manning was made a cardinal in 1875.

[4]   Susan: O'Brien, "Terra Incognita: The Nun in Nineteenth Century England", *Past and Present: A Journal of Historical Studies,* Number 121, November 1988, pp. 110–140; p. 111.

[5]   Francesca M Steel, *The Convents of Great Britain and Ireland,* John Griffin, (Roehampton,1901), p. 1.

[6]   Quoted in O'Brien, "Terra Incognita", p. 110.

[7]   J.N. Murphy, *Terra Incognita: Or the Convents of the United Kingdom* Burns & Oates, (London, 1876), Chapter XXXIII. The 'statistics' given are rough estimates only. There are no accurate statistic of the actual numbers of religious women in the convents of Great Britain at this time.

[8]   Anne Murphy, SHCJ, "Old Catholics, New Converts, Irish Immigrants: A Reassessment of Catholicity in England in the Nineteenth Century," *A Paper Delivered at the Cherwell* Conference (San Diego, California) Cherwell Conference Papers 1:3 (1993) p. 6. See also Susan O'Brien, "Terra Incognita", p. 110.

[9]   J.N. Murphy, *Terra Incognita,* p. 7. Murphy cites this as the figure for the 1871 census: England and Wales had a total population of 22,704,108, which was constituted by 11,040,403 males and 11,663,705 females. The female population was in the order of 1.056% higher than the male population.

[10]   For an overview of the emergence of Anglican Communities of women see: A.M. Allchin, *The Silent Rebellion: Anglican Religious Communities 1845*–1900, SCM Press (London, 1958), passim. See also P. Anson, *The Call of the Cloister: Religious Communities And Kindred Bodies in the Anglican Communion,* SPCK (London, 1956), passim.

[11]   Prior to the restoration of the hierarchy women aspirants to religious life, left England and joined European based congregations in France, or Belgium, the monasteries of England having vanished with the reformation. In the main, they were members of the Catholic minority within the landed gentry. On the dissolution of the monasteries see E. Duffy, *The Stripping of the Altars, Traditional Religion in England 1400–1580,* Yale University Press (New Haven, 1992), passim.

[12]   Cardinal Nicholas Wiseman (1802–1865), Cardinal Archbishop of Westminster 1850–65.

[13]   O'Brien, "Terra Incognita", p. 114.

[14]   By canonical definition the distinction between simple and solemn vows rests solely in the legislative mind of the church which defined a solemn vow as "solemn" when recognised as such by the Church. See Joseph Cruesens SJ. *Religious Men and Women in Church Law,* trans. E. Garesche, SJ, Bruce Publishing Co., (Milwaukee, 1931), p. 159. The solemnity of vows pertained to the type of religious life, and referred, according to church law, to monastic communities. Following the French Revolution, the establishment of communities of religious life which were not "monastic", and which took simple vows only, was permitted. Such a

decision released them from the binding of enclosure and other restrictions pertaining to the life of the older Religious Orders.

[15] Sarah Maitland, *A Map of the New Country, Women and Christianity*, Routledge and Kegan Paul, (London, 1983), p. 54.

[16] In 1849, the London District, which included Middlesex, Berkshire, Hampshire, Hertfordshire, Essex, Surrey, Sussex, Kent and the Isles of Wight, Guernsey and Jersey, – had 156 priests. In the same year, the ecclesiastical register indicates that there were 897 priest serving the whole of England, Scotland and Wales (an increase of 57 on the previous year). Forty-one convents were scattered throughout the country. *Ordo Recitandi Officii Divini et Missae Celebranmdae Pro Anno Domini MDCCCXLIX,* Apud C.Dolman (London: 1849), pp. 99–100. According to the *Ordo* of 1878, the number of priests had increased to 1,874, but these were unevenly spread across the country. See the figures for each diocese of England in The *Catholic Directory, Ecclesiastical Register and Almanac for the year of Our Lord, 1878*, Burns and Oates, (London, 1878), passim.

[17] For a breakdown of the European congregations in England see Susan O'Brien, "French Nuns in Nineteenth Century England," in *Past and Present* 154 (1997), 142–180, pp. 154–157.

[18] By an English Catholic, "The Condition and Prospects of Catholics in England", in *The Catholic World*, vii, 40, July 1868, p. 494.

[19] Roger Swift and Sheridan Gilley, *The Irish in the Victorian City*, Croom Helm (London, 1985), p. 8. See also W.L. Arnstein, *Protestant versus Catholic in Mid-Victorian England: Mr. Newdegate and the Nuns*, Columbia (London, 1982), chapters 5 & 6.

[20] See W. L. Arnstein, *Protestant versus Catholic*, pp. 62–73. E Hamer, *Elizabeth Prout 1820–1864: A Religious Life for Industrial England*, Downside Abbey (Bath, 1994), pp. 140–148.

[21] See S. M. Griffin, "Awful Disclosures: Women's Evidence in the Escaped Nun's Tale," *Publications of the Modern Language Association of America,* 111, 1, pp. 93–107. See also Rebecca Sullivan, "A Wayward from the Wilderness: Maria Monk's Awful Disclosures and the Feminization of Lower Canada in the Nineteenth Century," *Essays on Canadian Writing* 62, (1997) pp 201–222. J.N Murphy *Terra Incognita*, p. 3.

[22] See Susan Casteras, "Virgin Vows: The Early Victorian Artist's Portrayal of Nuns and Novices," in Gail Malmgreen (ed.), *Religion in the Lives of English Women, 1760–1930,* Croom Helm, (London, 1986) pp. 129–160.

[23] W.L. Arnstein, *Protestant versus Catholic*, pp. 108–122.

[24] See S. Casteras, "Virgin Vows", passim. See also P. Ingram, "Protestant Patriarchy and the Catholic Priesthood in Nineteenth Century England" in *Journal of Social History*, 24: 1991, passim; John Shelton Reed, *Glorious Battle: The Cultural Politics of Victorian Anti Catholicism*, Vanderbilt University Press, (Nashville & London, 1996), pp 201–209.

[25] Dale A. Spender, *Women in English Religion 1700–1925*, Studies in Women & Religion Vol. 10, Edwin Mellen Press (New York, 1983), p. 175.

[26] Mrs. S.M.D. Fry, writing in the *Ladies Repository* of 1872 saw women's religious orders as providing a place in which women's energies could be used. She believed that the Roman Catholic religious orders showed that "woman should not be not only a teacher and cherisher of home, but also a purifier of society." See "Ancient and Modern Sisterhoods" in *The Ladies Repository* Vol. 10, Issue 4, October 1872. The same view was held by Mrs. Anna Jameson, who saw that the Catholic Church "…had the good sense to turn to account and assimilate to itself," women's "singular and beneficent power." See A. Jameson, *The Sisters of Charity, Catholic & Protestant,* Ticknor & Fields, (Boston, 1857, Hyperion Reprint Edition, 1976), p. 44.

[27] This is the contention of John Shelton Reed in his study of Anglican women's religious orders, and there is no reason to suspect that the new orders did not prove to be equally troubling to middle-class Catholics to whom and for whom religious life was a new reality. See John Shelton Reed, "A Female Movement: The Feminization of Nineteenth Century Anglo-Catholicism," *Anglican and Episcopal History*, 57 (1988): 199–238.

[28] See G. A. Beck (ed), *The English Catholics, 1850–1959,* Burns Oates, (London, 1950); J. Bossy, *The English Catholic Community, 1570–1850,* (London, 1975); A. McLeod, *Religion and Society in England, 1850–1914,* MacMillan, (Hampshire 1996); D. Mathew, *Catholicism in England, 1535–1935,* Longmans, Green and Co. (London, 1936); J. Derek Holmes, *More Roman that Rome: English Catholicism in the Nineteenth Century* Burns & Oates (London, 1978).

29 See for example: M Vicinus, *Independent Women: Work and Community for Single Women* 1850–1920, Virago Press Ltd (London, 1985). See also A.M. Allchin, *The Silent Rebellion,* and P. Anson, *The Call of the Cloister.*

30 The notable exception to this is the work of Dr. Susan O'Brien. Her small but valuable corpus of works on the role of Catholic religious communities remains the most significant in the field. See S. O'Brien, "Terra Incognita: The Nun in Nineteenth Century England" in *Past & Present:* no. 121, November 1988; "French Nuns in Nineteenth Century England," *Past & Present.* No 154, February 1997, pp. 142–180; "Lay Sisters and Good Mothers: Working Class Women in English Convents 1840–1910," in W.J. Shields and D. Wood (eds.), *Women in the Church: Studies in Church History 27,* Ecclesiastical History Society, Blackwell, (Oxford, 1990) and "Making Catholic Spaces: Women Decor, and Devotion in the English Catholic Church, 1840–1900" in D. Wood, (ed.), *The Church and the Arts: Studies in Church History* no. 28, Blackwell, (Oxford 1992).

31 Susan O'Brien gives a conservative estimate of eleven native English congregations. The actual number of foundations is hard to estimate because of the propensity of small groups to begin, splinter off, then fade from existence. According to O'Brien's estimates, however, those that can be identified with clarity are: Poor Servants of the Mother of God founded by Fanny Taylor (1869), Missionary Franciscan Sisters of the Immaculate Conception founded by Elizabeth Hayes (1859), Mill Hill Franciscans, founded by Mary Francis Basil (1868), Sisters of the Holy Child Jesus, founded by Cornelia Connolly (1846), Sisters of the Cross and Passion founded by Elizabeth Prout (1852), Sisters of St. Joseph of Peace, founded by Margaret Ann (Mother Clare) Cusack (1884), Alice Ingham's Franciscan Missionaries of St. Joseph(1871), Mary Potter's Little Company of Mary (1877), Margaret Hallahan's Dominican Sisters of St. Catherine of Siena (1829), Margaret Murphy's Franciscan Sisters Minoresses(1888), Mother M. St. Basil Larmenier's Poor Sisters of Nazareth (1854). Other communities emerged towards the end of the century such as Mary Manning's Home Mission Sisters (1896). Some of these eventually became the Franciscan Missionaries of Divine Motherhood, while others of the same founding group amalgamated with a French order the Franciscan Missionaries of Mary. See Susan O'Brien, "Terra Incognita," p. 135.

32 Caritas McCarthy, *The Spirituality of Cornelia Connolly: In God, For God, With God,* Edwin Mellen Press (Lewiston and Queenstown, 1991); J. Wadham, *The Case of Cornelia Connolly,* Collins (London, 1956). Radegunde Flaxman, *A Woman Styled Bold: The Life of Cornelia Connolly 1809–1879,* Darton, Longman and Todd (London, 1991); Mother Marie Therese, SHCJ, *Cornelia Connolly, A Study in Fidelity,* Burns & Oates (London, 1963).

33 E Hamer, *Elizabeth Prout 1820–1864: A Religious Life for Industrial England,* Downside Abbey (Bath, England, 1994).

34 See for example: *Sister Mary Ignatius of Jesus (Elizabeth Hayes) Foundress of the Missionary Franciscan Sisters of the Immaculate Conception – Diary,* privately published by the Missionary Sisters of the Immaculate Conception, (Kedron, Qld., 1994). See also, *Life Sketch of Mother St. Basil (Larmenier), Foundress of the Congregation of the Poor Sisters of Nazareth,* privately printed (n.d.). F.C Devas, *Mother Magdalen Taylor of the Sacred Heart,* Burns Oates & Washbourne, Ltd (London, 1927), and M. A. Dicens, *Mother Magdalen Taylor, Poor Servants of the Mother of God* (Bristol, n.d.). Ruth G Wells, *A Woman of Her Time and Ours: Mary Magdalen Taylor, SMG.* Laney-Smith (Charlotte, NC, 1988). S.M.C, *Steward of Souls: A Portrait of Mother Margaret Hallahan* (London: Longmans, Green & Co, 1952).

35 Gail Malmgreen, *Religion in the Lives of English Women, 1760–1930,* Croom Helm, (London, 1986), p. 3.

36 E Rapley, *The Dévotes: Women and the Church in Seventeenth Century France,* McGill-Queens University Press (Montreal, Kingston, London, 1990).

37 M. Ewens, *The Role of the Nun in Nineteenth Century America,* Arno Press (New York, 1978), M.A. Donovan, *Sisterhood as Power,* Crossroad (New York, 1989); Mary J. Oates " 'The Good Sisters': The work and position of Catholic Church Women in Boston, 1870–1940," in Josephine White (ed.), *The American Catholic Religious Life,* p. 277–06, Garland Publishing (New York, 1988); Margaret Susan Thompson, "Women and American Catholicism 1789–1989," in Stephen Vicchio and Virginia Geiger (eds), *Perspectives on the American Catholic Church, 1789–1989,* Christian Classics, (Westminster Md, 1989), Margaret Susan Thompson, "Sisterhood and Power: Class, Culture and Ethnicity, in the American Convent," *Colby Literary Quarterly* 25, Autumn 1989. I am grateful to Dr. Thompson for making a copy of this available to me.

38 Leslie Liedel, "Indomitable Nuns and a Determined Bishop: Property Rights, Women Religious and Diocesan Power in Nineteenth-Century Cleveland," PhD diss., Kent State University, (1998).

39 Lyn Jarrell, O.S.U, "The Development of Legal Structures for Women Religious Between 1500 and 1900: A Study of Selected Institutes of Religious Life for Women," Doctorate in Canon Law diss., School of Religious Studies, Catholic University of America (1984).

40 Margaret MacCurtain, "Late in the Field: Catholic Sisters in Twentieth-Century Ireland and the New Religious History." *Journal of Women's History* 7, 1, (1995): 49–63.

41 A. Fahey, "Female Asceticism in the Catholic Church: A Case Study of Nuns in Ireland in the Nineteenth Century", Ph.D. diss., University of Illinios at Urbana-Champaign, (1982). Catriona Clear, "The Limits of Female Autonomy: Nuns in Nineteenth Century Ireland," in M. Luddy, and C. Murphy (eds.), *Woman Surviving: Studies in Irish Women's History in the 19th and 20th Centuries*, Poolbeg, (Dublin, 1990). Catriona Clear, *Nuns in Nineteenth Century Ireland*, Gill & MacMillan (Dublin, 1987). M. P. Magray, *The Transforming Power of the Nuns*, Women, *Religion, and Cultural Change in Ireland, 1750–1900*, Oxford University Press, New York, (1998).

42 Susan O'Brien, opera cit.

43 See Martha Vicinus and Bea Nergaard (eds.) *Ever Yours, Florence Nightingale: Selected Letters*, Harvard University Press (Cambridge, 1990), p. 19.

44 See Josephine Butler, *The Hour Before Dawn*, Trubner Pty. Ltd. (London, 1876), p. 99.

45 Allen, K. "Representation and Self-Representation: Hannah Whitall Smith as Family Woman and Religious Guide." *Women's History Review* 7, 2 (1998): 227–239, p. 239.

46 Strictly speaking, religious orders within the Catholic tradition are those enclosed, monastic communities, who profess solemn vows. Common usage has come to speak of institutes or congregations of unenclosed, simple vowed religious communities as religious orders in broader definition. The terms "religious order" and "religious institute" are, for the purposes of this paper, interchangeable, and refer, unless specified otherwise, to both religious of solemn and simple vows.

47 As O'Brien has pointed out, European religious were more acceptable in terms of culture, and presumed more solidly Catholic – having emerged from traditionally Catholic cultures – and had proven ability as workers. Susan O'Brien, "French Nuns in Nineteenth Century England." p. 149.

48 loc. cit.

49 Margaret Susan Thompson, "Charism or Deep Story? Towards a Clearer Understanding of the Growth of Women's Religious Life in Nineteenth Century America", paper delivered to the History of Women Religious Conference, Chicago, 1998, passim. I am grateful to Dr. Thompson for a copy of this paper.

50 1 Cor. 12: 28ff.

51 Cited in Juan Manuel Lorenzo CMF, "Founder and Community: Inspiration and Charism," *Review for Religious*, 37, 2 (1978) p. 214.

52 Manuel Luis Jurado, SJ "Consecrated Life and the Charisms of the founders" in Rene Latourelle (ed.), *Vatican II: Assessment and Perspectives Twenty-five Years After (1962–1987)*, Paulist Press, (NJ, 1989), p. 8.

53 Sacred Congregation of Religious and Secular Institute (S.C.R.S.I) *Mutuae Relationes* in A. Flannery, (ed.), *Vatican Council II: More Postconciliar Documents*, Costello, (N.Y, 1982). Hereafter *MR*.

54 MR #10.

55 MR #11.

56 MR #12.

57 John Paul II: *Redemptionis Donum*, St. Paul's Press, Homebush, 1984, *#15*. Hereafter *RD*.

58 Eve Healy, *Mother Mary Potter*, (London, 1933); Rev. Patrick Dougherty *Mother Mary Potter, Foundress of the Little Company of Mary*, Sands & Co, (London, 1961); Dick Wordley *No One Dies Alone* Little Company of Mary (Sydney, 1976). Carefully researched but undocumented, the first two titles trace the evolution of the founding of the congregation, and early expansion. Substantially hagiographic in nature they do not examine the relationship between the spirituality of the founder and her charism. The third volume is the result of a creative writing process within the Australian Province of the Little Company of Mary. This work, privately published through the Australia Creative Workshop for the Little Company of Mary offers little in terms of the founder or her charism, it is focused upon the Little Company of Mary in its Australian expansion and ministry.

Notes for Section 1

1   F. Bedarida, *A Social History of England 1851–1990*, Routledge (London, 1994), p. 4.

2   loc. cit.; see also H.J Dyos and M Wolff, eds., *The Victorian City:* 2 vols., Routledge & Keagan Paul (London, 1973), passim; Fredrick Engels, *The Condition of the Working Class in England*, Granada/Panther Publishing Ltd. (London, 1969) passim.

3   H.J Dyos, "The Slums of Victorian London," *Victorian Studies*, 11 (1975), pp. 5–40; Fredrick Engels, *The Condition of the Working Class*, p. 62.

4   F. Bedarida, *A Social History of England 1851–1990*, p. 16–25; Asa Briggs, "The Language of Class in Early Nineteenth Century England," in Asa Briggs, *The Collected Essays of Asa Briggs Volume 1: Words, Numbers, Places, People*, The Harvester Press (Sussex, 1985); See also G Best, *Mid-Victorian Britain 1851–1875* Fontana Books, (London, 1979), passim.

5   F. Bedarida, *A Social History of England* 1851–1990, p. 52.

6   ibid.

7   Gail Malmgreen, *Religion in the Lives of Englishwomen*, p. 7.

8   Kenneth Hudson, *Pawnbroking: An Aspect of British Social History*, Bodley Head, (London, 1982), p. 67. A more comprehensive account of pawnbroking and its relationship to the working class poor is to be found in Melanie Tebbutt's *Making Ends Meet: Pawnbroking and Working Class Credit*, Leicester University Press (Leicester, 1983).

9   Postal Directory for the London District, 1849. In this directory Thomas Martin is also listed as owning a premises at 70 Snow Hill.

10 Tebbutt, *Making Ends Meet* p. 12.

11 ibid., pp. 106–107.

12 ibid., p. 13.

13 ibid., p. 25.

14 loc. cit.

15 William (c.1839), Thomas (1842), Henry (1844), and George (1845).

16 Thomas Potter to Father Francis Potter, March 23,1910, Letters P, Little Company of Mary Archives, Tooting Bec, London.

17 Bedarida, *A Social History of England 1851–1990*, pp. 53–5; 91–2. For further explorations of these themes see Walter E. Houghton, *The Victorian Frame of Mind, 1830–1870*, Yale University Press (New Haven, 1957, reprinted 1985); Gertrude Himmelfarb, *Poverty and Compassion*, Vintage Books (New York, 1992), pp 282–283; H. McLeod, *Religion and Society in England, 1850–1914*, MacMillan Press Ltd (Hampshire, London, 1996).

18 For an overview of bankruptcy within the Victorian era see V. Markham Lester, *Victorian Insolvency: Bankruptcy, Imprisonment for Debt and Company Winding up in Nineteenth Century England*, Oxford Historical Monographs, Oxford University Press (New York, 1995), passim.

19 Shirley Nicholson, *A Victorian Household: Based on the Diaries of Marion Sambourne*, Allan Sutton Publishing Ltd (Gloucestershire, UK, 1994), pp 97–98. For the Sambourne family, the bankruptcy of a family member meant ultimate disgrace and suicide – perhaps an "honourable" exit.

20 G Robb, "Victorian Insolvency: Bankruptcy, Imprisonment for Debt, and Company Winding up in Nineteenth Century England," *American Historical Review* 101, 5, (December 1996), pp. 1542–1543.

21 No dates can be found for Mary Ann's reception into the Catholic faith. It is recorded that Dr. Doyle, Provost of St. George's in the Fields (later to become St. George's Cathedral, Southwark), received her into the Catholic church.

22 Thomas Potter to his son Father Francis Potter, March 27, 1910, Little Company of Mary Archives, Tooting Bec, London.

23 loc. cit., Thomas remembered being taken to the Hammersmith Church: "I must have been about three, I fancy, which would make the date around 1845".

24 By 1847, the year of Mary Potter's birth, the family was living in Jamaica Road, Bermondsey. Mary Potter recalled "I was baptised and called only 'Mary', to my father's wrath". Mary Potter, *Autobiographical Notes*, p. 2, Little Company of Mary Archives, Tooting Bec, London. Hereafter *Autobiographical Notes*. See also Letter of Thomas Potter to Mother M. Cecilia, October 2, 1902, Letters P, Little Company of Mary Archives, Tooting Bec.

25 Mary Ann was at this point three months pregnant. Her fear of losing the child she carried was legitimate. In the Southwark area, infant mortality stood at a rate of 160 deaths to 1000 live births as late as 1901. The figure for 1850 was much higher. See Ellen Ross, "Labour and Love: Rediscovering London's Working Class Mothers, 1870–1918" in Jane Lewis (ed.), *Labour and Love*, pp. 74–96: p. 76 ff. For an excellent discussion of the whole terrible reality of infant mortality in the nineteenth century, see Anthony Wohl, *Endangered Lives: Public Health in Victorian Britain*, Harvard University Press, (Cambridge, Ma., 1983), chapter 2: Mary Ann's fear for her own life was also justified, as tuberculosis was a major cause of female mortality in the first half of the nineteenth century. See George Rosen, "Disease, Debility, and Death" in H.J. Dyos and M. Wolff, (eds.), *The Victorian City: Images and Realities*, vol. II, pp. 625–225, passim.

26 George Rosen, "*Disease, Debility, and Death*", p. 643.

27 Charles Kingsley to his wife in 1849. Cited in the home pages of Dicken's London **http://mars.acnet.wnec.edu/ &grempel/courses/wc2lectures/dickens.html** These are pages established at the site of "Dickens London" maintained by Dr. G. Rempel. Accessed November 1998. For an even more graphic description of the manner in which disease translated itself from poor to rich through the lack of sanitation see Charles Dicken's *Bleak House*, Chapter 46.

28 Rosen, "*Disease, Debility, and Death.*" passim.

29 Obituary Notice: Dr. Thomas Doyle, *The Tablet*, June 14, 1879. "The editor of The Times, in a leading article afterwards spoke most highly of Father Doyle's exertions among the poor of the Borough, and greatly extolled the excellent manner in which he had distributed the alms given to him for his suffering flock."

30 Church records indicate Mary Ann was confirmed at Holy Trinity Church, Dockhead on May 25, 1847. Copy of confirmation certificate held by Little Company of Mary Archives, Tooting Bec, London.

31 Potter's chronic illnesses form a sub-text to her life. Her heart condition limited her activities and constant lung infections made her life a misery. In later life she would develop malignant tumours of the shoulder and breast, and, as will be seen, faced the relative barbarity of nineteenth century surgery.

32 Mary Potter, *Autobiographical Notes*, p. 1.

33 ibid. p. 2.

34 Thomas Potter to Father Francis Potter, March 27, 1910. No records of William's entry into the colonies have yet been found. If a known debtor, he could have changed his name on the passage lists. There are, however, further mysteries remaining unsolved: Family records in this letter state that the family learnt of William's death in a scientific magazine some years after it had occurred, and this record told of his exploits in vine-growing along the Murray River. Research has discovered two William Norwood Potters in Australia. One died in Melbourne as a cab driver, the other married and became a river boat captain, and ultimately a customs agent at Bordertown. This latter William Norwood Potter may well be Mary Potter's father, though no direct links back to the family can be traced. I am indebted for this information to research undertaken by Father Patrick Dougherty, Jan Worthington, and Dorothy Fellowes.

35 Thomas Potter to his son Father Francis Potter, March 27, 1910.

36 Cited in Eve Healy, *Mother Mary Potter*, Sheed and Ward (London, 1936), p. 21–22.

37 Mother Hilda Potter, *Reminiscences*, p. 3. Unpublished MS., Little Company of Mary Archives, Tooting Bec, London. Hereafter referred to as *Reminiscences*.

38 Cited in Anthony Wohl, *The Victorian Family, Structures and Stresses*, Croom Helm, London, 1978, p. 10. Ruskin uses the terms in his description of the dignity of the family.

39 Allen Horstman, *Victorian Divorce*, Croom Helm (London, Sydney, 1985), pp. 37, 41.

40 Mary Anne Potter to Father Selley, July 1876, Letters P, Little Company of Mary Archives, Tooting Bec London.

41 M Vicinus, *Independent Women*: pp. 2–3.

42 Mary Potter, *Autobiographical Notes*, p. 3.

43 Mother Hilda Potter, Conference given to the Sisters of the Little Company of Mary on her aunt, Mother Mary Potter, Rome, June 13, 1957. Copy held at Marian Spirituality Centre, Wagga Wagga, NSW.

44 loc. cit.

45 Arlene Young, "Virtue Domesticated: Dickens and the Lower Middle-classes," in *Victorian Studies*, 39, 4, (Summer, 1996), p. 487.

46 Mary Potter, *Obedience Notes*, Vol. 1, p. 4. Five volumes, Little Company of Mary Archives, Tooting Bec, London. Hereafter *Obedience Notes*.

47   Mary Potter, *Autobiographical Notes*, p. 1.

48   See George Potter to Mother Cecilia Smith, 1902; Mary Potter to her mother, Mary Ann Potter, July 3, 1860, in Letters P, Little Company of Mary Archives, Tooting Bec, London; Mother Hilda Potter *Reminiscences*, p. 4.

49   George Potter to Mother Hilda Potter, 1919, Letters P, Little Company of Mary Archives, Tooting Bec, London.

50   George Potter to Mother Hilda Potter, June 4, 1919.

51   Carol Dyhouse, "Mothers and Daughters in the middle-class Home c. 1870–1914" in Jane Lewis, (ed.), *Labour and Love*, pp. 27–47, p. 28.

52   See Dyhouse, C., *Girls Growing up in Late Victorian and Edwardian England*, Routledge and Kegan Paul, (London, 1981), p. 12.

53   M. Potter, *Autobiographical Notes*, p. 10; Bryan Letters, November, 1876, Letters F, Little Company of Mary Archives, Tooting Bec, London. Hereafter referred to as Bryan Letters.

54   ibid., p. 4.

55   Mary Potter to Mrs. Mary Ann Potter, July 3, 1860.

56   Woolf, Virginia, "Professions for Women', in Woolf L., ed. *Collected Essays, Vol. II*, Chatto & Windus, (London, 1967) p. 285.

57   Carol Dyhouse, "Mothers and Daughters in the Middle-Class Home, c. 1870–1914," in Jane Lewis, *Labour and Love,* p. 37.

58   *Catholic Directory* – 1856, Burns & Lambert, London p. 200.

59   loc. cit.

60   loc. cit. This advertisement refers to a Catholic Boarding School for young ladies in Clapham, run by Mrs. and Miss Butt. Miss Butt had "been duly qualified by a residence of 10 years abroad under the direction of eminent professors". Another institute boasted of the presence of "a Parisian" among its teaching staff.

61   Mary Potter *Autobiographical Notes* p. 10.

62   loc. cit.

63   Mrs. Sarah Stickney Ellis, *The Mothers of England: Their Influence & Responsibility*, Fisher and Sons, (London, 1893), pp. 338–9.

64   Dyhouse,"Mothers and Daughters in the Middle-Class Home, c. 1870–1914," in Lewis, *Labour and Love*, p. 37.

65   Barbara Welter, "The Cult of True Womanhood, 1820–1860,"in *American Quarterly*, 18 (1966), pp. 151–174.

66   Edmund Burke, "Letters on a Regicide Peace," *Works, Vol. V*, (London, 1910), p. 208, cited in Himmelfarb, *Victorian Minds*, Peter Smith, (Gloucester, Mass., 1975) p. 282.

67   Mary Potter to Mrs. Mary Ann Potter, November 1862.

68   Richard Challoner, *The Garden of the Soul: A Manual of Spiritual Exercises and Instructions for Christians*, Society of St. Peter & Paul, (First published in London, 1741: Reprinted from the original in 1916). For the impact of this prayer book on the piety of English Catholics, see Mary Heimann, *Catholic Devotion in Victorian England*, Oxford Historical Monographs. (Oxford, 1995).

69   According to the advertisement in the *Catholic Directory*, of 1856, Father Danell, later to become Bishop of the diocese of Southwark, was one of the clergy involved in teaching the children of the school.

70   Mary Potter, *Motherhood*, Our Lady's Library (Nottingham, 1885), p. 27. Hereafter *Motherhood*.

71   See J. Sharp, "Juvenile Holiness: Catholic Revivalism among Children in Victorian Britain." *Journal of Ecclesiastical History* 35 (1984): 220–238, passim. See also Gerald Parsons, "Emotion and Piety: Revivalism and Ritualism in Victorian Christianity," in G. Parsons (ed.), *Religion in Victorian Britain: Traditions, Vol.* 1, Manchester University Press, (Manchester, 1988), p. 225. See also Michael Wheeler, *Death and the Future Life in Victorian Literature and Theology*, Cambridge University Press (Cambridge, 1990), pp. 180–182.

72   George Potter to Mother Hilda Potter, January 12, 1920.

73   Mary Potter, *Motherhood*, p. 27.

74   ibid., p. 25.

75   Mary Potter to Monsignor John Virtue n.d. Letter no. 13. Little Company of Mary Archives, Tooting Bec, London. The originals of these letters are to be found in the Roman Archives of the College of Propaganda Fide. The copies held by the LCM Archives (London) are by courtesy of the Roman College. The letters are undated but numbered. Hereafter referenced as Virtue Letters, with numbering as per copies held in LCM Archives, Tooting Bec.

76 Mary Potter, *Motherhood*, p. 23.

77 loc. cit.

78 John Ruskin, "Of Queens Gardens" in *Sesame and Lilies*, Thomas Nelson & Sons, (London, 1865) p. 82; see also Julie Melnyk, (ed.), *Women's Theology in Nineteenth Century Britain: Transfiguring the Faith of Their Fathers* Garland Publishing Inc. (New York, 1998), Introduction.

79 "A Chronology of Happenings and Development the Little Company of Mary during Mother's lifetime", MS. Little Company of Mary Archives, Tooting Bec, London. The author of this is unknown, but as it is a first person narrative it is possible that it is the work of either Mother Hilda Potter or Mother Cecilia Smith.

80 Gertrude Potter to Mother M. Hilda Potter, April 30, 1933, Letters J, Little Company of Mary Archives, Tooting Bec, London.

81 Letter Mrs Mary Ann Potter to Father Selley, June, 1876; letter from George Potter to Mother Hilda Potter, January, 1902; letter from Thomas Potter to Mother Cecilia Smith, January, 1902.

82 Portsmouth's ethnic origins were mixed. Irish soldiers made up 30% of the inhabitants and a surprising number of Polish refugees were part of its makeup. The garrison was the centre of activity within the city, along with the naval dockyards, which employed numbers of poor Irish labourers. See H.J. Hanham, "Religion and Nationality in the Mid-Victorian Army" in M.R.D.Foot (ed.), *War and Society*, (London, 1973), p. 161; V.J.L. Fontana, *Rebirth of Roman Catholicism in Portsmouth*, The Portsmouth Papers No 56, (City of Portsmouth, 1989), p. 19 ff.

83 Mary Potter *Autobiographical Notes,* p. 10.

84 Mary Potter to Father Selley, August 1876, Letters B, Little Company of Mary Archives, Tooting Bec, London. Hereafter referred to as Selley Letters.

85 On the evolution of leisure and entertainment in 19th Century Britain see: J. Lowerson and J. Myerscough, *Time to Spare in Victorian England*, Harvester Press, (Brighton, 1977); P. C. Bailey *Leisure, Culture and the Historian*, Leisure Studies 8, E & F. M. Spon Ltd., (1989), pp. 109–122.

86 Mrs. Potter to Rev. Father Selley, July 12, 1876.

87 William Fredrick Faber converted to Catholicism in 1845, and was superior of the Brompton Oratory from 1850 to his death. A prolific and somewhat neglected spiritual writer, he was highly influential in Catholic revivalism. His works include *All for Jesus* (1853), *The Creator and the Creature* (1848), *Growth in Holiness* (1855), *The Precious Blood* (1860). Translator of Grignon De Montfort's *Treatise on True Devotion to the Blessed Virgin*, in 1862, he was also the author of the highly contentious Mariological work entitled *The Foot of the Cross* (1856).

88 On the evolution of the Roman revival of English Catholicism see Sheridan Gilley, "Roman Catholicism" in D.G Paz, (ed.), *Nineteenth Century English Religious Traditions: Retrospect and Prospect*, Contributions to the Study of Religion, no. 44 Greenwood Press, (Westport, Connecticut, 1995), pp. 33–56. See also G Parsons, (ed.), *Religion in Victorian Britain: Vol I Traditions*, Manchester University Press (Manchester, 1988); H. McLeod, *Religion and Society in England, 1850–1914*, MacMillan Press Ltd (Hampshire, London, 1996); J. Derek Holmes, *More Roman Than Rome*, Burns & Oates Ltd. (London, 1978).

89 On the evolution of the cult of Our Lady of Victories, and its associated confraternity see: Thomas A Kselman, *Miracles and Prophecies in Nineteenth-Century France*, Rutgers University Press (New Brunswick, 1983), pp. 167–178. For the evolution of Marian cults see also Ralph Gibson, *A Social History of French Catholicism 1789–1914*, Routledge (London, 1989), passim.

90 On this whole issue see Mark Girouard, *The Return to Camelot: Chivalry and the English Gentleman*, Yale University Press, (New Haven, London, 1981), particularly chapter 12.

91 Mary Potter, *Autobiographical Notes*, p. 16.

92 This volume is held at the Little Company of Mary Archives, Tooting Bec, London.

93 Mother Mary Potter, *Autobiographical Notes*, p. 3.

94 ibid., p. 16.

95 Mark Girouard, *The Return to Camelot: Chivalry and the English Gentleman,* ch. 12. It is also interesting to note that the parents of Therese of Lisieux were alleged to have desired to a very similar relationship as that proposed by Godfrey King. See Stephane J. Piat *The Story of a Family: The Home of the Little Flower*, Gill & Son (Dublin, 1948), p. 34, 37ff.

96 loc. cit.
97 Mary Potter, *Autobiographical Notes*, p. 16.
98 M. Vicinus documents the status of the unmarried daughter of the house in *Independent Women:* p. 14 and passim.
99 Mary Potter, *Autobiographical Notes*, p. 3. There is a remarkable similarity between this and the terms used by the Martin family to justify just such a celibate marriage. See Piat, *The Story of a Family*, p. 37.
100 *Manual of Instructions in Christian Doctrine*, Burns, Lambert & Oates, (London, 1865), p. 373.
101 ibid., p. 373.
102 Mary Potter, Autobiographical Notes, p. 3.
103 loc. cit.
104 Letter from Thomas Potter to Mother Cecilia Smith, October 2, 1902.
105 loc. cit.
106 loc. cit.
107 Mary Potter, *Autobiographical Notes* p. 5.
108 loc. cit.
109 ibid., p. 16.
110 P. Ingram, "Protestant Patriarchy and the Catholic Priesthood in Nineteenth Century England," *Journal of Social History*, 24: (1991), passim. See also John Shelton Reed, *Glorious Battle: The Cultural Politics of Victorian Anti-Catholicism*, Vanderbilt University Press, (Nashville & London, 1996), pp. 201–209.
111 On the evolution of community life for women see M Vicinus, *Independent Women.* For the development of the Anglican Sisterhoods see A.M.Allchin *The Silent Rebellion,* passim. For a nineteenth century account of the re-emergence of Catholic religious life in England in the period see J.N. Murphy, *Terra Incognita*, passim; Susan O'Brien "Terra Incognita", passim. Mother Mary Paul SHCJ, "The Religious Orders of Women: Active Work," chap. in *Mathews, D. (ed.) Catholicism in England 1535–1935: Portrait of a Minority: Its Culture and Traditions*, Catholic Book Club (London, 1938).
112 John Shelton Reed, *Glorious Battle*, p. 205; Martha Vicinus, *Independent Women:* pp. 52–53.
113 Newman, John Henry (Cardinal), *Historical Sketches, Vol. II,* (reprint) (Westminster Md., 1970), p. 42. See also Martha Vicinus, *Independent Women,* p. 5.
114 C.M Yonge, *Womankind*, Walter Smith (London, 1876/1881), p. 1–2. Whilst Yonge defended the notion of the consecrated virgin, or the nun, she also insisted on the "absolute need of the feminine nature for discipline and obedience".
115 F.K. Prochaska, *Women and Philanthropy in Nineteenth Century England*, Clarendon Press (Oxford, 1980).
116 Anne Summers, "A Home from Home – Women's Philanthropic Work in the Nineteenth Century", chapter in Sandra Burman, (ed.), *Fit Work for Women*, Croom Helm (London, 1979), pp. 33–65.
117 F. M. Edselas, 'Women's work in Religious communities' in *The Catholic World, Vol. 58*, Issue 346, (January 1894) , p. 514.
118 Mrs. A. B Jameson, *Sisters of Charity Catholic and Protestant & The Communion of Labour*, Ticknor & Fields (Boston, 1858). For further reason why women found convents a consolation see Peter Anson, *The Call of the Cloister*, p. 323 and passim; See also, Martha Vicinus, *Independent Women,* chapter 2; A. Allchin, *Silent Rebellion,* passim, Susan O'Brien, "Terra Incognita" passim.
119 See Sheridan Gilley "Roman Catholicism" in D. Paz, *Nineteenth Century English Religious Traditions: Retrospect and Prospect,* Greenwood Press, (Conn., 1995), p. 44.
120 Peter Ingram, "Protestant Patriarchy and the Catholic Priesthood in Nineteenth Century England" in *Journal of Social History*, 24: 1991, p. 786. See also Susan Casteras, "Virgin Vows" p. 132.
121 loc. cit.; see also Walter Arnstein, *Protestant versus Catholic:* p. 4, and "The Murphy Riots: A Victorian Dilemma" in *Victorian Studies, 19:* (1975/6), p. 59.
122 Peter Ingram, "Protestant Patriarchy and the Catholic Priesthood", p. 793–4; Lawrence Stone, *The Family, Sex and Marriage in England 1500–1800*, Harper and Row (New York, 1977), p. 109.
123 Accounts of riots outside convents where nuns were allegedly held against their will occurred in Spalding (1873). See G. Best, "Popular Protestantism in Victorian Britain," in R. Robson, (ed.), *Ideas and Institutions of Victorian*

Britain, Bell, (London, 1967), pp. 118, 122, 124; Owen Chadwick *The Victorian Church, Vol. 1*, Adam & Charles Black (London, 1966), p. 14.

124 *The Tablet,* May 7, 1853.

125 The Catholic Sisters at Norwood were taken to court in 1852 for alleged imprisonment of an orphan. The case was dismissed, but is indicative of the speculation that engaged the public mind. See the *Tablet,* August 14, 1852. See also Owen Chadwick, *The Victorian Church*, vol. 1, p. 509. For other views on anti-convent activities and riots in Lewes and Northhampton, see Edna Hamer, *Elizabeth Prout, 1820–1864*, pp. 142–150.

126 Such men as Charles Newdegate also fuelled this fear of and fascination with convents. See W. Arnstein, *Protestant versus Catholic*, and D.G. Paz, *Popular Anti-Catholicism in Mid-Victorian England*, Stanford University Press, (Stanford, 1992). Also see E. R. Norman, *The English Catholic Church in the Nineteenth Century*, Oxford University Press, (Oxford, 1984).

127 According to J.N. Murphy the 1871 census showed that England and Wales had a total population of 22, 704, 108, made up of 11,040,403 males and 11,663,705 females. The female population was in the order of 1.056% higher than the male population. From the rough statistics given by Murphy, the number of religious women in the English Catholic Church was in the order of 4,200 in England, or a minute 0.036% of the total female population. See Murphy, *Terra Incognita* , p. 7.

128 Murphy, *Terra Incognita*, p. 3. Murphy mentions both the impact of artistic representation of nuns and such titillating works as *Revelations of a Convent,* or *the Story of Sister Lucy*, which could be brought for one shilling outside the Royal Academy of Art, in 1868. The best selling work *The Awful Disclosures of Maria Monk* remained popular throughout the century. *Punch* lampooned convents, and their illustrations indicate the complex variety of responses to the "convent question" of the Victorian era. For more literary responses, see Charles Kingsley, *Yeast: A Problem*, Richard Edward King (London, 1851), particularly Ch. 10; See also Susan M. Griffen, "Awful Disclosures: Women's Evidence of the Escaped Nun's Tale." *PMLA* 111, 1, The Modern Language Association of America, (January 1996), pp. 93–107. See also Susan Casteras, "Virgin Vows", p. 132. The market for works written by ex-nuns was also profitable. Clare Cusack, the Nun of Kenmare, profited by sales from her works on her years within Elizabeth Sellon's Anglican community, and later by her work *The Nun of Kenmare*, Ticker & Co, (Boston, 1889), which gave an account of her years as member of Catholic sisterhoods. On the artistic representations of nuns see Susan Casteras, "Virgin Vows", passim.

129 Mary Potter, *Autobiographical Notes*, p. 16. See also Virtues Letters, no. 2., n.d.

130 Gertrude Potter to Mother Hilda Potter, April 30, 1933.

131 Mary Potter, *Autobiographical Notes*, p. 16.

132 Mother Cecilia Smith, *Personal Reminiscences*, p. 1 Little Company of Mary Archives, Tooting Bec, London. Hereafter *Personal Reminiscences.*

133 In 1861, Sunday Devotions at St. John's Church, Prince George Street consisted of a Sunday Mass at 8 a.m. for civilians, and exclusive Mass for the military at 9 a.m., a High Mass at 11 a.m. Rosary and Catechism at 4 p.m., Vespers and Benediction at 7 p.m. On Holy Days, Mass was at 8 a.m., with Vespers and Benediction at 7 p.m. With the advent of Father Horan as parish priest, devotions were increased to included Rosary and Benediction on Wednesday evenings, Rosary and night prayers on Fridays. *Catholic Directory* 1861, 1871.

134 Mother Cecilia Smith *Personal Reminiscences*, p. 1–2.

135 loc. cit.

136 loc. cit.

137 Mother Hilda Potter, Conference given to the Sisters of the Little Company of Mary on her Aunt, Mother Mary Potter, Rome June 13,1957, p. 4.

138 loc. cit.

139 Father Horan (d.1885) was appointed to the parish of Portsmouth in 1865. He was remarkable in the parish for his love of music, his commitment to education and building a grand church which expressed the confidence of the emergent Catholic community of the area, and would eventually become the Portsmouth Cathedral in 1882. V.J.L Fontana, *Rebirth of Roman Catholicism in Portsmouth,* Portsmouth Papers, no. 56, Portsmouth City Council, (Portsmouth, 1989), pp. 24–25.

140 Mother Hilda Potter, *Reminiscences D*, p. 2, Little Company of Mary Archives, Tooting Bec, London. Hereafter *Reminiscences*.

141 loc. cit.

142 Father Peter Burke (1830–1873). Burke was professed in the Redemptorist Order in 1859, and according to the *Catholic Directory* was stationed at the Redemptorist parish at Clapham in 1868.

143 Virtue Letters, no. 2., n.d.

144 Father Peter Burke to Mary Potter: November 14, 1868, Letters K, Little Company of Mary Archives, Tooting Bec, London.

145 loc. cit. Emphasis as in original.

146 In 1868, there were three Carmelite communities in England, The Convent of Our Lady of Mount Carmel and St. Joseph, Darlington, Durham, and the Carmel of Lanherne, Cornwall. A further community was established in Selerder in 1864, transferred to Plymouth in 1871 and then to Wells in 1875. A community was founded in Chichester in 1870, and in London (Bayswater) in 1878. See Anon, *The Religious Houses of the United Kingdom*, Burns and Oates Limited (London, 1887), p. 122.

147 Virtue Letters, no. 9.

148 The term Religious Order is here used in its classical definition – viz., a group of women bound by the profession of solemn vows, enclosure, and the recitation of the divine office. By canonical definition, they are distinct from religious institutes or congregations, in which members take only simple vows. In common usage, however, the term "religious order" has come to denote any group of men or women, bound under rule to the religious state. When used in its classical sense, it will be capitalised as above. When used as a generic term, lower case letters will apply. On the canonical evolution and distinction of Religious Orders, Institutes and Congregations see Elizabeth Makowski, *Canon Law and Cloistered Women: Periculoso and Its Commentators, 1298–1545* Catholic University of America Press (Washington, D.C., 1997). M. Dortel Claudot, *The Evolution of the Canonical Status of Religious Institutes of Simple Vows From the 16th Century Until the New Code* trans., M.R. McGinley (Sydney: Institute of Religious Studies, n.d.). See also D.I. Lanslots, *Handbook of Canon Law for Congregations of Women Under Simple Vows,* Frederick Pustet & Co., (Ratisbon, Cincinnati, 1909).

149 Dowries were fundamental to religious communities, providing not only a source of income, but also an assurance (always unstated) that the candidate was somehow "worthy" of the venture. Few women of the lower middle-classes or the working-class could afford the dowry of the contemplative communities, who often required as much as £500 stg. Other active religious orders also required a dowry, which again discriminated against the poorer sections of the community. On the dowry required by various religious orders see P. F. Anson, *The Religious Orders and Congregations of Great Britain and Ireland*, pp. 163–175, 239–242, 366–371. See also, Francesca Steele *The Convents of Great Britain and Ireland*, passim, and J. Hohn, *Vocations, Conditions of Admissions etc. into Convents, Congregations Societies, Religious Institutes etc.,* R & T Washbourne Ltd. (London, 1912), pp. 51–52.

150 Susan O'Brien, "Lay Sisters and Good Mothers", p. 460. See also Susan O'Brien "Terra Incognita", pp. 134–140.

151 O'Brien, "Lay Sisters and Good Mothers", loc. cit.

152 Traditionally, cloistered life was the province of "old" Catholics, and just as class structures placed their own barriers against the world of "trade" and "shop" in the world, they had the same affect in religious orders. As both Susan O'Brien and Ann Murphy point out, the new religious congregations offered an opportunity of community life for middle-class women. Few of these new religious congregations were contemplative, however. See O'Brien, "Terra Incognita", p. 133 and Anne Murphy SHCJ, "Old Catholics, New Converts, Irish Immigrants: A Reassessment of Catholicity in England in the Nineteenth Century," a paper delivered at the Cherwell Conference, *Cherwell Papers vol.1:3* Casa Cornelia Publications, (San Diego, Ca, 1993), p. 4. I am indebted to Dr. Murphy and Casa Cornelia publications for a copy of this paper.

153 Virtue Letters no. 2.

154 Mary Potter, *Autobiographical Notes*, p. 7. Potter was not to learn of the contents of this letter until she was leaving the Brighton community. "They had not told me, as they did not know about other orders, and they no doubt thought that as I was so happy with them, it was not necessary. "

155 ibid. p. 3. A postulant is an aspirant to religious life, who shares in the life of the community, and its various works as a means of testing the validity of a perceived call to the religious life. Usually a six-month period of trial, it is followed by reception as a novice. The time of the novitiate was usually one year. This is followed by a period of temporary vows, which lasts for between three and five years, and is finally fulfilled by taking vows for life.

156 ibid., p. 16.

157 loc. cit.

158 ibid., p. 8.

159 ibid., p. 16.

160 "Rule and Constitutions – Religious Sisters of Mercy," Chapter 20: "Of the Reception of Postulants," cited in Mary C. Sullivan *Catherine McAuley and the Tradition of Mercy*, Four Courts Press, (Dublin, 1995).

161 Letter from Sister M. Evangelist RSM, Convent of Mercy, Brighton, to Mother M. Cecilia, September 30, 1902, Little Company of Mary Archives, Tooting Bec, London.

162 Catherine McAuley was born in of Catholic parents in Dublin in 1787, and died in 1841. Following the death of her parents, Catherine and her brother and sister were taken into care by Protestant friends of her father. In 1803, McAuley took up residence with Catherine and William Callaghan. She remained with the Callaghans for twenty years, was adopted by them, and became heiress to their substantial property. From the Callaghans Catherine got much of her considerable scriptural knowledge, and was deeply influenced by their Quaker spirit. On Catherine's life see Angela Bolster, *Catherine McAuley, Venerable for Mercy*, Dominican Publications, (Dublin, 1990); C. Bourke, *A Woman Sings of Mercy*, E.J. Dwyer, (Australia, 1987); Mary C. Sullivan *Catherine McAuley and the Tradition of Mercy*, Four Courts Press, (Dublin, 1995).

163 The Mercy congregation had a unique method of government. Each foundation was self-sufficient, not bound to its parent community in any way. The Brighton foundation, whilst an off-shoot of the Bermondsey community was in no way tied to it, being self-governing and self-supporting. The ecclesiastical superior was the bishop of the diocese and the superior the locally appointed head of the community. See Sister Bertrand Degnan, *Mercy unto Thousands*, Browne & Nolan Ltd., (Dublin, 1958).

164 Bishop P Dougherty, cited in "Mary Potter: Postulant and Novice in the Convent of Mercy 1868–1870," research notes prepared for the Sisters of the Little Company of Mary 1974. Confirmed in 1995 in conversation with Sister Imelda Keene RSM, Archivist, Bermondsey Archives, Convent of Mercy Bermondsey, and Sister Immaculata Ryan, RSM, community historian, Convent of Merc y, Brighton.

165 Extract from "The London Manuscript" cited in Sister M. Bertrand Degnan, *Mercy Unto Thousands*, p. 71. See also the " Rule and Constitutions – Religious Sisters of Mercy", Chapter 1. Here, the aim of the institute is enunciated as "a most serious application to the Instruction of Poor Girls, Visitation of the Sick, and protection of distressed women of good character." In Sullivan, *Catherine McAuley and the Tradition of Mercy*, p. 295.

166 Anon. *Guide to the Religious Houses of the United Kingdom, containing a short history and description of every House*, Burns & Oates, (London, 1887) p. 182.

167 The *Catholic Directory* 1861, p. 280.

168 Mary Potter *Autobiographical Notes*, p. 9.

169 Information given by letter from Sister M. Imelda Keene, RSM Bermondsey Archives, letter December 8, 1995: See also the *horarium* cited in Sister Mary Ignatius Neumann, RSM, ed, *The Letters of Catherine McAuley 1827–1841*, Helicon Press (Baltimore, 1969), p. 249.

170 Information given by letter from Sister M. Imelda Keene, RSM Bermondsey Archives, letter December 8, 1995.

171 "Rules and Constitutions – Sisters of Mercy", Chapter 3 no. 8. "Of the Visitation of the Sick," in Sullivan, *Catherine McAuley and the Tradition of Mercy*, p. 298.

172 Letter from Sister M. Evangelist, Convent of Mercy, Brighton, to Mother M. Cecilia, September 30, 1902.

173 According to the *Catholic Directory*, of 1877, Canon Rymer was a canon of the Southwark diocese, resident at Upper James Street Brighton.

174 Newspaper account of Ceremony of Reception, July 30, 1869, cited in Eve Healy, *Mother Mary Potter*, p. 35.

175 loc. cit.

176 Mary Potter, *Autobiographical Notes* p. 9.

[177] The fact that Victorian women in general were not so repressed or prudish has been well documented. See for example Peterson, M. Jeanne, *Family, Love and Work in the Lives of Victorian Gentlewomen*, Indiana University Press, (Bloomington, 1989), particularly Ch. 3.

[178] Catherine McAuley, *Thoughts from the Spiritual Conferences of Mother M. Catherine McAuley*, M. Gill & Son Ltd. (Dublin, 1946), p. 11.

[179] Angela Bolster RSM, *Catherine McAuley, Venerable for Mercy*, Dominican Publications, (Dublin 1990), p. 98.

[180] Bermondsey Annals, (also known as the London Manuscript). Copy supplied by courtesy of Sisters of Mercy, Goulburn, N.S.W., Australia. See also Sullivan, *Catherine McAuley and the Tradition of Mercy*, p. 99–129.

[181] "Rules and Constitutions – Sisters of Mercy," Chapter 5, no. 1, in Sullivan, *Catherine McAuley and the Tradition of Mercy*, p. 300.

[182] ibid., no. 3.

[183] ibid., no. 5.

[184] ibid., Chapter 6, no. 1.

[185] ibid., Chapter 7, no. 1.

[186] ibid., Chapter 8, no. 1–5.

[187] McAuley had spent years in the house of the Quaker Callaghan family. Whilst remaining a Catholic, and ultimately being instrumental in the conversion of Mrs. Callaghan to the Catholic faith, her own spirituality, it is suggested, received much from the interchange between herself and the members of the Callaghan family. See Sheila Carney RSM, "The Legacy of Catherine McAuley and the Transformative Elements for Religious Life in the Future," *The MAST: Journal of the Mercy Association in Scripture and Theology*, Vol 3/1 (Fall, 1992).

[188] loc. cit.

[189] loc. cit.

[190] The term "walking nuns" was used for the new apostolic religious, whose presence on the streets and among the poor, was a new phenomenon within Irish and English Catholic experience.

[191] "Rules and Constitutions – Religious Sisters of Mercy," Chapter Six, no. 2, cited in Sullivan, *Catherine McAuley and the Tradition of Mercy*, p. 323.

[192] loc. cit.

[193] ibid., p. 310.

[194] loc. cit.

[195] Mary Potter *Autobiographical Notes*, pp. 9–10.

[196] loc. cit.

[197] ibid., p. 14.

[198] Mary Potter, *Autobiographical Notes* p. 14.

[199] Letter from Sister M. Evangelista RSM to Mother M. Cecilia, September 30, 1902.

[200] Bermondsey Convent of Mercy was founded by Catherine McAuley in 1839. The first superior was Mary Clare Moore (1814–1874). In 1841, she was replaced by Mary Clare Agnew. After Mother Clare Agnew left the Sisters of Mercy (see note 202 below), Mother Clare Moore again became superior.

[201] Sister Mary Ignatius Neumann, *Letters of Catherine McAuley: 1827–1841*, pp. 181–183.

[202] Mother Clare Agnew subsequently left the Sisters of Mercy and entered the Trappist Community in Dorsetshire. See Sullivan, *Catherine McAuley and the Tradition of Mercy*, p. 78.

[203] Moore would remain the Superior of the Bermondsey community until 1874. A great friend of Bishop Thomas Grant, she, along with four other sisters of this community, went to the Crimea as nurses for British, Scottish and Irish troops. Serving at Scutari in Turkey, from 1854–1856, Moore became a close friend of Florence Nightingale, and in some ways served as her spiritual counsellor. See Sullivan, *Catherine McAuley and the Tradition of Mercy*, p. 78–79; See also Martha Vicinus and B. Nergaard, eds., *Ever Yours*, p. 156–7, 194. See also JoAnn Widerquist, "Dearest Rev'd Mother" in Vern Bullough, Bonnie Bullough and Marietta P. Stanton, *Florence Nightingale and her Era: A Collection of New Scholarship*, Garland, (New York, 1990), pp. 188–308.

[204] McAuley, Catherine, "The Spirit of the Institute," in Neumann, *Letters of Catherine McAuley 1827–1841*, p. 389.

[205] Joanne Regan RSM and Isabelle Keiss RSM, *Tender Courage*, Franciscan Herald Press (Chicago, 1988), p. 106.

206   Mary Celeste Rouleau RSM, "The Prayer of Mercy: Rhythm of Contemplation and Action" in *The MAST: Journal of the Mercy Association in Scripture and Theology*, 6, 2 (Spring, 1996), p. 26.

207   Mary Ann Scofield, RSM, "Towards a Theology of Mercy," *The MAST: Journal of the Mercy Association in Scripture and Theology*, 2, 2 (Spring 1992), pp. 1–8.

208   Roland Burke Savage, *Catherine McAuley: First Sister of Mercy*, M.H. Gill & Son (Dublin, 1949), pp 18–19.

209   Father George Lambert (b.1821–?), a Jesuit, was appointed as the "extraordinary confessor" to the Brighton community – a title which is canonical in origin, and was a provision for members of a community to have opportunity to speak with someone other than the regular confessor or the superior of the house. Perceived as a means of protection for those within the community, the 'extraordinary confessor' was to visit the community at least four times a year. Lambert, however, appears to have been not simply the extraordinary confessor to the community, but a more regular spiritual director. He had been the rector of St. Bueno's College, St. Asaph, Wales, and in 1870 moved to the Roman Generalate of the Society of Jesus. *The Catholic Directory*, 1861; see also Patrick Dougherty, "Mary Potter: Postulant and Novice in the Sisters of Mercy," p. 52.

210   Mary Potter to Father Edward Selley, June 29, 1876. Little Company of Mary Archives, Tooting Bec, London. Hereafter Selley Letters.

211   The importance of the Ignatian influence in the evolution of and support for congregations of women has been examined by Caritas McCarthy. She makes the point that in the main, the Jesuit order "developed men of the Spirit with a great faith in the action of the Spirit in others…spiritual directors whose faith in the 'inner teaching of the holy Spirit' was stronger even than their male scepticism." Caritas McCarthy "Apostolic Congregations of Women and the Ignatian Charism" in *The Way Supplement, 20* (Autumn, 1973), 10–18; p. 12. Lambert's intervention into Potter's life was a means whereby she came to some understanding of the action of the Spirit in her own life, and could apply some levels of discernment for herself. See Virtue Letters. no. 13.

212   On the Ignatian spirit and spirituality see: Joseph F. Conwell, SJ *Impelling Spirit: Revisiting a Founding Experience*, Loyola Press (Chicago, 1997); Ladislas Orsy, "SJ Constitutions: Continuity and Change" in *The Way Supplement* 20: Autumn 1973, 3–9.

213   Virtue Letters, no.9.

214   Selley Letters, June 29, 1876.

215   Mary Potter Autobiographical Notes, p. 17.

216   loc. cit.

217   loc, cit.

218   Virtue Letters, no. 19. Potter stated that "they tried me in every way, even keeping me from Holy Communion."

219   "Rule and Constitutions – Religious Sisters of Mercy," Chapter 10, no. 3, cited in Sullivan, *Catherine McAuley and the Tradition of Mercy*, p. 327–8.

220   loc. cit.

221   loc. cit.

222   ibid., Chapter 3, no.2, p. 297.

223   Abuse of power by superiors of religious houses, particularly in relation to matters of disclosure of conscious and permission to receive the sacraments of both confession and communion resulted in the decree *Quemadmodem* of December 17, 1890. This decree noted the perversion of power by superiors who "took it upon themselves to permit, at their pleasure, their subjects to approach the Holy Table, or even sometimes to forbid them Communion altogether." Decree of the Sacred Congregation of Bishops and Regulars, text given in Lanslots, *Handbook of Canon Law for Congregations of Women Under Simple Vows* p. 276.

224   Extact from the Annals of St. Joseph's Convent of Mercy, Brighton, now held at the Convent of Mercy Archives, Bermondsey. Transcription provided through the kind offices of Sister Imelda Keene, Archivist, Convent of Mercy Archives, Bermondsey.

225   Francesca Steele, *The Convents of Great Britain and Ireland*, p. 271.

226   loc. cit.

227   loc. cit.

228   Virtue Letters, no. 9.

229 loc. cit.

230 Mary Potter *Autobiographical Notes,* pp. 16–17.

231 Virtue Letters, no. 9.

232 loc. cit.

233 Mary Potter *Autobiographical Notes*, p. 9.

234 Extract of Annals of St. Joseph's Convent of Mercy Brighton.

235 Sister Marie Marguerite, Superior of the Convent of the Assumption to Mary Potter, September, 1870, cited in Patrick Dougherty, "Mary Potter: Postulant and Novice" p. 54.

236 Thomas Potter to Mother M. Cecilia Smith, October 12, 1902. See also Gertrude Potter to Mother Hilda Potter, April 20, 1933.

237 Of Mother Joseph's assessment of his sister's capacity for religious life, Thomas later wrote: "No capacity! Ye Gods! The Reverend Mother must have been purblind." Thomas Potter to Francis Potter, March 27, 1910.

238 Mary Potter Virtue Letters, no. 9.

239 Patrick Dougherty, "Mary Potter, Postulant and Novice", p. 47.

240 Extract of Annals of the St. Joseph's Convent of Mercy, Brighton. As the archivist of the Bermondsey archives Sister Imelda Keene notes, this entry in the annals of the Brighton Mercy community is unusual. The normative practice of the day was that reports on novices were not recorded in the Annals, but in separate, private documents. Whilst the first part of the record is accurate, its ending is not. Evidence of the letter from Sister Marie Marguerite of the Sisters of the Assumption, dated September 1870, indicates that that community accepted Mary Potter. Even more obviously, the concluding sentence is of much later origin as Potter left in 1870, and did not found her congregation until 1877. There is no evidence of a meeting between Mary Potter and superior of the Assumption Sisters, and the extant letter, dated September 1870 indicates that the two had not met.

241 Mother Joseph Barrington RSM, to the Vicar Capitular of Southwark Diocese, June 27, 1897, cited in Dougherty, "Mary Potter: Postulant and Novice", p. 45.

242 On the rise of religious life and the ascetic tradition it represents see: Christopher Brooke, *Monasteries of the World: The Rise and Development of the Monastic Tradition*, Crescent, (New York, 1982). Henry Chadwick, "The Ascetic Movement" in *The Early Church*, Rev. ed., Penguin History of the Church 1, Penguin Books, (London, 1993), pp. 173–83. Penelope Johnson, *Equal in Monastic Profession: Religious Women in Medieval France*, University of Chicago Press (Chicago, 1991). Jo Ann McNamara *Sisters in Arms: Catholic Nuns through Two Millenia*, Harvard University Press (Cambridge, Ma., 1996). See also Fahey, "Female Asceticism in the Catholic Church", passim.

243 Laura Finke "Mystical Bodies and the Dialogic of Vision" in U. Wiethaus (ed.) *Maps of Flesh and Light: The Religious Experience of Medieval Women Mystics*, Syracuse University Press, (New York, 1993), pp. 23–44; See also Bruno Borchert, *Mysticism: Its History and Challenge*, Samuel Weiser, Inc. (York Beach, Me., 1994), pp. 3–47.

244 Mary Potter, *Autobiographical Notes*, p. 5

245 ibid., p. 14

246 ibid., p. 15; see also p. 17

247 loc. cit.

248 Jane Lewis (ed.), *Labour and Love, p.* 9. See also Beverley Kingston, *My Wife, My Daughter and Poor Mary Ann*, Thos. Nelson Australia Pty. Ltd (Melbourne, 1975) passim.

249 On the role of women within the nineteenth century see: Martha Vicinus, (ed.), *A Widening Sphere: Changing Roles of Victorian Women*, Methuen & Co., Ltd (London, 1980); and *Suffer and be Still: Women in the Victorian Age*, Indiana University Press (Bloomington & London, 1973). See also M.Jeanne Peterson, *Family Love and Work in the Lives of Victorian Gentlewomen*, Indiana University Press (Bloomington, 1989); Angela V John, (ed.), *Unequal Opportunities: Women's Employment in England 1800–1918*, Basil Blackwell (Oxford, 1986), passim, and Sandra Burman, (ed.), *Fit Work for Women*, Croom Helm (London, 1979).

250 Martha Vicinus, *Independent Women*, pp. 36–40; Colleen Hobbs, "Reclaiming Myths of Power: Women Writers and the Victorian Spiritual Crisis," *Victorian Studies*, Vol 39/2, (Winter, 1996), pp. 244–324.

251 Caroline Emilia Stephen, *Light Arising: Thoughts on the Central Radiance*, (Cambridge, 1908), cited in Martha Vicinus, *Independent Women*, p. 37.

252 On the effects of the mystical life see Evelyn Underhill, *Mysticism: The Nature and Development of Consciousness*, One World Publications (Oxford, 1993) chapter X. Bruno Borchert, *Mysticism Its History and Challenge*, in particular Section III. See also: F.C. Happold, *Mysticism: A study and an anthology*, Penguin Books (London, 1963); James Horne, *The Moral Mystic*, Wilfrid Laurier University Press (Ontario, 1983); F. von Huegel, *The mystical element of religion* 2 vols., Dent Publishing (London, 1908); William James, *The Varieties of Religious Experience*, Mentor Books (New York, 1958); Richard Woods, *Understanding Mysticism*, Image Books (New York, 1980).

253 Alexander Walker, psychologist, 1840, "Introduction: The Adult Woman: Work" in Erna Olafson Hellerstein, Leslie Parker Hume and Karen M. Offen (eds.) *Victorian Women: A Documentary Account of Women's lives in nineteenth century England, France and the United States*, Stanford University Press (Stanford, 1981), p. 274.

254 Elizabeth Sewell, noted educationalist 1856, cited in Hellerstein et al., *Victorian Women* p. 274.

255 Carol Dyhouse, "Mothers and Daughters in the Middle-class Home, c. 1870–1914," in Jane Lewis, (ed.), *Labour and Love*, pp. 41–42.

256 Elaine Showalter, *The Female Malady: Women, Madness and English Culture, 1830–1980,* Virago Press, (London, 1987), in particular chapters 5 and 6. On the ways other women coped with the stress of living independent lives see also Martha Vicinus and Bea Neergard (eds.) *Every Yours,* p. 4. Florence Nightingale became a psycho-neurotic personality, using her illness to shield her from the demands of family, friends, and strangers, thus permitting her to focus solely on her work. On the manner in which spiritual orientation assisted women in the integration of their own selves, see Gerda Lerner, *The Creation of Feminist Consciousness: From the Middle Ages to the Eighteenth Century*, Oxford University Press (Oxford, 1993).

Notes for Section 2

1 Mother Cecilia Smith, *Personal Reminiscences*, p. 6.

2 Letter from Mrs. Mary Ann Potter to Father Edward Selley, July 12, 1876.

3 Mary Potter, *Autobiographical Notes*, p. 8.

4 Selley Letters, August, 1876. For an analysis of the tensions between mothers and daughters within the Victorian family see Carol Dyhouse *Feminism and the Family in England 1880–1939*, Basil Blackwell, (Oxford, 1989), particularly Chapter 1.

5 Selley Letters no. 20, September 26, 1976.

6 Letter Thomas Potter to Mother Mary Cecilia, October 2., 1902.

7 Mary Potter *Obedience Notes*, Vol. 1A, p. 14, Unpublished MS., Little Company of Mary Archives Tooting Bec, London. Hereafter *Obedience Notes.*

8 See Pat Jalland, *Death in the Victorian Family*, Oxford University Press, (Oxford, 1996), and Michael Wheeler *Death and Future Life in Victorian Literature and Theology*, Cambridge University Press, (Cambridge, 1990). Both authors note the importance of the issues of death and dying, grief and loss to the Victorians.

9 The work done by Phillipe Ariès in *The Hour of our Death*, (Penguin, Harmondsworth, 1981) and Thomas Kselman in *Death and the Afterlife in Modern France*, Princeton Press, (Princeton, 1993) both deal with death within the Catholic cultural tradition. However, the English Catholic tradition was as much influenced by its surrounding worldview as by its Catholic European inheritance. The nineteenth century Catholic revival received much French devotional material on death and dying, but its application was, it is suggested, tempered, and influenced by English evangelical understanding.

10 Michael Wheeler points out the work done by the missionary priest Father Furniss in this regard. Furniss, whose grisly descriptions of the torture, despair and hopelessness of the damned, and of hell were published in *The Sight of Hell,* in 1861, was a popular missionary priest for children. See Michael Wheeler, *Death and Future Life,* p. 184. See also cited in J. Sharp, "Juvenile Holiness: Catholic Revivalism Among Children in Victorian Britain", *Journal of Ecclesiastical History,* Vol 35, (1984), pp. 220–238.

11 Mary Potter, *Mary's Call, or Devotion to the Dying*, Our Lady's Little Library, (Nottingham, 1880), p. 33.

12 On the nineteenth century concepts and belief in purgatory see Wheeler, *Death and the Future Life*, pp. 74–75, Kselman, *Death and Afterlife in Modern France*, pp 117–119. On the doctrine of Purgatory within the Catholic Church see F.X. Schouppe *Purgatory*, Tan Books, (Rockville, Ill, 1973. First published in France, 1893).

13 On the life and spiritual works of Pierre Cardinal de Bérulle, (1575–1629) see William M. Thompson (ed.) *Bérulle and the French School: Selected Writings*, (trans. M. Lowell), Classics of Western Spirituality, Paulist Press, (New York/Mahwah, 1989). See also Henri Brémond, *A Literary History of Religious Thought in France* vol. 3, trans. K.L. Montgomery, Society for Promoting Christian Knowledge, (London, 1928), passim; See also R. Deville, *The French School of Spirituality* trans. Agnes Cunningham, Duquesne University Press (Pittsburgh, 1994), passim.

14 Brémond, *A Literary History of Religious Thought*, vol. 3., pp. 3–4.

15 The most complete studies of the spirituality of the French School are to be found in Henri Brémond's, *A Literary History of Religious Thought in France*; R. Deville's *The French School of Spirituality*, and the immense volume of material on the Spirituality of the French school as expressed by Grignon de Montfort in Stefano De Fiores, (ed.), *Jesus Living in Mary: A Handbook of the Spirituality of St. Louis Marie de Montfort*, De Montfort Publications (Bayshore, N.Y, 1996). Additional information is to be found in Michael Downy, (ed.), *The New Dictionary of Catholic Spirituality*, Liturgical Press (Collegeville, Minnesota, 1993), under entries pertaining to the history of spirituality, spiritual schools and spiritualities.

16 Henri Brémond, *A Literary History of Religious Thought*, vol. 1, p. 109.

17 Pierre Bérulle *Oeuvres Completes*, p. 94, cited in Brémond, op. cit., p. 111.

18 Patrick Gaffney, "Mary" in Stefano De Fiores, *Jesus Living in Mary*, p. 703.

19 Stefano de Fiores, "Montfort Spirituality" in De Fiores, *Jesus Living in Mary*, p. 828; Canon Rène Laurentin, *Mother of the Church: History, Meaning and Merit*, unpublished MS., courtesy of Canon Laurentin and IMRI, University of Dayton (Dayton, Ohio July 1995), p. 497.

20 Canon Rène Laurentin, *Mother of the Church*, p. 498; Stefano De Fiores "Montfort Spirituality", p. 830.

21 Patrick Gaffney, "Mary", in De Fiores, *Jesus Living in Mary* p. 818.

22 For a seminal article on the place of Mary in the doctrine of Bérulle, see V. Vasey, "Mary in the Doctrine of Bérulle on the Mysteries of Christ," *Marian Studies*, 36, 1985, pp. 60–80.

23 This concept is traditional of the French school of mysticism which preached the message that all were "*un néant capable de Dieu,*" and that the aim of the spiritual life was to become – as Mary was – filled with God.

24 Montfort, L.G., *The Secret of Mary*, The Montfort Fathers (Liverpool, 1954),# 68.

25 loc. cit.

26 Louis Grignon De Montfort *Treatise on True Devotion,* Fathers of the Company of Mary (London, 1954), # 2, 110, 116.

27 This term was used by De Montfort to describe those men and women who understood the practice of the spirituality, and became "apostles" of Jesus, and whose ministry was directed particularly to the poor, the disenfranchised and the rejects of society. See Louis Grignon de Montfort, *Treatise on True Devotion.,* #47, 48, 114.

28 P. Gaffney, "Reign," in De Fiores, *Jesus Living in Mary* p. 1034; see also Louis Grignon De Montfort, *The Secret of Mary*, # 59.

29 Mary Potter, *Path of Mary,* Washbourne and Sons, (London, 1876), p. 85.

30 loc. cit.

31 John Virtue changed his name to "Vertue" prior to his episcopal ordination. In the Catholic directories up to 1875, he is referred to as "Vertue." In the records of the 1895 episcopal conference, in 1897,and in later documentation, he is referred to as Bishop "Vertue." Enquiries carried out by Sister Anita MacDonald as to when or why this change may have occurred have been unfruitful. For the sake of consistency, the name "Virtue" has been used throughout this study.

32 Sister Anita MacDonald LCM, "Monsignor John Virtue," in *Companions on the Way*, unpublished historical resources of the Little Company of Mary.

33 Edward Norman, *The English Catholic Church in the Nineteenth Century*, Clarendon Press, (Oxford, 1984) p. 237 ff.

34 Sister Anita MacDonald LCM, *Companions on the Way*. In the collation of resources regarding the life and work of Monsignor Virtue, no date given for the edition edited by him. The most likely edition would be that of 1856. For information regarding the various English editions of Richard Challoner's *Garden of the Soul*, see Mary Heimann, *Catholic Devotion in Victorian England*, Oxford Historical Monographs, Clarendon Press (Oxford, 1995), pp. 79–89.

35 Obituary of Bishop George Vertue, *The Tablet*, May 26, 1900.

36 loc. cit.

37 Tribute to Monsignor Vertue by John Hobson Matthews in the *Tablet*, May 26, 1900.

38 loc. cit.

39 loc. cit.

40 Selley Letters, June 1876.

41 Mary Potter *Autobiographical Notes*, p. 4. This consecration was made on December 8, 1872.

42 Virtue Letters, Nos. 1 & 2.

43 loc. cit

44 See D. Knowles, *What is Mysticism*, Burns & Oates, (London, 1967), p. 10–11, also F.E. Weaver, 'Port Royal', *Dictionary of Spirituality, Vol. 13,* cols. 1931–1952. On the question of quietism and the spirituality of the French School, see P. Pourrat, *Christian Spirituality: Later Developments, Part II: From Jansenism to Modern Times*, Newman Press (Westminster, Md., 1995), and L. Dupré, "Jansenism and Quietism" in L. Dupré and D. Saliers, eds., *Christian Spirituality: Post Reformation and Modern*, Crossroad Press (New York, 1989).

45 On the explosion of visions and visionaries through the nineteenth century see N. Perry and L Echeverria, *Under the Heel of Mary*, Routledge Kegan & Paul (London, 1989), Thomas A Kselman, *Miracles and Prophecies in Nineteenth-Century France*. Rutgers University Press, (New Brunswick, 1983); Anne Baude *Radical Spirits, Spiritualism and Women's Rights in Nineteenth Century America*, Beacon Press, (Boston, 1989).

46 W. R. Inge, *Christian Mysticism*, 1901, reprinted by Kessinger Publishing Co.(New York 1997), Introduction.

47 Symbolised by the "manly" Christianity of Charles Kingsley (1819–1875), F. D. Maurice (1805–1872) and Thomas Hughes (1822–1896) it was Christianity as much national as spiritual and coalesced with the on-going struggle of the Victorians to absorb the immense intellectual spiritual and social crisis that surrounded them. See Norman Vance, *The Sinews of the Spirit: The Ideals of Christian Manliness in Victorian Literature and Religious Thought*, Cambridge University Press (Cambridge, 1985), p. 41.

48 G. Parsons "Emotion and Piety: Revivalism and Ritualism in Victorian Christianity" in G. Parsons (ed.) *Religion in Victorian Britain: Traditions*, vol. 1, Manchester University Press, (Manchester, 1988) pp. 213–234, p. 223 ff. S. Gilley, "Vulgar Piety and the Brompton Oratory", 1850–1860' in R. Swift and S. Gilley (eds.), *The Irish in the Victorian City*, pp. 255–266. See also Philip Hughes "The Coming Century" in George Beck, (ed.), *The English Catholics 1850–1950*, Burns Oates, London, 1950, p. 20–21.

49 Philip Hughes, ibid.

50 *Quarant Ore*, or the Forty Hours devotion and adoration of the Blessed Sacrament was an Italianate devotion in memory of Jesus' forty hours in the tomb. On the emergence of this devotion in England see Heimann, *Catholic Devotion in Victorian England*, pp. 42, 44.

51 Evelyn Underhill, *Worship*, Crossroad Press, (New York, 1982), p. 182. For the emergence of these devotions in England, see Heimann, *Catholic Devotion in Victorian England*, particularly Chapter 2.

52 See Sheridan Gilley, "Vulgar Piety", p. 255.

53 On the manner in which women actually assisted in the creation of "sacred spaces" see Susan O'Brien, "Making Catholic Spaces: Women Décor, and Devotion in the English Catholic Church, 1840–1900," passim.

54 Annie Besant, *An Autobiography*, (1893) The Theosophical Press, (Philadelphia, reprinted 1939) p. 52.

55 Cited in Besant, *An Autobiography*, pp. 66–67.

56 loc. cit.

57 Julie Melnyk (ed.), *Women's Theology in Nineteenth Century Britain: Transfiguring the Faith of Their Fathers*, Garland Publishing Inc., (New York: 1998), p. xvii.

58 Besant, *An Autobiography*, p. 40. See also Fredrick Roden "The Kiss of the Soul: The Mystical Theology of Christina Rossetti's Devotional Prose," in Melnyk, *Women's Theology in Nineteenth-Century Britain*, pp. 37–55; Sarah Wilburn, "Victorian Women Theologians of the Mystical Fringe: Translations and Domesticity" in Melnyk, op. cit., pp. 189–207, passim. For the American experience, see Anne Baude *Radical Spirits, Spiritualism and Women's Rights in Nineteenth Century America*, Beacon Press, Boston, 1989.

59 Aldous Huxley, in Sisirkumar Ghose, *Mysticism as a Force for Change* Theosophical Publishing House, (Wheaton, Ill. 1981), p. xii.

60   Besant, *An Autobiography*, p. 40.

61   Cited in Cecil Kerr, *Teresa Helena Higginson: Servant of God "The Spouse of the Crucified" 1844–1905,* Sands &Co., (London, 1927), p. 167. Teresa Higginson was an alleged stigmatic, visionary, miracle worker and mystic, who lived in Bootle. Her various experiences and her promulgation of devotion to the "Sacred Head (of Jesus)" as the source of Divine Wisdom, were intensively investigated by the Church both during life and after death. Her cause was introduced to Rome but was denied. Subsequent to this, when the examination of the Cause of Venerable Mary Potter was underway (the cause commenced in 1920), there was a flurry of agitation when one of Mary Potter's letters asked if the recipient had heard of a prayer to the "Sacred Head." The investigation then had to prove that Mary had not been involved with this devotion.

62   Gerda Lerner, *The Creation of Feminist Consciousness*, p. 47.

63   Melnyk, *Women's Theology in Nineteenth Century Britain*, p. xv.

64   Virtue Letters, no. 1.

65   loc. cit.

66   loc. cit.

67   loc. cit.

68   loc. cit .

69   loc. cit. see also Virtue Letters no. 10.

70   Mary Potter, *Autobiographical Notes*, p. 10.

71   ibid., p. 11.

72   Virtue Letters, no. 2.

73   loc. cit.

74   "Rules for Perceiving and Knowing in some manner the Different Movements which are caused in the Soul" in David A. Fleming SJ, *The Spiritual Exercises of St. Ignatius: A Literal Translation and A Contemporary Reading,* Institute of Jesuit Sources (St. Louis Missouri, 1978), p. 206.

75   loc. cit.

76   loc. cit.

77   It was an insight that would not be received by the Church until 1971, when Pope Paul VI made an explicit link between spiritual gifts (charisms) given for the building up of the body of the church and religious life. See Paul VI, *Evangelica Testificatio,* Paulist Press, (New York, 1971), #11; *Mutuae Relationes,* Paulist Press, (New York, 1978), in particular # 11, 12; John Paul II, *Redemptionis Domun,* Paulist Press, (New York, 1984), in particular # 15; *Christefidelis Laici,* Paulist Press, (New York, 1989), in particular # 24 ff.; On the evolution of the understanding of religious life as charismatic utterance in the church see: Antonio Romano, *The Charism of the Founders,* Paulist Press, (UK, 1989), Manuel Luis Jurado, SJ "Consecrated life and the Charisms of the Founders" in Rene Latourelle (ed.), *Vatican II: Assessment and Perspectives Twenty-five Years After (1962–1987),* Paulist Press, (NJ 1989).

78   Melnyk, *Women's Theology in Nineteenth-Century Britain* pp. xi-xvii. On the contemporary restriction and rejection of women's insights into theological discussion see Ruskin, "Of Queen's Gardens" in *Sesame and the Lilies,* passim. See also Christine L. Krueger, *The Reader's Repentance: Women Preachers, Women Writers, and Nineteenth Century Social Discourse,* University of Chicago Press, (Chicago,1992), passim.

79   Acts 2:4.

80   Exodus 15:20.

81   Joel 2: 28–29.

82   Lucretia A. Flamming, " 'Your Sons and Daughters will Prophesy': The Voice and Vision of Josephine Butler", in Melnyk, *Women's Theology in Nineteenth-Century Britain* p. 159; Anne Lang, *Prophetic Woman: Anne Hutchinson and the Problem of Dissent in the Literature of New England,* University of California Press (Berkley, 1987), p. 42; Marina Warner *Joan of Arc*, Vintage Books, (London, 1981).

83   Herbert J. Thurston, *Suprising Mystics*, Burns & Oates (London, 1955), p. 132.

84   loc. cit.

85   Virtue Letters no. 2.

86   loc. cit.

87   loc. cit.

88   loc. cit.

89   loc. cit.

90   M. Potter, *Autobiographical Notes*, p. 10.

91   loc. cit.

92   Virtue Letters, no. 3.

93   See John 15:16; Mark 4:20; Luke 8:15; Luke 13:9; and John 15:2.

94   Cf. Jeremiah 1:1–8; Isaiah 42: 1ff.

95   2 Corinthians 12: 9–10.

96   Gerda Lerner, *The Creation of Feminist Consciousness*, p. 69. Not only medieval women experienced the trans-
      formatory power of religion and religious experience. Modern studies by Carol Gilligan, and Elizabeth Ozorak
      each point to point to the same reality, and are supported by the research by Hill. See Carol Gilligan, *In a
      Different Voice*, Harvard University Press (Cambridge, Ma., 1982); Elizabeth Ozorak, "The Power but not the
      glory: how women empower themselves through religion" in *Journal for the Scientific Study of Religion*, Vol 35,
      (March, 1996), pp. 17–29; P. Hill "Towards an attitude process model of religious experience," in *Journal for
      the Scientific Study of Religion*, Vol 33, 121–28.

97   Richard Woods, "Medieval and Modern Women Mystics: The Evidential Character of Religious Experience,"
      Founder's Day Lecture, Alistair Hardy Research Centre, Westminster College, Oxford, December 5, 1992. I am
      indebted to Richard Woods OP for a copy of this paper. Elizabeth Alvida Petroff, *Body and Soul: Essays on
      Medieval Women and Mysticism*, Oxford University Press (New York, 1994), particularly pp. 8–9; G. M. Jantzen,
      "Feminists, Philosophers, and Mystics," 1994, *Hypatia*, 9,4, pp. 186–206; G. M. Jantzen, *Power, Gender and
      Christian Mysticism*, Cambridge University Press (Cambridge, 1995), particularly ch. 5. Nineteenth century
      women, like their medieval sisters, also used experiences of God to validate their claim to spiritual authority and
      the right to work and act "in God's name". See in particular L. Huffman Hoyle, "Nineteenth-Century Single
      Women and Motivation for Mission," *International Bulletin of Missionary Research*, April 1996, 20, 2, pp.
      58–64. Charles Wallace Jnr., "The Prayer Closet as 'A Room of One's Own': Two Anglican Women Devotional
      Writers at the Turn of the Eighteenth Century", *Journal of Women's History*, 9, 2 (Summer, 1997) pp. 108–12;
      see also Gail Malmgreen, *Religion in the Lives of Englishwomen 1760–1930*, Croom Helm (London, 1986).

98   For a discussion on the relationship between mysticism and schizophrenia, see K Wapnick, "Mysticism and
      Schizophrenia," *Journal of Transpersonal Psychology* 1, 2 (1985); on mysticism and the psychology of conscious-
      ness, see R.K.C. Forman, "What Does Mysticism Have to Teach us About Consciousness?," *Journal of
      Consciousness Studies* (, 1996); E Hocking, "The Meaning of Mysticism as Seen through Its Psychology," in
      Understanding Mysticism, Woods, R. (ed.)Althone Press, (London: 1980).

99   Virtue Letters, no. 3.

100   Mary Potter, *Autobiographical Notes*, p. 13.

101   Mary Potter, *Obedience Notes*, 3, no. 5.

102   Mary Potter, *Obedience Notes*, 5, no. 122.

103   loc. cit.

104   E. Underhill, *Mysticism*, p. 238–240.

105   Mary Potter, *Obedience Notes*, 5, no. 2.

106   Virtue Letters, no. 10.

107   See Evelyn Underhill, *Mysticism*, p. 414 ff. Richard Woods, "Mysticism and Social Action: The Mystic's Calling,
      Development and Social Activity", *Journal of Consciousness Studies*, 3, 2., 1996, passim. See also Sisirkumar
      Ghose *Mystics as a Force for Change*, passim.

108   Catherine of Genoa, (1447–1507): Cited in Evelyn Underhill, *Mystics of the Church*, James Clarke & Co., Ltd.,
      Cambridge, 1975, p. 165.

109   Virtue Letters no. 6.

110   Mary Potter to Monsignor Virtue # 2, c. November 1874. Virtue's placing Mary under pain of mortal sin not
      to either attend to the experiences, or 'permit' them, was an extraordinarily heavy penalty. For a Catholic, mor-
      tal sin means total separation from God, and if one dies in such a state, eternal punishment. The penalty under

which Virtue placed Potter also speaks of his conviction that the experiences she was undergoing were not 'of God'.

111 Virtue Letters, no. 5.

112 Mary Potter, *Autobiographical Notes*, p. 13.

113 Mary Potter, *Obedience Notes,* vol. A, p. 12.

114 See for example the visions of Gertrude the Great of Hefta, of Angela of Foligno and those of Julian of Norwich. Each of these women speaks of being drawn into the wounded side of Christ. In Gertrude's vision, Jesus says: "The union that you see between her heart and my side indicates that she is thus at every moment able to drink from the flood of my divinity." Angela has a similar experience but draws from it a different understanding: "[H]e called me and said I should put my mouth to the wound in his side. And it seemed to me that I saw and drank his blood flowing freely from his side. And I was given to understand that by this he would cleanse me." For Julian of Norwich, the sense was different again. In her long text she speaks of "our tender Mother Jesus can lead us easily into his blessed breast through his sweet open side, and show us there a part of the Godhead and of the joys of heaven, with inner certainty of endless bliss." The resemblance of Potter's experience to those of these three women mystics is striking, and offers possibility of further research. See Gertrude of Hefta, *Oeuvres 2: Héaut,* bk.1, chap. 16, pp. 206–18, cited in Caroline Walter Bynum, *Jesus as Mother: Studies in the Spirituality of the High Middle Age,* University of California Press, (California, 1982), p. 193. Revelations of Angela Foligno, cited in Elizabeth A. Petroff, *Body and Soul: Essays on Medieval Women and Mysticism* Oxford University Press, (New York 1994), p. 213; Julian of Norwich *Showings,* trans. Edmund Colledge OSA and James Walsh SJ, Paulist Press (New York, 1978), p. 298.

115 Mary Potter, *Mary's Conferences,* Richardsons (London, 1877: Australian reprint of original, 1988), p. 136. Hereafter *Mary's Conferences.*

116 Mary Potter, *Conferences A.,* p. 33. Little Company of Mary Archives, Tooting Bec, London. Hereafter *Conferences A.*

117 M. Potter, *Motherhood,* p. 79.

118 Mary Potter, *Conferences M,* p. 96, circa 1875. Little Company of Mary Archives, Tooting Bec, London. Hereafter *Conferences M.*

119 Mary Potter, *Mary's Conferences,* p. 19.

120 M.Potter, *Message from the Mother Heart of Mary,* Our Lady's Little Library, Nottingham, 1878, p. 37. Hereafter *Message from the Mother Heart of Mary.*

121 Barbara Taylor, *Eve and the New Jerusalem,* Pantheon Books (New York, 1983); Robert M. Kachur "Envisioning Equality, Asserting Authority: Women's Devotional Writings on the Apocalypse, 1845–1900" in Melnyk, *Women's Theology in Nineteenth-Century Britain,* pp. 3–34; Catherine Keller, *Apocalypse Now and Then: A Feminist Guide to the End of the World* (Beacon Press: Boston, 1996).

122 Kachur, "Envisioning Equality, Asserting Authority", p. 6.

123 J. Butler, *The Hour before Dawn,* Trubner Pty. Ltd. (London, 1876), p. 109 – 99.

124 loc. cit.; see also Lucretia A. Flamming, "And your sons and daughters will prophecy: The voice and vision of Josephine Butler," in Melnyk, *Women's Theology in Nineteenth-Century Britain.,* pp. 151–163.

125 Mary Potter, *Message from the Mother Heart of Mary,* p. 37.

126 Mary Potter *Path of Mary,* Washbourne & Son, (London, 1876) p. 23. Emphasis as in original. Hereafter *Path of Mary.*

127 Virtue Letters no. 2.

128 Mary Potter, *Conferences E.,* p. 7. no. 16. Little Company of Mary Archives, Tooting Bec, London. Hereafter *Conferences E.*

129 Mary Potter, *The Human Life of Jesus,* Gustavus Campolmi (Florence, 1901) p. 157. Hereafter *The Human Life.*

130 Patrick Gaffney, "Reign," in De Fiores, *Jesus Living in Mary,* p. 1035.

131 Virtue Letters, no. 6.

132 Virtue Letters, no. 5.

133 See in particular Isaiah 61:1–11. The prophet sings of the good news of repentance and mercy by beginning: "The spirit of the Lord is upon me, because the Lord has anointed me, he has sent me to bring good news to

the oppressed, to bind up the broken hearted, to proclaim liberty to captives and release the prisoners." Compare
with Luke 3:18–19, where Jesus uses the words of the prophet to describe his own mission.

134 Virtue Letters, no. 10.

135 loc. cit.

136 loc. cit.

137 loc. cit.

138 loc. cit.

139 Margaret Anne Cusack (1829–1899), known as the 'Nun of Kenmare', was a convert to Catholicism in 1858.
     Mandated by Wiseman to devote her life to Catholic Literature, she was a prolific writer, even after entering the
     Newry Poor Clare Convent. Her writings covered a wide range of interests. Seminal works included *The Patriot's
     History of Ireland* (1869), *The life and revelations of St. Gertrude* (1865/1870), 'The Spouse of Christ* in Two
     Volumes (1872–1878); *Women's Work in Modern Society* (1874), After a strange and sad life of persecution
     within and without the Church, Cusack abandoned Catholicism and wrote two autobiographical studies *The
     Nun of Kenmare* (1888) and *The Story of my Life* (1893), moderately anti-Catholic in tone. Her life and work
     provided her with material to support herself through lecture tours of the United States, under the auspices of
     the Episcopalian Church. Potter and the Nun of Kenmare were to maintain intermittent contact for their rest
     of their lives. Throughout Potter's correspondence, there are references to communication with Cusack, but
     sadly much of the actual correspondence is missing. For details of Cusack's life, see Irene Ffrench Eagar,
     Margaret Anne Cusack: one Woman's Campaign for Women's Rights, Arlen House, (Dublin, 1979) and
     D. A. Vidulich, *Peace Pays a Price,* Sisters of St Joseph of Peace (Washington, 1990).

140 Mary Potter *Path of Mary,* p. 111.

141 ibid., p. 108–109.

142 loc. cit.

143 ibid., p. 102.

144 ibid., pp. 91–105.

145 ibid., p. 15 ff.

146 Melnyk, *Women's Theology in Nineteenth Century Britain*, p. xii.

147 Virtue Letters, no. 13.

148 Selley Letters, June 16, 1876.

149 Virtue Letters, no. 14.

150 Virtue Letters, no. 17.

151 Mary Potter, *Autobiographical Notes*, p. 10.

152 loc. cit.

153 loc. cit.

154 V.J.L. Fontana, *Rebirth of Roman Catholicism in Portsmouth*, The Portsmouth Papers no.56, (City of
     Portsmouth), 1989, p. 19 ff.

155 Mrs Mary Ann Potter to Father Selley, July 11, 1876.

156 Mary Potter to Mary Fulker, n.d. 1875: Letters D, Little Company of Mary Archives, Tooting Bec, London.

157 On the relationship between domestic servants and employers and family members see Pam Taylor, "Daughters
     and mothers – maids and mistresses: domestic service between the Wars" in John Clarke, Chas Crichter and
     Richard Johnson, (eds.), *Working Class Culture: Studies in History and Theory,* Hutchinson (London, 1979),
     p. 125. For a fuller exploration of "the servant problem" and the relationship between servants and their mas-
     ters and mistresses see Leonora Davidoff, "Class and Gender and Victorian England," Judith Newton, Mary
     Ryan and Leonara Davidoff, (eds.), *Sex and Class in Women's History,* Routledge & Kegan Paul (London, 1983),
     esp. pp. 27–8.

158 Mrs Mary Ann Potter to Father Selley, July 11, 1876.

159 Mary Potter to Mary Fulker, n.d.

160 loc. cit.

161 Personal reminiscences of Mme Marguerite Potter (nee Faveraux), to her daughter Diddy Potter, April 30, 1933.
     Little Company of Mary Archives, Tooting Bec, London.

[162] Mary Potter to Mary Fulker, n.d.

[163] Mary Potter to Mary Fulker, November, 1875.

[164] loc. cit.

[165] Mme. Marguerite Potter to her daughter Diddy Potter, April 30, 1933, Little Company of Mary Archives, Tooting Bec.

[166] loc. cit.

[167] James Danell was in the Southwark diocese. Born July 14, 1821, he was consecrated Bishop of Southwark by Cardinal Manning on March 25, 1871.

[168] Selley Letters, n.d.

[169] Selley Letters, May 1876.

[170] loc. cit.

[171] P.J. Hickey, OSA, *The Life of the Rev. E.A. Selley OSA and Mary Potter,* unpublished manuscript n.d. pp 3–4.

[172] ibid. p. 10.

[173] The Marist Fathers or Society of Mary, were founded by Père Claude Colin in France in 1816, and formally approved by the Church in 1836. See J. Costé, SM, *Lectures on Society of Mary History (Marist Fathers), 1786–1854,* (Rome, 1965), passim.

[174] Hickey, *Life of Father Selley,* pp. 3–4.

[175] Selley Letters, no. 1. n.d.

[176] Selley Letters, no. 2. June, 1876.

[177] Selley Letters, no. 3. June, 1876.

[178] Selley Letters, no. 4, June 13, 1876.

[179] Susan O'Brien, "Terra Incognita," p. 115.

[180] ibid., p. 114.

[181] Raymond Deville "The French School of Spirituality," in De Fiores, *Jesus Living in Mary.*,p. 447. See also H.J. Jungmann, "Mystic" in De Fiores, op. cit., p. 855.

[182] Martha Vicinus, *Independent Women,* p. 49 ff. Of the new Catholic communities of England all had a clear social purpose, as had the Irish foundations of the same period. See Susan O'Brien, "Terra Incognita" pp. 110–140; Edna Hamer, *Elizabeth Prout,* pp. 82–87, and Rosemary Raughter, "A Discreet Benevolence: female philanthropy and the Catholic resurgence in eighteenth century Ireland," *Women's History Review,* Vol. 6/4, (1997); p. 479. On the American experience of women's foundations in the nineteenth century see M. Ewens, *The Role of the Nun* , passim, and Mary J. Oates *The Catholic philanthropic Tradition in America,* University of Indiana Press (Bloomington, Indiana, 1995).

[183] Mary Potter "On Devotion to the Dying", *Conferences M.,* 1875/1876. Hereafter "On Devotion to the Dying".

[184] loc. cit.

[185] loc. cit.

[186] This was also the view of the founders of the Sisters of the Cross and Passion, Elizabeth Prout (1820–1864). According to Edna Hamer, Prout's explicit purpose was to provide religious life for working women, who were denied entry to mainstream congregations due to the problem of dowry costs and lack of education. Potter's vision shared much of this earlier congregation's ideals – the unity of active and contemplative life and the engagement in outside work as a means of supporting the essential inner life. See Edna Hamer *Elizabth Prout: 1820–1864. A Religious life for Industrial England,* p. 81.

[187] Fulker, a machinist in a factory in Spitalfields, would have had no right of entry to a contemplative community as a choir member.

[188] Mary Potter "On Devotion to the Dying".

[189] loc. cit.

[190] loc. cit.

[191] loc. cit.

[192] loc. cit.

[193] loc. cit.

194   Mary Potter to Mrs. Elizabeth Bryan, November 22, 1876. Letters F, Little Company of Mary Archives, Tooting Bec, London. Hereafter Bryan Letters.

195   Selley Letters, June, 1876.

196   loc. cit.

197   loc. cit.

198   loc. cit.

199   The Marist vision, as expressed by its founder Colin, was essentially bound up in a Marian spirituality. Costé makes the point that within the Marist tradition lie three closely linked ideas, that of the imitation of Mary, the possession of her spirit and the living of her life. For Colin, Mary, the Mother of the Lord, was a living person: The obligation Marist Fathers took upon themselves under the inspiration of the founder, was to live a Marian life. Imitation of Mary led to the "more profound obligation of capturing her spirit." According to Costé, the spirit of Mary was "basically a capacity for modest and humble actions and the hidden life, all of which seemed to animate the Blessed Virgin during her earthly existence. …[but]… the essential thing was Mary herself and not a list of virtues by which her spirit is described." Selley had no difficulty in understanding or valuing the spirit of Mary that Potter proposed, finding within it an echo of a similar, though different vision to that of his own founder. See J. Costé, SM. *Lectures on Society of Mary History (Marist Fathers), 1786–1854* (Rome, 1965), passim.

200   Mary Potter to Mary Fulker, June 1876.

201   Mary Potter to Mary Fulker, July 1876.

202   loc. cit. Fulker did enter the Little Company of Mary but she did not remain.

203   In traditional convents (enclosed communities), and in most of the "new" religious institutes of the nineteenth century, there was a class division which divided those who could provide a substantial dowry and were therefore of more "respectable classes" from those who could not. Candidates from wealthier middle and upper classes were admitted to 'choir', that is to the chanting of the offices and works of the community. Working class women who entered such communities did so as lay-sisters. Their dowry was less and in real terms, they provided a servant class to the community. As lay-sisters, their training, education and spirituality were often different from those of the choir sisters, thus reinforcing the difference in status. Susan O'Brien has documented the nature of such separation into "choir and lay", within religious orders in England the nineteenth century. See Susan O'Brien, "Lay Sisters and Good Mothers", 453–465.

204   See for example: Carol Dyhouse, *Feminism and the Family in England*, p. 25 and Joan Perkin, *Victorian Women*, New York University Press (New York, 1993), p. 160–163.

205   Selley Letters, no. 5, June 16, 1876.

206   Selley Letters, no. 3, June, 1876.

207   Selley Letters, no. 5, June 16, 1876.

208   Elizabeth Bryan, (d.1898) a widow some years older than Potter, was to become one of the founding members of the community.

209   Selley Letters, June 16, 1876.

210   loc. cit.

211   Mrs Potter to Father Selley, July 4, 1876.

212   Mrs Potter to Father Selley, July 11, 1876.

213   Mrs Potter to Mary Potter, July 11, 1876.

214   Mrs. Potter to Father Selley, July 12, 1876.

215   loc. cit. No records exist to point to the actual occupation of Mr. George Saul, and efforts to trace family records have thus far failed.

216   loc. cit.

217   Mrs Mary Anne Potter to Mary Potter, July 11, 1876.

218   loc. cit.

219   Henry Cardinal Manning, the second Cardinal Archbishop of Westminster, was the leader of the Catholic Community in England. On his life and works see: Robert Gray, *Cardinal Manning: A Biography*, Weidenfeld and Nicolson (London) 1985. Edmund Sheridan Purcell, *Life of Cardinal Manning: Archbishop of Westminster*,

2 vols. MacMillan (London, 1896); Lytton Stachey, *Eminent Victorians,* Weidenfeld & Nicholson (New York, 1989); Oliver P. Rafferty "Henry Cardinal Manning: Apostle of Social Justice," in *America*, 166, 2 (1992) pp. 36–37.

220 Mrs. A Craven, *Life of Lady Georgiana Fullerton,* translated by H.J. Coleridge, Richard Bentley & Son (London, 1888), and Fanny Taylor [Mother Magdalen Taylor], *The Inner Life of Lady Georgiana Fullerton*, Burns & Oates Ltd (London,1899).

221 A.W. Hutton, *Cardinal Manning* Methuen & Co. (London, 1892), p. 247.

222 Peter Anson, *The Call of the Cloister*: pp. 254–246.

223 On the efforts made by Manning to establish religious houses with the support of Lady Georgiana Fullerton and Fanny Taylor see F.C Devas, *Mother Magdalen Taylor of the Sacred Heart,* p. 69ff.

224 On Manning's spirituality and theology see H. Francis Davis, "Manning the Spiritual Writer" in Fitzsimons, *Manning Anglican and Catholic*, pp. 149–160. Davis points out that Manning believed passionately in the internal and hallowing presence of the Spirit in each individual soul, and expressed this in his work *The Internal Mission of the Holy Ghost*. On Manning's own life see A.W. Hutton, *Cardinal Manning*, Methuen & Co. (London, 1892).

225 Lady Dilke to Mr. Bodley, n.d. cited in Shane Leslie, "Manning and his Friends" in John Fitzsimons, (ed.), *Manning, Anglican and Catholic*, 66–72, p. 72.

226 A priest friend of George Potter gave this information to Manning or to one of his advisers. It is referenced in a letter to Selley from Mary Potter in which she notes: "it is likely that through this priest that the letters which were sent … by my relations, were forwarded to the Cardinal's secretary." Selley Letters, August 17, 1876.

227 Cited in, Dougherty, *Mother Mary Potter,* p. 64.

228 Selley Letters, July 26, 1876.

229 loc. cit.

230 Fullerton financed Taylor in a journey to Poland to explore the foundation and spirit of a Polish community – the Little Servants of the Mother of God – in order to assess if their rule and life would be suitable in England, and to see if the community would be willing to have an English Branch, which used its rule and constitutions whilst having a degree of independence. There was a good deal of sense in the undertaking, for gaining the rule of an established order had much to recommend it in terms of acceptance. In 1869, Taylor gained permission from the Archbishop of Posen and the founder of the order M. Bojanowski, to establish a branch in England. Taylor and Cardinal Manning finally rejected an amalgamation, but used the rule to establish the Poor Servants of the Mother of God. For the history of the foundation see Devas, *Mother Magdalen Taylor of the Sacred Heart* passim*;* and Dicens, *Mother Magdalen Taylor,* passim. See also Mrs. Augustus Craven, *Life of Lady Georgiana Fullerton*, J. Coleridge (trans.), Richard Bentley & Son, (London, 1888), p. 411 ff.

231 Selley Letters, July 26, 1876.

232 loc. cit.

233 loc. cit.

234 loc. cit.

235 Selley Letters, August 10, 1876.

236 Selley Letters, August 1876.

237 loc. cit.

238 In response to the threat of withdrawing consent for publication, Henry Potter wrote to Cardinal Manning August 16, 1876. In this letter Henry makes a plea that he hopes, "Your Eminence will not refuse to grant the necessary consent to her book being published." In similar vein, he wrote to Bishop Danell of Southwark on the same date: "I trust your Lordship… will not forbid my sister's book or books to be published, but rather give your full permission to her to have them published."

239 Selley Letters, August 17, 1876. In this letter Potter wrote: "There is little wonder … at the Bishop's opposition. My brother is thought well of (as he deserves to be) at the Cathedral."

240 loc. cit.

241 From 1871, the year of his appointment as bishop of Southwark, Danell had been involved in the emerging constitutional development of Cornelia Connolly's Sisters of the Holy Child. At the first Chapter of the Institute

in 1874, Danell had confounded Cornelia and her sisters by presenting them with a complete constitution which had no reference to the spirit of the institute as enunciated by the founder, and which named him as bishop superior of the institute. The conflict generated by this arbitrary act continued and almost resulted in schism within the congregation. See Caritas McCarthy, *The Spirituality of Cornelia Connolly: In God, For God, With God*, Edwin Mellen Press (Lewiston and Queenston, 1991), pp. 186–198.

242 Letter from Bishop Danell to Mary Potter, Little Company of Mary Archives, Tooting Bec, London, n.d.

243 Selley Letters, August 14, 1876.

244 Hickey, Life of Father Selley, p. 15.

245 Selley Letters, August 12, 1876.

246 loc. cit.

247 loc. cit.

248 On nineteenth century views of women see: Georges Perrot and Michelle Duby, (gen. eds), *A History of Women in the West: 1V. Emerging Feminism From Revolution to World War*, Belknap Press (Cambridge, 1993); Jane Lewis, (ed.), *Labour and Love: Women's Experience of Home and Family 1850 – 1940*, Basil Blackwell (Oxford, 1986). M. Jeanne Peterson, *Family Love and Work in the Lives of Victorian Gentlewomen*, Indiana University Press (Bloomington, 1989). Dale A. Spender, *Women in English Religion 1700–1925*, Edwin Mellen Press, (New York, 1983), J.M. Thompson, "Incarcerated Souls Women as Individuals in Margaret Fuller's Woman in the Nineteenth Century," 1995, *Communication Quarterly*, Vol 43/1, pp 53–63. Anthony S. Wohl, (ed.), *The Victorian Family: Structure and Stresses*, Croom Helm (London, 1978); M Vicinus, (ed.), *Suffer and be Still: Women in the Victorian Age*, Indiana University Press (Bloomington & London, 1973); Mrs. A. B Jameson, *Sisters of Charity Catholic and Protestant & The Communion of Labour*, Ticknor & Fields (Boston, 1858). Erna Olafson Hellerstein, Hume, Leslie Parker and Offen, Karen M., eds., *Victorian Women: A Documentary Account of Women's Lives in Nineteenth Century England, France, and the United States* Stanford University Press, (California, 1981). Joan Perkin, *Victorian Women*, John Murray, (London, 1993).

249 M. Vicinus, *Independent Women*, p. xiv.

250 George. S. Saul to Mary Potter, August 14, 1876

251 Perkin, *Victorian Women*, p. 161. See also Steven Mintz, *A Prisoner of Expectations: The family in Victorian Culture*, New York University Press (New York, 1983); Patricia Jalland, "Victorian Spinsters: Dutiful Daughters, Desperate Rebels, and the Transition to the New Women" in Patricia Crawford, (ed.), *Exploring Women's Past: Essays in Social History*, (Sydney, 1984), pp 129–170; Cecile Dauphin, "Single Women" in Genevieve Fraisse and Michelle Perrot (eds), *A History of Women: Emerging Feminism from Revolution to World War*, 427–441.

252 On the struggle of women to achieve self-realisation see Alison Booth, *Greatness Engendered: George Eliot and Virginia Woolf*, Cornell University Press (Ithaca and London, 1992), p. 157, and passim.

253 Selley Letters, August 14, 1876.

254 loc. cit.

255 Selley Letters, August 17, 1876.

256 Henry Potter to Mary Potter, August 17, 1876.

257 The *Spiritual Exercises of Mary* was published in Nottingham in 1878.

258 Selley Letters, September 4, 1876. In the *Treatise on True Devotion,* such a retreat is mentioned, but no record of it existed within the known works of De Montfort. Potter's work was an original attempt at facilitating entry into the spirituality she had espoused.

259 Published in Rome, 1910.

260 Selley Letters, September 4, 1876.

261 Selley Letters, September 18th, 1976.

262 See *The Catholic Times*, October 6, 1876 and *The Weekly Register*, September 30, 1876.

263 Bryan Letters, October 30, 1876.

264 loc. cit.

265 Exploration of the relationship between Mary Potter and Mother Clare Cusack, the Nun of Kenmare, whilst outside the scope of this study, would bear interest. Apparently drawn to a correspondence through a shared

interest in the mystical life, Cusack expressed interest in joining Potter in founding her religious order. Though this plan was thwarted when she became ill, the two maintained a correspondence, and met again in Rome. Following Cusack's separation from the Catholic church, the two appear to have remained in contact, and while few letters are extant, it appears that Potter not only admired but also supported Cusack. I am indebted to Brendan Fay for information of letters from Mary Potter to Mother Clare Cusack and Mother Evangelista Gaffney, held in the American archives of the Sisters of St. Joseph of Peace.

266 Mother Clare Cusack to Mary Potter circa 1876. Referenced and reproduced in a letter from Selley Letters, October 1876.

267 Selley Letters, October 1, 1876.

268 Selley Letters, September 26, 1876.

269 Selley Letters, September 21, 1876.

270 Cited in Joan Perkin, *Victorian Women*, p. 161. On women writers and devotional literature, see M. Maison, *The Victorian Vision: Studies in the Religious Novel*, New York, 1961; see also M. Maison "Thine Only Thine: Women Hymn Writers in Britain, 1760–1835", in Malmgreen, *Religion in the Lives of Englishwomen*, pp. 11–40.

271 Selley Letters, October 1, 1876.

272 Selley Letters, undated, 1876.

273 Selley Letters, September 18, 1876.

274 Bryan Letters, November, 1876.

275 Selley Letters, October 5, 1876.

276 loc. cit.

277 Bryan Letters, November, 1876.

278 Bryan Letters, December 22. 1876.

279 Hickey, *Life of Father Selley*, p. 18–19.

280 loc. cit.

281 Letter from Father Stephen Chaurain to Mary Potter, October 1876.

282 Lincoln City Reference Library. Obituary Notices: Lincoln, *Rutland and Stamford Mercury*, 1891. Further sources per kind favour Mrs. Loewenthal, Archivist, Diocesan Archives Nottingham.

283 loc. cit.

284 Bryan Letters, December 29, 1876.

285 Mary Potter to Mary Fulker, January 3, 1876.

286 Marguerite Potter to Mother Mary Dunstan, 1930.

Notes for Section 3

1 Edward Bagshawe was born in London in 1829. The third son of Henry Richard Bagshawe KC, a county court judge, and Catherine Gunning, eldest daughter of John Gunning, Inspector of Hospitals in the Peninsula and Waterloo, he had been educated at University College, London, where he graduated with a first in Classics. Turning from his initial desire to enter the legal profession, Bagshawe entered the London Oratory in 1849, and was ordained as an Oratorian priest in 1852. The next twenty-two years were spent in unremarkable fashion as a priest at Brompton Oratory, until on November 12, 1874, he was consecrated Bishop of Nottingham by Cardinal Manning. Obituary Notice, *The Tablet*, February 13, 1915, p. 6.

2 In 1851, the population of the diocese of Nottingham stood at 1,121, 910. In 1861, it had increased to 1,202,349. In 1878, Bagshawe had fewer than one hundred priests to meet the needs of his scattered flock. Of these, nine were retired, twenty-three were in religious communities, leaving sixty-seven 'missionary' priests to work within the counties which constituted the diocese. There were four communities of religious women scattered throughout the diocese in 1861. The Sisters of Mercy had four convents (Derby, Belper and two in Nottingham), the Sisters of Providence were in one convent in Loughborough, one community of the Sisters of Charity of St. Paul was in Glossop, and a group of Dominican Sisters of Penance in Leicester. By 1878, the number of communities resident throughout the diocese had increased to eight, scattered in sixteen convents: See

Ecclesiastical Statistics, Diocese of Nottingham, 1851, 1861, 1878, in *The Catholic Directory: Ecclesiastical Registers and Almanac* for the years 1851, 1861, 1878.

3 J. Derek Holmes, *More Roman Than Rome*, Burns & Oates Ltd (London, 1978), p. 172.

4 loc. cit.

5 Sheridan Gilley "Roman Catholicism" in D.G. Paz (ed.), *Nineteenth Century English Religious Traditions: Retrospect and Prospect*, Greenwood Press (Westport, Connecticut) 1995, p. 53.

6 In his desire to expand the church within his diocese, Bagshawe: "began at once to open new missions…there was a great shortage of priests, so he had to borrow these, many of whom came from Ireland, and were admirable, but again there were some, even from America and other lands who were most undesirable, and so gave great disedification. The Bishop refused no one who applied to him; hence the diocese got the name of *Refugium Peccatorum.*" Sister M. Michael LCM, *Annals* No. 12, Little Company of Mary Archives, Tooting Bec, London. The bias towards Irish clergy is to be noted. Sister M. Michael, the annalist of this passage, was Irish and her assessment of the Irish clergy as "most admirable" is not borne out by the historical reality. Other records demonstrate the problems of the "exported" priests, which included alcoholism, debt and fraudulent behaviour. For an historical assessment of Bishop Bagshawe see J. Derek Holmes, *More Roman than Rome*, pp. 172–175 and 182–183.

7 Gerard Connolly, "Irish and Catholic: Myth or Reality" in Swift and Gilley, *The Irish in the Victorian City*, p. 243, note 44.

8 See Archivo Propaganda Fide: *Scritture Riferite nei Congressi-Anglia: 1879–1880* Vol. 21: Pagine Archivio: 560–683. Transcrizione dal Microfilm nell' Archivio della Piccola Comapgnia di Maria. Copies in both Italian and English held in the Little Company of Mary Archives, Tooting Bec, London. Complaint continued throughout his long reign as Bishop (1874–1901), particularly in relation to his poor choice of ministers, his attempts at creating a diocesan seminary (1882), and his repudiation of the Primrose League (1886).

9 These accusations followed Potter to Nottingham, and eventually found their way to Propaganda in letters of complaint about Bishop Bagshawe by members of the local clergy. See: *Scritture Riferite nei Congressi-Anglia: 1879–1880* Vol. 21: Pagine Archivio: 560–564. Transcrizione dal Microfilm nell' Archivio della Piccola Comapgnia di Maria: p. 564.

10 Mary Magray, *The Transforming Power of the Nuns: Women, Religion and Cultural Change in Ireland, 1750–1900*, Oxford University Press (London, 1998), p. 109.

11 loc. cit.

12 Lynn Jarrell, "The Development of Legal Structures for Women Religious Between 1500–1900: A Study of Selected Institutes of Religious Life for Women," Ph.D. diss., Catholic University of America, (1984), p. 278f.

13 loc. cit.

14 J. Pelikan, *Mary Through the Centuries: Her Place in the History of Culture*, Yale University Press (New Haven, London, 1996); N. Perry and L Echeverria, *Under the Heel of Mary*, Routledge Kegan & Paul (London, 1989); C.W Atkinson, C.H. Buchanan, M.R. Miles, eds., *Immaculate and Powerful: The Female in Sacred Image and Social Reality*, Beacon Press (Boston, 1985); S Cuneen, *In Search of Mary, the Woman and the Symbol*, Ballantine Books (New York, 1996); Carol Marie Engelhardt "Victorians and the Virgin Mary: Religion, National Identity and the Woman Question in England, 1830–1880," Ph.D diss., Department of History, University of Indiana, (1997).

15 Bryan Letters, January 14, 1877.

16 loc. cit. The Sisters of Bon Secours de Paris were founded in France in 1822. Formally approved by the Vatican in 1875, the work of the sisters was to nurse both rich and poor in their own homes. They had one house in England, in Westbourne Grove, London W. See Francesca Steele *The Convents of Great Britain and Ireland* p. 234.

17 Bryan Letters, January 14, 1877.

18 loc. cit.

19 19 Priests from the Portsmouth diocese had notified several of the disaffected clergy in Nottingham of Potter's arrival. Their assessment led to her being presented first to Bagshawe, and later Rome, as a hysteric, a self-confessed visionary, utterly wanting in humility and docility. See, *Archivo: Propaganda Fide: Scritture Riferite nei Congressi-Anglia: 1879–1880 Vol. 21*: Page 9 of transcript from microfilm.

20 Bryan Letters, January 16, 1877.

21 loc. cit.

22 Bryan Letters, January 22, 1877.

23 Mary Potter, *History of the Institute*, MS. Notes on the formation of the institute, Little Company of Mary Archives, Tooting Bec, London. Mr. Young, upon hearing that Potter had "taken up with the Bishop" withdrew his support, in what Potter recorded as a painful interview. In 1878, however, he again offered her a place and financial assistance to establish a community. In spite of desperate need, the bishop would again refuse the offer.

24 loc. cit.

25 Hyson Green and New Lenton were two new villages to emerge in Lenton Parish as a result of this expansion. Between 1801 and 1901, the population of Lenton Parish increased from 893 in 1801 to 23,872 in 1901. In 1851, there were approximately 5,589 people living within the Lenton Parish to which Hyson Green belonged.. See *Whites Directory Nottinghamshire*, 1853.

26 Letter from Theresa Tinsley, April 24, 1951. Therese Tinsley was a friend of the Tacey family, and lived near the property in Lenton Street. A friend of the community in her older years, she accompanied the sisters on some of the cases among the poor.

27 Little Company of Mary *Annals* 12, Unpublished MS., 1877, Little Company of Mary Archives, Tooting Bec, London. Hereafter *Annals*.

28 Garrett Sweeney, *History of the Diocese of Nottingham*, Unpublished MS., Diocese of Nottingham Archives.

29 *Annals* 12.

30 Potter had given to Bishop Bagshawe the same outline of the congregation as she had given to Selley. That document clearly stated the focus of the group – a twinned community of contemplative and active sisters whose primary concern was prayer for and care of the dying. Cf. Mary Potter, "On Devotion to the Dying", *Conferences M*. pp. 1–4.

31 *The Catholic Directory, 1878,* Burns and Oates, London, 1878. According to the directory, the Sisters of Nazareth ran Nazareth House, the Asylum for Aged Poor and Destitute Children in Nottingham, whilst the Sisters of Mercy staffed the House of Mercy for servants and two orphanages, as well as a school for girls. Across the diocese, there were other religious women. The Dominican Sisters of Penance were in Leicester, there was a community of Norbetines in Spalding. The Servants of the Sacred Heart were in Boston. There were also three communities of Sisters of Charity of St. Paul, and two communities of Sisters of Providence.

32 loc. cit. See also *Centenary monograph, St. Mary's Parish, Hyson Green Nottingham 1880–1980*, privately printed, (Leicester, 1980), p. 5. There were few parish churches or Mass centres in the Nottingham surrounds. The Catholic communities were not large, and the limited number of priests prevented many villages from having their own services. Hucknall did not have Mass until 1879, the village of Bulwell not until 1881.

33 Bryan Letters, January 20, 1877. Letter from Therese Tinsley April 24, 1951.

34 Mary Potter, *Autobiographical Notes*, p. 18.

35 Scrap MS., Little Company of Mary Archives, Tooting Bec, London.

36 These were Louise Roskell, 25, Contemplative or Active; Agnes Smith, 18, Active; Mary Hanlon, 18, Active; Jane Torkington, about 30 (sic), Contemplative; Mary Ann Reilly, 19, Active. These were women who through what Selley termed "the temporary opposition of parents" or "some little worldly complication" were prevented from coming immediately. This document is preserved in the archives of the Little Company of Mary, Tooting Bec, London.

37 Bryan Letters, January 23, 1877, continued January 25, 1877.

38 Mary Potter *Mary's Conferences*, p. 21. This statement of Potter is almost identical to that found in Faber's *The Creator and the Creature,* Burns & Oates, (London, 1856), p. 33. Faber writes: "There is a peculiar service, a distinct glory which God desires to have from … man different from the service and the glory of any other man in the world, and the man's dignity and happiness will result from his giving God that service and glory and no other." That Potter had read at least some of Faber's works is known. How much she actually utilised his theological opinion in her own writings would require far greater exploration than this study can undertake. It is however clear that she was influenced by it, and often echoed it.

39 Mary Potter "On Devotion to the Dying", p. 2.

40 loc. cit

[41] Mary Potter, *Come Follow Me*, Reprint from *The Human Life of Jesus,* Tipogrpaphica Poliglotta Vaticana, (Rome, 1947), p. 9.

[42] loc. cit.

[43] Mary Potter to Edward Selley Letter no. 3, June 1876. See also Mary Potter, "Outline of the Institute," 1875/1876, in *Conferences M.*, pp 1–3.

[44] On this issue, see Anne Murphy SHCJ, "Old Catholic, New Converts, Irish Immigrants: A Reassessment of Catholicity in England in the Nineteenth Century," also Gerard Connolly, "The Transubstantiation of a Myth: Towards a New Popular History of Nineteenth Century Catholicism," in *Journal of Ecclesiastical History* 35, 1 (1984), p. 78.

[45] Murphy, loc. cit.

[46] loc. cit.

[47] Mother Cecilia Smith *Personal Reminiscences*, p. 8.

[48] Mary Potter, *Autobiographical Notes*, p. 22.

[49] Mary Potter, *Conferences R,* p. 57. Unpublished MS., Little Company of Mary Archives, Tooting Bec, London. Hereafter *Conferences R.*

[50] Bryan Letters, March 16, 1877.

[51] loc.cit.

[52] Bryan Letters, February 4, 1877

[53] M .S. Thomson "Sisterhood and Power: Class, Culture and Ethnicity in the American Convent," *Colby Library Quarterly*, 25 (1989) pp. 149–175. See also O'Brien, "Lay Sisters and Good Mothers" pp. 449–464, passim.

[54] See O'Brien, "Terra Incognita," pp. 136–139, also "Lay Sisters and Good Mothers," p. 454. See also Thompson, "Sisterhood and Power", passim.

[55] O'Brien, "Lay Sisters and Good Mothers", p. 461. For details on the foundation and vision of Alice Ingham, I am indebted to the Franciscan Sisters of St. Joseph, Mill Hill for their provision of photocopy materials on their Foundress and her work. I am also indebted to Mr. Anselm Nye, of Queen Mary and Westfield College, University of London, for a copy of *Franciscan Missionary Sisters of St. Joseph: The preparation period, 1870–1880: Rochedale to Mill Hill.*

[56] ibid., p. 456. For details of Prout's vision and foundation see E Hamer, *Elizabeth Prout 1820–1864: A Religious Life for Industrial England*, passim.

[57] O'Brien, "Lay Sisters and Good Mothers," p. 464.

[58] loc. cit.

[59] loc. cit.

[60] Magray, *The Transforming Power of the Nuns*, p. 128.

[61] loc. cit.

[62] On the issue of subservience and "good religious" see Magray, *The Transforming Power of the Nuns*, pp. 128–130 and Catriona Clear *Nuns in Nineteenth Century Ireland*, pp. 62–68.

[63] Mother Mary Cecilia Smith, *Personal Reminiscences,* p. 6.

[64] Selley Letters, March 25, 1877.

[65] Mary Potter *Autobiographical Notes*, p. 20. Potter was not alone in her belief that her patronage of artisans contributed to their later fortunes. Mother Margaret Hallahan's contribution to the wealth of a Bristol artist is documented in her *Life* by a Dominican Sister in the following manner: "She…induced an artist in Bristol to make a mould from Degere's well-known statue, and paid him £16 for doing so…From this mould a vast number of very small statues were cast, …and so many were sold that the artist realised a handsome profit." *Life of Mother Margaret Mary Hallahan*, (London, 1869), p. 147, cited in Susan O'Brien, "Making Catholic Spaces," p. 457.

[66] Carol Marie Engelhardt, "Victorians and the Virgin Mary: Religion, National Identity, and the Woman Question in England, 1830–1880" p. 11.

[67] The decree was promulgated in 1854.

[68] Frances Power Cobbe, *Italics*, Truber and Co. (London, 1864), p. 330.

[69] Carol Marie Engelhardt, "Victorians and the Virgin Mary: Religion, National Identity, and the Woman Question in England, 1830–1880", passim.

70 Anna Jameson, *Legends of the Madonna as Reflected in the Fine Arts*, Longmans, Green & Co. (London, 1891), p. xviii.

71 Margaret Fuller, *Woman in the Nineteenth Century*, John P. Jewett & Company, (Boston, 1855) reprinted by W.W Norton & Co. (New York, 1971), p. 176–177.

72 Elizabeth K Helsinger, et al, *The Woman Question: Society and Literature in Britain and America 1837–1883*, vol. 3., University of Chicago Press, (Chicago, 1989), p. 52.

73 Anna Jameson, *Legends of the Madonna as Reflected in the Fine Arts*, p. xii.

74 ibid., p. 12.

75 ibid., p. 298.

76 Frances Power Cobbe, "Social Science Congresses and Women's part in them," *MacMillan's Magazine* (December, 1861), pp. 91–2, cited in Eileen James Yeo, "Social Motherhood and the Sexual Communion of Labour in British Social Science, 1850–1950", *Women's History Review*, 1,1 (1992) p. 68.

77 Frances Power Cobbe, "The Final Cause of Women" in *Women's Work and Women's Culture*, (ed.) Josephine Butler, (London, 1869), p. 21.

78 For a well-developed overview of the range and complexity of Cobbe's ideas, see Barbara Caine, *Victorian Feminists* Oxford University Press, (New York, 1992).

79 Cobbe, *Italics*, p. 330. Emphasis as in original text.

80 ibid. p. 331.

81 ibid. pp. 331–332.

82 Mary Potter, *The Attributes of God Reflected in the Person of Mary*, Burnes Oates and Washbourne (London, 1909), p. 149.

83 John 19:26.

84 Mary Potter, *Motherhood*, Thomas Richardson & Son (London, 1885), p. 3.

85 ibid. p. 79.

86 Mary Potter *The Attributes of God*, Burns & Oates (London, 1910), p. 18.

87 On the development of the "devotional revolution" in England see Rev. John Sharp "The Influence of St. Alphonsus Liguori in Nineteenth Century Britain," *The Downside Review*, Vol.101, (1983), pp. 60–67; Sheridan Gilley, "Vulgar Piety", pp. 255–266. For the Irish influence see Emmet Larkin, "The Devotional Revolution in Ireland, 1850–1875," *American Historical Review*, Vol.78, (1972), pp. 625–652. On its effects on the American Catholic church see Anne Taves, *The Household of Faith: Catholic Devotions in Mid-Nineteenth Century America*, University of Indiana Press (Indiana, 1986). See Susan O'Brien, "Making Catholic Spaces": Women, Décor, and Devotion in the English Catholic Church, 1840–1900". For the origins of this devotional revolution in Europe see Ted Campbell, *The Religion of the Heart: A Study of European Religious Life in the Seventeenth and Eighteenth Centuries*, University of South Carolina Press (Columbia, South Carolina1991).

88 Ted Campbell, Campbell, *The Religion of the Heart*, p. 177.

89 ibid. p. 175.

90 Susan O'Brien, "Making Catholic Spaces," p. 458. As O'Brien points out Margaret Hallahan pioneered much of the early restoration devotion to the Virgin Mary in Britain; Cornelia Connelly not only promoted but actively engaged in the construction of images to assist in the promulgation of devotion to the Madonna, as well as to female saints. The Hon. Laura Petrie erected the first public statue of Mary in England, and actively promoted Marian devotion as well as being a patron for the expansion of devotional artefacts and the arts in general.

91 loc. cit.

92 loc. cit.

93 John 19: 26–2.

94 See for example: John Keble, "The Annunciation of the Blessed Virgin Mary," *The Christian Year, 1827*, Thomas Y. Cromwell, (New York, 1890), p. 232. Charles Thomas, *Christ's Dying Hours: A sermon preached on the occasion of the Re-opening of St. Margaret's Church, Hilston, Holderness, on Thursday, July 31, 1862*, (London, 1862), pp. 15–17. William Ullathorne, *The Immaculate Conception of the Mother of God: An Exposition*, John Murch and Co. (Pittsburgh, 1855)..

95   Mary Potter *May Papers*, Propaganda Fide (Rome, 1906), Introduction.

96   Mary Potter, *Man Mirroring his Maker: The Priest in God's* Church, The Art and Book Company (Westminster, 1908), p. 153.

97   loc. cit.

98   ibid. p. 77. Throughout this work on the priesthood, Potter consistently uses the term "we priests." Whilst never expressing a desire for priesthood, there is an undoubted sense of sharing in the ministry of the priest. It is an aspect of her life that would profit by greater analysis than this present study allows.

99   Mary Potter *Our True Spirit*, Unpublished MS., p. 1.

100 Mary Potter, *Autobiographical Notes*, p. 19, see also Mother M. Cecilia Smith *Reminiscences*, p. 2.

101 Mary Eleanor Smith (1859–1940) was an associate of Mary Potter's from Portsmouth. Younger than Potter, she had spoken of her desire to enter a convent prior to Potter's leaving the district. Potter's response was to introduce her to Father Selley, and Smith, once she had turned eighteen years of age (1877), was given permission by her parents to join Potter in her new venture. She was given the religious name of Cecilia and became the annalist of the community. She had a wicked eye for detail, as some of her records demonstrate, and became a loyal and very close friend of Potter.

102 Mary Potter to Mary Eleanor Smith, March 29, 1877. Little Company of Mary Archives, Tooting Bec, London, Letters to Mary Eleanor Smith (Mother Cecilia Smith), hereafter Smith Letters.

103 A Miss Pritchard led the choir, which was made up of members of the "Children of Mary." Miss Pritchard was to become a member of the Little Company of Mary, and proved to be a thorn in the side of the community. See Mother M. Cecilia Smith, Personal *Reminiscences*, p. 4ff.

104 A *missa cantata* is a sung mass.

105 Mother Cecilia Smith, *Personal Reminiscences,* p. 4.

106 loc. cit.

107 ibid., p. 33.

108 Hickey, *Life of Father Selley*, p. 22.

109 loc. cit.

110 Bryan Letters, January 23, 1877. Conflict between religious orders of men and the official hierarchy of the church had marked the re-emergence of Catholicity within England. Wiseman had sought to bring religious communities to Britain to undertake the work of missionaries. There grew up an invidious distinction between secular clergy and religious orders. Religious were often seen as living in a higher "state of perfection" than the ordinary priest: they were not subject to the authority of the local bishop, but to their religious superiors, and this latter point brought them into some conflict with men like Cardinal Manning, whose investment was in the pastoral care of Catholic Britain. See J. Derek Holmes, *More Roman than Rome*, pp. 88–90 and 168–169.

111 Bryan Letters, January 30, 1877.

112 Bishop Bagshawe to Edward Selley, April 4, 1877.

113 Mother Cecilia Smith, *Personal Reminiscences*, p. 3; Bishop Bagshawe to Father Selley, April 2, 1877.

114 Mary Potter to Mary Eleanor Smith, April 1877, cited in Mother Cecilia Smith, *Personal Reminiscences*, p. 7.

115 Mother Cecilia Smith, *Personal Reminiscences,* p. 8.

116 loc. cit.

117 loc. cit.

118 Mary Potter, *Autobiographical Notes*, p. 25.

119 Mother M. Cecilia Smith, *Personal Reminiscences,* p. 8.

120 ibid. p. 5.

121 ibid. p. 6

122 Mary Potter, *Autobiographical Notes*, p. 22.

123 loc. cit.

124 Mother M. Cecilia Smith, *Personal Reminiscences* , p. 6.

125 The "imprimatur" of a book is an "official" recognition that the work is published with ecclesiastical approval and that it is without doctrinal error.

126 Bishop Bagshawe to Father Selley, June 13, 1877.

127 Hickey, *Life of Father Selley*, p. 22. Selley left the Marists and transferred to the Augustinian Fathers in September 1878, but remained a close friend of Potter and the Little Company of Mary for the remainder of his life.

128 Bishop Bagshawe to Edward Selley, June 13, 1877.

129 Those who lived with her made this assessment of Edith Coleridge, and the truth of the allegations was borne out in the conflicted relationship between herself and Mary Potter. A woman of great passion with an extraordinarily violent temper, her rages led her to physically assault Potter. Letter to Father Henry Walker, October 19, 1879. Little Company of Mary Archives, Tooting Bec, London. Hereafter Walker Letters. See also Mother Mary Cecilia, *Reminiscences*, p. 8.

130 The clothing ceremony or ceremony of reception of the habit is a public occasion, where the candidates for religious life are examined by the bishop in order to ensure that they have not been forced or unduly influenced in their decision. A prescription of the Council of Trent, it sought to stamp out abuses such as parents forcing unmarried daughters into convents. It also sought to ensure that the candidates act with full knowledge of the step they are about to take. Following the examination by the bishop, the candidate "takes the veil," or puts on the habit of the institute. To "receive the habit" is the formal initiation into a period of discernment, in which the novices receive instruction in the spiritual life of a given institute, are tested in their ability to live under the vows of poverty, chastity and obedience, and are introduced to the ministry or works of the congregation. See Lanslots, *Handbook of Canon Law for Congregations of Women under Simple Vows* p. 57. Only two of the founding members of the Little Company of Mary had previous experience of religious life. Mary Potter had eighteen months in the Mercy Novitiate, and Mary Thompson – according to the annals of the Little Company of Mary – had been in another religious order. The details of her length of stay or experience are unknown. The reception of the group as novices presupposed that Bagshawe or Potter had established a rule and a formation program for the members of the institute. This was not so, and, as will be seen, created much tension.

131 See Margaret Susan Thompson "Sisterhood and Power," pp. 149–175.

132 Bishop Bagshawe to Mary Potter, June 1877.

133 Scrap MS., Little Company of Mary Archives, Tooting Bec, London.

134 Mother Cecilia Smith *Personal Reminiscences*, 1877, p. 9.

135 ibid. p. 2 (a). Some of these "pets" mentioned so disparagingly by the young Mother Cecilia, were to enter the community and create much difficulty.

136 M. Potter, *Conferences I*, p. 93, Little Company of Mary Archives, Tooting Bec, London. Hereafter *Conferences I*.

137 Johannes Metz, "Tempo di religiosi?" cited in Antonio Romano, *The Charism of the Founders*, Paulist Press, (UK, 1989), p 146 See also Jurado, "Consecrated Life and the Charisms of the Founders". p. 7.

138 M. Potter, *Mary's Conferences*, 11, p. 119.

139 Mary Potter, *Conferences M*, p. 8.

140 Mary Potter to Henry Potter, n.d. 1876.

141 Mary Potter *Conferences A*, p. 33.

142 Up to 1947, there was no official definition within the Roman Catholic Church of what was characterised by the word "founder" or "foundress" as it pertained to religious life. Debate over the issue has continued to the present day, and is the subject of Antonio Romano's, *The Charism of the Founders*, translated by Sister Francis Teresa, St. Pauls, (Slough, 1994), passim. Romano's work clearly illustrates that the founder of a religious institute is that person who clearly sees that he or she has been called to found an institute – that he or she and no other has been charged with a charismatic responsibility. Jean Marie Tillard in his *Carisma e sequela* (Bologna, 1978), p. 72 makes the point clear, when he states that founders are historical mediators of a definite charismatic economy through which God continues to speak to his people.

143 Barbara Charlesworth Gelpi, "Introduction" in Hellerstein, *Victorian Women*. For specific reference to religious women, see Catriona Clear, *Nuns in Nineteenth Century Ireland*, Ch. 2 and passim.

144 Barbara Gelpi, "Introduction", p. 5.

145 Catriona Clear, *Nuns in Nineteenth Century Ireland*, p. 47.

146   This point is made brutally clear in the discussion mounted by Clear in *Nuns in Nineteenth Century Ireland*, pp.
      62–68. Women religious were at the mercy of clerics who believed that they alone had authority and insight in
      regard to spiritual matters.

147   A diocesan congregation is an association of pious persons founded and continuing to exist on the approbation of
      the bishop of a diocese, which has taken no steps to obtain approval from the Holy See. In such congregations, the
      bishop is responsible for the congregation, for approval of the rule and the vowed life of its members. Up until
      1906, bishops or local ordinaries could approve a new congregation within the limits of their diocese without any
      permission needed from the Holy See. This situation changed following the *Motu Proprio* of Pope Pius X, who
      determined that no bishop could establish a congregation within a diocese without recourse to the then Sacred
      Congregation of Regulars. For an analysis of the shifts and changes in the canonical status of institutes of religious
      women, see M. Dortel-Claudot SJ, *The Evolution of the Canonical Status of Religious Institutes with Simple Vows from
      the 16th Century until the New Code*, passim. See also M. S. Thompson, "The Validation of Sisterhood: Canonical
      Status and Liberation in the History of American Nuns," in Margot H. King (ed.), *A Leaf from the Great Tree of
      God: Essays in honor of Ritamary Bradley, SFCC*, Perigrina Publishing Co. (Toronto, Ontario, 1994), pp 47–48.

148   Catriona Clear illustrates the fragile position of women's congregations in relation to episcopal authority. See
      Nuns in Nineteenth Century Ireland, p. 63.

149   loc. cit.

150   This issue of episcopal control plagued many religious congregations in the nineteenth century. The level of con-
      flict generated is examined in Leslie Liedel, "Indomitable Nuns and a Determined Bishop: Property Rights,
      Women Religious and Diocesan Power in Nineteenth-Century Cleveland," Ph.D diss., Kent State University,
      (1998). See also Michael Hill, *The Religious Order: A study of virtuoso religion and its legitimation in the nine-
      teenth century Church of England*, Heinemann Education Books, (London, 1973); See also Catriona Clear, *Nuns
      in Nineteenth Century Ireland*, pp. 47–48.

151   Hill, *The Religious Order*, p. 9. Catriona Clear, *Nuns in Nineteenth Century Ireland*, p. 48.

152   Hill, loc. cit.

153   "Catholic Progress in London" originally published in the *London Review* 1865, and reprinted in *The Catholic
      World*, August 1865, pp. 703–707.

154   A. Murphy SHCJ, "Remembering the future: 150 Years of SHCJ History;" *History: Society of the Holy Child
      Jesus: Issue* 1: *Beginnings*, privately printed, (1996), pp. 5–11, passim. See also Susan O'Brien, "Terra Incognita,"
      passim; W.J. Battersby, "Educational Work of the Religious Orders of Women, 1850–1950" in George A Beck,
      (ed.), *The English Catholics 1850–1950*, Burns Oates (London, 1950), pp. 337–364; Maud Monahan
      "Religious Communities of Women," in *Catholic Emancipation, 1829–1929: Essays by Various Writers*,
      Longmans Green and Co., (London, 1929), pp. 201–222; V. A. McClelland, *Cardinal Manning: His Public Life
      and Influence, 1865–1892*, O.U.P. (London, 1961), p. 41.

155   J.N. Murphy, *Terra Incognita*, p. 484.

156   loc. cit. See also Mother Mary Paul SHCJ, "The Religious Orders of Woman: Active Work", pp. 281–286;
      Susan O'Brien, "10,000 nuns: Working in Convent Archives," *Proceedings of the Catholic Archivists
      Association*,Vol 9 (1989), pp. 26–32; V. A. McClelland, *Cardinal Manning*, p. 41.

157   The phrase is used to describe William Fredrick Faber's particular brand of eccentric proselytism in Sheridan
      Gilley's "Catholic Faith in the Irish Slums" in H.J. Dyos and Michael Wolff, (eds.) *The Victorian City: Images
      and Realities*, Vol. 2., p. 839. It is used here, as it seems to describe his novice's own beliefs and behaviours.

158   Gerard Connolly, "Irish and Catholic: Myth or Reality" in Swift and Gilley, *The Irish in the Victorian City*,
      p. 228.

159   Mary Potter *Autobiographical Notes*, p. 20.

160   Mary Potter, *Conferences A*, p. 33.

161   Bryan Letters. December 29, 1876.

162   Bishop Bagshawe to Mary Potter, June 1877.

163   loc. cit.

164   loc. cit.

165 Mary Potter, undated note in Potter's own handwriting, prepared for submission to Holy See circa 1881, Little Company of Mary Archives, Tooting Bec, London.

166 J.M.R. Tillard, *There are Charisms and Charisms: The Religious life*. Lumen Vitae Press, Brussels, 1977, p. 30.

167 ibid. p. 126.

168 As Tillard points out, the whole meaning of a rule or way of life in any religious project, was simply to prescribe the conduct to the freely chosen ideal. See Tillard, *There are Charisms and Charisms*, p. 34–35.

169 Mary Potter, *Mary's Conferences*, p. 24.

170 loc. cit.

171 loc. cit.

172 On the *Devotio Moderna* and the Brothers and Sisters of the Common life see: John Van Engen *Devotio Moderna: Basic Writings*, Classics of Western Spirituality, Paulist Press (New York, 1988), particularly introduction.

173 This was a particular characteristic of De Montfortian spirituality and the devout humanism that shaped it, in which the foolishness of the Cross of Jesus, confounds the wise of "the world." See de Fiores *To Jesus through Mary*, passim.

174 Dorothee Soelle, "Mysticism, Liberation and the Names of God," *Christianity and Crisis*, 41, 11 (June22, 1981), pp. 179–85, p. 179.

175 Eleanor McLaughlin, "Women, Power and the Pursuit of Holiness in Medieval Christianity," in Rosemary Ruether and Eleanor McLaughlin (eds.) *Women of Spirit: Female leadership in the Jewish and Christian Traditions*, Simon and Schuster (New York, 1979), pp. 101–130: p. 123.

176 On the evolution of the Beguines see: Carol Noel, 'The Origins of the Beguines' *Signs* 14, (Winter 1989): 322–341; Lynda L Coon, et al, *That Gentle Strength: Historical Perspectives on Women in Christianity*, University Press of Virginia (Charlottesville, 1990). Robert E. Lerner *The Heresy of the Free Spirit in the Later Middle Ages*, Notre Dame University Press (Notre Dame, 1993). Ernest McDonnell, *The Beguines and the Berghards in Medieval Culture* Rutgers University Press, (New Brunswick, NJ, 1969). Oliver Davis (trans) *Beguine Spirituality: Mystical Writings of Mechtild of Magdeburg, Beatrice of Nazareth and Hadewijch of Brabant*, Crossroad (N.Y. 1990).

177 On the whole issue of the charismatic nature of religious life – which is a still evolving consideration within the Roman Catholic church – see J.M.R. Tillard, *There are Charisms and Charisms:* passim. See also Antonio Romano, *The Charism of the Founders*, passim; James R. Cain, "Cloister and the Apostolate of Religious Women," *Review for Religious*, 27, 2 (1968): esp. p. 267.

178 E. I. Watkin, *The Church in Council*, Darton, Longman and Todd, (London, 1960), p. 117.

179 ibid. p. 139. The decision of the Fourth Lateran Council was affirmed by the Council of Vienne (1311–1312), in which other "new" societies – and the Beguines in particular – came under attack.

180 Elizabeth Makowski, *Canon Law and Cloistered Women: Periculoso and its Commentators, 1298–1545*, Catholic University of America Press (Washington D.C.), 1997, p. 1.

181 ibid. p. 2. See also Cain, "Cloister and the Apostolate of Religious Women" especially p. 267, and Caritas McCarthy, *The Rule for Nuns of St. Caesarius of of Arles*. Studies in Medieval History n.s., 16, Catholic University of America Press (Washington, D.C.), 1960, p. 65.

182 For closer examination of the impact of the Council of Trent and the controls applied to women religious see Lyn Jarrell OSU, "The Development of Legal Structures for Women Religious Between 1500 and 1900" pp. 15–17.

183 ibid. p. 18.

184 *Decori* was promulgated by Pius V in response to the confusion that had resulted from the early *Circa Pastoralis*. It affirmed full enclosure and laid down the three reasons for leaving the monastic enclosure as fire, leprosy and an epidemic. The last two had to be verified by the bishop. See Lyn Jarrell, "The Development of Legal Structures for Women Religious between 1500 and 1900," p. 22.

185 Active in orientation, the communities founded by Catherine of Sienna, Merici and Ward (viz. Dominican Tertiaries, Ursulines, and Sisters of the Institute of the Blessed Virgin Mary), were constrained and contained by the application of canonical structures, most noticeably by enclosure. In the case of Mary Ward, her institute was suppressed in 1630 and again in 1631, receiving final legitimisation in 1749.

[186] On the evolution of institutes of active religious life see E Rapley, *The Dévotes,* passim.

[187] ibid., p. 196.

[188] For fuller detail on the evolution of canonical structures for religious women see M.R MacGinley, *A Dynamic of Hope: Institutes of Women Religious in Australia*, Crossing Press (Sydney, 1996), Chs. 1–3, M. Dortel-Claudot SJ, *The Evolution of the Canonical Status of Religious Institutes with Simple Vows from the 16th Century until the New Code*, passim. On the growth of women's apostolic communities in the seventeenth century, and the associated canonical legislation see E Rapley, *The Dévotes*. On the nature of contemplative life and women's role see G Lerner, *The Creation of Feminist Consciousness: From the Middle Ages to the Eighteenth Century*, passim.

[189] For a detailed portrayal of the early rules adapted for the new religious communities see D. J. Fladenmuller and K. S. McMilan, eds., *Regular Life: Monastic, Canonical and Mendicant Rules*, Western Michigan University, (Kalamazoo, Mich., 1997).

[190] Anson, *The Call of the Cloister*, p. 323.

[191] loc. cit.

[192] See Mary Ewens, *The Role of the Nun* p. 254ff.

[193] ibid., p. 282.

[194] On the evolution of middle-class women's role in nineteenth century European society, see Bonnie Smith *Ladies of the Leisure Class: The Bourgeoises of Northern France in the Nineteenth Century*, Princeton (New Jersey, 1981). On the explosion of religious communities of apostolic life in Ireland in the same period, see Catriona Clear, *Nuns in Nineteenth Century Ireland*, chapter 5. For the missionary outreach of European congregations in the Australian context, see M. R. MacGinley, *A Dynamic of Hope*, passim.

[195] Dortel-Claudot, *The Evolution of the Canonical Status of Religious Institutes*, passim. See also Ewens, *The Role of the Nun in Nineteenth Century*, pp. 14–21.

[196] Mary Potter, *Mary's Conferences,* p. 115.

[197] Jo Ann Kay McNamara, *Sisters in Arms: Catholic Nuns through Two Millennia*, Harvard University Press (Harvard, 1996), p. 240.

[198] Mary Potter, On Formation*, Conferences M*, p. 8.

[199] Mary Potter *Mary's Conferences*, p. 115.

[200] Mary Potter, *Mary's Conferences*, p. 152.

[201] loc. cit.

[202] loc. cit.

[203] Mother M. Cecilia Smith, *Personal Reminiscences*, p. 6.

[204] loc. cit.

[205] *Archivo: Propaganda Fide: Scritture Riferite nei Congressi-Anglia: 1879–1880 Vol. 21: Pagine Archivio: 560–5683.* Transcrizione dal Microfilm nell 'Archivio della Piccola Comapgnia di Maria: Complaint continued throughout his long reign as Bishop (1874–1901).

[206] As the complaints against him indicate, his manner – as much as anything else – served to alienate him from many of the clergy and aristocratic laity of Nottingham. Archives of Propaganda indicate, he was noted for discourtesy shown to his clergy. One of the complaints issued against him was the manner in which he told senior priests of their moves. Deciding to remove the head of the cathedral clergy, Bagshawe notified that priest by a note pinned to a table in his room which read: "Leave Nottingham at once, and go and reside in Louth." For other complaints against the idiosyncratic bishop see Edward Norman, *More Roman than Rome*, pp. 173–174.

[207] ibid.

[208] Mother Catherine Crocker, *Personal Recollections*, p. 3. Mother Cecilia Smith, *Personal Reminiscences*, p. 6.

[209] Mary Potter, *Autobiographical Notes*, p. 25.

[210] The role of a "spiritual director" was perceived as the prerogative of males, and usually, though not always, priests. As Faber makes very clear in his *Growth in Holiness*, Burns & Oates (London, 1864), note, p. 313, the director was a "supernatural *man*" [sic]. Faber links the work of spiritual direction with that of a confessor, and, it is true, that within the nineteenth century, "spiritual direction" where it was given at all, was given within the confessional situation. Yet, as Faber also makes clear, spiritual direction was given by women, to women, and in

terms of religious life, a spiritual direction, in addition to that available from external confessors, was indeed practised by those in charge of novices.

211 Selley Letters, March 1878.

212 Bishop Bagshawe to Mary Potter, March 23, 1878. Appended to the end of the missive in Potter's handwriting is the comment: "The Bishop perhaps forgets he himself told me, to do all that a Novice Mistress would do except tell the Sisters of their faults or listen to their trials and difficulties."

213 As Leslie Liedel points out, this was a ploy used by many bishops and priests to control and manipulate religious orders of women. See Liedel, "Indomitable Nuns and a Determined Bishop,"p. 32. There was a constant struggle between bishops and women founders. As Cornelia Connolly, founder of the Sisters of the Holy Child noted, "Bishops prefer diocesan orders where their power is without appeal". Cited in Caritas McCarthy *The Spirituality of Cornelia Connolly*, p. 181.

214 Mother M. Cecilia Smith, *Personal Reminiscences*, p. 30.

215 loc. cit.

216 Archivo: Propaganda Fide: *Scritture Riferite nei Congressi-Anglia*: 1879–1880 Vol. 21. p. 9.

217 loc. cit.

218 loc. cit.

219 loc. cit.

220 loc. cit.

221 loc. cit.

222 ibid. p. 10.

223 loc. cit.

224 The spectre of women incarcerated in convents was one of the great themes of the anti-Catholic and anti-convent crusade. The immensely popular *Awful Disclosures of the Hotel Dieu Nunnery*, by Maria Monk (1836), and Rebecca Reed's *Six Months in a Convent* (1835) were two early examples of sensationalism which not only titillated the public mind, but provided the background for the traditional Protestant suspicion of convents and monasteries. It was a theme which continued through the century in popular literature and art. See J.N Murphy *Terra Incognita*, particularly chapter 1; Susan Casteras, "Virgin Vows"; Susan M. Griffen, "Awful Disclosures: Women's Evidence of the Escaped Nun's Tale"; Jenny Franchot, *Roads to Rome: The Antebellum Protestant Encounter with Catholicism*, University of California Press (Berkeley, 1994); Edward Norman *Anti-Catholicism in Victorian England*, George Allen & Unwin (London, 1968) and Walter Arnstein *Protestant versus Catholic*, particularly chapter 5.

225 Mother M. Cecilia Smith *Personal Reminiscences*, MS., Little Company of Mary Archives, Tooting Bec, London. What is interesting here, is that this reference is missing from later "editions" of Mother Cecilia's reminiscences. Originally written with great verve and great colour, their more startling presentations were gradually expurgated, to provide a more "sanitised" collection.

226 Walker Letters, October 19, 1879.

227 Letters of Mother Mary Philip Coleridge to her director Father Kirby, Little Company of Mary Archives, Tooting Bec, London, passim.

228 M Vicinus, *Independent Women*, pp. 53–56.

229 Addiction to alcohol or opiates was common within the nineteenth century and in part, medically induced. By the last quarter of the century, doctors began to give morphine to women to numb the pain of "female troubles", or transform women considered to be hysterics into manageable invalids. The use of laudanum was common – both as a means of seeking relief from pain, and as an equivalent to Valium as an antidepressant. Women religious were not exempt from these issues. On the issue of female addiction in the nineteenth century see Mara L. Keire "Dope fiends and degenerates: the gendering of addiction in the early twentieth century", in *Journal of Social History*, 3, 4, 1998, pp. 809–22, passim. David T. Courtwright, "The Female Opiate Addict in Nineteenth Century America" in *Essay in Arts and Sciences* 10 (1982): 163–4; Wayne Morgan, *Drugs in America. A Social History, 1800–1980*, Syracuse University Press, Syracuse, NY, 1981, in particular pp. 39–40.

230 Bryan Letters, undated, circa August/September 1877.

231 These would finally be published as *Mary's Conferences to her Loving Children both in the world and in the Cloister* in 1878, and became the foundational texts of the institute.

232 Mother Cecilia Smith *Personal Reminiscences*, p. 32.

233 loc. cit. The enmity with which the activities of Sister Francis White are recorded by the members of the first community would indicate that the woman was indeed troublesome and vindictive if not pathological in her behaviour, particularly towards the founder.

234 Mother Cecilia Smith, *Personal Reminiscences,* p. 33.

235 loc. cit. Begging for funds was "regularised" in the decree *Singulari Quidem* of March 27, 1896, where rules and prescriptions regarding how alms should be collected were laid down for women religious.

236 loc. cit.

237 Bryan Letters, August 11, 1878. No record is given of the convent at which the sisters stayed, nor the board required of the visitors.

238 loc. cit.

239 Catholic Directory, 1878, p. 374.

240 loc. cit.

241 The Little Sisters of the Poor were founded in France in 1840 by Jeanne Jugan.

242 Cited in Dom Aidan Bellinger "France and England: The English Female Religious from Reformation to World War" in Frank Tallett and Nicholas Atkin (eds), *Catholicism in Britain and France since 1789,* The Hambeldon Press, (London, 1996), p. 9.

243 The support Lady Georgiana Fullerton gave to the institute of the Poor Servants of the Mother of God is a case in point. Yet, the calls on her charity were legion, and even with the support offered by Fullerton, the sisters lived poor and hard. Cf. Craven, *Life of Lady Georgiana Fullerton*, pp. 411–413 passim. Devas, *Mother Magdalen Taylor of the Sacred Heart.*, passim.

244 Scrap MS. This note is written in Potter's handwriting and is a scrap of a letter which she would ultimately present to Rome when seeking papal approbation of the rule in 1882. Little Company of Mary Archives, Tooting Bec, London. Potter's initial discussions with the bishop had included the possibility of a small, middle-class school for fee-paying students, but this was no longer possible, as work among the poor kept on increasing and engaged all the members of the institute.

245 loc. cit.

246 Bishop Bagshawe to Mary Potter, August 2, 1878.

247 Bishop Bagshawe to Mother Elizabeth Bryan, Nov. 16, 1878, see also letters dated November 27, 1878, and December 3, 1878.

248 The Sisters of Nazareth were an off shoot of the Little Sisters of the Poor. In 1851, at the invitation of Cardinal Wiseman, a foundation of Little Sisters of the Poor was made in London. Due to poor communication and a lack of finance, this branch house faltered, and finally separated from its French foundation in 1854. Under Mother St. Basil, (Victoire Larmenière, 1827–1877), who had come to London with the foundation group, the English branch was renamed the Sisters of Nazareth, and in 1858, with the support of Wiseman, sought approbation from Rome. Their recognition as a separate institute came in 1864. The works of the order were directed to the poor, in particular, to the aged, and to incurable children: *Life Sketch of Mother St. Basil (Larmenière)*, privately published by the Sisters of Nazareth, n.d.

249 ibid, p. 39.

250 loc. cit.

251 ibid. p. 40. Sister Alphonsus was ultimately deposed as superior of the Nottingham house and sent to the Mother House in Hammersmith.

252 Bryan Letters, undated, circa November 1878.

253 ibid.

254 Bishop Bagshawe to Mother Elizabeth Bryan, November 16, 1878.

255 loc. cit.

256 Bishop Bagshawe to Mother Elizabeth Bryan, November 27, 1878.

257 Bishop Bagshawe to Mother Elizabeth Bryan, December 3, 1878.

258 *Annals* 18, Little Company of Mary Archives, Tooting Bec, London.

259 Bishop Bagshawe to Mother Elizabeth Bryan, December 3, 1878.

260 Mother Cecilia Smith *Personal Reminiscences* B, p. 6.

261 Bishop Bagshawe to Mother Mary Potter, February 14, 1879.

262 Bishop Bagshawe to Mother Mary Potter, February 17, 1879.

263 Walker Letters, May 1879.

264 Walker Letters, October 15, 1879.

265 Walker Letters, October 19, 1879.

266 There is a terrible sadness in the small scraps of paper which are to be found in the *Miscellanea* in the archives. They are notes signed "your loving daughter", and plead with Potter not to turn away from her, but pray that this "pass from me".

267 Letters of Mother Philip Coleridge to Monsignor Kirby. The English College returned copies of these letters to the Little Company Archives. They are undated, but all are written from 1882 onwards.

268 Walker Letters, loc. cit.

269 According to the Hyson Green register, apart from Potter, Bryan, Coleridge, Bray and Smith, there were six other members admitted to postulancy.

270 Walker Letters, circa April 1880.

271 Margaret Susan Thompson, "The Validation of Sisterhood: Canonical Status and Liberation, in the History of American Nuns," Margot H. King, (ed.) *A Leaf from the Great Tree of God: Essays in Honour of Ritamary Bradley*, Peregrina Publishing, (Toronto, 1994), p. 56–58.

272 Mary Oates, "The Good Sisters': The Work and Position of Catholic Churchwomen in Boston, 1870–1940," in Joseph M. White, (ed.), *The American Catholic Religious Life*, Garland Publishing, (New York1988), pp. 286–287.

273 Henry Walker was a priest of the Diocese of Birmingham, stationed at Kenilworth in Warwickshire. He had met Mary Potter through a mutual friend (Father William Herbert), who was a priest of Nottingham Diocese. Walker was drawn to the writings of Mary Potter, and to the spirituality of De Montfort. His continued support over the years 1879–1883 was of considerable importance to Potter, as he not only provided a friendship and a shared spiritual vision, but also aided her in the editing and publishing of her books. His introductions to her writings reflect not only his admiration for the woman, but the spirituality he shared with her.

274 Walker Letters, June 27, 1880.

275 Mary Potter *Autobiographical Notes*, p. 44.

276 This point has been discussed in relation to American religious women in Dolores Liptak, RSM, "Full of Grace: Another Look at the 19th Century Nun," *Review For Religious: Christian Heritages and Religious Living*, 55, 6 (1996) pp. 625–639.

277 Mary Potter *Autobiographical Notes*, p. 44. One cannot help but wonder if this comment is the result of the women who surrounded Bishop Bagshawe, and who were so disruptive when they sought entry to Potter's community.

278 loc. cit.

279 Anon, "Missionary Work of one of the Sisters of the Little Company of Mary from March 1882 till September of the same Year," MS., Little Company of Mary Archives, Tooting Bec, London.

280 Infant mortality and deaths of young children remained high over the whole of the nineteenth century. As Anthony Wohl demonstrates in *Endangered Lives: Public Health in Victorian Britain* J.M.Dent (London, 1983), the epidemics of infectious diseases which swept urbanised areas across Britain were the result of poor sanitation, overcrowding and the rapidity with which cities grew. Housing for the working classes, and the problems that it engendered in terms of public health were further problems, which Bishop Bagshawe himself sought to address in a pastoral letter of 1885, entitled *Mercy and Justice for the Poor*, Kegan Paul Trench & Co, (London, 1885). The enormous demographic pressure which led to social distress, and lay at the heart of public health and housing issues is discussed further in: Anthony Wohl, *The Eternal Slum: Housing and Social policy in Victorian London*, Edward Arnold, (London, 1977); Stanley D. Chapman, (ed.), *The History of Working Class Housing: A Symposium*, David and Charles (Newton Abbot, 1971); and Enid Gauldie's *Cruel Habitations: A History of Working Class Housing 1780–1918*, Barnes and Noble (New York, 1974). Nottingham, whilst more "enlightened" in its housing patterns, still failed to eradicate the problems associated with rents, overcrowding, and the constant threat of epidemic illness amongst the overcrowded homes of the poor.

[281] The Stapleton family of Nottingham lost three children – Clara 11, Arthur 8 and Ada 4 years old – to scarlet fever in April 1882. All of them were baptised by the mission sister. The two eldest children – though Methodist – had attended the convent school at Hyson Green and the parents appear to have had little problem with permitting these children being baptised close to death. The baptism of the third child proved a little more difficult, the mother only consenting if the father were not told "for, poor foolish man, he had begun to fear that if she were baptised death would immediately follow." The records tell of Charles Henry Brooks, aged 4 years who "was attacked with Bronchitis. His mother came to the convent late on the evening of Friday 17th February, to ask for a little help, as they were very poor, and wished for a sister to call to see her little boy. The reverend mother, ever on the watch for souls…sent the mission sister and she saw that the poor child had but a poor chance humanely speaking of recovery. The parents told her that he had never been baptised, and consented to have the sister perform the ceremony, which she did. In the next room lay a dead child who died the day before…Cited in Anon, "Missionary Work of one of the Sisters of the Little Company of Mary from March 1882 till September of the same Year", MS., Little Company of Mary Archives, Tooting Bec, London, p. 4.

[282] loc. cit.

[283] ibid., p. 2.

[284] As the congregation was not yet "regularised," or fully canonically erected, these vows were private vows made to the bishop.

[285] Mother Cecilia Smith, *Personal Reminiscences*, p. 7.

[286] loc. cit. Mother Cecilia was a foundation member of the Quordon Mission.

[287] Walker Letters, July 10, 1880.

[288] loc. cit.

[289] Mary Potter *Autobiographical Notes*, p. 29.

[290] Walker Letters, September 11, 1880.

[291] Walker Letters, September 4, 1881.

[292] Walker Letters, September 2, 1881.

[293] Walker Letters, January 1881.

[294] Walker Letters, July 23, 1881.

[295] Walker Letters, August 11, 1881.

[296] Walker Letters, September 2, 1881.

[297] Walker Letters, April 19, 1882.

[298] Walker Letters, August 16, 1882.

[299] Bishop Bagshawe to Mother Mary Potter, July 18, 1882.

[300] loc. cit.

[301] Bishop Bagshawe to Mother Mary Potter August 19, 1882.

[302] Patricia Wittberg, *The Rise and Fall of Catholic Religious Orders: A Social Movement Perspective*, State University of New York Press (New York, 1994), p. 95. See also Caritas McCarthy, "Constitutions for Apostolic Religious" in the *Way Supplement*, 14, (1971), pp. 33–45 and "Apostolic Congregations of Women and the Ignatian Charism," *Way Supplement*, 20 (1973), pp. 10–16.

[303] Mary Potter to Sacred Congregation of Propaganda Fide, n.d., p. 1. Handwritten MS., Little Company of Mary Archives, Tooting Bec, London.

[304] ibid. Pp. 15–17.

[305] Mother Cecilia Smith *Personal Reminiscences* p. 8.

Notes for Section 4

[1] James McCaffrey, *History of the Catholic Church in the Nineteenth Century (1789–1908)*, Vol. I: M.H. Gill and Sons, Ltd (Dublin & Waterford, 1910). P. 471; H. Daniel-Rops *The Church in an Age of Revolution 1789–1870*, J.M. Dent and Sons Ltd., (London, 1965), p. 471; Hugh McLeod, *Religion and the People of Western Europe, 1789–1970*, Oxford University Press, (New York, 1981), p. 36.

2   Hugh McLeod, *Religion and the People of Western Europe, 1789–1970*, Oxford University Press, (New York 1981), p. 36.

3   Mary Anne Donovan, *Sisterhood as Power: The past and passion of ecclesial women*, Crossroad, (New York, 1989), p. 51.

4   Patricia Byrne, "American Ultramontanism" in *Theological Studies*, 5:56, (1995), p. 322.

5   Hugh McLeod, *Religion, and the People of Western Europe, 1789–1970*, , p. 36. See also Jay P. Dolan, *The American Catholic Experience: A History from Colonial Times to the Present*, Doubleday (New York, 1985).

6   Magray, *The Transforming Power of the Nuns*, p. 129.

7   Margaret Susan Thompson, "Charism or Deep Story?" passim.

8   Rosemary Raughter, "A Discreet Benevolence: Female Philanthropy and the Catholic Resurgence in Ireland," *Women's History Review*, 6, 4 (1997), p. 465.

9   Catriona Clear, "The limits of Female Autonomy: Nuns in Nineteenth Century Ireland," in Maria Luddy and Cliona Murphy (eds) *Women Surviving: Studies in Irish Women's History in the Nineteenth and Twentieth Centuries*, p. 43.

10 M. Dortel-Claudot, SJ, *The Evolution of the Canonical Status of Religious Institutes*, passim.

11 Pope Paul VI, *Ecclesia Sanctae*, St. Paul Publications (Homebush NSW, 1966), #II.

12 ibid. #11.

13 Montanism emerged in Christianity in the late second century. Condemned by Bishop Eutherus as heretical, it was an apocalyptic and prophetic movement. Called the "Phrygian heresy" it was named after its first prophet Montanus, who was accompanied by prophetesses (Priscilla and Maximilla). They believed they were under the direct guidance of the Holy Spirit, and whist they treasured the Gospel of John, they tended to undermine traditional authorities such as Scripture and the office of the bishop. Tertullian (c.155–c.225 CE), was the most famous of the Montanist converts, and was the first to use the word *Trinitas* (trinity) to describe the Godhead. His use of the term paved the way for the orthodox development of Trinitarian Christological doctrine. See: *New Catholic Encyclopedia*, Catholic University of America (eds.), McGraw Hill (New York, 1967).

14 These norms would find their expression in the two major documents on religious life promulgated by Pope Leo XIII – *Conditae a Christo* (1900), and the *Normae* of 1901.

15 Margaret Susan Thompson "The Validation of Sisterhood: Canonical Status and Liberation in the History of American Nuns" in King, *A Leaf From the Great Tree of God*, p. 64.

16 *Little Company of Mary Rule*, 1893. Little Company of Mary Archives, Tooting Bec, London. Hereafter *LCM Rule*.

17 Sarah Maitland, *Map of the New Country*, RKP, (London, 1983), p. 57. See also *LCM Rule*, 1893. Little Company of Mary Archives Tooting Bec, London.

18 *Annals* 18, p. 20.

19 ibid. p. 21.

20 Mother Cecilia Smith, *Personal Reminiscences*, p. 20–1.

21 Letter from Mother Philip Coleridge, *Annals* 18, p. 21.

22 Mother Cecilia Smith, *Personal Reminiscences.*, p. 20.2.

23 loc. cit. It is quite conceivable that this is exactly what it was, a women's prison, an undertaking the Sisters of the Good Shepherd Sisters carried out in Europe, but not in England.

24 ibid. p. 20.4.

25 Mother Cecilia Smith, *Personal Reminiscences,* p. 14.

26 loc. cit.

27 loc. cit.

28 ibid. p. 20.5.

29 *Annals* 18, p. 22: Pope Leo XIII, (Cardinal Vincenzo Gioacchino Pecci 1810–1903) was elected to the papacy on February 20, 1878.

30 ibid., p. 20.6.

31 Walker Letters, September 1882; see also *Annals* 18, p. 23.

32   *Annals* 18, p. 23.

33   loc. cit.

34   McCaffrey, *History of the Catholic Church in the Nineteenth Century*, p. 473.

35   loc. cit.

36   As Potter wrote to her brother Thomas: "The convents here have had their property taken away from them; 4d. a day allowed each professed; no novices allowed to enter; inventory of all Church goods and many other sad things; poor priests, etc., so that those who have money have many ways of disposing of it…" Mary Potter to Thomas Potter, 1883.

37   loc. cit.

38   Patricia Byrne, "American Ultramontanism" *Theological Studies*, V. 56: January, 1995; 301–327, p. 322. See also McLeod, *Religion and the People of Western Europe*, p. 36.

39   Walker Letters, February circa 1883.

40   *Annals*, 18, p. 52.

41   Mary Potter to Thomas Potter, September 16, c.1882; J. McCaffrey, op. cit., pp. 469–487; M.V. Caprani, *The Spirit and the Heritage*, privately printed, (Rome, 1978), p. 38. For contemporary accounts of visitors to Rome see Jesse Albert Locke, "A Recent Convert's Pilgrimage to Rome, Part II," *Catholic World*, 57, 341 pp. 655–667.

42   Mother Cecilia Smith *Personal Reminiscences*, p. 44.

43   Walker Letters, April 24, 1883.

44   Mary Potter to Thomas Potter, September 16, c. 1882.

45   Mother Cecilia Smith, *Personal Reminiscences*, p. 21ff; Mary Potter to Mrs Mary Ann Potter, September 16, 1883. The Glesley family also provided carpets for the rooms the sisters were living in.

46   loc. cit.

47   ibid. p. 24; *Annals 18*, p. 26.

48   *Annals 18*, p. 26. Potter's community had no such numerical strength, nor did their rule stipulate the need for a sister to be accompanied by another in district nursing.

49   Mother Cecilia Smith, *Personal Reminiscences*, p. 20.

50   loc. cit.

51   loc. cit.

52   Mrs. L. St. John Eckel (Mrs. St. John Harper), was also the author of *Maria Monk's Daughter: An Autobiography*, United States Publishing Co., (New York, 1874). See Ewens, *The Role of the Nun in Nineteenth Century America*, pp. 156–157.

53   Mother Cecilia Smith, *Personal Reminiscences*, p. 18.

54   *Annals 18*, p. 24.

55   Mother Cecilia Smith, *Personal Reminiscences*, p. 18.

56   Father Gomair Peeters OSF to Alice Ingham, January 10, 1878: Extracted from: *Letters: Father Gomair Peeters to Alice Ingham*," *The Preparation Period 1870–1880*. Privately printed for the Centenary of the Franciscan Missionary Sisters of St. Joseph, 1882–1983, n.d. p. 58.

57   *Annals 18*, p. 24.

58   Mary Potter *Autobiographical Notes*, p. 34.

59   loc. cit.

60   This desire not to insert her charism into an already existing form or rule has been identified by J.M.R. Tillard as part of a "founder's charism." This he accords to those men and women who, under the guidance of a spiritual insight or intuition, are forced to create new expressions of religious life which express more fully the spiritual reality they hold, and: "instead of inserting their charism into an already existing form of religious life…changed the shape of religious life, adapting it to their purpose, so as to provide a new form for their design." It was a matter of choice made based on the visionary imperative. J.M.R.Tillard "Founder's Charism or Founding Charism," *Religious Life Review: Supplement to Doctrine and Life*, 22:105, (Nov-Dec. 1983), p. 318.

61   *Annals, 18*, p. 25.

62   Mary Potter, *Mary's Conferences*, C.2, p. 20.

63   Tillard, "Founder's Charism or Founding Charism," p. 324.

64   *Annals* 18, p. 25.

65   Mother M. Catherine Croker *Early Recollections*, p. 4.

66   This point is made in Catriona Clear's *Nuns in Nineteenth Century Ireland*. It was delivered a considerable degree
     of "kudos" to be nursed by a "blue sister" in Limerick. And one suspects that there was a mutual benefit. The
     sisters moved among "the rich and famous", even as they provided what was tantamount to a "nurse compan-
     ion" service. See Clear, op. cit., p. 132.

67   In Charles Williams (ed.) *The Letters of Evelyn Underhill*, Longmans, Green & Co. (London, 1947), p. 115.

68   ibid, pp. 117–118.

69   Mary Potter, MS., "On devotion to the Dying" *Conferences M*, 1876.

70   Hand-written MS., Copy of the Rule: Chapter II.

71   Mary Potter, *Mary's Conferences*, p. 64.

72   Mary Potter *Spiritual Exercises of Mary*, pp. xxxii–xxxiii.

73   Mary Potter, "Compendium of Rule – (Spirit), *Conferences M*, 1893, p. 31.

74   Mary Potter MS., "Rules Regarding Novices in the Future State of our Institute," *Conferences M*, 1876, p. 6.

75   Mary Potter, MS., "Compendium of Rule – (Spirit), *Conferences M*, 1893, p. 31.

76   loc. cit.

77   Mary Potter, MS., "Regarding Missionary Work," First Rule (1877), *Conferences M*, p. 30.

78   Mary Potter, *Obedience Notes*, 5, p. 4.

79   Mary Potter, *Obedience Notes*, 4, p. 37.

80   Whilst recognising the dangers of imputing any form of feminism onto Potter, or the women who embraced
     religious life in the nineteenth century, the fact remains that Potter's view of the role of the women of the LCM
     bears a striking resemblance to that uttered by Margaret Fuller and other apocalyptic feminists of the period.
     See Elizabeth Helsinger et al., *The Woman Question: Society and Literature in Britain and America, 1837–1883*,
     Vol. I, The University of Chicago Press, (Chicago, 1983), p. 52. See also Catherine Keller, *Apocalypse Now and
     Then: A feminist guide to the end of the world*, Beacon Press (Boston, 1996) passim.

81   Barbara Welter, "The Cult of True Womanhood, 1820–1860" in *American Quarterly* 18(1966), 151–74.

82   Theologically defined, mission is the participation in the evangelising mission of the church. It is distinct from
     ministry in so far as it is concerned with preaching the gospel, whereas ministry is the work of Christian service
     performed in the name of the gospel.

83   Mary Potter, "Our Lady's New Family," *Conferences S*, p. 21.

84   Mary Potter, Primitive Rule, 1877, *Conferences M*, p. 4.

85   Mary Potter, Letter, "To my children in the Antipodes," *Conferences A*, p. 33

86   If, as Michael Buckley and others theologians have suggested, an authentic "charism" of religious life "always
     effects a particular configuration to Jesus," then there can be little doubt that Potter's insight into the charismatic
     nature of her own institute was valid. Michael Buckley "The Charism and Identity of Religious Life," *Review
     for Religious*, 44, 5 (1985), p. 661. See also Romano, *The Charism of the Founders*, passim. Jean Marie Renfro,
     SSS, "Religious Charism: Definition, Rediscovery and Implications," *Review for Religious*, 45, 4 (July/August,
     1986); Johannes B. Metz *Followers of Christ* Burns & Oates, (London, 1977), p. 15.

87   Handwritten MS., Copy of First Rule, Part I, Chapter I.

88   loc. cit.

89   Mary Potter, *Conferences F*, p. 8.

90   Leo XIII *Conditae a Christo*, in D.I. Lanslots, OSB., *Handbook of Canon Law for Congregations of Women under
     Simple Vows* Frederick Pustet & Co., Publishers (New York, 1909), 246–258, pp. 249–250. Hereafter *Conditae*.

91   Bishop Bagshawe to Mary Potter, Letter no. 20.

92   Mary Potter, *Autobiographical Notes*, p. 32. According to Potter, "We were indeed offered a letter of praise, but advised
     not to accept it, as they would think then that they had done sufficient for us for some years, this being the usual way."

93   *Annals*, p. 28.

94   loc. cit.

95   This was a "gratuity," given by a Count Plunkett for the care given to his wife during a serious illness. Count
     Plunkett paid the rent for two years, after which the community took control of the building. See *Annals* 18, p. 28.

96   loc. cit.

97   ibid. p. 36a.

98   ibid.

99   Clear is actually referring to the Irish situation in this passage, it is however one that I think pertains to the Roman situation as well. See Catriona Clear, *Nuns in Nineteenth Century Ireland*, p. 132.

100 Dortel-Claudot, *The Evolution of the Canonical Status of Religious Institutes.*, p. 17.

101 Copy of the First Rule, Hand-written MS., Chapter II.

102 loc. cit.

103 loc. cit.

104 See Kari Vogt "Becoming Male: one aspect of early Christian Anthropology," E.S. Fiorenza and Mary Collins (eds.) *Concilium: Women Invisible in Church and Theology,* T and T. Clark, (Edinburgh, 1985) pp. 72–83; Katherine E Zappone, "Christian Feminism: the spirituality of bonding," in Fiorenza and Collins, op. cit., pp. 17–24. See also Sara Maitland *A Map of the New Country*, passim.

105 Mary Potter, "On the Affiliated" in *Conferences S.* Little Company of Mary Archives, Tooting Bec.

106 Hand-written MS., Copy of the Rule, Chapter II. It is an interesting comment on the nature of the carnality of ordinary women and the angelic purity of religious.

107 At the request of Bishop Bagshawe, Potter and the community had taken up midwifery to provide care for unmarried mothers in the Nottingham area where they were forbidden entrance to the lying hospitals. Handwritten notation, First Rules, Little Company of Mary Archives, Tooting Bec.

108 On at least one occasion, explicit permission was given by Cardinal Parrochi, Vicar of Rome, for sisters to be present at childbirth. See Dougherty *Mother Mary Potter, Foundress of he Little Company of Mary*, pp. 237–241.

109 op. cit., p. 239.

110 *Rule of the Little Company of Mary*, 1886, Little Company of Mary Archives, Tooting Bec, London.

111 Dortel-Claudot, *The Evolution of the Canonical Status of Religious Institutes*, passim.

112 Sister Brigid Rosser, *Diary* unpublished MS., p. 1.

113 Mary Potter, "To my children in the Antipodes," 1890.

114 loc. cit.

115 Bishop Bagshawe to Mary Potter, May 19, 1884.

116 Dr. Moran was called to Rome and created cardinal on July 27, 1885.

117 Mary Potter "To my Children in the Antipodes, 1890, p. 2.

118 loc. cit.

119 loc. cit.

120 Liedel, "Indomitable Nuns and a Determined Bishop", p. 167.

121 Mary Potter to the first mission sisters n.d., 1885. Between 1877 and 1885, membership to the community had waxed and waned as prospective postulants came and went. Irish postulants were on the increase, but most of these were still postulants or novices. In 1883, the community numbered thirty-three: there were six postulants, five "indoor" novices, eight "outdoor" novices, three professed (first profession), and eleven sisters "finally professed." This latter group had taken vows for three years publicly, but had made private vows for life to the bishop. The Roman community accounted for five members and the sisters either at Hyson Green or in the surrounding missions for the rest. By 1885, there was no marked numerical increase.

122 Mary Potter, *Autobiographical Notes*, p. 35: Mother Rose would have a breakdown in Sydney and be returned to the Mother House. She eventually left the order, physically and mentally unable to take the strain of life.

123 Mary Potter to His Eminence, Cardinal Moran, August 6, 1885. Little Company of Mary Archives, Australian Province Ryde.

124 Mary Potter to Mother Raphael Byrne Farrar, Feast of the Holy Cross, November 1885.

125 Mary Potter to the Australian Pioneers. 1885.

126 loc. cit.

127 These included two Sacred Heart nuns, who were "reinforcement" for the Rose Bay convent, six sisters of the Faithful Companions of Jesus and the six Little Company of Mary sisters. Sister Brigid Rosser's *Diary*, p. 8.

128 Sister Geraldine Fitzgerald, *A Vision of Hope*, Treaty Press Ltd., (Dublin, 1979), p. 9.

129   Mary Potter, *Autobiographical Notes*, p. 39.

130   loc. cit.

131   Records from the Register of Hyson Green for the period 1877–1886.

132   Bryan Letters, December 30, 1885.

133   Devas, *Mother Magdalen Taylor of the Sacred Heart*, p. 254.

134   loc. cit.

135   Devas, *Mother Magdalen Taylor of the Sacred Heart*, p. 261.

136   Bryan Letters, December 30, 1885.

137   loc. cit.

138   loc. cit.

139   loc. cit.

140   loc. cit.

141   loc. cit.

142   ibid., p. 45.

143   Mary Potter, *Autobiographical Notes*, p. 41.

144   ibid.

145   Bishop Bagshawe to Mary Potter, letters numbered 30, 33. See also Bryan Letters, May 5, 1886 and Mary Potter, *Autobiographical Notes*, p. 36.

146   Bryan Letters, April 1886.

147   Mother Cecilia Smith, *Personal Reminiscences*, p. 2.

148   Little Company of Mary *Annals* 18, p. 33. Bishop Bagshawe to Mary Potter, letter no. 33.

149   Catriona Clear, *Nuns in Nineteenth Century Ireland*, p. 42.

150   *Annals 18*, p. 35; Count Moore to Mary Potter, Letters 9 &, 10; Mary Potter, *Autobiographical Notes*, p. 31.

151   This altercation was caused by the Bishop O'Dwyer accusing Mother Veronica of entering his diocese without notifying him. Mother Veronica, knowing that the good bishop had been notified of her arrival, smartly told him that if he did not want the presence of the sisters, other bishops would gladly have them. For some of the trials of this foundation see Clear *Nuns in Nineteenth Century Ireland*, pp. 63–64, 67, 96.

152   Mary Potter, *Autobiographical Notes*, p. 40.

153   Clear, *Nuns in Nineteenth Century Ireland*, p. 64.

154   Mary Potter to Mother Catherine Crocker, n.d.. 1891.

155   loc. cit.

156   Liedel, "Indomitable Nuns and a Determined Bishop" p. 14 ff.

157   *LCM Rule*, 1896, p. 12.

158   The three foundations were Commercial Road, The Guardian Angels Home for Unmarried Mothers, and a hospital for crippled children at Isleworth.

159   W. Booth, *In Darkest England and the Way Out*, Salvation Army Press (London, 1890), p. 9.

160   Mary Potter, *Mary's Conferences*, p. 252.

161   Mary Campion, LCM, Place of Springs: The First One Hundred Years of the Province of the Maternal Heart, privately printed, (London, 1977), p. 38.

162   If Sheridan Gilley is to be believed, nuns were "the single most unpopular group in Victorian England," whilst the accuracy of this statement is suspect, it is true to say that anti-convent sentiment was common throughout the whole of the nineteenth century, and extended through to the twentieth. See Roger Swift and Sheridan Gilley *The Irish in the Victorian City*, p. 8; Susan O'Brien, also questions Gilley's hyperbole in "10,000 Nuns: Working in Convent Archives," *Catholic Archivist*, no. 9, (1989), p. 27.

163   *Annals* 18, p. 36.

164   loc. cit.

165   Street preaching was long the province of the evangelicals and Catholic revivalism borrowed its intensity. For an interesting, contemporary account of the call for Catholicism to embrace street-preaching see Rev. A. Young, "Street-Preaching" in *Catholic World*, 46, 274, January 1888, pp. 499–504.

166   loc. cit.

167 Mary Potter, *Autobiographical Notes* Vol. 1, p. 45.

168 *LCM Rule* 1886/1893, Part the Second: "The Principal Charges of the Congregation".

169 ibid. Article 2.

170 ibid. Article 5.

171 ibid. Article 6.

172 Liedel, "Indomitable Nuns and a Determined Bishop", p. 36; Oates, *The Catholic Philanthopic Tradition in America*, pp. 286–7.For further insight into the manner in which Australian bishops sought to control the "good sisters" see M. M. K. O'Sullivan *'A Cause of Trouble'? Irish Nuns and English Clerics*, Crossing Press, (Sydney, 1995); Sister Mary Xaverius O'Donoghue, *Mother Vincent Whitty: Woman and Educator in a Masculine Society* (1972: Melbourne University Press); Osmond Thorpe *Mary McKillop*, Burns & Oates, (London, 1957).

173 Sister Brigid Rosser's *Diary*, Unpublished MS., p. 38.

174 loc. cit.

175 loc. cit.

176 loc. cit.

177 ibid. p. 57.

178 ibid. p. 61.

179 Mary Potter, *Obedience Notes,* no. 4. p. 34.

180 Mary Potter "To my dear Children in the Antipodes," *Conferences A*, p. 34.

181 Cardinal Patrick Moran to Mary Potter, August 14, 1895.

182 St: Mary's Cathedral Archives: Ref: 286: Sacred Congregation of the Propagation of the Faith to Cardinal Patrick Moran, August 28, 1899.

183 St. Mary's Cathedral Archives: Ref: 276: Sacred Congregation of the Propagation of the Faith, to Cardinal Patrick Moran, April 18, 1899.

184 Liedel, "Indomitable Nuns and a Determined Bishop", p. 197–198. See also Margaret Susan Thompson "Women, Feminism and the New Religious History: Catholic Sisters as a case study" in Phillip R. VandelMeer and Robert P. Swierenga, (eds), *Belief and Behaviour: Essays in the New Religious History*, Rutgers University Press (Rutgers, NJ, 1991), p. 144; See also Thompson's "'Father Didn't Always Know Best': Sisters Versus Clerics in Nineteenth-Century American Catholicism." 1993 Annual Address for the Women's Studies Program, University of Florida, Gainesville, Fl. I am grateful to Dr. Thompson for this resource.

185 Thompson "Validation of Sisterhood", passim; Liedel, "Indomitable Nuns and a Determined Bishop", p. 35.

186 Brigid Rosser *Diary*, Unpublished MS., p. 54; See also St. Mary's Cathedral Archives: Ref: 267: Sacred Congregation of the Propagation of the Father to Cardinal Patrick Moran, Rome, April 18, 1899.

187 Mary Potter to Mother Raphael, May 1894.

188 These issues are variously dealt with in Mary Ewens, *The Role of the Nun in Nineteenth Century America*, Catriona Clear, *Nuns in Nineteenth Century Ireland*; Mary Magray, *The Transforming Power of the Nuns,* and Margaret Susan Thompson,"The Validation of Sisterhood".

189 Margaret Susan Thompson "The Validation of Sisterhood," p. 64.

190 Mother Philip Coleridge to Monsignor Virtue, August 23, 1891.

191 ibid. There is a possibility that Dr. Thompson was the father or brother of an unhappy ex-member of the institute, Sr. M. Josephine, who entered the community in 1877 and left some two years later. No evidence exists to support this however.

192 Mother Philip Coleridge to Monsignor Kirby, August 1892. A member of the institute had incurred the debts by charging items to the convent accounts. This was not only against the rule, but it meant that the debts incurred were now the responsibility of the convent.

193 Mother Cecilia Smith to Monsignor Kirby, August 2, 1891.

194 Mary Potter to Mother Cecilia Smith, Letter no. 107, 1892.

195 Mary Potter, *Conferences M*, p. 4.

196 Karl Rahner, "Experience of Self and Experience of God," translated by David Bourke, in *Theological Investigations Vol. 13¸* Seabury Press (New York, 1975) p. 126.

197 Mary Potter, *Conferences R*, p. 100.

[198]   Mary Potter, *Life in God's Human Family*, Little Company of Mary, (London, 1900) p. 25.

[199]   This relaxation of rule and discipline was voiced in the rule, where it was stated that: "The ordinary rule cannot always be kept in its entirety in the branch houses. The superioress of these, before fixing the time table, should agree with the superioress general upon the changes which local circumstances require and should then keep to the instructions she may receive upon the subject, and see that they are punctually observed." *LCM Rule*, 1896, Chapter 15.

[200]   Kenneth Wapnick, "Mysticism and Schizophrenia," *Journal of Transpersonal Psychology*, Vol 1/2, pp. P.53. See also William Ernest Hocking "The Meaning of Mysticism as seen through its Psychology" in Richard Woods OP., *Understanding Mysticism*, Athlone Press, (London, 1980), p. 235ff.

[201]   loc. cit.

[202]   Mary Potter, *Path of Mary*, 1877 edition, reprinted Catholic Book Club, (Chicago, 1957) p. 168.

[203]   Mary Potter, "Letter to Congregation", *Obedience Notes*, Vol. 4, pp. 32–35.

[204]   Mary Potter, *Conferences R*, p. 41. On the importance of the figure of Moses to the contemplative life see *From Glory to Glory: Texts from Gregory of Nyssa's Mystical Writings*, selected and with an introduction by Jean Daniélou SJ, trans. Herbert Musurillo SJ, St. Vladimir's Seminary Press, (New York, 1979), passim. Gregory of Nyssa's treatise *The Life of Moses*, is a *logos*, or formal treatise which asks the question, "What is perfection for those leading a life of virtue"? The figure of Moses is a *hypodeigma*, an example of the doctrine of mystical perfection.

[205]   Cf. Exodus 32: 11–14.

[206]   Mary Potter, *Conferences R*, p. 104.

[207]   cf. Exodus 33:11–23; 34:510. Mary Potter, *Conferences R.*, p. 41.

[208]   Mary Potter, *Mary's Conferences*, p. 246.

[209]   According to the primitive rule, all sisters engaged in active works were to return to the Mother House each year to make a thirty-day retreat on the *Spiritual Exercises of Mary*. They would also be "recalled to the Motherhouse [sic] for a longer of shorter period to re-animate their fervour; to renew their love of the hidden life." Mary Potter, 'Primitive Rule of 1876', in *Conferences M*, no. 2.

[210]   loc. cit.

[211]   ibid., Mary Potter to Mother Cecilia Smith, Letter 104, n.d.

[212]   Mary Potter, *Conferences M*, p. 89.

[213]   Mary Potter to Mother Cecilia Smith, n.d.

[214]   Mary Potter, *Conferences J*, p. 15.

[215]   Studies that demonstrate the ways in which women used their religious beliefs to expand their control and influence are numerous. See for example: Carroll Smith-Rosenberg, *Disorderly Conduct: Visions of Gender in Victorian America* Oxford University Press, (New York, 1985); Kathryn Kish Sklar, *Catharine Beecher: A Study in American Domesticity*, W.W. Norton (New York, 1973). See also Malmgreen, *Religion in the Lives of Englishwomen*, and Prochaska, *Women and Philanthropy in Nineteenth Century England*, for examples of the manner in which religion and the religious imperative empowered women.

[216]   Little Company of Mary Australian Archives, copy of Letter to Cardinal Moran, 1899.

[217]   Little Company of Mary Australian Archives, copy of Letter to Cardinal Ledochowski, Sacred Congregation of Propaganda.

[218]   Elizabeth McDonough, "Charisms and Religious life." *Review for Religious*, (September-October, 1993), p. 648.

[219]   Mary Magray, *The Transforming Power of Nuns*, p. 129.

[220]   Mary Potter, *Obedience Notes*, 5. p. 99–126.

[221]   *LCM Rule*, 1893, p. 41.

[222]   Over the years 1877–1894, thirty-seven English-born women entered the Hyson Green Novitiate, compared with twenty-four Irish-born women over the same period. Between 1895 and 1909, the ratio of Irish to English born had changed with thirty-seven Irish entering as against twenty-five English. From 1909 to 1918, overall numbers entering had declined but English entrants more so than Irish, with twenty-one Irish women joining the congregation as against ten English. By 1918, out of a total recorded entry of 167, there were seventy-two English to eighty-two Irish. Over half were Irish nationals. See Appendix A.

[223] Grainne O'Flynn "Some Aspects of the Education of Irish Women through the Years," *The Capuchin Annual*, Dublin, (1977), p. 178; see also Anne V. O'Connor, "The Revolution in Girls' Secondary Education in Ireland 1860–1910," in Mary Cullen (ed.), *Girls don't do Honours: Irish women in Education in the Nineteenth and Twentieth Centuries*, Women's Education Bureau, (Dublin, 1987); Catriona Clear, *Nuns in Nineteenth Century Ireland*, p. 27.

[224] Whist unafraid of admitting postulants, she was equally unafraid of sending them away if unsuited to the life: "Let them enter the path of Mary, but never urge them farther than they have grace to go. Oh, the unspeakable evil that is done in religious houses by having members unsuited." Mary Potter, *Mary's Conferences*, p. 306.

[225] Mary Potter *Conferences A*, p. 82. At least one case of illiteracy was discovered only after the sister in question had been in the community for a considerable length of time – had been appointed as novice mistress in the Australian mission. It was a source of amazement to Potter that the sister had managed to disguise the fact for so long, and it only became apparent when the woman was returned to Rome, having created much dissension.

[226] Margaret MacCurtain, "Late in the Field: Catholic Sisters in Twentieth Century Ireland and the new Religious History," *Journal of Woman's History*, 7, 1 (Winter, 1995), p. 58.

[227] *LCM Rule*, 1893, "On the Instructions Necessary."

[228] loc. cit.

[229] Mary Potter to Mother Cecilia Smith n.d.

[230] Mary Potter to Mother Raphael, n.d.

[231] Mary Potter Circular Letter in *Obedience Notes*, no. 4, p. 24.

[232] Mary Potter *To the Novices* n.d.

[233] Mary Potter *Obedience Notes*, Vol. 4, p. 50.

[234] ibid., p. 49.

[235] Mary Potter, *Brides of Christ*, Little Company of Mary (Chicago, 1957), p. 53.

[236] Not all congregations took all three vows: some took none. See Patricia Wittberg, *The Rise and Fall of Catholic Religious Orders: a social movement perspective*, The State University of New York Press, (New York, 1994), p. 49–50.

[237] The relevant scripture passages upon which the principle of the vows rested are: Matthew 16:24; Matt 19:21 and Matt: 19:12.

[238] Wittberg, *The Rise and Fall of Catholic Religious Orders*, p. 49–50 and 241–256.

[239] Mary Potter, *Conferences M.*, 1–3.

[240] Mary Potter to Mother Xavier Lynch, in *Conferences R*, p. 35.

[241] Mary Potter, *Conferences R*, p. 36.

[242] Mary Potter *Brides of Christ* (Chicago edition.) p. 42.

[243] loc. cit.

[244] ibid. p. 41–42.

[245] Mary Potter, *Mary's Conferences* p. 28.

[246] See McLeod, *Religion and the People of Western Europe* p. 36. McCaffrey, *History of the Catholic Church* in *the Nineteenth Century*, p. 471. Daniel-Rops, *The Church in an Age of Revolution 1789–1870.*, p. 347 ff. J. Derek Holmes, *The Triumph of the Papacy: A Short History of the Papacy in the Nineteenth Century*, Burns & Oates (London, 1978), p. 287. Umberto Benigni "Ultramontanism" in The Catholic Encyclopædia 15, (1912). Barbara Corrado Pope "Immaculate and Powerful: The Marian Revival in the Nineteenth Century" in Clarissa W. Atkinson et al., (eds.), *Immaculate and Powerful The female in Sacred Image* and *Social Reality*, Beacon Press, (Boston, 1985), p. 182. Patricia Byrne, "American Ultramontanism" p. 314.

[247] Mary Potter, *Mary's Conferences*, p. 28.

[248] loc. cit.

[249] Mary Potter, *Man Mirroring his Maker*, Propaganda Fide Press (Rome, 1908), p. 176

[250] Mary Potter, *Mary's Conferences*, p. 135.

[251] Mary Potter, *Conferences R*, p. 52.

[252] ibid., p. 88.

[253] ibid., p. 166.

[254] Helsinger et al., The Woman Question: Society and Literature in Britain and America, Vol. I, p. xiv.

255 These figures are loose approximations only. In 1913, there were 313 sisters of the Little Company of Mary scattered across four continents. In 1906, there were 53 finally professed sisters in Australia, somewhere in the vicinity of 124 in Hyson Green. There were four novitiates operating. Hyson Green continued to train novices for England and Ireland, and some novices were sent to the Roman novitiate, Australia followed this practice too. The American Novitiate was not formally established until the first quarter of the twentieth century. Rome, Australia and US registers are, however, inaccurate and in some cases the necessary episcopal returns are missing from archives. See Appendix A.

256 St. John's Hospital Limerick and the Workhouse Infirmary at Fermoy.

257 Lewisham Hospital, Sydney (1889); Mount St. Margaret's Asylum, Ryde (1890); and Calvary Hospital, Adelaide (1890).

258 The Malta House was opened in 1894, and the hospital (Casa Leone XIII) finally opened in 1910.

259 Raphael Cardinal Merry del Val (b. 1865) was probably the most conspicuous ecclesial figure in Rome. Born in London of Spanish parents, he had been educated in England and had risen to swift fame as a Vatican diplomat. He was a noted Anglophile, had been the Papal Envoy at the time of Queen Victoria's Jubilee, and held much influence among the English and European aristocrats of Rome. This he used to affect when Mary Potter persisted in refusing to build on the site he had selected – a plot of land just behind St. Peter's Basilica. M.V. Caprani, *The Spirit and the Heritage*. Privately Published. Rome, 1978, pp. 80–82.

260 Cf. *Report by the Congregation for the Cause of Saints*, October 9, 1972. I am grateful to Mr. Guido Dughetti for the transcription of this document.

261 Caprani, *The Spirit and the Heritage,* p. 96. By 1928, the nursing school had graduated one hundred and sixty nurses, and gained approval of the Italian government as an "accredited" training school.

262 ibid.

263 Mother Cecilia Smith *Personal Reminiscences*, p. 11.

264 The first hospital opened by the English community was in 1897, when the ground floor of Gunnersby House, Isleworth, was converted to become a children's hospital. It was never particularly successful, and the works of the institute in England remained centred on district nursing, and working among the poor. In 1897, a home for unmarried mothers called "The Guardian Angels Home" was opened firstly in Charlotte Street, London. It moved to St. John's Wood in 1911.

265 Mary Potter, "Conference on the Confraternity of Calvary", n.d.

266 Written by Mary Potter in 1883, given to Mother Cecilia by Mary Potter, and contained in Mother Cecilia Smith, *Personal Reminiscences*, p. 43.

267 There is a remarkably similar passage to Potter's experience in Mary Sinclair's *Mary Oliver: A Life*. Sinclair's character, Mary Oliver, describes a moment of spiritual awakening in the following manner: "This is an awful feeling. Dying must be like this. One thing going after another. Something holding down your heart, stopping its beat; something holding down your chest, crushing the breath out of it…Let everything go except yourself. Hold onto yourself, you feel yourself going. Going and coming back; gathered together, incredibly free…" in Mary Sinclair *Mary Oliver: A Life*, Virago Press (London, 1980: First Published London, 1914), p. 351. Willingness to give up the self to the darkness resulted for Mary Oliver in a new freedom to act, a new life, free from the bondage of the angelic ideal and constraining cultural mores. For Mary Potter, ego death – either in mystical experience or in reality – was the entry into a new freedom, a "true" self, which was, of course, "in God". This is the essence of her understanding of the end of the spiritual life and of life itself.

268 Mary Potter *Loves in the Heart of Mary,* Little Company of Mary, London, p. 101.

269 Michael Wheeler *Death and the Future Life in Victorian Literature & Theology*, Cambridge University Press (Cambridge, 1990), p. 32.

270 Mary Potter, *Conferences E,* p. 16.

271 Mary Potter, *Conferences A,* p. 33.

272 *Conditae a Christo* was promulgated by Pope Leo XIII on December 8, 1900.

273 Leo XIII, *Conditae a Christo*, in D.I. Lanslots, OSB, *Handbook of Canon Law for Congregations of Women under Simple Vows*, Frederick Pustet & Co., Publishers (New York, 1909), pp. 246–258. The document was signed by Potter's old friend, Monsignor, now Cardinal Macchi.

274 ibid. p. 250.

275 *LCM Rule*, 1893, p. 8.

276 Lanslots, *Handbook of Canon Law*, p. 5.

277 op. cit., p. 6.

278 loc. cit.

279 *Normae* #42 in Lanslots, op. cit.

280 *Normae* # 43, 45, ibid. p. 35.

281 *Normae #32,* ibid. p. 3.

282 *Normae* #27, ibid.

283 *Normae # 51,* ibid., p. 37.

284 *Normae* # 51, ibid.

285 loc. cit.

286 *Normae* #13, ibid.

287 *Normae* #14, 15, ibid.

288 cf. Mary Ewens *The Role of Nun*, p. 19–21.

289 Mary Potter, Circular Letter no. 5, *Conferences E*, p. 10–11.

290 loc. cit. Punctuation as in original.

291 Mary Potter, *Conferences R*, pp. 37, 61, 62.

292 ibid. p. 61.

293 Mary Potter, *Conferences E*, pp. 7, 16.

294 Tillard, *There are Charisms and Charisms*, pp. 30–36.

295 The significance of the various decrees on renewal of religious life emerging from the Second Vatican Council rests in the charge given to all communities to renew themselves in the spirit or the charism of the founder. For some communities, the call to renewal has led to the discovery that their foundation was the result of the functionalism mentioned in this thesis. For others, it has led to the discovery that the founding charism of their institute was significantly different from the historical evolution of the particular community. On the impact of Vatican II on religious life and the understanding of the charism of the various expressions of that life see: Manuel Ruiz Jurado, "Consecrated Life and the Charisms of the Founders" in René Latourelle *Vatican Two: Assessment and Perspectives Twenty-five Years After*, Vol. 3, Paulist Press (Mahway, NJ, 1989), pp. 3–26; *Religious Life in the Light of Vatican II*, Compiled by the Daughters of St. Paul, Daughters of St. Paul Press (Boston, 1967), passim. Romano *The Charism of the Founders*, passim.

296 The record of her spiritual journey can be found in her personal notes contained in *Obedience Notes*, Vols. 1–4. These books constitute a spiritual diary begun c.1903 and continuing until her death. They record her ongoing mystical experiences.

297 Mary Potter, *Obedience Notes*, Vol. 3, p. 21.

298 ibid. p. 17.

299 Mary Potter, *Obedience Notes*, Vol. 5, p. 4.

300 ibid. p. 99.

301 ibid. p. 122.

302 Mary Potter to Mother Philip Coleridge, 1913.

303 Mother Cecilia Smith, *Personal Reminiscences*, p. 11.

304 Circular Letter to the Houses of the Little Company of Mary, April 11, 1913.

305 ibid.

306 Elizabeth Bryan predeceased Mary Potter, dying in Rome in July 1898.

307 ibid.

308 Mother Cecilia Smith lived to a ripe old age, and died on June 18, 1940. Agnes Bray followed her one year later (June 18, 1941). The last of the "boon companions" of the early days of Hyson Green and Rome, Mother Catherine (Minnie) Croker died in Rome in 1949. With their deaths, the foundation period of the Little Company of Mary can be said to have ended.

Appendix

Primary Sources: Contemporary Printed Materials

A Guide to the Religious Houses of Great Britain and Ireland. London: Burns & Oates, Ltd., 1887.

Burdett-Coutts, A.G., (ed.) *Woman's Mission A Series of Congress Papers on the Philanthropic Work of Women by Eminent Writers*. Sampson Low, Marston & Company. London, 1893.

Besant, Annie, *An Autobiography*. T. Fisher Unwin, London, 1908.

Booth, W. *In Darkest England and the Way Out*. Salvation Army Press: London, 1890.

Bowden, J. E. *The Life and Letters of Fredrick William Faber D.D.* Burns & Oates Ltd. London, 1869

Butler, J. *The Education and Employment of Women*. T. Brakell. Liverpool, 1868.

—   (ed.), *Women's Work and Women's Culture*. MacMillan & Co London. 1869

—   *The Hour Before Dawn*. Trubner Pty. Ltd: London, 1876.

Catholic Directory. *The Catholic Directory Ecclesiastical Register, and Almanac, for the Year of Our Lord 1878*. Burns Oates. London, 1877.

Clinton, A., (trans.) *The Characteristics of True Devotion*. Translated from the French of The Rev J.N.Grou. Benziger Bros, New York, 1895.

Cobbe, F. Power. "Social Science Congresses and Women's Part in them." *Macmillan's Magazine* December (1861).

—   *Italics*. Trubner & Co. London, 1864.

—   The Final Cause of Women. In J. Butler (ed.), *Women's Work and Women's Culture*. MacMillan & Co. London. 1869

Craven, A. *Life of Lady Georgiana Fullerton* (trans. from the French by H.J. Coleridge). Richard Bentley & Son, London, 1888.

Cusack, M. *The Nun of Kenmare – An Autobiography*. Ticknor & Company. Boston, 1889

De Lehen, F. *The Way of Interior Peace*. Dedicated to Our Lady of Peace 2nd ed. Benziger Brothers, New York, 1888.

Ellis, Sarah Stickney. The Mothers of England, Their Influence and Responsibility. Fisher & Sons. London:1890.

Faber, F. W. *The Foot of the Cross*. The Peter Reilly Co. Philadelphia, 1956.

—   *All For Jesus*. Burns & Oates. London, 1853.

—   *Bethlehem*. The Peter Reilly Co. Philadelphia, 1955.

—   *Growth in Holiness: Or the Progress of the Spiritual Life*. Burns & Oates Ltd. London, 1854.

—   *The Blessed Sacrament*. Burns & Oates. London, 1854.

—   *Hymns*. Thomas Richardson & Son. London, 1871.

—   *The Precious Blood*. Burns & Oates. London, 1860.

Froude, J. A. *Short Studies on Great Subjects* Vol. 4: *The Oxford Counter Reformation*. London, 1888.

Hutton, A.W. *Cardinal Manning*. Methuen & Co. London, 1892.

Jameson A. B. *Legends of the Madonna as Presented in the Fine Arts*. Longmans, Green & Co. London, 1891.

—   *Sisters of Charity Catholic and Protestant & The Communion of Labour*. Ticknor & Fields. Boston, 1858.

Keble, J, "The Annunciation of the Blessed Virgin Mary. *The Christian Year*. Thomas Y. Cromwell: New York, 1890.

— *Manual of Instructions in Christian Doctrine*. Second Edition. Burns, Lambert, & Oates, London, 1865.

Kingsley, C. *Yeast: A Problem*. Richard Edward King. London, 1851

Murphy, J.N. *Terra Incognita or The Convents of Great Britain*. Burns & Oates. London, 1876.

Ordo. *Ordo Recitandi Officii Divini et Missae Celebrandae Pro Anno Domini MDCCCLI*. [Including the Catholic Directory, Ecclesiastical Register and Almanac] London: Apud C.Dolman, 1850.

Ordo. *Ordo Recitandi Officii Divini et Missae Celebrandae Pro Anno Domini MDCCCLVI*. [Including the Catholic Directory, Ecclesiastical Register and Almanac] London: Apud Burns et Lambert, 1856.

Ordo. *Ordo Recitandi Officii Divini et Missae Celebranmdae Pro Anno Domini MDCCCXLIX*. [Including the Catholic Directory, Ecclesiastical Register and Almanac] London: Apud C.Dolman, 1849.

Ordo. *Ordo Recitandi Officii Divini Sacrique Peragendi Pro Anno Domini Bissextili MDCCCLX*. [Including the Catholic Directory, Ecclesiastical Register and Almanac] London: Apud Burns et Lambert, 1860.

Ordo. *Ordo Recitandi Officii Divini Sacrique Peragendi Pro Anno Domini MDCCCLXI*. [Including the Catholic Directory, Ecclesiastical Register and Almanac] London: Apud Burns et Lambert, 1861.

Purcell, Sheridan. *Life of Cardinal Manning: Archbishop of Westminster*. 2 Vols. MacMillan: London, 1896.

Taylor, F (Mother Magdalen Taylor). *The Inner Life of Lady Georgiana Fullerton*. Burns & Oates Ltd. London, 1899.

Ullathorne, W. *The Immaculate Conception of the Mother of God: An Exposition*. John Murch & Co. Pittsburgh, 1855.

Thomas, C. *Christ's Dying Hours: A Sermon Preached on the Occasion of the re-Opening of St. Margaret's Church Hilston, Holderness on Thursday July 31, 1862*. London, 1862.

Yonge, C.M. *Womankind*. Walter Smith. London, 1876/1881.

Secondary Sources:

à Kempis, T. *The Imitation of Christ*. St Paul Publications. Homebush NSW, 1983.

Abel-Smith, B. *A History of the Nursing Profession*. Heinemann. London, 1975.

Adams, C. "A Choice Not to Wed? Unmarried Women in Eighteenth-Century France." *Journal of Social History*. 29, 4 (1996).

Adams, K.V. "The Madonna and Margaret Fuller." *Women's Studies Journal* 25, 4 (1996): 385–406.

Ahles, M.A. "Her Days in an Anglican Sisterhood (Ch.2)." *In the Shadow of His Wings A History of the Franciscan Sisters*. The North Central Publishing Company. St Paul, Min, 1977.

Akenson, D. H. *Small Differences: Irish Catholics and Irish Protestants 1815–1922*. Gill & Macmillan. Dublin, 1988.

Allen, K. "Representation and Self-Representation: Hannah Whitall Smith as Family Woman and Religious Guide." *Women's History Review* 7, 2 (1998): 227–239.

Allchin, A.M. *The Silent Rebellion: Anglican Religious Communities 1845–1900*. SCM Press. London, 1958.

Almond, P.C. *Mystical Experience and Religious Doctrine: An investigation of the study of mysticism in World Religions*. Mouton Publishers. Berlin, 1982.

Altizer, T.J.J. "Apocalypticism and Modern Thinking." *Journal for Christian Theological Review*. 2:2 [http://apu.Edu/~CTRF/articles/1997_articles/altizer.Html] (1997).

Anderson, K.M. "Muscular Christianity Embodying the Victorian Age." *College Literature* 24, 3 (1997).

Anson, P. *The Call of the Cloister: Religious Communities and Kindred Bodies in the Anglican Communion*. SPCK, London, 1956.

Arbuckle, G. A. *Out of Chaos: Refounding Religious Congregations*. Paulist Press. New Jersey, 1988.

— *Strategies for Growth in Religious Life*. St Paul Publications. Homebush, NSW, 1987.

— "Refounding Congregations From Within: Anthropological Perspectives." *Review For Religious*, 45:4. July/August 1986: 538–553

Armstrong, K. *The Gospel According to Woman*. Fount. London, 1986.

Arnstein, W. "Queen Victoria and the Challenge of Roman Catholicism." *The Historian*. 58, 2. (Winter 1996) 295–315

— *Protestant Versus Catholic in Mid-Victorian England Mr. Newdegate and the Nuns*. University of Missouri Press. Columbia & London, 1982.

— "The Murphy Riots: A Victorian Dilemma." *Victorian Studies* (1975/6): 51–71.

Arseniev, N. *Mysticism and the Eastern Church*. St Vladimir's Seminary Press, New York, 1979.

Aspinwall, B. "Changing Images of Roman Catholic Religious Orders in the Nineteenth Century." *Studies in Church History* 22 (1985): 351–363.

Atkinson, C. W., Buchanan, C. H., and Miles, M. R., (eds.) *Immaculate and Powerful: The Female in Sacred Image and Social Reality*. Beacon Press, reprinted by Crucible. Boston, 1985.

Bancroft, A. *Women in Search of the Sacred*. Arkana Penguin. London, 1996.

Barmann, Lawrence F., (ed.) *Newman at St. Mary's: A Selection of the Plain and Parochial Sermons*. Newman Press. Westminster, Maryland, 1962.

Barnard, S. *To Prove I'm Not Forgot: Living and Dying in a Victorian City*. Manchester University Press. Manchester, 1990.

Barnes, P. L. "Rudolf Otto and the Limits of Religious Description." *Religious Studies*. 30 (1994). 219–230.

Barry, C J. (ed.) *Readings in Church History Volume 111*. The Modern Era 1789 to the Present. The Newman Press. Westminster Ma., 1965.

Barry, W. A. *What Do I Want in Prayer?* Paulist Press. New York, 1994.

— and Maloney, K.A., (eds.) *A Hunger for God*. Ten Approaches to Prayer. Sheed & Ward. Kansas City, 1991.

Basham, D. *The Trial of Woman: Feminism and the Occult Sciences in Victorian Literature and Society*. New York University Press. New York, 1992.

Battersby, W.J. "Educational Work of he Religious Orders of Women, 1850–1950." Chap. in *The English Catholics: 1850–1950*. Burns & Oates. London, 1950: 337–364.

Bearsley, P.J. "Mary the Perfect Disciple: A Paradigm for Mariology." *Theological Studies* (1980) 41: 461–504.

Beck, George A. (ed.) *The English Catholics 1850–1950*. Burns Oates, London, 1950.

Bedarida, F. *A Social History of England 1851–1990* (trans. A.S. Forester). Methuen & Co. Ltd. London, 1979.

Beggiani, S.J. "Theology at the Service of Mysticism Method in Pseudo-Dionysius." *Theological Studies*. Vol. 57 No 2 201–223 (1996)

Beinert, W. "Mary and feminism." *Theology Digest*. 31, 3 (1984): 235–239.

Bellinger, Dom Aiden. "France and England: The English Female Religious From Reformation to World War." Chap. in Tallett, F., and Atkin, N (eds.) *Catholicism in Britain and France Since 1789*. Hambeldon Press. London: 1996:3–10

Belshaw, G.P.M., (ed.) *Lent with Evelyn Underhill*. Mowbrays, London, 1966.

Bennett, J. M., Clark, E.A., O'Barr, J.F., Vilen, B.A., and S. Westphal-Wihl. (eds.) *Sisters and Workers in the Middle Ages*. University of Chicago Press. Chicago, 1989.

Berlin. I. *The Age of Enlightenment: The 18th Century Philosophers*. Mentor Books. New York, 1956.

Bernard of Clairvaux, St. *On the Love of God*. A. R. Mowbray & Co. London. 1950.

— *On the Song of Songs: Sermons in Cantica Canticorum*. Translated and Edited by A religious of C.S.M.V. A. R. Mowbray & Co. London, 1952.

Best, G. *Mid-Victorian Britain 1851–1875*. Fontana Books. London, 1979.

Bielak, V. *The Servant of God Mary Theresa Countess Ledochowska 2nd ed*. Foundress of the Sodality of Saint Peter Claver. The Society of St Peter Claver. St. Paul, Min, 1944.

Billington, R. A. "Maria Monk and Her Influence." *Catholic Historical Review* 22 (1936–7): 283–296.

Black, E. C., (ed.) *Victorian Culture and Society*. Harper & Row. New York, 1973.

Blake, C. *The Charge of the Parasols: Women's Entry Into the Medical Profession*. The Women's Press. London, 1990.

Blaquiere, G. *The Grace to be Woman*. Alba House. New York, 1983.

Boff, C. "The Poor of Latin America and their new Ways of Liberation." *Concilium* 191, 3 (1987): 33–44.

Boff, L. *The Maternal Face of God*. Collins. London, 1989.

Boland, T.P. *Quiet Women*. Sisters of Perpetual Adoration. Brisbane, 1974.

Bolster, A. *Catherine McAuley: Venerable for Mercy*. Dominican Publications. Dublin, 1990.

Booth, A. *Greatness Engendered: George Eliot and Virginia Woolf*. Cornell University Press. New York, 1992.

Borchet, B. *Mysticism Its History and Challenge*. Samuel Weiser Inc. York Beach, Maine, 1994.

Bossy, J. *The English Catholic Community 1570–1850*. London, 1975.

Boultwood, A. *Christ in Us Reflections on Redemption*. The Liturgical Press. Collegeville, Minn., 1970.

Bouyer, L. *A History of Christian Spirituality*. 3 Vols. Burns & Oates. Tunbridge Wells, 1967–8.

—   *Newman His Life and Spirituality*. Burns & Oates. London, 1958.

Bowie, F., (ed.) *Beguine Spirituality An Anthology*. Translations by Oliver Davies. SPCK. London, 1989.

Bradley, R. *Julian's Way*. A Practical Commentary on Julian of Norwich. Harper Collins Religious. London, 1992.

—   *Praying with Julian of Norwich*. Twenty-third Publications. Mystic Connecticut, 1995.

Braude, A. *Radical Spirits Spiritualism and Women's Rights in Nineteenth-century America*. Beacon Press. Boston, 1989.

Bremond, H. *A Literary History of Religious Thought in France:* Vols 1–3 Society for Promoting Christian Knowledge. London, 1928, 1936.

Brennan, W.T. "Faith, Mary, Culture." *Marian Studies* XLVI (1995): 10–25.

Briggs, A. *The Collected Essays of Asa Briggs Volume 1: Words, Numbers, Places, People*. The Harvester Press. Sussex, 1985.

            The Collected Essays of Asa Briggs Volume 11 Images, Problems, Standpoints, Forecasts. The Harvester Press. Sussex, 1985.

—   "Cholera and Society in the Nineteenth Century." *Past and Present* 19 (1961): 76–96.

Brooke, C. *Monasteries of the World: The Rise and Development of Monastic Tradition*. Crescent Books, New York, 1982.

Brown, L. B. *The Psychology of Religion an Introduction*. SPCK. London, 1988.

Brown, R. *Portsmouth's Pictorial Past*. Milstone Publications. Hampshire, 1985.

Brown, R. E., Donfried, D. P., Fitzmyer J. A, and J. Neumann, (eds.) *Mary in the New Testament*. Fortress Press. Philadelphia, 1978.

Brozyna, A. E. "The Right to Labour, Love and Pray: the Creation of the Ideal Christian Woman in Ulster Roman Catholic and Protestant Religious Literature, 1850–1914." *Women's History Review* 6, 4 (1997): 505–528.

Buckley, M. "The Charism and Identity of Religious Life." *Review for Religious* 44, 5 (1985).

Buckley, M.J. "Ecclesial Mysticism in the Spiritual Exercises of Ignatius." *Theological Studies* 56, 3 (1995): 441–463.

Buehrle, M.C. *Raphael Cardinal Merry Del Val*. Sands & Co Ltd. London, 1957.

Bullough, Vern L, Bonnie Bullough, and Stanton, Mariella P. (eds.) *Florence Nightingale and Her Era: A Collection of New Scholarship*. Garland Reference Library of Social Science Vol. 629. Garland Publishing. New York & London, 1990.

Burkhardt, W., (ed.) *Woman New Dimensions*. Paulist Press. New York, 1975.

Burman, S., (ed.) *Fit Work for Women*. Croom Helm. London, 1979.

Busfield, J. "The Female Malady? Men, Women and Madness in Nineteenth Century Britain." *Sociology* 28, 1 (1994): 259–277.

Butler, C. *Western Mysticism*. Arrow Books. London, 1960.

Byrne, P. "American Ultramontanism." *Theological Studies* 56, January (1995).

Cada, L., Fitz, R., Foley, G., Giardino, T. and Lichtenberg, C. (eds.) *Shaping the Coming Age of Religious Life*. The Seabury Press. New York, 1979.

Cahill, S, (ed.) *Wise Women*. W.W. Norton & Co. New York W.W. Norton & Co, 1997.

Cain, James R. "Cloister and the Apostolate of Religious Women." *Review for Religious* 27, 2 (1968).

Caine, B. *English Feminism 1780–1980*. OUP. New York, 1997.

— "Feminist Biography and Feminist History." *Women's History Reviw*. Vol 3, No 4. 1994

Campbell, A. V. *Professional Care. It's Meaning and Practice*. SPCK, London, 1984.

Campbell, T. A. *The Religion of the Heart*. A Study of European Religious Life in the Seventeenth and Eighteenth Centuries. South Carolina University Press. Columbia, 1991.

Campion, E. *Australian Catholics*. The Contribution of Catholics to the Development of Australian Society. Viking. Ringwood Vic, 1987.

— (ed.) *Lord Acton and the First Vatican Council A Journal*. Catholic Theological Faculty. Sydney, 1975.

Campion, M. *Place of Springs*. Privately published. Bootle, Merseyside, 1977.

Caprani, M.V. *The Spirit and the Heritage*. Privately Published. Rome, 1978.

Carey, A. *Sisters in Crisis*. The Tragic Unravelling of Women's Religious Communities. Our Sunday Visitor Inc. Huntingdon, Ind. 1997.

Carey, T, (ed.) *Therese of Lisieux: A Discovery of Love – Selected Spiritual Writings*. New City Press. New York, 1992.

Carney, S., RSM. "The Legacy of Catherine McAuley and the Transformative Elements for Religious Life in the Future." *The MAST Journal* 3, 1 (Fall, 1992).

Carondelet Conference. *The Future of Religious Life*. Proceedings of the Carondelet Conference. The Liturgical Press. Collegeville, 1990.

Carr, A. & Schussler Fiorenza, E. (eds.) *Motherhood Experience, Institution, Theology*. Concilium. T and T Clark. Edinburgh, 1989.

Carr, A. E. *Transforming Grace*. Christian Tradition and Women's Experience. Harper & Row. San Francisco, 1988.

Carroll, Michael P. "Rethinking Popular Catholicism in Pre-Famine Ireland." *The Journal for the Scientific Study of Religion*. 34, 3 (1995): 354–366,.

Cary-Lewis, C. *Experiences with God A Dictionary of Spirituality and Prayer*. Sheed and Ward. London, 1986.

Casey, Ellen Miller. "Edging Women Out? Reviews of Women Novelists in the Atheneum 1860–1900." *Victorian Studies*. 39, 2 (1996: 151–172.

Casteras, S. "Virgin Vows." Chap. in Gail Malmgreen, (ed.) *Religion in the Lives of Englishwomen 1760–1930*. Croom Helm. London, 1986.

Catholic Emancipation 1829 – 1929: Essays by various writers. Longmans, Green and Co. London, 1929.

Catholic Truth Society. *Publications of the Catholic Truth Society Vol. V*. Catholic Truth Society. London, 1891.

Catterall, M. *Teresa Higginson: M.Catterall's Narrative*. W.Watson & Co. Preston, 1936.

Celine, M. *A Woman of Unity: Mother Lurana of Graymoor*. Franciscan Sisters of the Atonement. New York, 1956.

Centenary Monograph: St Mary's Parish Hyson Green, Nottingham. Privately printed: Leicester, 1980.

Chadwick, O. "The Ascetic Movement." In *The Early Church*. Rev. edition. Penguin History of the Church, Chadwick O. 173–183. Penguin Books. London, 1993.

— *From Bossuet to Newman*. 2nd ed. Cambridge University Press. Cambridge, 1987.

— *The Secularization of the European Mind in the 19th Century*. Cambridge University Press. - Cambridge, 1975.

— *The Victorian Church, Vols I & II*. Adam & Charles Black. London, 1966.

— (ed.) *Western Asceticism: Vol XII The Library of Christian Classics*. SCM Press Ltd. London, 1958.

Challoner, R. *The Garden of the Soul: A Manual of Spiritual Exercises and Instructions for Christians*. Society of St Peter & Paul. London, 1741/1916.

Chapman, S. D., (ed.) *The History of Working Class Housing 1780–1918: A Symposium*. David and Charles. Newton Abbot, 1971.

Chittister, J. "The Fall of the Temple A Call to Formation in the Prophetic Tradition." *Signum,* August (1996): 15–20.

—   *Wisdom Distilled From the Daily. Living the Rule of St Benedict Today.* Harper San Francisco, 1991.

—   *Women, Ministry and the Church.* Paulist Press. New York, 1983.

Christ, C. P., and J. Plaskow, (eds.) *Womanspirit Rising: A Feminist Reader in Religion.* Harper. San Francisco, 1972/1991.

Church, R.A. *Economic and Social Change in a Midland Town: Victorian Nottingham.* Franck Cass & Co. Ltd. London,1966.

Clark, E. A. *Women in the Early Church.* Michael Glazier Inc. Wilmington Delaware, 1983.

Clarke, E.A, Richardson, H, (eds.) *Women and Religion: Sourcebook of Women in Christian Thought.* Harper Collins. San Francisco, 1977.

Clarke, J., (trans.) *Story of a Soul.* The Autobiography of St Therese of Lisieux Third Edition. ICS Publications. Washington DC, 1996.

Clear, C. "The Limits of Female Autonomy: Nuns in Nineteenth-Century Ireland." In Luddy M. and Murphy C., (eds.) *Women Surviving Studies in Irish Women's History in the 19th & 20th Centuries.* Poolbeg. Dublin, 1990.

—   *Nuns in Nineteenth Century Ireland.* Gill & MacMillan. Dublin, 1987.

Colledge, E. & Walsh, J., (trans.) *Julian of Norwich Showings.* The Classics of Western Spirituality. Paulist Press. New York, 1978.

Congar, Y. *Jesus Christ.* Geoffrey Chapman. London, 1968.

—   *Power and Poverty in the Church.* Geoffrey Chapman. London, 1965.

Congregation for Catholic Education. *The Virgin Mary in Intellectual and Spiritual Formation.* University of Dayton. Dayton Ohio, 1988.

Connolly, G.P. "The Transubstantiation of Myth: Towards a New Popular History of Nineteenth-Century Catholicism in England." *Journal of Ecclesiastical History* 35 (1984): 78–104.

Conwell, J.F., SJ. *Impelling Spirit: Revisiting a Founding Experience.* Loyola Press. Chicago, 1997.

Cook, Sir Edward. *The Life of Florence Nightingale.* Macmillan. London, 1913.

Coon, L., Haldane, K., and Sommer, E. *That Gentle Strength: Historical Perspectives on Women in Christianity.* University Press of Virginia. Charlottesville, 1990

Cor Mariae Commission, (eds.) *Far Beyond Pearls: Documents of Research Servants of the Holy Heart of Mary.* SSCM. Quebec, 1978.

Corish, Patrick A. "Women and Relgious Practice." In MacCurtain, M. and O'Dowd, M. (eds.). *Women in Early Modern Ireland.* Edinburgh University Press. Edinburgh, 1991.

Costé, J. *Lectures on Society of Mary History.* Tipographia S. pio X. Roma, 1965.

Courtwright, D. "The Female Opiate Addict in Nineteenth Century America." *Essays in Arts and Sciences* 10 (1982): 163–4.

Creusen, J. *Religious Men and Women in Church Law.* The Bruce Publishing Company. Milwaukee, 1931.

Crews, C. F. *English Catholic Modernism: Maud Petre's Way of Faith.* University of Notre Dame Press. Notre Dame, Indiana, 1984.

Cullen, M., (ed.) *Girls Don't Do Honours: Irish Women in Education in the Nineteenth and Twentieth Centuries.* Women's Education Bureau. Dublin, 1987.

Cuneen, S. *In Search of Mary, the Woman and the Symbol.* Ballantine Books. New York, 1996.

Cunningham, L., (ed.) *The Catholic Faith.* Paulist Press. New York, 1988.

Danielou, J. & Musurillo, H., (eds.) *From Glory to Glory.* Charles Schribner & Sons. New York, 1961.

Daniel-Rops, H. *The Church in an Age of Revolution 1789–1870.* J.M.Dent & Sons Ltd. London, 1965.

Daughters of St Paul (eds.). *Religious Life in the Light of Vatrican 11.* St Paul Press. Boston, 1967.

Dauphin, C. "Single Women." In Fraisse G and Perrot M (eds.). *A History of Women: Emerging Feminism From Revolution to World War.* Belknap Press. Cambridge, Ma. (1993) 427–441

Davidoff, L. "Class and Gender in Victorian England." In Newton J., Ryan, M., and Davidoff L., (eds.) *Sex and Class in Women's History,* Routledge & Kegan Paul. London, 1983.

Davies Celia. *Re-Writing Nursing History*. Croom Helm. London, 1980.

Davies, N. *Europe A History*. Pimlico. London, 1997.

Davies, O. *God Within*. The Mystical Tradition of Northern Europe. Darton, Longman and Todd. London, 1988.

—— (trans.) *Beguine Spirituality: Mystical Writings of Mechtild of Magdeburg, Beatrice of Nazareth and Hadewijch of Brabant*. Crossroad. New York, 1990.

Davies Celia. *Re-Writing Nursing History*. Croom Helm. London, 1980.

Dawson, C. *The Spirit of the Oxford Movement*. Sheed & Ward. London, 1933.

De Fiores, Stefano. Edited by *Jesus Living in Mary: Handbook of the Spirituality of St. Louis Marie de Montfort*. Montfort Publications. Bay Shore NY, 1994.

De Guibert, J. *The Theology of the Spiritual Life*. Sheed & Ward. London, 1954.

De Jaegher P. *One with Jesus*. Burns Oates & Washbourne Ltd. London, 1929.

De Montfort, L.G. *The Secret of Mary*. The Montfort Fathers. Liverpool, 1954.

—— *True Devotion to the Blessed Virgin Mary*. The Montfort Fathers. New York, 1946.

—— *Treatise on The True Devotion to the Blessed Virgin Mary*. Fathers of the Company of Mary. London, 1954.

—— *The Secret of Mary or The Slavery of the Blessed Virgin*. The Montfort Fathers. Liverpool, 1954.

de Vinck, J. *Revelations of Women Mystics From Middle Ages to Modern Times*. Alba House. New York, 1985.

Degnan, M. B. *Mercy Unto Thousands*. Browne and Nolan Ltd. Dublin, 1958.

Denison, G. *Time to Remember A Collection of Photographs from the Nottingham Historical Film Unit*. T.Bailey Forman Ltd. Nottingham. n.d.

Devas, F.C. *Mother Magdalen Taylor of the Sacred Heart*. Burns Oates & Washbourne, Ltd. London, 1927.

Deville, R. *The French School of Spirituality* (trans. Agnes Cunningham). Duquesne University Press, Pittsburgh, 1994.

Dicens, M. A. *Mother Magdalen Taylor*. Poor Servants of the Mother of God. Bristol, nd.

Dickens, C. *Hard Times*. Wordsworth Classics. Ware, Hertfordshire, 1995.

Dirvin, J. I. *The Soul of Elizabeth Seton*. Ignatius Press. San Francisco, 1990.

Doheny, W.J, and J. P Kelly, (eds.) *Papal Documents on Mary*. Bruce Publishing Co. Milwaukee, 1954.

Dolan, A. "Nottingham Diocese Archives." *Catholic Archives No 3*: (1983).9–17.

Dolan, Jay P. *The American Catholic Experience: A History From Colonial Times to the Present*. Doubleday. New York, 1985.

Donnelly, D. (ed.) *Mary Woman of Nazareth: Biblical & Theological Perspectives*. Paulist Press. New York, 1989.

Donovan, M. A. *Sisterhood as Power*. Crossroad. New York, 1989.

Dortel-Claudot, M., S.J. *The Evolution of the Canonical Status of Religious Institutes with Simple Vows From the 16th Century until the New Code*. (Trans. R. MacGinley PBVM). Institute of Religious Studies. Sydney, 1989.

Dougherty, P. *In the Garden of God's Church: A Commentary on the Writings of Mother Mary Potter*. Unpublished work. circa 1964.

—— *Mary Potter Postulant and Novice at the Convent of the Sisters of Mercy*. Paper prepared for the Sisters of the Little Company of Mary. Sydney, 1972

—— *Mother Mary Potter*. Sands & Co. London, 1961.

Douglas, A. *The Feminization of American Culture*. Anchor Doubleday. New York, London, 1977.

Downey, M., (ed.) *The New Dictionary of Catholic Spirituality*. The Liturgical Press. Collegeville, 1993.

Drake, E. F. *What a Young Wife Ought to Know*. The Vir Publishing Company. Philadelphia, 1909.

Dreyer, E. *Passionate Women*. Paulist Press. New York, 1989.

Drury, N. *The Visionary Human*. Mystical *Consciousness & Paranormal Perspectives*. Element Books. Dorset, 1991.

Duby, G. And Perrot, M., (eds.) *A History of Women in the West: 1V. Emerging Feminism From Revolution to World War*. Belknap Press. Cambridge, 1993.

Duffy, E. *The Stripping of the Altars: Traditional Religion in England 1400–1580*. Yale University Press. New Haven, 1992.

Dulles, A. *A Church to Believe In: Discipleship and the Dynamics of Freedom*. Crossroads. New York, 1984.

—   "The Ignatian Charism and Contemporary Theology." *America*. 176,14 (1997): 14–22.

Dunbar, Janet. *The Early Victorian Women: Some Aspects of Her Life*. Harraps: London, 1953.

Dupre, L. & Saliers, D.E., (eds.) *World Spirituality Volume 3. Christian Spirituality Post-Reformation and Modern*. SCM Press. London, 1990.

Durwell, F-X. *Mary. Icon of the Spirit and of the Church*. St Paul Publications. Middlegreen, 1991.

Dyhouse, Carol. *Girls Growing up in Late Victorian and Edwardian England*. Routledge & Kegan Paul. London, 1981.

—   *Feminism and the Family in England 1880–1939*. Basil Blackwell Ltd. Oxford, 1989.

Dyos H.J. and Wolff, M. (eds.) *The Victorian City: 2Vols*. Routledge & Keagan Paul. London, 1973.

Dyos, H. J. "The Slums of Victorian London." *Victorian Studies* 11 (1975): 5–40.

Egan, H. *Christian Mysticism*. Peublo Publishing Company. New York, 1984.

Elkins, S. "Gertrude the Great and the Virgin Mary." *Church History 66, 4.* (1997):720–734.

Engelhardt, C.M. "Victorians and the Virgin Mary: Religion, National Identity, and the Woman Question in England, 1830–1880." Ph.D. thesis, Department of History, University of Indiana. 1997.

Engels, F. *The Condition of the Working-Class in England*. Panther Books Ltd. London, 1969.

English, J.J. *Spiritual Freedom: From an Experience of the Ignatian Exercises to the Art of Spiritual Direction*. Loyola House. Guelph, Ont, 1987.

—   *Choosing Life*. Paulist Press. New York, 1978.

Eudes, St. J. *The Admirable Heart of Mary*. P.J.Kennedy & Sons. New York, 1948.

Ewens, M. *The Role of the Nun in Nineteenth Century America*. Arno Press. New York, 1978.

Fabella, V, and Oduyoye M.A. (eds.) *With Passion and Compassion*. Orbis Books. New York, 1988.

Fales, E. "The Case of St. Teresa." *Religious Studies*. 32, 2. (1996): 143–164.

Faricy, R. & Blackborow, S. *The Healing of the Religious Life*. McCrimmons. Great Wakering, Essex, 1986.

Faricy, R. *The End of Religious Life*. Winston Press. Minneapolis, 1983.

Fastnedge, R. *English Furniture Styles From 1500 to 1830*. Penguin Books, Harmnondsworth, 1955.

Fahey, A. "Female Asceticism in the Catholic Church: A Case Study of Nuns in Ireland in the Nineteenth Century." Ph.D. thesis, University of Illinois at Urbana-Champaign, 1982.

ffrench Eagar, Irene. *Margaret Anne Cusack: One Woman's campaign for women's rights*. Revised edition. Arlen House. Dublin, 1979

Fiand, B. *Living the Vision Religious Vows in an Age of Change*. Crossroad. New York, 1992.

—   *Wrestling with God: Religious Life in Search of Its Soul*. Crossroad Herder. New York, 1997.

Fielding, S. *Class and Ethnicity*. Open University Press. Buckingham Philadelphia, 1993.

Fields, Stephen. "Balthasar and Rahner on the Spiritual Senses." *Theological Studies*. 57, 2 (1996):224–242.

Fifth Congress of Religious Sisters of Australia. *A Theology of Renewal in Religious Life: Proceedings of the Fifth Congress of Religious Sisters of Australia, New Zealand and Oceania*. Leader Press, Brisbane, 1969.

Finke, R. "An Orderly Return to Tradition: Explaining the Recruitment of Members into Catholic Religious Orders." *Journal of the Scientific Study of Religion* 36 (1997): 218–230.

Finley, J. *Merton's Palace of Nowhere: A Search for God through Awareness of the True Self*. Ave Maria Press. Notre Dame, Ind., 1978.

Fitzgerald, G. *A Vision of Hope*. Treaty Press Ltd. Dublin, 1979.

Fitzpatrick, J. *Characteristics from the Writings of Father Faber*. R&T Washbourne, London, 1903.

Fitzsimons, J, (ed.) *Manning: Anglican and Catholic*. Burns Oates. London, 1951.

Flannery, A. OP (ed.) *Vatican Council II. Vol 2: More Post Conciliar Documents*. Costello Publishing Co. New York, 1982.

Flannery, A., and L. Collins, (eds.) *Light for my Path: The New Code of Canon Law for Religious*. E.J.Dwyer. Sydney, 1983.

Flaxman, R. *A Woman Styled Bold: The Life of Cornelia Connelly 1809–1879*. Darton, Longman & Todd. London, 1991.

Fleming, D. *Modern Spiritual Exercises*. Image Books. New York, 1983.

— *The Spiritual Exercises of St Ignatius*. Institute of Jesuit Resources. St Louis, 1978.

— (ed.) *The Fire and the Cloud*. An Anthology of Catholic Spirituality. Geoffrey Chapman, London, 1978.

Flint, K. *The Woman Reader 1837–1914*. Clarendon Press. Oxford, 1993.

Fontana, V.J.L. "Rebirth of Roman Catholicism in Portsmouth." *The Portsmouth Papers No. 56*. Portsmouth City Council. Portsmouth, 1989

Forman, R.K.C *Meister Eckhardt: Mystic as Theologian*. Element Inc. Rockport, MA, 1991.

— "What Does Mysticism Have to Teach us About Consciousness?." *Journal of Consciousness Studies:* 1996.

Fowler, M. *The Embroidered Tent: Five Gentlewomen in Early Canada*. Anasi Press Ltd. Toronto, 1982.

Fox, M., (ed.) *Western Spirituality*. Bear & Co. Sante Fe, New Mexico, 1981.

Frances Teresa, "Theological Reflection on Our Thirty Year Post-Conciliar Experience of Women's Contemplative Life." *UISG Bulletin* 97 (1995): 32–39.

Franchot, J. *Roads to Rome: The Antebellum Protestant Encounter with Catholicism*. University of Califormia Press. Berkley, 1994.

Franciscan Missionary Sisters of St. Joseph. *The Preparation Period: Rochdale to Mill Hill*. Privately Printed: n.d.

Franklin, F.F. "The Merging of Spiritualities: Jane Eyre as Missionary of Love." *Nineteenth Century Literature*. 49, 4. (1995): 456–483

Fry, T. (ed.) *The Rule of St Benedict in English*. The Liturgical Press. Collegeville, 1982.

Fullenbach, J. "Reflections on the Theological Foundation for Lay Association into Religious Institutes." *UISG Bulletin* 97 (1995): 22–31.

Fuller, M. *Woman in the Nineteenth Century*. W.W. Norton & Co. London, New York, 1971.

Futrell, John C. "Discovering the Founder's Charism." *The Way Supplement*. 14 (1971): 62–70

Gaffney, J.P. "Reform the Reform (editorial)." *Queen, '96*, (1996) 9–43.

— *Louis Marie Grignion de Montfort*. Paper Obtained from Marian Library, Dayton University OH. n.d.

— (ed.) *God Alone: The Collected Writings of St. Louis Marie de Montfort*. Montfort Publications. Bayshore NY, 1987.

Gard, R. "Catholic Lay Societies in England and Wales, 1870–1970 A Preliminary List." *Catholic Archives* 10 (1990): 48–57.

Garrigou-Lagrange, R. *The Mother of the Saviour and Our Interior Life*. Golden Eagle Books Ltd. Dublin, 1941.

— *The Three Ages of the Interior Life Volume Two: Prelude of Eternal Life*. B.Herder Book Co. St. Louis, 1955.

— *The Three Ways of the Spiritual Life*. Oates & Washbourne Ltd. London, 1938.

Gauldie, E., *Cruel Habitations: A History of Working Class Housing, 1780–1918*. Barnes and Noble. New York, 1974.

Gebara, I. & Bingemer, M.C. *Mary Mother of God, Mother of the Poor*. Burns & Oates. Tunbridge Wells, 1989.

Gendrot, M. (ed.) *Make Way for Jesus: The Message of St. Louis de Montfort*. Montfort Publications. Bay Shore NY.

George, M.D. *London Life in the Eighteenth Century*. Penguin Books. Middlesex, 1925.

Connolly, G. "The Transubstantiation of a Myth: Towards a New Popular History of Nineteenth Century Catholicism." *Journal of Ecclesiastical History* 35, 1 (1984): 78–104

Ghose, S. *Mystics as a Force for Change*. The Theosophical; Publishing House. Wheaton, Il, 1981.

Gibbard, M. *Twentieth-Century Men of Prayer*. SCM Press Ltd. London, 1974.

Gibson, R. *A Social History of French Catholicism 1789–1914*. Routledge. London, 1989.

Gilbert, S.M, Gubar, S, (eds.) *The Madwoman in the Attic: The Woman Writer and the Nineteenth-Century Literary Imagination*. Yale University Press. New Haven, London, 1979/1984.

Gill, S. *Women and the Church of England From the Eighteenth Century to the Present*. SPCK. London, 1994.

Gilley, S. "Vulgar Piety and the Brompton Oratory, 1850–1860." Chap. in *The Irish in the Victorian City*. Swift R, and Gilley, S. (eds.) Croom Helm. London, 1985.

—   "Roman Catholicism." Chap. in Paz, D. G., (ed.) *Nineteenth Century English Religious Traditions*, Greenwood Press. Westport, Connecticut, 1995.

—   & Sheils, W.J., (eds.) *A History of Religion in Britain: Practice & Belief from Pre-Roman Times to the Present*. Blackwell. Oxford, 1994.

Gilligan, C. *In A Different Voice*. Psychological Theory and Women's Development. Harvard University Press. Cambridge Mass, 1982.

Girouard, M. *The Return to Camelot: Chivalry and the English Gentleman.*: Yale University Press. New Haven and London, 1981.

Glasscoe, M., (ed.) *Julian of Norwich A Revelation of Love*. University of Exeter. Exeter, 1976.

Ghose, S. *Mystics as a Force for Change*. The Theosophical Publishing House. Wheaton, Illinois, 1981.

Gourvish, T.R, and A O'Day, (eds.) *Later Victorian Britain 1867–1900*. Macmillan Press Ltd. London, 1988.

Graef, H. *Mary: A History of Doctrine and Devotion*. Sheed & Ward. London, 1985.

Gray, C. "Nineteenth Century Women of Freethought." *Free Inquiry*. Spring 15(2) (1995): 32–35.

Gray, R. *Cardinal Manning: A Biography*. Weidenfeld & Nicholson. London, 1985.

Green, D. *Gold in the Crucible: Teresa of Avila and the Western Mystical Tradition*. Element Books. Longmead, 1989.

Greene, D., (ed.) *Evelyn Underhill: Fragments From an Inner Life*. Morehouse Publishing. Harrisburg, 1993.

Grey, M. *Redeeming the Dream: Feminism, Redemption, and Christian Tradition*. SPCK. London, 1989.

Grieve, N. & Burns, A., (eds.) *Australian Women: New Feminist Perspectives*. Oxford University Press. Melbourne, 1986.

Griffin, L. "Women in Religious Congregations and Politics." *Theological Studies* 49 (1988): 417–444.

Griffin, S.M. "Awful Disclosures: Women's Evidence in the Escaped Nun's Tale." *Publications of the Modern Language Association of America* 111, 1 (1996): 93–107.

Groeschel, Bt J. *Spiritual Passages*. The Psychology of Spiritual Development. Crossroad. New York, 1984.

Grou, J. *Manual for Interior Souls: A Collection of Unpublished Writings*. Burns Oates & Washbourne. London, 1952.

Gwynn, D. *The Second Spring 1818–1852: A Study of the Catholic Revival in England*. The Catholic Book Club. London, 1944.

Haggis, J. "'A Heart that has felt the love of God and longs for others to know it': Conventions of Gender, Tensions of Self and Constructions of Difference in Offering to be a Lady Missionary." *Women's History Review* 7, 2 (1998): 171–193.

Hales, E.E.Y. *The Catholic Church in the Modern World*. Eyre & Spottiswood. London, 1958.

Halevy, E. *A History of the English People in the Nineteenth Century, Vol. 4: Victorian Years 1841–1895* (trans. E.I Watkin). Ernest Benn Ltd. London, 1951.

Hamer, D.S. "The Whole Story? Using Archives to Write Biography: Elizabeth Prout, Foundress of the Cross and Passion Sisters." *Catholic Archives* 16 (1996): 27–36.

—   *Elizabeth Prout 1820–1864: A Religious Life for Industrial England*. Downside Abbey. Bath, 1994.

Hampl, P. *Virgin Time*. Ballantine Books. New York, 1992.

Hanham H.J. "Religion and Nationality in the Mid-Victorian Army." Chap. in Foot, M.R.D (ed.). *War and Society*. London:1961.

Harding, M. E. *Psychic Energy*. Its Source and Its Transformation. Princeton University Press. New Jersey, 1948.

Hardy, A. *The Divine Flame*. An Essay Towards a Natural History of Religion. The Religious Experience Research Unit. Oxford, 1966.

Hartzer, F, and L. Hartzer. *Fire upon the Earth: The Life of Mother Marie Louise Hartzer – Foundress of the Daughters of Our Lady of the Sacred Heart*. E.J. Dwyer. Sydney, 1948.

Haskins S. *Mary Magdalen Myth and Metaphor*. Harcourt Brace & Company. New York, 1993.

Haughton, R. *The Passionate God*. Darton, Longman & Todd. London, 1981.

—   *The re-creation of Eve*. Templegate Publishers. Springfield, Il, 1985.

Healy, E. *The Life of Mother Mary Potter*. Foundress of the Congregation of the Little Company of Mary. Sheed & Ward. London, 1936.

Hebblethwaite, M. *Motherhood and God*. Geoffrey Chapman. London, 1984.

Heeney, B., *The Women's Movement in the Church of England: 1850–1930*. Clarendon Press. Oxford, 1988.

Heilman, A. "Mona Caird (1854–1932)." *Women's History Review*. 5, 1. (1996):

Heimann, M. *Catholic Devotion in Victorian England*. Oxford Historical Monographs, Clarendon Press. Oxford, 1995.

Hellerstein, E.O., Hume, L.P., and Offen, K.M., (eds.) *Victorian Women. A Documentary Account of Women's Lives in Nineteenth Century England, France, and the United States*. Stanford University Press, Stanford Ca, 1981.

Helsinger, E. K., Sheets, R. L. And Veeder, W. *The Woman Question. Society and Literature in Britain and America 1837–1883 Volume 1 Defining Voices*. The University of Chicago Press, Chicago, 1983.

—   *The Woman Question. Society and Literature in Britain and America 1837–1883 Volume 3 Literary Issues*. The University of Chicago Press, Chicago, 1989.

Herzig, A. "Mary-Hopeless Ideal or Sister in Faith?" *Theology Digest* 39, 3 (1992): 209–213.

Hick, J. *An Interpretation of Religion*. Yale University Press. New Haven, 1989.

Hickey, J. *Mary at the Foot of the Cross: Teacher and Example of Holiness*. Ignatius Press, San Francisco, 1988.

Hilkert, M.C. "Feminist Theology: Key Religious Symbols: Christ and God." *Theological Studies*. 56(2): June (1995) 341–352.

Hill, M. *The Religious Order: A Study of Virtuoso Religion and Its Legitimation in the Nineteenth-Century Church of England*. Heinemann Educational. London, 1973.

Hill, M. and Deacon, A. The Problem of "Surplus Women" in the Nineteenth Century. In *A Sociological Yearbook of Religion in Britian – 5*, Hill, Michael. London: S.C.M. Press, 1972.

Hill, P.C. "Toward an Attitude Process Model of Religious Experience." Journal for the Scientific Study of Religion. 33, 4 (1994): 303 – 314.

Himmelfarb, G. "Can Lost Morality be Restored to Modern Societies?." *American Enterprise*. 6, 6 (1995):72–73.

—   *Poverty and Compassion: The Moral Imagination of the Late Victorians*. Vintage Books, New York, 1992.

—   *Victorian Minds*. Peter Smith. Gloucester, Mass, 1975.

Hinnebusch, P. *Salvation History and the Religious Life*. Sheed and Ward. New York, 1966.

—   *The Signs of the Times and the Religious Life*. Sheed & Ward. New York, 1967.

Hobbs, C. "Reclaiming Myths of Power: Women Writers and the Victorian Spiritual Crisis." *Victorian Studies* 39, 2 (1996): 244–246.

Hobsbawm, E. *Age of Extremes 1914–1991*. Abacus Books, London, 1995.

Hocking, E. "The Meaning of Mysticism as Seen Through Its Psychology." Chap. in *Understanding Mysticism*, Woods, R., (ed.) Althone Press. London, 1980.

Hogan, A. & Bradstock, A. (eds.) *Women of Faith in Victorian Culture: Reassessing the Angel in the House*. McMillan Press Ltd. London, 1998.

Hohn, H. *Vocations Conditions of Admission Etc. Into the Convents, Congregations, Religious Institutes*. R & T Washbourne Ltd. London, 1912.

Hollingworth, P. *Kingdom Come*. Anglican Information House. Sydney, 1991.

Hollis, C. *Newman and the Modern World*. Hollis & Carter. London, 1967.

Holm, J, and K. Bowker, *Women in Religion.* Pinter Books. London, 1994.

Holmes, J. D. *More Roman Than Rome.* Burns & Oates Ltd. London, 1978.

——   *The Triumph of the Papacy: A Short History of the Papacy in the Nineteenth Century.* Burns & Oates. London, 1978.

Homberger, E., and Charmley, J., (eds.) *The Troubled Face of Biography.* The Macmillan Press Ltd. London, 1988.

Honore, J. *The Spiritual Journey of Newman.* Alba House. New York, 1992.

Horne, James. *The Moral Mystic.* Wilfrid Laurier University Press. Ontario, 1983.

Horstman, Alan. *Victorian Divorce.* Croom Helm. London, 1978.

Horton, R.F. & Hocking, J. *Shall Rome Reconquer England?* National Council of Evangelical Free Churches. London, 1910.

Houghton, W. E., *The Victorian Frame of Mind, 1830–1870.* Yale University Press. London, 1957/1985.

Hoyle, L.H. "Nineteenth-Century Single Women and Motivation for Mission." *International Bulletin of Missionary Research* 20, 2 (1996): 58–64.

Hudleston, R., (ed.) *The Spiritual Letters of Dom John Chapman.* Sheed and Ward. London, 1954.

Hudson, K. *Pawnbroking: An Aspect of British Social History.* Bodley Head. London, 1982.

Iliffe, R. & Beguley,W. *Victorian Nottingham A Story in Pictures Vols. 8,9,10,11,13,14,17.* The Nottingham Historical Film Unit. Nottingham, 1972–6.

Inge, Dean W. R. *Christian Mysticism.* Reprint. Kessinger Publishing Company. New York, 1997.

——   *A Rustic Moralist.* Putnam. London, 1937.

Inglis, K.S. *Churches and the Working Classes in Victorian England.* Routledge & Kegan Paul. London, 1963.

Ingram, P. "Protestant Patriarchy and the Catholic Priesthood in Nineteenth Century England." *Journal of Social History,* 24, 4. (1990): 783–797.

Jackson, H. *The 1890s.* The Cresset Library. London, 1988.

Jaffe, J. "Religion, Gender and Education in a Durham Parish during the Early Nineteenth Century." *Journal of Ecclesiastical History* (1997) 48, 2: 282–301.

Jalland, P. "Victorian Spinsters: Dutiful Daughters, Desperate Rebels and the Transition to the New Woman." Chap. in Crawford, P. (ed.) *Exploring Women's Past: Essays in Social History.* Allen & Unwin. Sydney,1984.

——   *Women, Marriage and Politics 1816–1914.* Oxford University Press. Oxford, 1986.

——   *Death in the Victorian Family.* Oxford University Press. Oxford, 1996.

James, William. *Varieties of Religious Experience.* Mentor Books. New York, 1958.

Jantzen, G. *Julian of Norwich.* SPCK. London, 1987.

——   "Feminists, Philosophers, and Mystics." *Hypatia* 9, 4 (1994): 186–206.

——   *Power Gender and Christian Mysticism.* Cambridge University Press. Cambridge, 1995.

Jarrell, L.M. "The Development of Legal Structures for Women Religious Between 1500 and 1900: A Study of Selected Institutes of Religious Life for Women." PhD in Canon Law diss. Catholic University of America. 1984

Jegen, C.L F., (ed.) *Mary According to Women.* Sheed and Ward. London, 1985.

John Paul 11. *Letter to Company of Mary, Christian Instruction of Saint-Gabriel and Daughters of Wisdom on Occasion of Fiftieth Anniversary of Canonisation of St Louis-Marie Grignon de Montfort.* Photocopy of address per kind favour of De Montfort Missionaries. 1997

John, A. V., (ed.) *Unequal Opportunities: Women's Employment in England 1800–1918.* Basil Blackwell. Oxford, 1986.

John Paul II. *Redemptionis Donum.* Paulist Press. New York, 1984.

——   *Cristefidelis Laici.* Paulist Press. New York, 1989.

Johnson, D. A. *Women in English Religion 1700–1925.* Edwin Mellen Press. New York, 1983.

Johnson, E.A. *She Who is: The Mystery of God in Feminist Theological Discourse.* Crossroad. New York, 1994.

Johnson, P. *A History of Christianity.* Penguin Books. London, 1976.

Johnson, Penelope. *Equal in Monastic Profession: Women in Medieval France*. University of Chicago Press. Chicago, 1991.

Johnston, W. *Lord Teach us to Pray*. Fount Paperbacks. London, 1990.

— *Mystical Theology. The Science of Love*. Harper Collins. London, 1995.

— *The Mystical Way*. Fount Paperbacks. London, 1993.

— *The Mysticism of the Cloud of Unknowing*. Anthony Clarke. Wheathampstead, Hert, 1974.

Jones, C., Wainwright, G. Yarnold, E., (eds.) *The Study of Spirituality*. SPCK. London, 1986.

Joy, M, and P Magee, (eds.) *Claiming Our Rites: Studies in Religion by Australian Women Scholars*. The Australian Association for the Study of Religions. Adelaide, 1994.

Judd, C. *Bedside Seductions: Nursing and the Victorian Imagination, 1830–1880*. St. Martin's Press. New York, 1998.

Julian of Norwich. *The Revelations of Divine Love*. Anthony Clarke Books. Wheathampstead, Hert, 1961.

Jung, C.G. *Aion: Researches Into the Phenomology of the Self*. (trans. R.F.C. Hull), Bollingen Series XX. Princeton University Press, Princeton, 1959.

— *Modern Man in Search of a Soul*. Ark Paperbacks. London, 1933.

Jurado, Manuel, Luis, S.J. "Consecrated LIfe and the Charisms of the Founders." Chap. in Latourelle, R. (ed). *Vatican II: Assessment and Perspectives Twenty-Five Years After (1962–1987) Volume Three*. Paulist Press. N.Y, 1989:

Kane, P. *Victorian Families in Fact and Fiction*. St Martin's Press. New York, 1995.

Katz, S.T. (ed.) *Mysticism and Religious Traditions*. Oxford University Press. Oxford, 1983.

Kavanaugh, K. & Rodriguez, O., (trans.) *The Collected Works of St Teresa of Avila, Volume One*. ICS Publications. Washington, DC, 1976.

— *The Collected Works of St. John of the Cross*. ICS Publications. Washington DC, 1973.

Kavanaugh, K., (ed.) *John of the Cross: Selected Writings*. The Classics of Western Spirituality. Paulist Press, New York, 1987.

Keire. "Dope Fiends and Degenerates: the Gendering of Addiction in the Early Twentieth Century." *Journal of Social History* 3, 4 (1998): 809–22.

Keller, C. *Apocalypse Now and Then*. Beacon Press. Boston, 1996.

Kelly, G.A. "Rebellion in the Convent." *Religious Life* (April, 1998) 10–11.

Kenny, J.P. *The Meaning of Mary for Modern Man*. Spectrum Publications. Melbourne, 1980.

Kerr, C. *Teresa Helena Higginson*. Sands & Co. London, 1927.

King, A.S. "Spirituality: Transformation and Metamorphosis." *Religion* 26 (1996): 343–351.

King, M., (ed.) *A Leaf from the Great Tree of God*. Essays in Honour of Ritamary Bradley SFCC. Perigrina Publishing Co. Toronto, 1994.

King, U. *Women and Spirituality Voices of Protest & Promise*. MacMillan Education. London, 1989.

Kingston, B. *My Wife, My Daughter and Poor Mary Ann*. Thos. Nelson Australia Pty. Ltd. Melbourne, 1975.

Kittel, G. & Friedrich, G., (eds.) *Theological Dictionary of the New Testament*. Abridged in One Volume by Geoffrey W. Bromiley Reprinted 1990. William B. Eerdmans Publishing Company. Grand Rapids, 1985.

Knowles, D. *What is Mysticism*. Burns & Oates. London, 1967.

Kolbenschlag, M. *Women in the Church 1*. The Pastoral Press. Washington DC, 1987.

Kolodny, A. "Inventing a Feminist Discourse: Rhetoric and Resistance in Margaret Fuller's 'Woman in the Nineteenth Century.'" *New Literary History* 25, 2 (1994): 355–383.

Konya, P. *To Answer Her Call The Sisters of the Little Company of Mary in Southern Africa*. Privately Published. Port Elizabeth SA, 1979.

Kopp, L. *Sudden Spring 6th Stage Sisters*. Sunspot Publications. Waldport, 1983.

Kselman, T. A. *Death and Afterlife in Modern France*. Princeton University Press. Princeton, 1993.

— *Miracles and Prophecies in Nineteenth-Century France*. Rutgers University Press. New Brunswick, 1983.

Kung, H. *On Being A Christian*. Simon & Schuster. New York, 1976.

LaCugna, C.M. "Catholic Women as Ministers and Theologians." *America* 167, 10. (1992): 238–248.

LaFountaine, Charles V. *Essays in S.A. History*. Franciscan Friars of the Atonement. Graymoor/Garrison, New York, 1984.

Langland, E. *Nobody's Angels: Middle-Class Women and Domestic Ideology in Victorian Culture*. Cornell University Press. Ithaca, 1995.

Lanslots, D. I. *Handbook of Canon Law for Congregations of Women Under Simple Vows – 4th Edition*. Fredrick Pustet & Co. Ratisbon, 1909.

Larkin, Emmett. "The Devotional Revolution in Ireland, 1850–1875." *American Historical Review* 78 (1972): 625–652

Larsen, T. "'How Many Sisters Make a Brotherhood?' A Case Study in Gender and Ecclesiology in Early Nineteenth-Century English Dissent." *The Journal of Ecclesiastical History* 49, 2. (1998): 282–292.

Latourelle, K.S. *A History of Christianity. Vol II: Reformation to the Present: AD 1500–1975*. Harper and Row Associates. San Francisco, 1955/1975.

Latourelle, R. (ed.) *Vatican 11 Assessment and Perspectives Twenty-five Years After (1962–1987)*. 3 Vols. Paulist Press. New York, 1987.

Laurence, A. *Women in England 1500–1760: A Social History*. Weidenfeld and Nicolson. London, 1994.

Laurentin, R. "Fifth Period The Post-Tridentine Marian Movement (1563–1958)." *A Short Treatise on the Virgin Mary*. AMI Press, Washington, NJ, 1991: 126–141

—   *A Year of Grace with Mary*. Rediscovering the Significance of her role in the Christian Life. Vertias. Dublin, 1987.

—   *Mary's Place in the Church*. Burns & Oates. London, 1965.

—   *Mother of the Church: History, Meaning and Merit*. Manuscript of Course offered IMRI (International Mariological Institute). University of Dayton, Dayton Oh., July 1995.

Lavelle, L. *The Meaning of Holiness*. Burns & Oates. London, 1954.

Leavey, C., and O'Neill, R. *Gathered in God's Name*. Crossing Press. Sydney, 1996.

Leetham, C. "Gentili's Reports to Rome." *The Wiseman Review no.* 498 (1963): 395–414.

Leonard, R. *Beloved Daughters 100 Years of Papal Teaching on Women*. David Lovell. Melbourne, 1995.

Lerner, G. *The Creation of Feminist Consciousness: From the Middle Ages to the Eighteenth Century*. Oxford University Press. Oxford, 1993.

—   *The Creation of Patriarchy*. Oxford University Press. New York, 1986.

Lerner, R. E. *The Heresy of the Free Spirit in the Later Middle Ages*. Notre Dame University Press. Notre Dame, 1993.

Lester, V. M. *Victorian Insolvency: Bankruptcy, Imprisonment for Debt and Company Winding up in Nineteenth Century England*. Oxford Historical Monographs. Oxford University Press. New York, 1995.

Lewis, G. J. and Lewis, J. (trans.) *Gertrud the Great of Helfta Spiritual Exercises*. Cistercian Publications. Kalamazoo, 1989.

Lewis, J. (ed.) *Labour and Love: Women's Experience of Home and Family 1850 – 1940*. Basil Blackwell. Oxford, 1986.

Leys, M.D.R. *Catholics in England*. The Catholic Book Club. London, 1961.

Librera Editrice Vaticana/The Canon Law Society Trust, (eds.) *The Code of Canon Law*. Collins. London, 1983.

Libreria Editrice Vaticana. *Catechism of the Catholic Church*. St Paul Publication. Homebush NSW, 1994.

Liedl, L.L. "Indomitable Nuns and a Determined Bishop: Property Rights, Women Religious, and Diocesan Power in Nineteenth-Century Cleveland." PhD diss., Kent State University. 1998.

Ligouri, St. A. *The Love of God in Practice*. Majellan Press. Ballarat Vic, 1963.

—   *The Glories of Mary*. Redemptorist Fathers. Brooklyn, 1931.

Liptak, D. "Full of Grace: Another look at the 19th Century Nun." *Review for Religious* 56, 6 (1996): 625–639.

Livingston, K.T. *The Emergence of an Australian Catholic Priesthood 1835–1915*. Catholic Theological Faculty. Sydney, 1977.

Lombard, H. *Discussion Paper on the Distinctive Role of Religious*. Unpublished Paper. 1985

Lonergan, M. "The Archives of the Anglo-Scottish Province of the Little Sisters of the Assumption." *Catholic Archives* 11 (1991): 17–24.

Long, T.L. 1995. *Julian of Norwich's "Christ as Mother" and Medieval Constructions of Gender*. Presented at Madison Conference on English Studies, James Madison University March 18, 1995. [http://users.Visi.Net/`longt/julian.html].

Lorenzo, Juan Manuel. "Founder and Community: Inspiration and Charism." *Review for Religious* 37, 2 (1978): 214–16.

Loudon, M. *Unveiled Nuns Talking*. Vintage. London, 1993.

Louth, A. *The Origins of the Christian Mystical Tradition From Plato to Denys*. Clarendon Press. Oxford, 1981.

Lowerson J. and Myerscough, J. *Time to Spare in Victorian England*. Harvester Press. (Brighton, 1977)

Luddy, M., and Murphy, C. (eds.) *Women Surviving: Studies in Women's History in the Nineteenth and Twentieth Centuries*. Poolbeg. Dublin, 1989.

MacCaffrey, J. *History of the Catholic Church in the Nineteenth Century (1789–1908)*. Volume 1, Second Edition Revised. M.H.Gill and Son Ltd. Dublin and Waterford, 1909.

MacCurtain, M. "Late in the Field: Catholic Sisters in Twentieth-Century Ireland and the New Religious History." *Journal of Women's History* 6 (1995): 49–63.

MacCurtain, M. And O'Dowd, M., (eds.) *Women in Early Modern Ireland*. Edinburgh University Press. Edinburgh, 1991.

McDonnell, E. *The Beguines and the Berghards in Medieval Culture*. Rutgers University Press. New Brunswick, N.J., 1969

MacDougall, H.A. *Lord Acton on Papal Power*. Sheed and Ward. London, 1973.

MacEoin, G. (ed.) *The Papacy and the People of God*. Orbis Books. Maryknoll NY, 1998.

MacGinley, M.R. *A Dynamic of Hope: Institutes of Women Religious in Australia*. Crossing Press. Sydney, 1996.

Mackerell, G. *Thoughts for Religious*. St Paul Publications. Slough, 1984.

Macquarrie, J. *Mary For All Christians*. Harper Collins. London, 1991.

—   *Paths in Spirituality 2nd ed*. SCM Press Ltd. London, 1992.

Magray, M. P. *The Transforming Power of the Nuns. Women, Religion, and Cultural Change in Ireland, 1750–1900*. Oxford University Press, New York, 1998.

Maison, M. *The Victorian Vision: Studies in the Religious Novel*. New York, 1961.

Maitland, S. *A Map of the New Country*. Women and Christianity. Routledge and Kegan Paul, London, 1983.

Makowski, E. *Canon Law and Cloistered Women*. Periculoso and its Commentators 1298–1545. The Catholic University of America Press, Washington, DC, 1997.

Malmgreem, G. *Religion in the Lives of Englishwomen 1760–1930*. Croom Helm. London, 1986.

Maloney, G. *Mary, the Womb of God*. Dimension Books. New Jersey, 1976.

Maloney, G.A. *God's Incredible Mercy*. Alba House. New York, 1989.

Maloney, R. "The Cross Yesterday and Today." *Review for Religious* 53, 4 (1994): 544–559.

Manton, J. *Sister Dora: The Life of Dorothy Pattison*. Quartet Books Inc. London, 1971.

Marcus, S. *The Other Victorians*. Basic Books Inc, New York, 1966.

Marmion, C. *Christ in His Mysteries*. Sands & Co. London, 1924.

Martini, C. *The Ignatian Exercises in the Light of St John*. Translated by Joseph Gill SJ. Gujarat Sahitya Prakash, Anand India, 1981.

Martinsoskice, J. *Metaphor & Religious Language*. Clarendon Press. Oxford, 1985/87.

Massam, K. *Sacred Threads*. UNSW Press. Sydney, 1996.

Mathew, D. *Acton, The Formative Years*. Eyre & Spottiswoode. London, 1946.

—   *Catholicism in England 1535–1935*. Portrait of a Minority: Its Culture and Tradition. Longmans, Green and Co, London, 1936.

Matthews, J.J. *Good and Mad Women: The Historical Construction in Twentieth Century Australia.* George Allen & Unwin, Sydney, 1984.

May, G.G. *Will & Spirit.* Harper & Row. San Francisco, 1982.

Mayhew, H. *London Labour and the London Poor.* Penguin Books. Middlesex, 1985.

Mazeau, H. *The Heroine of Pe-Tang: Helene de Jaurias, Sister of Charity 1824–1900.* Burns Oates & Washbourne Ltd. London, 1928.

McAuley, C. *The Bermondsey Manuscript.* Convent of Mercy Archives. Parramatta, Sydney. n.d.

—   *Thoughts From the Spiritual Conferences of Mother M. Catherine McAuley.* M. Gill & Son. Dublin, 1946.

McBrien, R. P. *Ministry A Theological, Pastoral Handbook.* Harper & Row. San Francisco, 1987.

McCabe, J. *Twelve Years in a Monastery.* Watts & Co. London, 1930.

McCaffrey, J. *History of the Catholic Church in the Nineteenth Century. 2 Vols.* M. H. Gill & Sons: Dublin and Waterford, 1910.

McCarthy, C. *The Spirituality of Cornelia Connelly: In God, for God, with God.* Studies in Women and Religion Vol. 19. Edwin Mellen Press. Lewiston, 1991.

—   "Apostolic Congregations of Women and the Ignatian Charism." *The Way Supplement* 20, Autum (1973): 10–18.

McClelland, V.A. *Cardinal Manning: His Public Life and Influences, 1865–1892.* O.U.P. London, 1961.

MacDonald, Anita LCM. *Companions on the Way.* Privately printed for the Little Company of Mary. England: n.d.

McDonnell, T. P. (ed.) *A Thomas Merton Reader.* Image Books. New York, 1989.

McDonough, E. "Charisms and Religious Life." *Review for Religious* 52, 5 (1993): 646–659.

McGinn, B. (ed.) *Meister Eckhart Teacher and Preacher.* Paulist Press. New York, 1986.

McKean, M. *Karl Rahner's Theology of Religious Life: A Recentering of the Christian Vision.* UMI Dissertation Services. Ann Arbor, 1997.

McLaughlin, E. "Women, Power and the Pursuit of Holiness in Medieval Christianity." Chap. in Rosemary Ruether and Eleanor McLaughlin (eds.) *Women of Spirit: Female leadership in the Jewish and Christian Traditions,* Simon and Schuster. New York, 1979.

McLay, A. *Women on the Move: Mercy's Triple Spiral.* Sisters of Mercy. Adelaide, 1996.

McLeod, H. *Religion and Society in England, 1850–1914.* MacMillan Press Ltd. Hampshire, 1996.

—   *Religion and the People of Western Europe, 1789–1970.* Oxford University Press: New York, 1981.

McMilan, D. J., and Fladenmuller, K. S., (eds.) *Regular Life.* Monastic, Canonical and Mendicant Rules. Western Michigan University, Kalamazoo, Mich., 1997.

McNamara, J.A. *Sisters in Arms: Catholic Nuns through Two Millennia.* Harvard University Press. Cambridge Ma, 1996.

Medical Missionaries of Mary. *Medical Missionaries of Mary.* Covering the First Twenty-five Years of the Medical Missionaries of Mary. Medical Missionaries of Mary, Dublin, 1962.

Melnyk, J., (ed.) *Women's Theology in Nineteenth-Century Britain.* Transfiguring the Faith of Their Fathers. Garland Publishing Co, New York, 1998.

Merkle, J. *Committed by Choice.* The Liturgical Press. Collegeville, 1992.

Metz, J., *Followers of Christ.* Burns & Oates: London, 1977.

Michael, C. P., and Norrisey, M. C. *Prayer and Temperament.* Different Prayer Forms for Different Personality Types. The Open Door Inc., Charlottesville, 1984.

Michaels, A. *Fugitive Pieces.* Bloomsbury Publishing. London, 1997.

Mieth, D. "Continuity and Change in Value-Orientations." *Concilium* 191, 3 (1987).

Minz, S. *A Prisoner of Expectation: The Family in Victorian Culture.* New York, 1983.

Misciattelle, P. *The Mystics of Siena.* English Version by M.Peters-Roberts. W.Heffer & Sons Ltd, Cambridge, 1929.

Mole, D.E.H. "Challenge to Church: Birmingham 1815–65." In Dyos H.J., Wolff M. (eds.) *The Victorian City Images and Realities Vol. 2.* London: Routledge & Kegan Paul, 1973. 815–871

Moll, E., (ed.) *The Church and Women A Compendium.* Ignatius Press. San Francisco, 1988.

Moltmann, J. *The Trinity and the Kingdom of God: The Doctrine of God.* SCM. London, 1981.

Monahan, M. *The Life and Letters of Janet Erskine Stuart.* Longmans. London, 1922/1960.

— "Religious Communities of Women." Chap. in *Catholic Emancipation, 1829–1929: Essays by Various Writers.* 201–222. London: Longmans Green & Co, 1929.

Moore, J. R., (ed.) *Religion in Victorian Britain: Vol III, Sources.* Manchester University Press, Manchester, 1988.

Moore, S. *The Crucified is No Stranger.* Darton, Longman & Todd. London, 1977.

Moorhouse, G. *Against All Reason.* Stein and Day. New York, 1969.

Morgan, W. *Drugs in America: A Social History 1800–1980.* Syracuse University Press. Syracuse, New York, 1981.

Mottola, A., (trans.) *The Spiritual Exercises of St. Ignatius.* Image Books. New York, 1964.

MSA Secretariat. "Faith, Mary, Culture." *Marian Studies Volume XLVI* Marian Library. Dayton, Ohio. (1995).

Mumm, S. "Not Worse Than Other Girls": the Convent-Based Rehabilitation of Fallen Women in Victorian Britain. *Journal of Social History* 29, 3 (1996): 527–546.

Murk-Jansen, S. *Brides in the Desert: The Spirituality of the Beguines.* Orbis Books, Maryknoll NY, 1998.

Murphy, Anne, SHCJ. "Old Catholics, New Converts, Irish Immigrants: A Reassessment of Catholicity in England in the Nineteenth Century." *A Paper Delivered at the Cherwell Conference* (San Diego, California) Cherwell Conference Papers Vol 1:3 (1993).

— "Remembering the Future: 150 Years of SHCJ History." *History: Society of the Holy Child Jesus: Issue 1: Beginnings* (Privately Printed) (1996).

Murphy, D. *The Death and Rebirth of Religious Life.* E.J.Dwyer. Alexandria NSW, 1995.

Murphy, G. "The Marian Doctrine and Devotion of Father Faber." *Extract From a Dissertation Entitled Marian Doctrine and Devotion of Father Faber, Submitted to the Faculty of Sacred Sciences of the University of Ottawa.* Copy obtained from Marian Library, University of Dayton, Ohio.

Murray, R. *The Forsaken Fountain.* Hollis and Carter. London, 1948.

Murtagh, J. G. *Australia The Catholic Chapter.* The Polding Press. Melbourne, 1969.

Nash, D.S. "'Look in Her Face and Lose Thy Dread of Dying': The Ideological Importance of Death to the Secularist Community in Nineteenth-Century Britain." *Journal of Religious History* 19, 2. (1995).

Nelson, C. & Vallone, L. (eds.) *The Girl's Own: Cultural Histories of the Anglo-American Girl, 1830–1915.* University of Georgia Press. Athens and London, 1994.

Nelson, J. and Walter, L. *Women of Spirit: Woman's Place in Church and Society.* St. Marks. Canberra, 1989.

Nelson, S. "Pastoral care and moral government: early nineteenth century nursing and solutions to the Irish question." *Journal of Advanced Nursing* 26 (1996): 6–14.

Nemeck, F. K., and Coombs, M.T. *Called by God: A Theology of Vocation and Lifelong Commitment.* The Liturgical Press, Collegeville Min., 1992.

Neubert, E. *Life of Union with Mary* (trans: Sylvester Juergens S.M.), Bruce Publishing Co., Milwaukee, 1959.

Neumann, M. I. (ed.) *Letters of Catherine McAuley 1827–1841.* Helicon. Baltimore, 1969.

Newman, John Henry. *Historical Sketches.* Vol. II. Westminster MD,1970.

    The Dream of Gerontius. James Hewetson & Son. London, 1907.

Newton, J., Ryan, M., and Davidoff L., (eds.) *Sex and Class in Women's History,*: Routledge & Kegan Paul. London, 1983.

Nicholson, S. *A Victorian Household: Based on the Diaries of Marion Sambourne.* Allan Sutton Publishing Ltd. Gloucestshire, 1994.

Noffke, S. (ed.) *The Prayers of Catherine of Siena.* Paulist Press. New York, 1983.

Nolan, M. M. *Medical Missionaries of Mary.* Privately Published. Dublin, 1967.

Norman, E. *The English Catholic Church in the Nineteenth Century.* Oxford University Press. Oxford, 1984.

—   *Roman Catholicism in England: From the Elizabethan Settlement to the Second Vatican Council.* Oxford University Press. Oxford, 1986.

—   *Anti-Catholicism in Victorian England.* George Allen and Unwin Ltd. London, 1968.

Oates, Mary J. "The 'Good Sisters': The Work and Position of Catholic Church Women in Boston, 1870–1940." Chap. in White, J. (ed.). *The American Catholic Religious Life.* Garland Publishing. New York, 1988.

—   *The Catholic Philanthropic Tradition in America.* University of Indiana Press. Bloomington, Indiana, 1995.

O'Brien, E. M. *Life and Letters of Archpriest John Joseph Therry Volume 11.* Angus & Robertson Ltd. Sydney, 1922.

O'Brien, Susan. "Terra Incognita: The Nun in Nineteenth-Century England." *Past & Present* 121, November (1988): 110–140.

"10,000 Nuns Working in Convent Archives." *Catholic Archives* 9 (1989): 26–32.

—   "Making Catholic Spaces: Women, Decor, and Devotion in the English Catholic Church, 1840–1900." In *The Church and the Arts: Studies in Church History 28*, Woods, D. Oxford: Basil Blackwell, 1992.

—   "French Nuns in Nineteenth Century England." *Past and Present* 154 (1997): 142–180

O'Carroll, M. *Theotokos.* Michael Glazier. Inc. Wilmington, 1983.

Ochs, C. *Women and Spirituality.* Rowman & Allanheld. New Jersey, 1983.

O'Collins, G. *The Calvary Christ.* SCM Press. London, 1977.

O'Connor, Anne V. "The Revolution in Girl's Secondary Education in Ireland 1860–1910." Chap. in Cullen, M. (ed) *Girls Don't do Honours: Irish Women in Education in the Nineteenth and Twentieth Centuries.* Women's Educational Bureau. Dublin, 1987.

O'Donnell, C. *Life in the Spirit and Mary.* Michael Glasier Inc. Delaware, 1981.

O'Flynn, G. "Some Aspects of the Education of Irish Girls Through the Years." *Capuchin Annual* Dublin, 1977.

Ogata, S. *Zen for the West.* For the Buddhist Society of London. Greenwood Press. Westport, 1959.

O'Leary, M. B. "The Archives of the Religious Sisters of Charity." *Catholic Archives* 17 (1997): 28–41.

O'Murchu, D. *The Prophetic Horizon of Religious Life.* Excalibur Press. London, 1989.

O'Neill, M. A. "The Nature of Women and the Method of Theology." *Theological Studies* 56, 4 (1995): 703–743.

Orsay, Ladislas, SJ. "SJ Constitutions: Continuity and Change." *The Way Supplement* 20, Autumn (1973): 3–9.

O'Sullivan, M.M.K. *'A Cause of Trouble? Irish Nuns and English Clerics.* Crossing Press. Sydney, 1995.

Ozorak, E.W. "The power, but not the glory: how women empower themselves through religion." *Journal for Scientific Study of Religion* 35: 17–29.

Paredes, J. *Mary and the Kingdom of God.* St. Paul. Slough, 1991.

Parish, D.L. "The Power of Female Pietism: Women as Spiritual Authorities in Seventeenth-Century England." *The Journal of Religious History* 17, 1. (1992): 33–46.

Parrinder, G. *Mysticism in the World's Religions.* Oneworld Publications. Oxford, 1995.

—   (ed.) *Collinc Dictionary of Religious & Spiritual Quotations.* HarperCollins Publishers. Glasgow, 1992.

Parsons, G. (ed.) *Religion in Victorian Britain: Vol I Traditions.* Manchester University Press. Manchester, 1988.

       "Emotion and Piety: Revivalism and Ritualism in Victorian Christianity." Chap. in Parsons G. (ed.), *Religion in Victorian Britain: Vol 1 Traditions.* Manchester University Press. Manchester, 1988.

Paul, M. Mary SHCJ. "The Religious Orders of Women: Active Work." Chap. in Mathews, D.(ed) *Catholicism in England 1535–1935: Portrait of a Minority: Its Culture and Traditions.* 281–286. London: Catholic Book Club, 1938.

Paul VI. *Evaglica Testificatio.* Paulist Press. New York, 1971.

Paz, D.G., (ed.) *Nineteenth-Century English Religious Traditions Retrospect and Prospect.* Greenwood Press. Westport, Con., 1995.

—   "Popular Anti-Catholicism in England, 1850–1851." *Albion* 11 (1979): 331–359.

—   *Popular Anti-Catholicism in Mid-Victorian Britain.* Stanford University Press: Stanford, 1992.

Peckham, M. L. *Catholic Female Religious Congregations and Religious Change in Ireland, 1770–1870.* UMI Dissertation Services. Ann Arbor, 1997.

Pelikan, J. *Mary Through the Centuries: Her Place in the History of Culture.* Yale University Press. New Haven and London 1996.

Pennington, B. *A Retreat with Thomas Merton.* Amity House. New York, 1988.

Perkin, J. *Victorian Women.* John Murray Publisher Ltd. London, 1993.

Perrin, J-M. *Mary, Mother of Christ and of Christians.* Alba House. New York, 1977.

Perry, N., & L. Echeverria. *Under the Heel of Mary.* Routledge Kegan & Paul. London, 1989.

Peterson, M. J. *Family Love and Work in the Lives of Victorian Gentlewomen.* Indiana University Press. Bloomington, 1989.

Petroff, E. A. *Body and Soul Essays on Medieval Women and Mysticism.* Oxford University Press. New York, 1994.

Plumb, J.H. *England in the Eighteenth Century.* Pelican Books. Middlesex, 1965.

Plus, R. *Mary in Our Soul-Life.* Frederick Pustet Co. New York, 1940.

—   *The Folly of the Cross.* Burns Oates & Washbourne Ltd. London, 1927.

Pollock, G. 1997. "Imaging the Others; Other Imageries The Avant-Garde, the Feminine and Religious Discourse in the Late Nineteenth Century." *Plenary Lecture 3, Leeds University.*

Poor Sisters of Nazareth. *Life Sketch of Mother St. Basil.* Privately Published. Poor Sisters of Nazareth, London, nd.

Pope, Barbara Corrado. "The Marian Revival in the Nineteenth Century." Chap. in Atkindson, Clarrisa W., (ed.) *Immaculate and Powerful: The Female in Sacred Image and Social Reality.* Beacon Press. Boston, 1985.

Porter, J. "Perennial and Timely Virtues: Practical Wisdom, Courage and Temperance." *Concilium* 191, 3 (1987): 60–68.

Pound, J.N. *From Oak to Kowhai.* Little Company of Mary. New Zealand, 1977.

Pourrat, P. *Christian Spirituality: Later Developments From Jansenism to Modern Times.* Newman Press. Westminster, Md., 1995.

Powell, J. *The Christian Vision.* Argus Communications. Texas, 1984.

Press, M. M. *From Our Broken Toil: South Australian Catholics 1836–1906.* Catholic Archdiocese of Adelaide. Adelaide, 1986.

Preston, M. "Women and Philanthropy in Nineteenth-Century Dublin." *The Historian* 58, 4 (1996): 763–786.

Prochaska, F.K. *Women and Philanthropy in Nineteenth Century England.* Clarendon Press. Oxford, 1980.

Przywara, E., (ed.) *A Newman Synthesis.* Sheed & Ward. London, 1930.

Pugh, T. *The Church of St John the Baptist Brighton 1835–1985.* St John the Baptist's Church. Brighton.

Rafferty, O.P. "Henry Cardinal Manning Apostle of Social Justice." *America* 166, 2 (1992): 36–37.

Rahner, K. *Grace in Freedom.* Herder and Herder. New York, 1969.

—   *Mary Mother of the Lord.* Anthony Clarke. Wheathampstead, 1963.

—   *Mission and Grace I.* Essays in Pastoral Theology Sheed & Ward, London, 1963.

—   *Mission and Grace.II.* Essays in Pastoral Theology. Sheed and Ward, London, 1964.

—   *The Dynamic Element in the Church.* Burns & Oates, London, 1964.

—   *Theological Investigations Volume 1.* God, Christ, Mary and Grace. Darton, Longman & Todd, London, 1961.

—   *Theological Investigations Volume 11.* Man in the Church. Helicon Press, Baltimore, 1963.

—   *Theological Investigations Volume 4.* More Recent Writings. Darton, Longman & Todd, London, 1966.

— *Theological Investigations Volume 5. Later Writings.* Darton, Longman & Todd, London, 1966.

— (ed.) *The Teaching of the Catholic Church.* The Mercier Press. Cork, 1967.

Raphael, F. *The Daily Life of a Religious.* Sands & Company. London, 1914.

Rapley, E. *The Dévotes: Women and the Church in Seventeenth Century France.* McGill-Queens University Press. Montreal, Kinston, London, 1990.

Raughter, R. "A Discreet Benevolence: Female Philanthropy and the Catholic Resurgence in Eighteenth-Century Ireland." *Women's History Review* 6, 4 (1997): 465–487.

Raymond of Capua, *The Life of St Catherine of Siena.* Harvill Press. London, 1960.

Raymond, J.G. "Nun's and Women's Liberation." *Andover Newton Quarterly* 12, 4 (1972): 201–212.

Read, E. Et al., (eds.) *The Collected Workls of C.G.Jung Volume 9, Part 11.* Aion Researches into the Phenomenology of the Self Bollingen Series XX Second Edition. Princeton University Press, Princeton, 1979.

Reed, J. S. *Glorious Battle: The Cultural Politics of Victorian Anglo-Catholicism.* Vanderbilt University Press. Nashville, 1990.

— "A Female Movement: The Feminization of Nineteenth Century Anglo-Catholicism." Anglican and Episcopalian History, 57. (1988): 199–238.

Reinhart, C.J., Tacardon, M., and P. Hardy. "The Sexual Politics of Widowhood: The Virgin Rebirth in the Social Construction of Nineteenth- and Early-Twentieth-Century Feminine Reality." *Journal of Family History* 23, 1 (1998).

Renfro, J.M. "Religious Charism: Definition, Re-Discovery and Implications." *Review for Religious* 45, 4 (July-Aug 1986).

Rouleau, Mary Celeste RSM. "The Prayer of Mercy: Rhythm of Contemplation and Action." *The Mast Journal* 6, 2 (Spring, 1996): 23–28.

Richards, I., (trans.) *Discernment of Spirits.* The Liturgical Press, Collegeville, 1970.

Rigault, G. *Blessed Louis-Marie Grignon de Montfort.* Burns Oates & Washbourne Ltd. London, 1932.

Robb, G. "Victorian Insolvency: Bankruptcy, Imprisonment for Debt, and Company Winding-Up in Nineteenth-Century England (Oxford Historical Monographs)." *American Historical Review* 101, 5 (1996): 1542–1543.

Robson, R., (ed.) *Ideas and Institutions of Victorian Britain.* London, 1967.

Roden, F. "The Kiss of the Soul: The Mystical Theology of Christina Rossetti's Devotional Prose." Chap. in Melnyk J., (ed) *Women's Theology in Nineteenth-Century Britain: Transfiguring the Faith of Their Fathers.* Garland. New York. 1998

Roebuck, J, *The Making of Modern English Society From 1850.* Routledge & Kegan Paul. London, 1973.

Romano, A,. *The Charism of the Founders.* (trans.) Sr. Francis Teresa. St. Pauls Puboications. Slough, 1994.

Rosen, G. "Disease, Debility and Death." Chap. in *Dyos, H.J and Wolff, M (Eds) The Victorian City: Images and Realities, Vol 2.* 125–225. London: Routledge & Kegan Paul, 1973.

Ruddick, S. *Maternal Thinking. Towards a Politics of Peace.* The Women's Press. London, 1989.

Ruether, R. R. *Gaia & God. An Ecofeminist Theology of Earth Healing.* Harper. San Francisco, 1992.

Mary – The Feminine Face of the Church. Westminster Press. Philadelphia, 1977.

— and Eleanor McLaughlin (eds.) *Women of Spirit: Female leadership in the Jewish and Christian Traditions.* Simon and Schuster. New York, 1979.

Ruskin, John. *Sesame and the Lilies.* London. Thomas Nelson & Sons, 1865

Sacred Congregation for Religious and for Secular Institutes. *Religious and Human Promotion, The Contemplative Dimension of Religious Life.* St Paul Publications. Sydney, 1981.

Saudreau, A. *Mystical Prayer According to St Jane de Chantal.* Sheed & Ward. London, 1929.

Saward, J. *Perfect Fools.* Oxford University Press. London, 1980.

— *Redeemer in the Womb.* Ignatius Press. San Francisco, 1993.

Schillebeeckx, E. *The Church with a Human Face. A New and Expanded Theology of Ministry.* SCM Press. London, 1985.

— & Halkes, C. *Mary Yesterday Today Tomorrow.* Crossroad. New York, 1993.

Schimmel, A. *My Soul is a Woman: The Feminine in Islam* (trans. Ray, Susan H.). Continuum. New York, 1997.

Schneiders, S. M. *New Wineskins: Re-Imagining Religious Life Today*. Paulist Press. New York, 1986.

— "Contemporary Religious Life Death or Transformation?" *Cross Currents* 46, 4 (1997): 510–535.

Schussler Fiorenza, E. *In Memory of Her. A Feminist Theological Reconstruction of Christian Origins*. SCM Press. London, 1983.

— *Bread Not Stone: The Challenge of Feminist Biblical Interpretation*. Beacon Press. Boston, 1984.

Schwarz, T. *The Complete Guide to Writing Biographies*. Writer's Digest Books. Cincinnati, Oh, 1990.

Scofield, Mary Ann. "Towards a Theology of Mercy." *The Mast Journal* 2, 2 (Spring, 1992): 1–8.

Scott, M. P. *A Virgin Called Woman*. Bethlehem Abbey Press. Portglenone, 1986.

Scullion, M. 1992. *The 100th Year Anniversary of the Newman Centre*. As presented to Penn Newman December 2, 1992.

Sharp, J. "The Influence of St Alphonsus Ligouri in Nineteenth-Century Britain." *Downside Review*. 101: 342 (1983).

— "Juvenile Holiness: Catholic Revivalism among Children in Victorian Britain." *Journal of Ecclesiastical History* 35 (1984): 220–238.

Shaw, M. F., (ed.) *The Diary of Sister Mary Ignatius of Jesus (Elizabeth Hayes) 1823–1894, Foundress of the Missionary Sisters of the Immaculate Conception*. Privately Printed. Kedron, Australia, 1994.

— *Companion to the Diary: Sister Mary Ignatius of Jesus*. Privately Published. Bardon, Qld, 1995.

Shelton Reed, J. "A Female Movement: The Feminization of Nineteenth-Century Anglo-Catholicism." *Anglican and Episcopelian History* 57 (1988): 199–238.

Sheeran, M.J. *Beyond Majority Rule: Voteless Decisions in the Religious Society of Friends*. Religious Society of Friends. Philadelphia, 1983.

Sheils, W.J., Wood, D. (eds.) *Women in the Church*. Studies in Church History Vol. 27. Ecclesiastical History Society. Basil Blackwood, Cambridge, 1990.

Showalter, E. *The Female Malady: Women, Madness and English Culture, 1830–1980*. Virago Press. London, 1988/1995.

— "Victorian Women and Insanity." *Victorian Studies* 23, 2 (1980): 157–181.

Shuster, G.N. *The Catholic Spirit in Modern English Literature*. The McMillan Company. New York, 1922.

Simpson, D.P. *Cassell's New Latin-English Dictionary*. Cassell. London, 1959.

Sinclair, M. *Mary Oliver: A Life*. First Published London, 1914. Reprinted. Virago Press: London, 1980.

Singleton, J. "The Virgin Mary and Religious Conflict in Victorian Britain." *The Journal of Ecclesiastical History* 43, 1 (1992): 16–34.

Sisters of St. Joseph. *Their Story 1882–1982*. Sisters of St. Joseph of Goulburn. Goulburn, nd.

Sisters Servants of Mary. *Salve*. No 2. Sisters Servants of Mary. Rome, 1984.

Sisters, Servants of the Immaculate Heart of Mary. *Building Sisterhoods*. A Feminist History of the Sisters, Servants of the Immaculate Heart of Mary. Syracuse University Press. Syracuse, 1997.

Skerrett, E., Kantowocz. E.R., and Avella, S.M. *Catholicism, Chicago Style*. Loyola University Press. Chicago, 1993.

Sklar, K. K. *Catharine Beecher: A Study in American Domesticity*. W.W. Norton & Co, Inc. New York, 1973.

Smart, N., Clayton, J., Sherry, P., Katz, S.T., (eds.) *Nineteenth Century Religious Thought in the West 3 Vols.* Cambridge University Press. Cambridge, 1985.

Smith, Bonnie. *Ladies of the Leisure Class: The Bourgeoisie of Northern France in the Nineteenth Century*. Princeton University Press: New Jersey, 1981.

Smith-Rosenberg, C. *Disorderly Conduct: Visions of Gender in Victorian America*. Oxford university Press: New York, 1985.

Smyth, A., (ed.) *Irish Women's Studies Reader*. Attic. Dublin, 1991.

Society of Mary. *Principles of the Spiritual Life*. According to the Ven. Johnn Claude Colin Founder of the Society of Mary. Paschal Press, Harrow, 1953.

Society of the Holy Child Jesus. *History Society of the Holy Child Jesus Issue 1:Beginnings*. Privately Published, n.d.

Soelle, D. *Choosing Life*. SCM Press Ltd. London, 1981.

— "Mysticism, Liberation and the Names of God," *Christianity and Crisis*, 41, 11 (June22, 1981), pp. 179–85.

Spender, D. A. *Women in English Religion 1700–1925*. Studies in Women & Religion Vol. 10:. Edwin Mellen Press, New York, 1983.

St John of the Cross, *Spiritual Canticle*. E.Allison Peers ed. Image Books, New York, 1961.

St John-Stevas, N. "The Victorian Conscience." *The Wiseman Review* 493 (1962): 247–259.

Stacpoole, A., (ed.) *Mary's Place in Christian Dialogue*. St Paul Publications. Slough, 1982.

— (ed.) *Mary and the Churches*. Columba Press. Dublin, 1986.

Steele, F. M. *The Convents of Great Britain and Ireland*. Sands & Co. London, 1902/1925.

Steinberg, D., M.L. O'Hara, and H. Coughlan, (eds.) *The Future of Relgious Life: Proceedings of the Carondolet Conference*. Liturgical Press. Minnesota, 1990.

Stone, L. *The Family, Sex and Marriage in England 1500–1800*. New York: Harper and Row, 1977. New York.

Strachey, L. *Emminent Victorians*. Chatto & Windus. London, 1918.

Strahan, L. *Out of the Silence: A Study of a Religious Community of Women: The Community of the Holy Name*. Melbourne: Oxford University Press, 1988.

Strolz, M.K., (ed.) *In Search of Light Life Development Prayer*. Three Essays on John Henry Newman. International Centre of Newman Friends, Rome, 1985.

Stuart, A Moody. *The Three Marys*. The Banner of Truth Trust. Edinburgh, 1862/ 1984.

Sullivan, B. "Grown Sick with Hope Deferred": *Christina Rossetti's Darker Musings. Papers on Language and Literature* 32, 3 (1996): 227–243.

Sullivan, M. C. *Catherine McAuley and the Tradition of Mercy*. Cambridge University Press. Cambridge, 1995.

— "Catherine McAuley's Spiritual Reading and Prayers." *The Irish Theological Quarterly, Vol. 57 No.1*. Maynooth, 1991.

Sullivan, R. "A Wayward From the Wilderness: Maria Monk's Awful Disclosures and the Feminization of Lower Canada in the Nineteenth Century." *Essays on Canadian Writing*, 62 (1997): 210–222.

Summers, A. *Damned Whores and God's Police*. Penguin Books Australia Ltd., Ringwood, 1975/1994.

— "A Home From Home: Women's Philanthropic Work in the Nineteen Century." *Fit Work for Women*. London: Croom Helm, 1979.

— *Angels and Citizens: British Women as Military Nurses 1854–1914*. London,: Routledge & Kegan Paul, 1988.

Sweeney, G. *History of the Diocese of Nottingham*. Unpublished Mss. Diocese of Nottingham Archives.

Swift, R.R and Gilley, S., eds. *The Irish in the Victorian City*. Croom Helm. London, 1985.

Tallet, F. and Atkins, N. eds. *Catholicism in Britain and France Since 1789*. Hambeldon Press: London, 1996.

Talor, P. "Daughters and Mothers – Maids and Mistresses: Domestic Service Between the Wars." In Clarke, J., Crichter Chas., Johnson R., eds. *Working Class Culture: Studies in History and Theory*, London: Hutchinson, 1979.

Tamburello, D. *Ordinary Mysticism*. Paulist Press. New York, 1996.

Tavard, G. *The Thousand Faces of the Virgin Mary*. The Liturgical Press. Collegeville, 1996.

Taylor, Barbara. *Eve and the New Jerusalem*. Pantheon Books: New York, 1983.

Taylor, P. Daughters and Mothers – maids and mistresses: domestic service between the Wars. In *Working Class Culture: Studies in History and Theory*, Clarke, J., Crichter C., and Johnson R., eds. London: Hutchinson. 1979

Tebbutt, M. *Making Ends Meet*. St Martin's Press. New York, 1983.

Teresa of Avila, St. *The Way of Perfection*. E.Allison Peers (ed.) New York, 1964.

Thaden, B. Z. *The Maternal Voice in Victorian Fiction. Rewriting the Patriarchal Family*. Garland Publishing, Inc., New York, 1997.

The Canon Law Society of Great Britain and Ireland. *The Code of Canon Law*. Collins. London, 1983.

The Commission on Nursing, Ireland 1998, (ed.) *Report of the Commission on Nursing: The Evolution of the Nursing Profession in Ireland Until the Early 1980's*. [http:www.Nursingboard.Ie/NCReport/Chp02.html].

The Sisters of Charity, eds. *Treasure of the Sanctuary*. Easton & Son Ltd. Dublin, 1911.

Therese, M. *Cornelia Connolly, A Study in Fidelity*. Burns & Oates. London, 1963.

Theriault, M. "The Challenge for Apostolic Women Religious: To be in the World, Presence, Symbol and Word." *UISG Bulletin*, 97, (1995): 13–21.

Thompson, J.M. "Incarcerated Souls: Women as Individuals in Margaret Fuller's 'Woman in the Nineteenth Century'." *Communication Quarterly* 43, 1 (1995): 53–63.

Thompson, Margaret S. "Women and American Catholicism 1789–1989." In *Perspectives on the American Catholic Church, 1789–1989*, Stephen Vicchio and Virginia Geiger. Westminster, MD: Christian Classics, 1989.

— "Catholic Women's Relegous Archives: A Historian's Perspective." *Copy of Paper Delivered to Catholic Archives Society (UK)*. May, 1997.

— "The Validation of Sisterhood: Canonical Status and Liberation in the History of American Nuns." In *A Leaf from the Great Tree of God: Essays in Honour of Ritamary Bradley*. Peregrina Publishing Co. Toronto, 1994.

— *Charism" or "Deep Story? Toward a Clearer Understanding of the Growth of Women's Religious Life in Nineteenth-Century America*. Paper presented at the History of Women Religious Conference, Chicago 1998. Copyright 1998, Margaret Susan Thompson.

— "Sisterhood and Power: Class Culture and Ethnicity in the American Convent." *Colby Library Quarterly* (1989) Autumn, 25: 883–994.

Thompson, T.A. "The Virgin Mary in the French School of Spirituality." Paper by courtesy of the Marian Library, University of Dayton OH.

Thurian, M. *Mary, Mother of the Lord, Figure of the Church*. Mowbray. London, 1963.

Thurner, M. "Subject to Change: Theories and Paradigms of U.S. Feminist History." *Journal of Women's History* 9, 2 ([http://www.Indiana.Edu/~iupress/journals/jwh-art6.html].).

Thurston, H. *Modern Spiritualism*. Sheed & Ward. London, 1928.

— *Surprising Mystics*. Burns & Oates. London, 1955.

Tillard, J.M.R. *A Gospel Path The Religious Life*. 2nd edition. Lumen Vitae, Brussels, 1975.

— *There are Charisms and Charisms: The Relgious Life*. Lumen Vitae. Brussels, 1977.

— "Founder's Charism or Founding Charism." *Religious LIfe Review: Supplement to Doctrine and Life* 22, 105 (Nov-Dec 1983): 313–323.

Toner, J. J. *A Commentary on Saint Ignatius' Rules for Discernment*. A Guide to the Principles and Practice. The Institute of Jesuit Sources, St. Louis, 1982.

Trevelyan, G.M. *A Shortened History of England*. Penquin Books. Middlessex, 1959.

English Social History. Longmans Green & Co. London, 1944.

Illustrated English Social History 3 Vols. Longmans, Green & Co. London, 1942/1949.

Trevor, M. *Newman. The Pillar of the Cloud*. MacMillan & Co Ltd, London, 1962.

— *Newman*. Light in the Winter. MacMillan & Co Ltd, London, 1962.

Truman, T. *Catholic Action and Politics*. Georgian House. Melbourne, 1959.

Turner, N. *Catholics in Australia*. A Social History Volume 2. Collins Dove, North Backburn Vic, 1992.

Uglow, J. *Elizabeth Gaskell*. Faber and Faber. London, 1993.

Underhill, E. *Abba*. Compiled by Roger L.Roberts. Morehouse-Barlow Co, Inc, Wilton, Conn, 1982.

— *Life as Prayer*. And other writings of Evelyn Underhill. Moorehouse Publishing, Harrisburg, 1946.

— *Light of Christ*. Compiled by Roger L. Roberts. Morehouse-Barlow Co Inc., Wilton. Conn, 1982.

— *Mysticism*. Bracken Books. London, 1995.

— *Mysticism: The Nature and Development of Consciousness.* OneWorld Publications. Oxford, 1993.

— *Mystics of the Church.* James Clark & Co Ltd. Cambridge, 1975.

— *The Essentials of Mysticism and Other Essays.* One World Press. Oxford, 1995.

— *The Spiritual Life.* Mowbray. London, 1984.

— *Worship.* Crossroad. New York, 1982.

Van Der Leeuw. *Religion In Essence and Manifestation 2 Vols.* Harper Torchbook. The Library of Religion and Culture. Harper & Row, New York, 1963.

Van Engen, J., (trans.) *Devotio Moderna.* Paulist Press. New York, 1988.

van Mens-Verhulst, J. "Reinventing the mother-daughter relationship." *American Journal of Psychotherapy* (1995) 49, 4: 526–539.

Vance, N. *The Sinews of the Spirit: The Ideals of Christian Manliness in Victorian Literature and Religious Thought.* Cambridge University Press. Cambridge, 1985.

Vandelmeer, P.R., & R.P. Swierenga, eds. *Belief and Behaviour: Essays in the New Religious History.* Rutgers University Press: Rutgers, N.J., 1991.

Vasey, V. "Mary in the Doctrine of Bérulle on the Mysteries of Christ." *Marian Studies* 36 (1985): 60–80.

Venard, J. "Vocation to Consecrated Life – Convictions." *UISG Bulletin,* 97 (1995): 3–12.

Vicinus, M. (ed.) *Suffer and be Still: Women in the Victorian Age.* Indiana University Press. Bloomington & London, 1973.

— (ed.) *A Widening Sphere: Changing Roles of Victorian Women.* Methuen & Co., Ltd. London, 1980.

— & Nergaard, B, eds. *Ever Your, Florence Nightingale: Selected Letters.* Virago Press. London, 1989.

— *Independent Women: Work and Community for Single Women 1850–1920.* Virago Press Ltd. London, 1985.

Vidler, A.R. *The Church in an Age of Revolution.* Pelican History of the Church Volume Five. Penquin Books, Middlesex, 1961.

Vidulich, D. A. *Peace Pays a Price.* Sisters of St Joseph of Peace. Washington, 1990.

Vogt, Kari. "Becoming Male: One Aspect of Early Christian Anthropology." Chap. in Fiorenza, E.S., and Collins, M. (eds.) *Concilium: Women Invisible in Church and Theology.* T & T Clark. Edinburgh, 1985. 72–83.

von Balthasar, H. U. *Two Sisters in the Spirit. Therese of Lisieux and Elizabeth of the Trinity.* Ignatius Press. San Francisco, 1992.

von Heugel, F. *The Mystical Element of Religion 2 Vols.* Dent Publishing: London, 1908.

Vortgrimler, H., (ed.) *Commentary on the Documents of Vatican 11, Volume One`.* Burns & Oates/Herder & Herder. London, 1967.

Wadham, J. *The Case of Cornelia Connolly.* Collins. London, 1956.

Waldersee, J. *Catholic Society in New South Wales 1788–1869.* Sydney University Press. Sydney, 1974.

Walker, C. Bynum, *Fragmentation and Redemption: Essays in Gender and the Human Body in Medieval Religion.* Zone Books. New York, 1991.

— *Jesus as Mother.* Studies in the Spirituality of the High Middle Ages. University of California Press. Berkeley CA, 1982.

Wallace, C. "The Prayer Closet as a 'Room of One's Own'": Two Anglican Women Devotional Writers at the Turn of the Eighteenth Century. *Journal of Women's History Vol., no.* 9, 2 (1997): 108–121.

Walsh. J., (trans.) *The Revelations of Divine Love of Julian of Norwich.* Anthony Clarke Books. Wheathampstead, 1961.

Walters, A. *Religious in the Constitution on the Church.* Doctrinal Pamphlet Series. Paulist Press, New Jersey, 1966.

Wapnick, K. "Mysticism and Schizophrenia." *Journal of Transpersonal Psychology* 1, 2 (1985).

Ward, W. *Men and Matters.* Longmans Green & Co. London, 1914.

— *The Life of John Henry Newman Cardinal Newman 2 Vols.* Longmans, Green and Co. London, 1921.

Ware, A P, (ed.) *Midwives of the Future – American Sisters Tell Their Story.* Leaven Press. Kansas City, 1985.

Warner, M. *Alone of All Her Sex: The Myth and Cult of the Virgin Mary.* Pan Books Ltd. London, 1976.

— *Joan of Arc.* Vintage Books. London, 1981.

Watkin, E.I. *Roman Catholicism in England.* From the Reformation to 1950. Oxford University Press, London, 1957.

— *The Church in Council.* Darton, Longman & Todd. London, 1960.

Welch, J. *Spiritual Pilgrims: Carl Jung and Teresa of Avila.* Paulist Press, New York, 1982.

Welter, B. "The Cult of True Womanhood, 1820–1860." *American Quarterly* 18 (1966): 151–174.

West, E.A. *To Recapture the Dream: The Spiritual Heritage of the Little Company of Mary From the Writings of Venerable Mary Potter.* Unpublished, London, 1989.

Wheeler, M. *Death and the Future Life in Victorian Literature and Theology.* Cambridge University Press. Cambridge, 1990.

Heaven Hell and the Victorians. Cambridge University Press. Cambridge, 1994.

White, J., (ed) *The American Catholic Religious Life.* Garland Publishing. New York: 1988.

White, R.J. *Life in Regency Britain.* B.T. Bateson Ltd. London, 1963.

Whitmont, E.C. *Return of the Goddess: Femininity, Aggression and the Modern Grail Quest.* Routledge & Kegan Paul. London, 1982.

Wickins, W. "Archive Notes for the Congregation of the Sisters of the Holy Child Jesus." *Catholic Archives* 6 (1986): 61–64.

Widerquist, JoAnn. "Dearest R'vd Mother." Chap. in *Florence Nightingale and Her Era: A Collection of New Scholarship.* Garland. New York, 1990: 188–308.

Wiethaus, U., (ed.) *Maps of Flesh and Light.* Syracuse University Press. New York, 1993.

Wilkes, P. *The Good Enough Catholic: A Guide for the Perplexed.* Ballantine Books. New York, 1996.

Wilson, A.N. *Jesus.* Flamingo. London, 1993.

Wilson, M. *The Life of William Blake.* Granada Publishing. London, 1978.

Winter, M.T. *The Gospel According to Mary.* Crossroads. New York, 1993.

Wittberg, P. *Creating a Future for Religious Life: A sociological persepective* New York, Paulist Press, 1991.

— *The Rise and Fall of Catholic Religious Orders.* A Social Movement Perspective. The State University of New York Press. New York, 1994.

Wohl, A. S. *Endangered Lives: Public Health in Victorian Britain.* J.M.Dent & Sons Ltd. London, 1983.

The Eternal Slum: Housing and Social Policy in Victorian London. Edward Arnold. London, 1977.

(ed.) *The Victorian Family:Structure and Stresses.* Croom Helm. London, 1978.

(ed.) *The Victorian Family Structure and Stresses.* Croom Helm. London, 1978.

Wolffe, J. *God and Greater Britain.* Religion and National Life in Britain and Ireland 1843–1945. Routledge, London, 1994.

— *The Protestant Crusade in Great Britain, 1829–1860.* Clarendon Press. Oxford, 1991.

Women Religious at the Service of a New Humanity. Asian Trading Corporation. Bangalore, 1984

Wood, D., (ed.) *The Church and the Arts:* Studies in Church History:28. The Ecclesiastical History Society. Blackwell, Oxford, 1992.

Woodruff, S. *Meditations with Mechtild of Magdeburg.* Bear & Co. Sante Fe, 1982.

Woods, R. *Christian Spirituality. God's Presence Through the Ages.* Christian Classics. Burman & Allen. Texas, 1996.

— (ed.) *Understanding Mysticism.* Image Books. New York, 1980.

— "Medieval and Modern Women Mystics: The Evidential Character of Religious Experience." *Founder's Day Lecture, Alistair Hardy Research Centre, Westminster College.* Oxford. December 5 (1992).

— "Mysticism and Social Action: The Mystic's Calling, Development, and Social Activity." *Journal of Consciousness Studies.* 3,2 (1996).

Woodward, E. *Poets, Prophets & Pragmatists.* Collins Dove. Blackburn Vic, 1987.

Woolf, Virginia. "Professions for Women." In Woolf, L (ed.). *Collected Essays, Vol. II.* Chatto & Windus. London, 1967.

Woollen, W. *Father Faber.* Catholic Truth Society Publication. London, n.d.

Wordley, D.W. *No One Dies Alone.* The Australian Creative Workshop for the Little Company of Mary. Sydney, 1976.

Woywob, S. *A Practical Commentary on the Code of Canon Law.* Joseph F. Wagner Inc. New York, 1952.

Yeo, Eileen Janes. "Social Motherhood and the Sexual Communion of Labour in British Social Science, 1850–1950." *Women's History Review* 1, 1 (1992).

Young, A. "Virtue Domesticated: Dickens and the Lower Middle-class." *Victorian Studies* 39, 4. (1996): 483–511.

Zagarell, S.A. "The Consciousness of Her Age – Harriet Beecher Stowe: A Life by Joan D. Hedrick." *Women's Review of Books* 11, 7 (1994): 13–15.

Zappone, K.E. "Christian Feminism: the Spirituality of Bonding." Chap. in *Concilium: Women Invisible in Church and Theology.* T & T Clark. Edinburgh. (1985):17–24.

Zimdars-Swartz, S. L. *Encountering Mary: From La Salette to Medjugorje.* Princeton University Press. Princeton, 1991.

Zohar, D. *The Quantum Self. Human Nature and Consciousness Defined by the New Physics.* Quill/William Morrow. New York, 1990.